THE CENTURY PSYCHOLOGY SERIES

RICHARD M. ELLIOTT, *Editor*

KENNETH MACCORQUODALE, *Assistant Editor*

Dynamic Psychology

DYNAMIC PSYCHOLOGY

PERCIVAL M. SYMONDS, Ph.D.

Professor of Education
Teachers College
Columbia University

New *York*

APPLETON-CENTURY-CROFTS, INC.

Preface

This book is an abridgment and condensation of the writer's earlier book, *The Dynamics of Human Adjustment*. To the surprise of both the writer and the publisher, the original book, which was written and intended for clinical psychologists, psychological counselors, and other professional groups interested in the readjustment of the individual, was immediately adopted for use as a textbook in undergraduate classes in psychology. Its widespread use revealed a suspected but hitherto unverified interest in dynamic psychology and a demand for a text which could be used on the undergraduate level. The detail with which each topic is treated in the original book makes it valuable for the experienced clinician who wishes to use it for professional study and reference. For the requirements of undergraduate students and others who desire a more abridged and less comprehensive treatment of dynamic principles of psychology, this briefer text is now available. *Dynamic Psychology,* the title of this book, is designed to meet the requirements of the undergraduate student. It is intended to be used as an introductory text in psychology from the dynamic point of view.

Dynamic psychology in its present development is the outgrowth of the experience of clinicians rather than experimentalists. Many of the points of view expressed in this book received their first formulation by psychoanalysts who gradually accumulated impressions and hazarded generalizations concerning human nature from their intensive experience in penetrating into the complexity of human personality. These contributions have come particularly from Freud who pioneered in intensive study of the human personality and his followers, Abraham, Ferenczi, Rank, Jones, Alexander, Reik, Klein, Isaacs, Fenichel and many others. Some of the great psychologists have contributed to dynamic psychology, notably James with his discussion of unconscious processes and the self, and Woodworth with his concept of mastery. Kurt Lewin with his theoretical background of field theory also has contributed in an important way to dynamic principles. It is hoped that many of the generalizations presented in this book which are the result of clinical observations can sometime in the near future be experimentally verified. A beginning has been made in the experimental attack on dynamic principles and a good ground work has been laid, but much remains to be done.

The student should recognize that the psychology presented in these

pages by no means covers the whole range of topics with which psychologists are concerned. Herein will be found no treatment of the
nervous system and its relation to behavior, nor of attention, sensation,
perception, learning (except a brief sketch in chapter II), memory,
thinking, imagination, individual differences, or intelligence, and one
must turn to other texts for a treatment of these more orthodox and
descriptive aspects of the mind or of behavior. However, the book
should help a student to understand himself and also his friends and
acquaintances. In particular it will shed light on individual motivation
and will help to interpret the significance of behavior and personality
characteristics in oneself and in others.

From the longer book has been eliminated: (1) psychoanalytic interpretations which are least accessible to consciousness of most persons
and hence which seem least convincing; (2) dynamics of abnormal
states and conditions; and (3) unfamiliar vocabulary. In addition the
long bibliography is gone and in its place footnotes point out the more
important specific references. The chapters on displacement, reaction
formation, fantasy, miscellaneous mechanisms as well as the introductory
chapter on adjustment have been eliminated entirely. Retained are the
definitions, elementary principles and fundamental considerations and
the social, educational and therapeutic implications. To each chapter
has been added questions for discussion, as well as a selected list of sup-
plementary readings by which the student can extend his acquaintance
with each of the topics.

A new chapter on the "Ego and Self" has been added to round out
a phase of the treatment which was neglected in the original book. In
the preface to *The Dynamics of Human Adjustment* it was stated that
"reason and intellect are dethroned as the principal factors in adjustment" and this statement has troubled many persons. To be sure, I went
on to say that "reason is the crown of human achievement, and the use
of reason in meeting problems of adjustment is reached, if at all, only
in maturity as the result of high intellectual endowment and the capacity to profit by experience." The chapter on "Ego and Self" elaborates
this point and fittingly rounds out the treatment by pointing to some
of the possibilities of the individual as he achieves maturity and integration.

                                                          P.M.S.

Contents

Contents

Dynamic Psychology

I

Introduction

Man has always found himself of absorbing interest and the study of man takes its rightful place among the other sciences. Investigations of physical phenomena have resulted in control of the material world and there is hope that a better understanding of man may lead to more effective control of the forces within him.

DEFINITION OF PSYCHOLOGY

The science of experience, of the mind, and of behavior have all been offered as definitions of psychology, but none of these is wholly satisfactory. To be sure, the psychologist is interested in methods of experiencing. He attempts to answer such questions as: To what are we sensitive? How is experience organized? What use is made of experience? But experience is only one of the interests of the psychologist. He is concerned also with mental functioning and asks such questions as: What is the function of the mind? How does the mind operate? What factors lead to increased mental efficiency? How do people learn? How do individuals differ in their mental functioning? Again, psychology has sometimes been called the science of consciousness. However, it should be recognized that not all mental processes are conscious and much goes on in the mind which is below the conscious level. Even to-day psychology does not have a fully satisfactory explanation of the nature of consciousness, although conscious phenomena can be described and partially explained, and certain distinctions can be drawn between those processes which are conscious and those which operate without conscious awareness.

The definition of psychology as the science of behavior is again too partial to be wholly satisfactory. Admittedly, behavior is observable and its outcomes are of primary significance to an individual, but psychology is concerned as well with the experiencing side of personality and with the mind. With regard to behavior, the psychologist tries to answer such questions as: What are the varieties of behavior? What forces affect behavior? How does behavior develop? How do individuals differ in their behavior? Behavior is taken broadly to include not only habits and skills but also attitudes, interests, and appreciations. Psychology, then, must be defined broadly as the science of experience, of the mind, and of behavior. It conceives of man as an organism who is responsive to the world about and who is capable of affecting efficient adaptation to the environment through the operation of his mental processes.

The study of psychology applies to animals as well as to man. Animals, like men, perceive and respond. Although they function on more simple and rudimentary levels than man, they also affect a working relationship with their environment.

HUMAN BEHAVIOR AS VIEWED BY DIFFERENT SCIENCES

Biology. Human behavior and mental phenomena are the interests of many sciences. Biology, the science of life, which treats in the broadest sense the functioning of living organisms, is interested in phenomena relating to the origin, growth, and reproduction of organisms and it concerns itself with problems of heredity as well as those features of growth which are conditioned by the environment. Biologists are interested in the adjustment of an organism to its environment. Many of these topics are of common interest with psychology which, in its attempt to describe and explain experience, mind, and behavior, draws on observations made by biologists.

Physiology. Physiology also studies phenomena which concern psychology. In particular the physiologist studies the functioning of the nervous system, and the nervous system is believed to be intimately related to mental functioning. Note that it was said, "believed to be." Most psychologists today believe that every aspect of mental functioning is paralleled by corresponding operations in the nervous system, and the mind and the nervous system are held to be two aspects of the same phenomenon. Indeed, today there is reluctance to conceive of the mind as an independent entity whose functioning takes place in parallel fashion with the functioning of the nervous system. Rather, it is believed that as the nervous system carries out its functions the total process resulting in changes in behavior is what is recognized as the operation of the mind. To be sure, our knowledge of the nervous system has not gone far enough to permit description of a one-to-one correspondence between nervous and mental functioning. However, the fault lies in our imperfect knowledge. It is the belief of many scientists that a complete correspondence between the functioning of the nervous system and mental operations will be revealed when all the facts are in. At present this correspondence is so vaguely understood that there is little value to the student of psychology in acquiring a detailed knowledge of the nervous system.

Sociology. Another science interested in human behavior is sociology, the science of society. Sociology is particularly concerned with the functioning of social groups and of individuals in the group. Inasmuch as the behavior of groups is also one of the interests of psychologists, these two disciplines have much in common. As a matter of fact, sociology serves as a corrective to a distinctly biological point of view by pointing out the extent to which behavior is conditioned by the environment. Actually, sociology has had considerable influence on psychology in recent years, so that today human behavior is viewed by psychologists as the product of social experiences to a far greater extent than was true a few decades ago.

Anthropology. Anthropology, the science of races and of culture, also has many interests akin to those of psychology. As psychologists have become increasingly aware of the extent to which behavior is socially conditioned they are paying increasing attention to variations in society, in different races and cultures, and have drawn on anthropological findings for some recent interpretations and points of view.

VALUE OF PSYCHOLOGY TO THE STUDENT

Unlike the physical sciences, psychology appeals to the student in large measure because it helps him understand himself better, and in particular, because of a hope that he may find in psychology a solution for some of the problems that beset him. Specifically, students look to psychology for answers to three groups of personal questions: 1. How can I solve my problems of mental conflict and emotional adjustment and achieve happiness and peace of mind? 2. How can I become more adequate and successful, particularly in regard to my work in college? How can I develop better self-control? 3. How can I become more adequate socially and develop greater confidence and poise? These problems, it may be mentioned in passing, are not unique with students but are common to a large proportion of men and women in our civilization.

Brief descriptions of individuals will illustrate the kinds of personal problems which students face.

Eileen came to college under great difficulties. Her father did not believe that girls should receive higher education and he not only failed to coöperate with Eileen's plans but put every obstacle in her way. Her mother, a timid person, did not dare actively to assist her. Eileen's only encouragement came from an aunt who lived in a college town in a neighboring state. It took considerable courage for Eileen to announce that she intended to attend college by living with her aunt during her college years. Although her aunt makes a good home for her, Eileen looks forward to the day when she can be wholly independent and will no longer feel that she is under obligations to her parental home.

Jack, as long as he can remember, felt that he took second place in his family to his older sister. She was always pointed out as being an excellent student throughout elementary and high school, and in college she made a brilliant record. This older sister had always been held up to Jack as a shining example which he was expected to emulate and he felt that he was a constant disappointment to his parents because his record was never equal to that of his sister. This same fate pursued him in college and he could not throw off the feeling of his inferiority because his marks ranged between B and C. Although he enjoyed the fellows in his fraternity and took part in athletics, he felt that he was failing to live up to expectations his parents held for him.

Eddie, the much sheltered son from a strict and puritanical home, found a new world when he came to college. His sheltered home did not prepare him for the many experiences and temptations with which college life confronted him. He was in a constant conflict between going out with the fellows on beer parties or petting parties and the feeling that these experiences would not meet the approval of his parents or of his minister at home. Although he enjoyed his class work he never was able to shake off the feeling that other aspects of his college life forced him to do things which, although they were enjoyable, gave him a deep sense of guilt.

Esther is a perfectionist. With high ideals as to what she would like to accomplish in college, she strives to carry out each assignment so as to surpass every other member of her class. She holds high standards for her own work and puts in long and tedious hours in polishing up papers or in doing extra assignments. Many times she is unable to bring herself to commence a task because, half consciously, she feels that she will not be able to carry it through to meet her own standards of excellence. This obsession drives her ceaselessly and causes her to feel dissatisfied with almost everything that she attempts.

Tom's greatest fear is over the impending examination. He commences each semester confidently and then when the first examination is announced he feels the sinking feeling creeping over him again. The approaching examination throws him into a panic. He wakens at night filled with dread and his appetite suffers. Although he has prepared faithfully he feels that the questions he will be asked will be strange and unknown to him. When he reaches the examination he is so tense and excited that his handwriting will become hardly legible and this will be an additional factor which he fears may go against him.

E. B. has difficulty with concentration. He has read many books on how to study and has arranged his desk in his room according to the most exacting requirements. However, when he sits down and opens his book his mind flits away to other things. He thinks about the coming game on Saturday, about the girl with whom he has a date that evening, the letter from his mother which he received that morning and her complaints about her ill health. When the time is up he finds that he has made no headway with his studies but he seems unable to control himself or to do anything about it.

Alice is much concerned over her popularity. She envies other girls on the campus about whom everyone talks, who have many dates and who are recognized as beauties. She feels that she is overlooked and that other girls secretly ridicule her. She would like to have many dates and feels that in a way this is expected of her, but she has more or less resigned herself to being left out when it comes to joining a group for an evening.

Sue is an example of perpetual motion. She must be doing something from early morning until late at night. She is in a great many college activities,—serves on student committees, sings in the college choir, and has editorial responsibility on the college paper. Sue rarely sits down to do nothing or to fool away the time but seems relentlessly driven from one activity to another. Vacation periods are unhappy times for Sue. She feels worthless and depressed and is glad when classes reassemble so that she again can throw herself into her many activities.

The student should recognize that psychology does not provide ready-made answers to personal problems. A textbook in psychology cannot be looked upon as a "fix-it" manual but rather as containing the fundamental knowledge which will give one a basic understanding of the principles of personality development and adjustment. One should not expect to use a psychology textbook as the automobile owner uses the manual accompanying his car which informs him how to drive and care for his car and what to do when any part of the car fails to function. Rather, to extend the analogy, the psychology text may be compared with the textbooks in physics and engineering which supply basic principles.

In addition to these personal problems for which students hope to find the clues to a solution from psychology, there are many mysteries in the mind for whose understanding one looks to psychology. Among these mysteries are the unconscious, hypnotism, the split personality, telepathy and clairvoyance, and dreams. Many persons are curious as to whether the character of another person can be sized up from physiognomy, handwriting, physique and other external signs. Various groups of individuals, such as the insane, the criminal, and the feebleminded are little understood by many persons and there is fear of these pathological conditions. All of these mysteries evoke the fear of the unknown and psychology is turned to for light so that these little understood phenomena will become less awe-inspiring and anxiety-provoking. Certain of these topics, including the unconscious, and more briefly hypnotism and dreams, are discussed in this book. Most of these phenomena, when understood, are seen to be exaggerations of mental processes which are common to all individuals, and as they are understood, they lose their fearsome qualities.

SCHOOLS OF PSYCHOLOGY

Introspectionism. The number of schools of psychology which have developed, each of which presents its own data and interpretations, is a challenge to the validity of psychology as a science. The fact that there are numerous kinds of psychologies makes many persons distrust the findings of psychology in general. The existence of these separate schools, however, testifies to the gaps in our present knowledge, and indicates that the total field is still being explored by different methods which have not yet brought agreement as to fundamental principles. One school of thought known as *introspectionism,* or more technically as structural or existential psychology, was developed by Titchener, for many years a distinguished professor of psychology at Cornell University. Titchener was concerned only with data which were observable by the perception of one's own mental processes as they revealed themselves in one's own sensation and feelings. Introspectionism attempted to be a pure psychology of the mind, but owing to its failure to relate mental processes to their biological and social functions, it remained sterile and today has largely disappeared as a separate school.

Behaviorism. Another school of psychology, popularized by John B. Watson, was known as *behaviorism.* Distrusting the subjective nature of introspection, Watson restricted the data of psychology to observable behavior. While behaviorism helped to make psychology objective and advanced the scientific approach to psychological problems, it too is recognized as being partial because of the exclusion of a considerable body of data in the form of sensations, feelings, emotions, and the awareness of mental states.

Gestalt psychology. Still another school of psychology originally concerned with experience and perception is known as *Gestalt* psychology, spearheaded by a trio of German psychologists, Wertheimer, Koehler, and Koffka. In Gestalt psychology, emphasis is placed on the functional unity of perception as contrasted with the building up of perception out of separate units. According to Gestalt psychology one perceives as a whole. This school of psychology interests itself in the pattern or figure or organization that perceptions assume against a background. Somewhat later Lewin, another German psychologist, showed how these same gestalt principles could apply equally to motor processes. In passing it is worthy of note that of these four German psychologists who have resided in America in recent years and have had considerable influence on American psychological thinking, only Koehler is now alive.

Dynamic psychology. This book deals with *dynamic psychology* which is interested in many states and processes, and particularly with those driving forces within the individual which seek their satisfactions in the world about. Dynamic psychology therefore becomes a psychology of the organism. Dynamic psychology is concerned with the action of forces within the personality. It conceives of personality as a structured affair, which it views as operating on different levels. Basically an individual is stimulated by his physiological needs, and these needs serve as the foundation of all behavior. As the individual matures, thinking and controlling processes enable him to find ways of meeting these physical needs by adapting himself to his surroundings. Finally, the individual must grow up to take his place as a member of society. In society he finds the most adequate satisfaction of his needs, yet at the same time society expects of him in return certain adjustments and conformities. These various phases of personality may fail to work together harmoniously and the study of these conflicts becomes an important topic in dynamic psychology. Dynamic psychology relates the present personality with the past and conceives of personality as having a natural history of development. The characteristics of the adult, it is believed, have been formed in infancy and childhood. The experiences of a child help to form his character in the future while the behavior trends of the adult can be traced back to experiences in early life.

In defense of contemporary psychology it should be noted that in recent years a process of integrating and consolidating the several schools of psychology has been in progress exemplified by the work of Woodworth, Murphy, G. Allport, Dashiell, Munn and others.

SCIENTIFIC METHOD USED IN PSYCHOLOGY

The data of psychology are round about us everywhere. One does not have to travel widely or bring in special apparatus in order to study the traits of individuals. Consequently, everyone makes common observations which can be used as the basic data of psychology. The inadequacy of random observations of individuals is found in their hit or miss character and possible subjectivity. However, common observation is not to be entirely despised or discounted for in every science observation of the phenomena to be studied is the basic source of data. Psychology may also use as its data human experience as recorded in literature, history, and biography. Gordon Allport,[1] for instance, has recently ad-

[1] G. W. Allport, "The Use of Personal Documents in Psychological Science," *Bulletin of the Social Science Research Council*, No. 49. (New York, Social Science Research Council, 1942.)

vocated the use of personal documents as data to be used by psychologists. Many novelists and poets have made sage observations of human behavior which at least serve as fruitful hypotheses for further study.

The *observation* of individuals over extended periods of time becomes particularly appropriate as a method in the study of children, and by means of it many facts with regard to growth and development have been discovered. In the developmental approach the psychologist serves as a passive observer and does not interject himself into the situation.

Another method, coming into favor in recent years, is the *clinical study* resulting in the comprehensive case history. Clinical study is essentially the detailed study of an individual using not only first hand observation, but also applying certain more rigorous and standardized tests. The standardization of tests makes possible a close and accurate comparison of one individual with another. The case history not only provides a cross-section of an individual at a given time, but also includes a report on his development. Although psychologists have not been willing to place too much credence on intensive studies of individuals as a basis for general laws and principles, it is possible to accumulate in the clinical study of many persons facts which may be used to formulate general hypotheses.

Psychologists place their greatest faith in *experimentation* carried out under controlled conditions so that variation in behavior can be noted with respect to changes in only one or a few factors in the situation. Because of the greater control of the surroundings, the opportunity for more accurate observations, and the study of larger numbers, it is believed that experimentation is the method best designed to study the laws of mental processes.

OBJECTIVE VERSUS SUBJECTIVE DATA IN DYNAMIC PSYCHOLOGY

One of Watson's arguments for behaviorism was the fact that many mental phenomena are not accessible for objective observation. However, behaviorism was limited to the extent that the methods which it employed forced it to neglect important mental phenomena. Inaccessible to study by behaviorism were wishes, impulses, feelings, emotions, and the affects—anxiety, guilt, shame, disgust, et cetera. Since these processes are very much the concern of dynamic psychology, methods by which they may be studied are of particular concern. A considerable proportion of the material of dynamic psychology has been derived from clinical case studies. In particular, dynamic psychology has drawn on the findings of psychoanalysis. Psychoanalysis is a term which has three different meanings: a method of psychotherapy, a method of individual study, and a body of theory growing out of these studies during psychotherapeutic interviews. The method of psychoanalysis traditionally has been free association, which consists of putting a person at ease and encouraging him to let his mind wander as it will and to reveal to the analyst the fantasies, desires, and anxieties that flow through. This method has been characterized by psychologists as the acme of subjectivity. Not only is the person being analyzed reporting utterly uncontrolled feelings, desires, thoughts, and fantasies, but he is reporting them to only one individual so that there is no way of verifying them. One of the requirements of the scientific method is that experiments shall be repeatable and therefore subject to verification. Psychoanalytic sessions cannot be repeated and the data are subject to the error of the analyst who reports and interprets them. If dynamic psychology were limited to such subjective data its teachings would indeed be under suspicion. However, by this time hundreds, indeed, thousands of reports of interviewing and analytic sessions have been reported and there is a repetition and consistency in them which go far toward overcoming the subjectivity of separate individual reports. Many observations have been repeated and verified scores of times until now they have gained general credence. To be sure, it is the goal of psychologists to subject all such observations made from interviewing sessions to controlled experimental tests. But the evidence that has now accumulated from the case history method seems on the whole to be dependable and trustworthy.

One must distinguish with care fact from theory in psychology. It is one thing to have facts which are reliable and dependable, it is another thing to have theories which have been tested adequately. Theories may be based upon a modicum of observation and experience or they may be drawn from extensive observation and careful inquiry into relationships. It is the purpose of every science to base theories on adequate and reliable data and to frame theories so that they will stand the test of time and will apply in every situation with a high degree of generality. Most of the material in the present book is based on factual data derived from psychoanalytic and other case experience, but the results of experimental findings have been included when these are available. There has been a minimum of theorizing, and so far as possible general statements have been based on all the evidence available.

Many persons are misled as to what to expect from findings of dynamic psychology. Many of its statements are not in terms of laws and principles which must *always* follow, but rather in terms of *possible* outcomes or sequences. For instance in Chapter III there will be found a discussion of responses to frustration. One common response to frustration is aggressive behavior. However, it is not asserted that all frustration will be followed by aggression for it is recognized that frustration may also be followed by regressive behavior, by fantasy, or by withdrawal. Nor has theory reached the point where it can be said under what circumstances frustration will be followed by one or the other of these responses. At the present time the most that dynamic psychology can do is to point out the variety of possible responses that may be expected to follow certain conditions or the variety of motivations which may precede and activate a certain type of response. When it is said that regressive behavior may be a result of a birth of a new child in a family, this should not be interpreted to mean that all regressive behavior is the result of a new child in the family, nor that the birth of a child will cause all older children in the family invariably to regress. The most that can be done at our present state of knowledge is to report that in certain instances regressive behavior on the part of an older child has followed a birth. It is believed that such observations are helpful in interpreting either the results of certain experiences or in explaining the meaning of behavior as it is repeated in another setting.

QUESTIONS FOR DISCUSSION

1. What professions does psychology serve as a basic science and what should the student in these professions expect to get from psychology?

2. Psychology is beginning to think of itself as a profession. What services does the professional psychologist render?

3. If psychology is a science how can there be several "schools of psychology"? What does the existence of these several schools imply?

4. What can a student expect to get from psychology that may help him with his own personal problems?

5. Why does psychology place greatest confidence in experimentation as a method by which valid principles may be determined?

RECOMMENDED READING

1. DASHIELL, J. F., *Fundamentals of General Psychology* (Boston: Houghton Mifflin Company, 1937).

2. HEIDBREDER, EDNA, *Seven Psychologies* (New York: Appleton-Century-Crofts, Inc., 1933).

3. MENNINGER, K. A., *The Human Mind* (New York: Alfred A. Knopf, 1930, 1937, 1945). Third edition.

4. MUNN, N. L., *Psychology* (Boston: Houghton Mifflin Company, 1946).

5. RUCH, F. L., *Psychology and Life* (Chicago: Scott, Foresman and Company, 1937, 1941). Second edition.

6. SHAFFER, L. F., The Psychology of Adjustment (Boston: Houghton Mifflin Company, 1936).

7. WOODWORTH, R. S. and MARQUIS, D. G., *Psychology* (New York: Henry Holt and Company, Inc., 1921, 1929, 1934, 1940, 1947). Fifth edition.

II

Drive

This book deals with the process of adjustment and, in particular, the dynamic or motivating factors that govern the process of adjustment in the individual. Living is a process of adjustment, and like any biological process, man does not have to understand it in order that it may function smoothly; yet the process of adjustment may be subjected to human inquiry, and a better understanding of it can lead to improved methods of controlling it.

For one who would understand an individual personality, there is nothing more important than insight into the inner forces which drive him to action. The argument of this book is based on the hypothesis that all behavior originates in response to urges within an individual. His frustrations and conflicts, his modes of adjustment and all of the details of daily conduct follow in response to certain fundamental motivating forces within him.

In order to tell the story of these dynamic driving forces, it is necessary to talk first in terms of living organisms in general. The fact cannot be denied that human beings are part of the total family of living organisms, and that the basic understanding of human behavior is rooted in biology and physiology. However, these fundamental concepts will be only briefly touched upon, inasmuch as our main interest is in human behavior.

Every organism has two main necessities or purposes. One is *self-maintenance* and the other, the *perpetuation of the species* of which he sex is a member. If an organism is to exist at all, it has to maintain itself in an environment often barely tolerant and frequently hostile. Likewise, unless organisms within each species have within themselves mechanisms by which they can reproduce and consequently perpetuate their species, these organisms never would have appeared on this planet as separate individuals in the series of generations. It is because of these two characteristics of every organism that the driving forces within it arise.

BASIC PHYSIOLOGICAL CONCEPTS

Equilibrium and disequilibrium. A basic principle which seems to characterize all living matter is known as *equilibrium*. Every organism has a tendency to maintain itself and to resist change or decay. If, for instance, organisms did not have within them this resistant force, there would be nothing to maintain the identity of the individual, and the world of living matter would lose its stability. Cannon,[1] the eminent physiologist, following the lead of Bernard [2] over half a century ago, has described the various processes within the body which work to maintain equilibrium and to bring the organisms back from a state of disequilibrium into equilibrium. He called this process "homeostasis." That the human body, for example, possesses mechanisms for maintaining a constant internal temperature while external temperatures range from far below freezing to extreme heat is among the marvels of nature.

need to balance

Tissue needs. *Tissue needs* is the second concept which is important in building up the theory of drives. Every living organism, by virtue of the fact that it is forced to keep itself intact and to maintain certain equilibria in order to accomplish this, must consume energy in the process of adapting to a reluctant environment. Just as an engine does work through the release of energy and must be provided with fuel as a source of this energy, so an organism requires raw material which we call food as a source of its energy. Behavior becomes an interaction between the organism and the outside world which the forces driving for equilibrium demand in order to service these continually depleting tissue needs.

It is important to note that several of these tissue needs are *cyclical* in nature. Energy is constantly being depleted, not only in the more active processes of adjustment to the outside world, but by the mere operation of the internal processes themselves, so that there is a constantly recurring need for the intake of food. Likewise, the fluid contents of the blood are being continually lost, partly through excretion, partly through breathing, and partly through perspiration. Consequently, it is imperative that every organism periodically replenish the fluid contents of the body. The intake of oxygen necessitates a continuous rhythmic process of breathing which cannot be postponed for more than a minute or so. Just as food and water must be periodically taken into the body, so waste products must be periodically disposed of. Finally, there is the daily cycle of activity and rest which coincides naturally with the cycle of day and night to which the body is attuned.

In general, the longer the time before a need is satisfied, the stronger the tissue need becomes. If eating food is postponed, the need for food increases. Likewise, if rest is postponed, the need for rest and sleep grows.

[1] W. B. Cannon, *The Wisdom of the Body* (New York: W. W. Norton & Company, Inc., 1932, revised edition, 1939).

[2] Claude Bernard, *Leçons sur les Propriétés Physiologiques et les Altérations Pathologiques des Liquides de l'Organisme* (Paris: J.-B. Baillière et Fils, 1859).

Immediately after a tissue need is met the need itself is at or close to zero but increases in amount with the passage of time.

Visceral tension. A third concept is that of _visceral tension_. As a tissue need grows in amount, certain tensions arise in the body. These tensions are the observable indices of disequilibrium. One might define equilibrium as a state in which tension is absent, whereas disequilibrium is a state in which tension is present. These tensions are actually physical or physiological states within the body such as the tension of muscle groups, the stretch or contraction of tissue, the presence of disturbing or irritating substances in different parts of the body.

Inner stimuli. The meaning of visceral tension which was described in general terms in the last paragraph can be better understood in terms of the concept of _inner stimuli_. First, there are the irritating or painful inner stimuli. These are best illustrated by the signs of hunger within the body which arise in response to the depletion of energy supplies. For many years physiologists were at a loss to identify the exact nature of hunger. In 1911, however, Cannon [3] suspected that contractions of the smooth muscle in the wall of the stomach might be related to the sensations which are known as hunger. He came to this conclusion as a result of some experimental observations which he was able to make with the help of one of his assistants, A. L. Washburn, who swallowed a rubber balloon which permitted the recording of the stomach contractions on a kymograph. As Cannon pursued his inquiry, he finally came to the conclusion that hunger is precisely the uncomfortable sensations caused by these muscle contractions. It is as though all of the depleted energy needs in the body are made known through these muscle contractions which serve as distressing stimuli. More recent research by Bash [4] has demonstrated that there is a hunger drive in which afferent nerve impulses from the stomach play no part. However, the earlier work of Cannon undoubtedly still holds, and the major stimuli or warnings that there is a nutritional deficit in the body come from uncomfortable 'stimuli in the stomach. The possible secondary stimuli for organic drives will be discussed in a later section under the heading of "Appetite" (pp. 24–26).

Likewise, Cannon [5] believes that thirst is a stimulus in the mucous membrane of the mouth and throat arising from the unpleasant sensation of dryness or stickiness in those tissues. This sensation of thirst is

[3] W. B. Cannon and A. L. Washburn, "An Explanation of Hunger," _American Journal of Physiology_, 29 (1912), 441–454.

[4] K. W. Bash, "Contributions to a Theory of the Hunger Drive," _Journal of Comparative Psychology_, 28 (1939), 137–160; K. W. Bash, "An Investigation into a Possible Organic Basis for the Hunger Drive," _Journal of Comparative Psychology_, 28 (1939), 109–135.

[5] W. B. Cannon, _Bodily Changes in Pain, Hunger, Fear and Rage_ (New York: Appleton-Century-Crofts, Inc., 1915; second edition, 1927). Ch. V.

the body's signal that its fluid content has been depleted. But just as it has been demonstrated that contractions of the stomach do not wholly account for the hunger drive, so work by Bellows [6] has demonstrated that the sensations of thirst arising from dryness of the tissues do not provide a complete explanation for the thirst drive, although these stimuli still hold first place as a signal of fluid depletion in the body.

Pressures within the body serve as painful or irritating stimuli and as the basis for other important drives. For instance, in the male, pressure of the accumulated secretions in the gonads is undoubtedly one factor in accounting for the sex drive, although it is by no means the only factor. Likewise, distention of the bladder by urine, or of the large intestine by feces becomes a stimulus which eventually sets in action the reflexes of the processes of urination and defecation. These distentions and pressures act as specific stimuli and serve as signals for the need for elimination.

Glandular secretions operate in ways not wholly clear as signals or stimuli of organic needs. This accounts for the larger part of the sex drive. Both males and females secrete hormones which not only determine the secondary sexual characteristics of hair, voice, contour of the body, and so forth, but serve as driving forces leading to behavior which is recognized as sexual. Similarly, in a much less specific way the secretions of the thyroid gland in the neck produce variations in general bodily activity by regulating chemical change in the body. In less well-known ways chemical changes in the blood or tissues serve as a basis for drive although it is probable that these chemical states or changes themselves do not serve as stimuli. Young [7] believes that the nutritive deficits which produce physical and chemical changes in the body at the same time produce changes in the taste mechanisms, and that these are in part responsible for variations in appetite and are consequently indirectly related to hunger. The actions of internal stimuli which are activated by chemical changes within the body are not wholly clear at the present time but there seems to be little doubt that mechanisms of this order are present and operative. When the physiological means for maintaining a constant inner environment are damaged the organism itself makes an effort through behavioral control to maintain the necessary inner constancy.

Protective needs. Finally, tissue damage is an obvious form of painful stimulus which calls forth instantaneously appropriate avoiding or protective behavior. The surface of the body is dotted with a close network of pain spots, and any strong or sharp stimulus which penetrates to these sensory nerve endings is immediately transmitted as a sharp sense of

[6] R. T. Bellows, "Time Factors in Water Drinking in Dogs," *American Journal of Physiology*, 125 (1929), 87–97.

[7] P. T. Young, "The Experimental Analysis of Appetite," *Psychological Bulletin*, 38 (1941), 129–164.

pain which evokes appropriate avoiding responses. Likewise, the skin is also supplied with heat and cold spots which serve as signals of contact with objects which are too hot or too cold and stimulate withdrawal or protective responses. To a modified degree, tissues inside the body are sensitive to harmful or destructive influences and activate reflexes which serve as protection. For instance, if some toxic substances are taken into the body they will be spit out or vomited. This is enough to show that needs in the body stimulate definite sensory nerve endings which in turn transmit their messages to the central nervous system and set in motion behavior appropriate to the interests of these bodily needs.

It may be serviceable at this time to make a distinction between *deficit* and *protective* needs. This distinction is psychological as well as physiological, because these two groups of needs lead to entirely different types of behavior. Deficit needs give rise to such drives as hunger and thirst and lead to *seeking* behavior—the search for the object which has the power to reduce the irritating stimulus. Protective needs, on the other hand, typically lead to *avoiding* behavior which will separate the organism from the damaging object in the interests of tissue protection.

THE PAIN-PLEASURE PRINCIPLE

There is a philosophic theory known as *hedonism,* originally a main tenet of the Epicureans, which asserts that good and bad can be defined in terms of pleasure and pain. Whatever is pleasurable is, by definition, good and whatever is painful is, by definition, bad. There is a corresponding psychological theory which asserts that all behavior without exception can be explained as an attempt to achieve pleasure and to avoid pain. This theory is an old one.[8] It was advanced by the English school of philosophy—Hobbes,[9] Hume,[10] Bentham,[11] J. S. Mill,[12]

---

[8] "Nature has placed mankind under the governance of two sovereign masters, pain and pleasure."—J. Bentham, *Principles of Morals and Legislation,* Ch. I.

"For the present, I hold it as a rule, beyond all dispute, that there is at the bottom of every genuine voluntary impulse, some one variety of the many fears wherein pain or pleasure takes possession of the conscious mind."—A. Bain, *The Emotions and the Will,* p. 355.

"The unavoidable conclusion is, then, that the intuition does not, and cannot, ignore the ultimate derivations of right and wrong from pleasure and pain."—H. Spencer, *The Data of Ethics.*

"It seems as if our entire psychological activity were directed toward gaining pleasurable stimulation, toward avoiding painful ones; that it is regulated automatically by the principle of pleasure."—S. Freud, *A General Introduction to Psychoanalysis,* p. 308.

[9] Thomas Hobbes, *Leviathan* (London: 1651; New York: Oxford University Press).

[10] David Hume, *An Inquiry Concerning the Human Understanding* (Edinburgh, 1777).

[11] Jeramy Bentham, *An Introduction to the Principles of Morals and Legislation* (Oxford: Clarendon Press. 1789; New York: Doubleday, Doran & Company, Inc., 1935). Ch. I.

[12] J. S. Mill, *Utilitarianism* (London: 1863, reprinted from *Fraser's Magazine,* 1861; tenth edition. 1888; New York: E. P. Dutton & Co., Inc., 1910).

Spencer,[13] Bain,[14] and Locke.[15] As often as this theory is proposed, it is challenged. When one recalls some of the martyrs in the world who have eagerly and joyfully sought out lives of pain, and individuals in our own time who endure extreme hardships and privations in order to achieve some end, it would seem as though this principle was far from being a satisfactory explanation of behavior. Certainly it is a poor principle which requires such extensive explanation for the exceptions to it, and yet the principle has a remarkable vitality. Early in his work Freud [16] initiated the "pleasure principle" and psychoanalytic discussions are frequently couched in terms of it.

Physiologically, there seems to be a sound basis for this principle, although in the complications and subsequent developments of human behavior the principle becomes modified and overrun by other forces. Basically, visceral tensions are unpleasant. We have seen this is true in our discussion of organic stimuli. Their very unpleasantness is the basis of the driving force which they possess. These visceral tensions as inner stimuli act as signs or signals of organic and tissue needs. Pain, as well as heat and cold stimuli on the surface of the body, acts in a similar manner as a signal of tissue damage. Consequently, it may be said that drives are unpleasant. On the other hand, the reduction of visceral tension and of the various organic stimuli gives relief or satisfaction. To say that man seeks pleasure is not an exact statement. A more precise statement is that man seeks to escape from pain or discomfort, and to achieve a state of equilibrium which is satisfying in the sense that pain or discomfort is absent. Fundamentally, the forces that motivate an organism are the discomforts. We shall have to wait until appetites are discussed before we speak about pleasures which have their own attractive qualities. As Schopenhauer has said: "A need is a push from the past rather than a pull from the future."

Pain or discomfort furnishes the momentum for activity and serves as the basis of drive. Although pain or discomfort furnishes momentum, it does not define direction, and we shall later discover that direction is a result of the process of learning. After learning has shown the organism the way in which drives can be satisfied, images of these anticipated goals will serve as additional stimuli to the drive and help to orient it in direction.

[13] Herbert Spencer, The Data of Ethics (New York: Appleton-Century-Crofts, Inc., 1879, 1939).

[14] Alexander Bain, The Emotions and the Will (London: Longmans, Green & Co., 1859; fourth edition, 1899).

[15] John Locke, An Essay Concerning the Human Understanding (London: 1690; New York: E. P. Dutton & Co., Inc.).

[16] Sigmund Freud, A General Introduction to Psychoanalysis (Garden City, New York, Garden City Publishing Company, Inc., 1920, 1935; first published in German, 1916).

PHYSIOLOGICAL PRINCIPLES THAT UNDERLIE DRIVES

All behavior in the service of reduction of organic needs. Drive can *[excludes religion]* now be defined as the activity of an organism to remove a painful or unpleasurable stimulus. Drive is intimately related to need. Need sets *[religion made to meet needs]* in motion the organic stimulus (stomach contractions, for example) which in turn, through the messages relayed to the central nervous system, sets in motion appropriate behavior destined, if successful, to reduce the stimulus. Fundamentally, then, all behavior arises from drives for the alleviation of organic needs, whether these be nutritive deficits in the body, the need to excrete waste products, the stimulation of chemical or glandular agents in the blood and tissues, or the need to protect the organism against injury. This stimulus-response psychology is deficient in that it does not take into account the dynamic processes of the organism itself and the fact that an organism behaves in response to its own needs. In these fundamental terms happiness may be traced back to the satisfaction of physiological needs.[17]

For those who wish to deal with the problems of individuals or the problems of society, whether in education, medicine, social work, or government, a psychology based on dynamic driving forces within the individual is imperative.

Drive persistent as long as need is present. A drive is *persistent* as *[baby hungry]* long as the need is present. The tissue needs of the body activate these stimuli for drives, and as long as the need persists the visceral or protective stimuli arouse discomfort. Organic drives, therefore, differ from peripheral stimuli (those which originate outside the body) in their unavoidableness.

Desire the subjective experience of drive. A drive may have subjective experiences accompanying it. We know of the presence of a drive by consciously felt desire or wish. However, many drives apparently operate unconsciously without an accompanying conscious experience. This is true of most drives originally, but particularly of drives which are later repressed and whose conscious counterpart is excluded from experience. Many conscious desires are indicators of more basic drives of which they are only the conscious representatives. For instance, the wish of a child in the clinic to have the worker give him some small gift such as a piece of paper or crayon to take home, in many instances is a representation of his underlying need for the love for and assurance of a secure relationship with the worker.

[17] Here again it may be more meaningful and realistic to say that happiness depends on the satisfaction of derived ego and social needs.

Drives are not always expressed in observable behavior. Frequently, their only form of expression is in the implicit activity of fantasy, and they may even become "stored" as it were, in the form of residual tensions. A drive may lie dormant for years, to be called into active expression finally by the appropriate stimulus. One may find in later years that he is strongly aroused emotionally when he returns to his childhood home as associations from the past arouse latent passions which have long been quiescent.

Cyclical nature of need. Strength of drives varies significantly in response to the cyclical character of the need to which it is a response. In the *active* stage, the drive itself initiates the activity. In the *ready period,* the drive itself is inactive but is susceptible to excitation by appropriate stimuli. In civilized society hunger operates infrequently. Our schedule of three meals a day provides nutriment before hunger actually has a chance to operate. The drive to eat, however, is ready when the appropriate outer stimulus is presented. A little child may be quite happy in his play, but if he hears that refreshments are being passed, his drive to eat is instantly aroused. In everyday life drives frequently get no further than the ready stage. Our routine of living takes us from one stimulus to another and forestalls drives in their active stages. We prepare a schedule of social events which does not permit us to get overhungry for the companionship of other people. We surround ourselves with beautiful objects that constantly impinge on our senses so that the craving for beauty never becomes intense. We organize our lives so that distressing or painful inner stimuli do not have an opportunity to operate. We catch drives when they are ready and in this way ward off the more intense and painful demands of a drive in the active stage. In the *refractory* period, that is, the period immediately after a need is satisfied, the drive itself is quiescent, and no incentive will arouse it. After a full meal, hunger is absent. In fact, food may actually be distasteful and repellent if one is urged to eat when he is not hungry.

Stimulating or depressing effect of peripheral factors on drive. The strength of drive, other things being equal, is in direct proportion to the intensity of the need. But drives are not entirely controlled in their strength by tissue needs. A drive requires some external incentive or stimulus in addition to the inner need in order to reach open expression in behavior. Seward [18] found, for instance, that there must be some external incentive to release the sex drive of the male guinea pig. If one is hungry or restless searching movements are initiated, but they are also in response to cues in the external environment. Drives can be stimu-

---

[18] G. H. Seward, "Studies on the Reproductive Activities of the Guinea Pig. V. Specificity of Sexual Drive in the Male," *Journal of Genetic Psychology,* 59 (1941), 389–396.

lated or depressed, especially by social factors. It is a common psychological experiment to demonstrate that motivation is increased by the presence of other individuals and even by distracting factors. Appetite for a meal is enhanced by the surroundings, the flowers, and appointments of the table, as well as by stimulating company. It is obvious that drives vary in degree of strength. Some drives are impelling and impetuous, others are weak.

On one occasion Bernard flies into a rage because his mother will not let him go to the movies with the other boys. For hours on end he whines and moans. On another occasion, however, this particular drive seems to be practically non-existent.

Precedence of strong need. Skard [19] points out many interesting laws relating to interplay among various drives. For instance, one principle which he elaborates is that if a strong need remains unsatisfied, other needs tend to remain unrecognized. If hunger becomes intense, its very intensity so grips the individual that other drives are temporarily eclipsed. During intense hunger the sex drive is weak; likewise the drive for recognition or success is for the time being in abeyance. A strong need becomes so imperative that the drive which it sets in motion seems to have full precedence.

PROCESS OF ADJUSTMENT

Theory of instinct. One major issue which embroiled the psychological world for many years concerned the question as to whether the basic drives were learned or unlearned. Following the interest in biology in the middle of the nineteenth century and particularly in the work of Darwin and others of the evolutionary school, it became fashionable to think in terms of instinct. In seeing man as one branch in the natural development of species and being part and parcel with other branches of the animal kingdom, it was only natural to ascribe to his behavior the same instinctive and innate quality of mind that was found to operate in lower animals. That was an assumption which seemed almost axiomatic. It was little wonder, therefore, that William James,[20] in 1887, should have made a tentative list of man's instincts and should have ascribed much of the primitive behavior of man to an instinctual basis, or that Thorndike [21] should have further elaborated this concept in his volume, *The Original Nature of Man.*

19 A. G. Skard, "Needs and Need-Energy," *Character and Personality,* 8 (1939), 28–41.
20 William James, "Some Human Instincts," *Popular Science Monthly,* 31 (1887), 160–170, 666–681; William James, "What Is an Instinct?" *Scribner's Magazine,* 30 (1887), 433–451; William James, *Psychology* (New York: Henry Holt and Company, 1890), Vols. 1, 2.
21 E. L. Thorndike, *Educational Psychology,* Vol. 1, *The Original Nature of Man* (New York: Bureau of Publications, Teachers College, Columbia University, 1913).

William McDougall [22] was another champion of instincts as the "essential springs or motive powers of all thought and action." McDougall defined instinct as an *"innate specific* tendency of the mind." With dogmatic abruptness he rejected the possibility of what he defined as instinctive actions being learned.

Because the lists of specific instincts became longer and longer, the elaborate theoretical structure finally broke beneath its own weight. It is interesting that the challenge to the instinct theory should have come from a group of sociologists.[23] The behavioristic school of thought, championed by John B. Watson,[24] also presented new evidence and advocated a new point of view, namely, that the behavior of the infant could well be explained as developing by a process of learning instead of being God-given through biological inheritance.

The instinct theory saw all instinctive behavior as having four characteristics: it served the purposes of individual and race survival; it was innate and unlearned and given in a state of primitive perfection through biological inheritance; it was universal, being found in all races of men and in all cultures; each separate instinct was accompanied by a characteristic emotion. The opposing view, and the one which psychologists favor today, is that the direction of a drive which gives the drive its specific behavior qualities is determined by experience based on learning. Gregariousness, or the "drive for affiliation" as Murray calls it, then, is not an innate, biologically inherited tendency, but one which originates and develops by a process of learning in situations which must of necessity surround every infant. This change in point of view is based largely on the results of intensive observation and experiments which have demonstrated how behavior develops, and how a process of learning seems to be operative from the movement of birth. As the natural history of the development of behavior is better understood, the tendency to describe it as preformed and innate grows less. Even drives—although we recognize that fundamentally and primitively they satisfy organic tissue needs—soon become adapted to the culture, and the particular forms that the many drives of an individual take are determined as much, if not more, by the culture and the society into which he is born and grows up as by the tissue needs themselves. Marriage is not merely a matter of satisfying the sex drive, but is also an institution which has been determined in the long process of social

[22] William McDougall, *An Introduction to Social Psychology* (New York: John W. Luce & Company, 1921; 1926), 20.

[23] L. L. Bernard, "The Misuse of Instinct in the Social Sciences," *Psychological Review*, 28 (1921), 96–119; L. L. Bernard, "Instinct and the Psychoanalysts," *Journal of Abnormal and Social Psychology*, 17 (1923), 350–366; Ellsworth Faris, "Are Instincts Data or Hypotheses?" *American Journal of Sociology*, 27 (1921–1922), 184–196.

[24] J. B. Watson, *Psychology from the Standpoint of a Behaviorist* (Philadelphia: J. B. Lippincott Company, 1919).

evolution to take care of a number of basic needs of men and women.

Elements of the adjustment process. In every case there would seem to be a final reaction which reduces or removes the painful stimulus. With regard to hunger, this reaction is the swallowing of food, bringing food to the stomach and consequently relieving the painful stomach contractions. Thirst subsides when water or other liquids are taken into the mouth and swallowed. The distentions of the bladder and of the large intestine are relieved by the peristaltic movement of evacuation and urination. In the male, pressure of the seminal fluid is relieved by ejaculation. Noxious substances taken into the body through the nose are ejected by sneezing or those taken into the mouth by spitting or vomiting. On the surface of the body of the new-born infant there are reactions for brushing a tickling or painful object from the skin.[25] Freud calls such a reaction the "aim of an instinct."[26] A drive sets in motion behavior which is calculated to release this final or consummatory reaction. A reaction which reduces or eliminates the painful stimulus produces satisfaction.

The final reaction is stimulated by some object in the environment brought into contact with the body so that the reaction can operate. This object is known as the *satisfier* or *goal-object*. With reference to hunger the satisfier (food) must be discovered and brought to the mouth, where the act of swallowing can be initiated. The substance that satisfies thirst (typically water) also must be discovered and brought to the mouth. With regard to the sex drive, a person of the opposite sex is the most fitting stimulus for setting off the ejaculatory reflex or orgasm. The object or person must all be brought to the individual so that contact can be made. In the case of harmful or noxious substances the reverse is true. By accident they come into contact with the body, and then the individual seeks to separate them from himself, as when a person tries to drive away an annoying mosquito.

In the case of hunger and thirst, the precise satisfier is not uniquely prescribed. Indeed, the stronger the need, the less particular one will be as to the satisfier. When hunger is intense, almost any kind of food will be eaten. When there is intense thirst, one may be tempted to drink water even though he is not assured of its purity. On a hike, for instance, members of the party who became intensely thirsty at lunch time drank from a small stream in disregard of a sign which read, "It is dangerous to drink this water."

It is still more true that one psychogenic drive can be substituted for

25 Leonard Carmichael, "The Experimental Embryology of Mind," *Psychological Bulletin*, 38 (1941), 16, 17.

26 Freud, *Collected Papers*, IV. "Instincts and Their Vicissitudes" (1915) p. 65, used the word *instinct* as practically synonymous with the word *drive* as we have defined it and are using it in this book. Consequently, Freud's statement that this final reflex is the aim of instinct would be interpreted in our terminology as the aim of the drive.

another.[27] The youth who is denied scholastic success may compensate by his social prowess. The traffic offender, not daring to express his anger to the policeman who tells him to pull over to one side of the road, may do so later to his wife sitting innocently beside him. On the other hand, everyone knows the child who has his heart set on possessing one particular toy will not be diverted from his wish. But in this last case the ego is probably involved, and a drive to dominate and control gives tenacity to the desire.

When a need is satisfied, the person, not merely a part of the person, is satisfied. Drives do not involve segments of the personality. When a drive is set in operation it is the whole person that is at work trying to serve the drive. The organism as a whole searches for food. Consequently, the person himself is satisfied whenever one of his needs is satisfied.

A drive, therefore, which seeks as its consummation the reflex which will still the discomforting inner stimuli, and which requires an object to set this reflex into motion, initiates random, restless activity in search of this object. This seeking is in the interests of reducing the painful inner stimulation: so the drive does not become dynamic and operative until it collaborates with exterior stimuli. Behavior, then, is the joint operation of the internal forces set into motion at the behest of an organic need and the given reaction stimulated by situations in the exterior environment.

The energy for this process of restless, seeking activity is provided by the nutritional process within the organism, that is, the energy of the muscles in the manipulative and locomotive systems of the body. We have here, then, a most interesting cycle. As the organism seeks for its source of energy, it uses energy within itself. This depletion of energy creates the need; the need stimulates the drive; the drive sets in operation this seeking activity in interaction with the environment, which again consumes energy. The process of adjustment, therefore, is a neat ring or cycle of energy depletion and rebuilding. When the object or satisfier is encountered, it is attended and responded to in such a way that it is brought into contact with the body so as to set off the appropriate reflex.

In the case of harmful objects, the process of learning would seem to be somewhat simpler. Rudimentary reflexes of avoidance are already available to the organism. These become perfected through experience. In general, two methods of avoiding harmful objects are available: one is to run away or *escape*, the other is to stand one's ground and attack in order to *defend* oneself.

The learning process. Through learning, a person proceeds rather directly and without error to the satisfaction of his needs, and to the

[27] The concept of "psychogenic drive" introduced here will be elaborated in detail on pp. 28–30.

reduction of the painful stimuli which initiate drives through a chain of behavior acts. It is these chains of behavior acts that constitute the day-to-day life and activity of human beings. In response to any drive, this behavior is at first imperfect, random, and blind. It seeks it knows not what and does not even recognize an object which it is seeking with any degree of clarity or sureness. Human beings are born into the world helpless, and the first objects to satisfy needs are provided by parents. The infant is directed to its mother's breast in the first place so that the sucking and swallowing reflexes will have an opportunity to operate. From these guided first responses, the growing infant gradually learns to identify objects which will satisfy his needs and learns to manipulate them. Gradually he acquires skill and independence until he reaches maturity. Thorndike [28] has demonstrated that of the various behaviors which are tried, those are selected for survival and repetition which actually succeed in reducing the drive and satisfying the need. This is the famous *law of effect*. It is interesting that this same satisfaction which comes as the result of reduction of a drive should also serve as the decisive factor in learning. In this very real sense, learning is adaptive behavior.

In the chain of behaviors which carries one from situation to situation until the final satisfying object is attained, an individual is guided by a multitude of *cues* or *signals,* and much of learning consists in acquiring recognition of these signals and learning to respond to them. When the drive is initiated the individual immediately becomes set for certan cues which will initiate the chain of behavior leading to the final consummatory action. Consequently, after learning has established some of these chains of behavior, there will be set into operation an immediate preparatory state of anticipation tension following the arousal of a drive.

This preparatory set may be in part muscular, but probably also, in large part, it is physiologically what has sometimes been called emotional tension. The action of the sympathetic nervous system in preparing the individual for vigorous and decisive activity has been described many times. The physiological decks are cleared, as it were, for prompt and vigorous action. Energy supplies are thrown into the blood stream for immediate uses by the muscular system. Adrenalin which serves as a stimulant is released. On the other hand, the secretions and activities of the digestive system are, for the time being, diminished. This emotional tension may persist for a considerable interval in case there is no immediate muscular discharge. In fact, an emotional tension in the form of anxiety can become, in a degree, chronic, indicating the inhibition of immediate

[28] E. L. Thorndike, *Animal Intelligence: Experimental Studies* (New York: The Macmillan Company, 1911); E. L. Thorndike, *The Fundamentals of Learning* (New York: Bureau of Publications, Teachers College, Columbia University, 1932).

discharge and satisfaction of the drive. This *emotional* tension which is part of the preparatory set of an individual in response to a drive that has been aroused, should not be confused with *visceral* tension which is the stimulus to the drive itself in response to an organic need. The sequence of events is something as follows: An organic need arises. This leads to visceral tension of an unpleasant nature which serves as a stimulus to the drive. Once the drive is aroused, the organism is set into a state of preparation for the activity which is to follow. This state of preparation is what is commonly called emotional tension.

It has been said the individual learns to respond to outer stimuli as cues for the direction of drive. The direction that the drive takes is a product of learning. In the interests of good adjustment there is a need for predictable and favorable surroundings in which the cues learned through experience can function. The life of a normal human being is built up around familiar surroundings which serve as cues for the satisfaction of his needs. It is a distinct threat to an individual to be plucked from his familiar surroundings and placed in new conditions where new adjustments must be made. The old cues and signals have disappeared or no longer guide one to the final goal and lead only to frustration. This experience requires new adjustments based on renewed learning. It is always a threat to a child's adjustment to have to change from one home or family to another.

Appetite and sensory pleasure as foresatisfier. Another important principle which can be illustrated now that the process of adjustment has been discussed concerns the nature of *appetite* and *sensory pleasure*. Activities stimulated originally by organic drives and originally serving these drives may have their own sensory pleasures which operate as foresatisfiers. There are two main groups of these foresatisfiers. The first are the pleasures from sensation—taste, smell, sight, hearing, and touch. Let us illustrate how these operate by discussing taste and its connection with hunger. Much has already been said describing how an organism, in response to the hunger drive, and through a blind trial-and-error process of learning, finally establishes efficient behavior patterns for reducing the drive. When food is taken into the mouth it stimulates the sense organs of taste which are, on the whole, pleasurable, although certain taste sensations are unpleasurable. By and large, valuable foods have a pleasant taste, whereas many noxious or poisonous food substances have an unpleasant taste. However, taste varies according to the stage of need and becomes one of the main determiners of appetite. These pleasures of taste, particularly in anticipation, can serve as stimuli for eating in the ready stage of the drive of hunger even before the drive of hunger becomes dynamically active. One has only to watch a little child tease for a sweet when he is obviously not ravenously hungry to see how this has its own driving qualities. Likewise, we are not only stimulated but driven in anticipation by pleasing odors, agreeable sights and sounds, and pleasing sensations of touch. We seek the art gallery, the concert, we bend over to smell the flowers, we reach out and touch silk or velvet in order to have the pleasure of the agreeable sensation.

Erogenous Zones. A second group of these foresatisfiers is composed of erogenous zones. These are surfaces of the skin at various orifices of the body which are highly endowed with sense organs, the stimulation of which have their own peculiar quality of pleasure. There is no doubt that there is peculiar pleasure in the stimulation of the lips. One has only to observe the infant who mouths everything within reach to see what a strong attraction this form of pleasure has. The intensity of pleasure in the stimulation of the lips diminishes after the first year, but throughout life people find pleasure in sucking objects, smoking, kissing, and the like. Likewise, there are equally pleasurable sensations in the anus, and the infant finds the process of defecation a pleasurable one. This is difficult for adults to appreciate because our culture has laid over this pleasure with disgust and loathing so that the pleasurable aspects of this process are submerged and deeply repressed. The highly sensitive and stimulating nature of the genital organs are well known and do not need to be elaborated. The stimulation of any of these sensitive areas has been recognized by psychoanalysts as having a sexual quality and perhaps as standing with respect to sex as a foresatisfier in much the same way that taste stands in respect to hunger. The hands can contribute to this pleasure by touching and rubbing, by grasping objects and bringing them to the mouth, and perhaps by the manipulation process itself. Lastly, the infant finds pleasure through looking, so that the eyes become another source of sensory satisfaction.

Distinction Between Appetite and Drive. These pleasurable sensations, therefore, must be distinguished from drive proper. Drives, as we have seen, are efforts to remove painful or unpleasant stimuli. On the other hand, appetite is the general term to be given to the driving force of these pleasurable sensations. Perhaps the pleasure principle, enunciated by Freud, applies more directly to the driving force of these foresatisfiers than to the inner organic drives themselves which, as we have seen, are annoying. If one wishes to be comprehensive in describing the nature of the dynamic origins of behavior, one ought in reality to speak of a pain-pleasure principle, rather than of the pleasure principle itself. In other words, fundamentally, all behavior looks toward the reduction of painful stimuli but is guided in this direction, following the process of learning, by seeking the stimulation of certain pleasurable stimuli.

As we have seen, drive is blind and without direction. It is partly through appetite that direction is given to the drive. Appetite is selective.

Any food within wide limits will satisfy hunger. It is appetite which is selective of the foods that we like and hence prefer and choose. Young [29] speaks of the partial hungers, by which he means the *specific* needs which develop in response to the depletion of *specific* food elements within the body. He believes that chemical changes produced in the body, following the depletion of specific nutritional elements, cause chemical changes in the sense organs of taste, raising or lowering certain taste thresholds. These variations in taste in their turn raise or lower appetites for different foods which influence an organism's choice of food. For instance, if there is a lowering of the salt content of the body there will be a corresponding lowering of the salt taste threshold which will result in a craving for salty foods until the depletion in the body is made up. This may serve as a pattern for other varieties of appetite which take their place in the general concept of drive, but serve, at the same time, in helping to determine the direction of drive. Appetite may change without a corresponding change in drive. Bring tempting food within sight of a person or permit him to smell the odor of a roast cooking, and immediately his appetite will increase even though there is no corresponding change in hunger.

It is interesting to note that what were originally the cues or signals for initiating a train of responses, eventually reducing a drive, may later themselves yield their own satisfaction. This is, of course, in line with the principle that habits may become drives. In this way we attach values and sentiment to personal possessions, to special foods, pictures, textures, fabrics, buildings, and the like. In this way one prizes distant tokens of affection in place of more immediate sensory gratification. A letter may bring tidings which are very nearly the equal of the sender's presence, and they affirm his continued allegiance and trust. Such tokens are more effective in the realm of sex than in the satisfaction of other basic physiological needs. A token of food hardly staves off hunger.

Replacement of one drive by another. Finally, among the psychogenic drives in particular, there is the possibility for a considerable amount of substitution and replacement of one drive for another. Psychogenic drives, as may be remembered, are always means toward ends, but human nature is extremely flexible in substituting one means for another, in case the old drive does not give promise of resulting satisfaction of the need which it is serving. A child may have a strong desire to dominate its parents by negativistic behavior; but if the parents are adamant in refusing requests or become too threatening, the child may change his tactics and strive to win his ends by becoming winsome and cute.

[29] P. T. Young, "The Experimental Analysis of Appetite," *Psychological Bulletin*, 38 (1941), 129–164.

CLASSIFICATION OF DRIVES

Having now discussed some of the physiological principles which underlie drive and the process of adjustment and learning by which drives are translated into action, we are now ready to present and discuss some of the drives. In the following discussion a number of pairs of opposites or dichotomies will be set forth. That these fundamental driving qualities in the individual exist in contrasting pairs is not due to some twist in the author's mind but goes back to certain dichotomous cleavages in the organism and its organization.

Desires and aversions. The first distinctions to be made is that between *desires* and the *aversions*. This concept was first enunciated and the names, desires and aversion, given to these two opposite tendencies by Hobbes nearly three centuries ago.[30] Craig [31] noted the distinction again more recently in a study of the instincts of doves. Certain drives require for their satisfaction bringing to the body some object or person. On the other hand, there are needs which are satisfied by the separation of objects (or persons) from the body, including both substances which are expelled from the body and objects which are separated from the body. Harmful substances on the surface of the body which stimulate the sense of pain, or extremes of heat and cold must be separated from the body either by throwing them off or retracting the body from them. A spider's web is brushed from the face as we unwittingly run into it. The child pulls his hand away quickly when he touches the lighted end of a cigarette.

These two groups of needs may be related generally in terms of the goals which are sought in order to satisfy the needs—*satisfaction* and *safety*. By satisfaction we refer to the satisfaction of inner needs or appetites; by safety the condition by which outer dangers are avoided or are prevented from threatening.

Self — **Ego and libido basic needs.** A second distinction already made on p. 11 exists between the *ego* and *libido* needs. This distinction may also be known as the drive toward *self-preservation* and the drive toward *race preservation,* based on *hunger and thirst,* on the one hand, and *love* or *sex,* on the other. This pair of fundamental and underlying needs or

---

[30] "This endeavour, when it is toward something which causes it, is called 'appetite,' or 'desire,' the latter being the general name, and the other oftentimes restrained to signify the desire for food, namely, 'hunger' and 'thirst.' And, when the endeavour is fromward something, it is generally called 'aversion.' "—Thomas Hobbes, *Leviathan* (London: edition of George Routledge & Sons), 28.

[31] Wallace Craig, "Male Doves Reared in Isolation," *Journal of Animal Behavior,* 14 (1914), 121–133; Wallace Craig, "Appetites and Aversions as Constituents of Instincts," *Biological Bulletin,* 34 (1918), 91–107.

need groups was enunciated by Freud [32] in his earlier work, as being the basic and fundamental instincts.

Basically the body has these two main groups of needs, the one having to do with maintenance of the individual, the other with preservation of the race. It is justifiable and convenient to split off drives according to whether they are serving one end or the other. In fact, one system of diagnosis of personality which was originated by Kenworthy attempts to classify all of the information gathered about an indvidual into these two categories, according to whether the personality trend seems to be in the interests of maintenance of the individual or of sex.[33] However, this distinction is difficult to make, as much behavior serves both purposes at the same time. For instance, a man's love-making to a girl obviously has a sexual reference but at the same time expresses his appreciation of her as an individual. Or to use another illustration, a woman may be attracted to a man because she is interested in gaining sex satisfactions, but at the same time she hopes to get a good home and a good provider. There are differences, however. The ego drives are, on the whole, more urgent than the libido drives, except within very narrow limits. Hunger, for instance, is not something that can be put off or delayed or for which substitute satisfactions can be used. Only eating can satisfy hunger, and only drinking can satisfy thirst. No other reflexes will suffice; no substitution can be made. Ego drives are relatively inflexible and consequently are amenable to educational influences out of sheer necessity. To exist at all is to adjust. On the other hand, the libido drives tend to be somewhat plastic. In the case of sex, substitutions are possible and one aim can take the place of another.

Viscerogenic and psychogenic drives. A third dichotomy is that mentioned by Murray, who divided drives into the two classifications: *viscerogenic* and *psychogenic*. Viscerogenic drives are those which have already been so thoroughly discussed in this chapter. They are the drives depending on bodily needs—the deficits, tensions, or tissue damages. Psychogenic drives have not been mentioned so far, except in passing. These drives are thought to be, in all instances, derivations of the viscerogenic drives. They are mental and emotional processes and behaviors which serve to prepare the way for the more fundamental organic satisfactions. Under psychogenic drives we would list such tendencies within the individual as the dominance of others or submissiveness to others, showing aggression toward others, striving for achievement, having a tendency to exhibit oneself prominently, showing a desire to learn about things and pry into the affairs of others, and so on. For none of these tendencies can

---

[32] Sigmund Freud, *Collected Papers*, IV. "Instincts and Their Vicissitudes" (1915), 67.

[33] See M. E. Watson, *Children and Their Parents* (New York: Appleton-Century-Crofts, Inc., 1932).

a specific somatic source of stimulation be found. They are behavior tendencies which prepare the way for the satisfaction of the more basic viscerogenic needs.

The accompanying table from Murray [34] quotes a list of twelve viscerogenic drives in a significant classification. In the first place, they are grouped according to the kind of need represented. The first four represent vital organic needs and have as consummatory reflexes an intake operation including oxygen, water, food, as well as various sensory pleasures. A second group includes those drives where the stimulus is a distention, and these are relieved by an output or disposal of something from inside the body. They include sex, lactation, expulsion of carbon dioxide, urination, and defecation. Then there is a group of harms or dangers which are reacted to by retractions or avoidances. Here Murray has included the avoidance of various toxic or irritating stimuli, avoidance of pain, and avoidance of extremes or heat and cold.

A List of Twelve Viscerogenic Drives [35]

a) *Lacks* (leading to intakes)		1. Inspiration (oxygen)	
		2. Water	
		3. Food	Positive
		4. Sensory gratification	Adient
b) *Distentions* (leading to outputs)	Secretion (life-sources)	5. Sex	
		6. Lactation	
	Excretion (waste)	7. Expiration (carbon dioxide)	
		8. Urination	
		9. Defecation	
c) *Harms* (leading to retractions)		10. Avoidance of repulsive, irritating, or nauseating substances	Negative Abient
		11. Avoidance of pain	
		12. Avoidance of extremes of heat or cold	

To illustrate how a psychogenic drive might originate, let us consider the drive to be *helped, advised,* or *guided* by another person. In the state of helplessness in earliest infancy, we know that the baby's wants are

[34] H. A. Murray, Jr., and others, *Explorations in Personality* (New York: Oxford University Press, 1938), 76, 88.

[35] From H. A. Murray, *Explorations in Personality,* 79. By permission of Oxford University Press, New York.

satisfied through the care of his mother. At first, of course, the fact that his satisfactions are at the mercy of the continued care and protection of another person is only dimly realized. When this nurture is given readily and regularly, a child may never clearly sense the fact that he is depending for the satisfaction of his needs on other persons. It is only when this nurture is irregularly or carelessly and unwillingly given that the child begins to respond to this need distinctly as apart from the satisfaction of the hunger itself. If, as a prerequisite for getting food, warmth, and other comforts, he has first to attract the attention of his mother and make her interested and willing to supply his needs, then the need for nurture becomes a drive on its own account. The child in school who demands a great deal of attention is sometimes one who is accustomed to having every need constantly and instantaneously satisfied, but also one who has learned to demand attention in order to get some of his other basic needs satisfied. This account of how the drive toward being sustained, protected, and guided by others originates will serve as a type illustration for the development of all psychogenic drives. They are forced on an individual as way-stations in the process of satisfying basic organic needs and eventually take on driving forces of their own. The child who has first to win the attention and interest of his parents will be the child in whom the drive for being protected and loved is most strongly developed, and this drive may persist even into adult life. Similarly, other drives may be developed to a high degree of strength in response to frustrations.

   Fundamental goals: security and adequacy. Every individual has two fundamental goals or aims: one to be secure, and the other to be adequate. Alexander [36] interprets the wish for security as an expression of dependence, while the wish for adequacy he interprets as an expression of self-expression and independence. He even goes so far as to call the wish for security an expression of a collectivistic trend, while the wish for adequacy he describes as an individualistic trend. Security is related to the desire to avoid frustration. On the ego side there is the goal of playing safe and avoiding dangers or harms. An important part of learning in infancy consists in recognizing dangers in order to avoid them. So, achieving security on the ego level is related to attempts to banish fear of outer danger and to rid oneself of feelings of insecurity. Security also relates to the avoidance of inner lacks and the privations due to lack of food, oxygen, and sensory stimulation. We speak of emotional security as being mainly concerned with the prevention of loss of love and affection and tenderness and all the other satisfactions that these carry with them. The most important phase of security to the little child is that he

[36] Franz Alexander, "Aggressiveness-Individual and Collective," in *The March of Medicine,* the New York Academy of Medicine Lectures to the Laity, 1943 (New York: Columbia University Press, 1943), 83–99.

shall continue to receive the warmth of his mother's love, because if he can be assured of the continuance of this love, he feels that it will bring with it the other satisfactions he needs. A major threat to a child's emotional security is the possibility of a cooling off in the intensity of the love which his parents feel for him. This need for security is not something that is felt only in infancy when one is helpless and when loss of love would be a real threat; this need continues all through life. One never grows away from the need to be loved by others, although in some persons this need may be clearly repressed. Gradually through childhood and particularly in adolescence, one seeks security in friendly relationships with one's contemporaries. Even in the adult the need for security persists, and typically one establishes a family of his own in which husband and wife continue to provide security for each other, perpetuating the same circle of security relationships into which the person originally was ushered into the world. In old age the need for emotional security and a family relationship returns with renewed insistence.

Adequacy is connected with the need to *achieve* satisfaction. In a general sense, every growing child wishes to learn how he may have his wishes come true and achieve satisfaction. We can think of adequacy along the two lines of the ego and the libido. To maintain the self the individual needs to learn mastery over his environment. As the child begins to get about he proceeds to learn certain skills with hand and eye. Instead of being limited to objects within reach, he can move about to bring himself into contact with objects beyond his reach. The child begins to explore, learn the relationships of objects, and gain skill in manipulating them. He also learns to manage himself and to run and jump, to swim and ski. In his individual psychology Adler [37] has fully elaborated the importance of adequacy for individual adjustment. On the side of the libido, an individual can be adequate in gaining for himself various pleasures. On the sensory level one may also secure skill. One thinks of the acquisition of skill in producing music or painting, or in enjoying music or appreciating painting. On the purely sexual level securing satisfaction is also something that is subject to learning. To become adequate sexually is no more innate than to become adequate in adapting to the world about one, yet this is often forgotten by adults, due to sensitiveness and prudery in regard to sex. Many parents are afraid of sex and believe that pleasure is wicked, so that instead of permitting their children to learn how to become sexually adequate, they attempt to stamp out all sexual expression.

These two goals of security and adequacy are basic to good adjustment. Whenever one finds a person who shows signs of poor adjustment,

[37] Alfred Adler, *Study of Organ Inferiority and Its Psychical Compensation*, Nervous and Mental Disease Monograph Series, No. 24 (New York: Nervous and Mental Disease Publishing Company, 1917).

one may be certain that he has failed to achieve reasonable goals of adequacy or security or both. Adequacy and security are two conditions which are essential for normality in living, and a society which makes possible the accomplishment of these goals achieves stability.

Fundamental emotional responses. Two fundamental responses in the adjustment process are *love* and *hate*. These two feelings, which again represent two opposite poles, are derived directly through the adjustment process. We have already seen that the need which produces a drive is unpleasant, annoying, or unsatisfying. *Love* is related to *gratification* and is an outgrowth of the pleasant feelings resulting from the reduction of a need. Love can be traced back originally to relief of hunger and other basic needs and to the sensual pleasures.

The new-born infant seemingly gets *gratification* from nursing and processes of excretion. Later, however, as learning develops, he begins to recognize the persons and objects which are related to the process of gaining gratification. Just as taking nourishment is pleasant and satisfying, so he learns to attach his feelings of well-being to the persons (and objects) which are connected with or related to these satisfying experiences. Speaking more plainly, he begins to like, find pleasure in, and love his mother who is always associated with the experience of nursing. Toward the good mother who contributes to his satisfactions there are friendly feelings expressed by gurgling and cooing and later by return of caresses and affection. This is the beginning of the love response. By a slow process of learning, it spreads and eventually takes in all objects to which the infant is attracted and by which he finds pleasure or which even contribute to these experiences in later life. Love, then, is the generic and basic term (although it is a somewhat strong and emotionally charged term) to stand for all our positive emotionally toned attitudes toward people, objects, events, and conditions.

Hate, on the other hand, is related to frustration.[38] As needs remain unsatisfied and drives do not find a solution, the painful or uncomfortable stimuli persist. We have already made this clear with regard to both hunger and sex. These feelings of frustration, irritation, or unpleasantness then become projected on and attached to persons or objects associated with the withholding of satisfactions. The inner annoyance becomes associated with the person responsible for denying the satisfaction of pleasure. The bad mother who is associated with his continued deprivations is hated in a primitive way by the infant who storms against her by wailing, and, when older, by attempts either to harm her or to rob her of the nourishment which she possesses. This is the origin of hate. Hate again is a general term (perhaps emotionally

[38] John Dollard, L. W. Doob, N. E. Miller, O. H. Mowrer, R. R. Sears, *Frustration and Aggression* (New Haven: Yale University Press, 1939).

overtoned) to stand for all negative feelings and attitudes toward persons, objects, events, and circumstances which are frustrative.

This pair of responses describes the basic attitudes that an individual takes toward all subsequent experiences. The external mother can both withhold nourishment, and hence call up these painful feelings, and provide relief from painful internal stimuli. These good and bad internal states, therefore, become identified with a good and bad external object—the mother or nurse. Further than that there develops a tendency to project these inner states onto external objects and persons and attribute to them characteristics which are comparable to these inner states. So the image of a person develops which is a reflection of one's inner states, and the qualities and characteristics which are ascribed to a person are as much the product of one's own inner states of comfort and discomfort, satisfaction and dissatisfaction, as they are the result of one's observation of the characteristics of the person himself. Every individual has a capacity for loving and also for hating, and these become attached to parents and siblings as well as to objects and circumstances in the early environment. One can certainly count on love and hate directed toward both father and mother as being present in everyone. If we find an individual in whom hate, anger, aggression, or hostility is absent or an individual in whom love for father and mother is absent, we have to assume that these attitudes have been repressed, because, by the nature of the developmental process, they must have been there originally. The process of therapy consists, to a large extent, in enabling the individual to express these two basic attitudes more freely in the various situations that he has to face.

Directions That Love May Take. Love may take one of two directions. First of all, love is directed toward the self—every individual is fundamentally interested in satisfying his own needs. Later one can direct his love to other persons, which is the customary meaning, or one can again refer the love given to other persons back onto the self. Love, as we saw, grows out of the conditions which surround gaining of satisfaction. It is a transference of feelings of well-being which accompany satisfaction to the objects or situations or circumstances which were associated with achieving the satisfaction. Original satisfactions are very specific kinds of sensory pleasure arising from stimulation of the erogenous zones, as well as from the deeper satisfactions which represent the reduction of visceral tension. Such sensory pleasures are originally stimulated by other persons, but as the infant grows older and acquires skill in manipulation he learns that he can stimulate these pleasures in himself. Instead of getting mouth pleasure from his mother's breast he may suck his own thumb. Instead of becoming aroused and excited from the gentle stimulation of the pressure of the napkin on his genitals he may learn that he can stimulate himself as in masturbation. Those sensory pleasures stimulated by other persons are called *alloerotic;* those stimulated by the person himself are called *autoerotic.* Alloerotism and autoerotism are pleasures out of which love is built.

As intelligence develops, discriminations are made so that the infant begins to distinguish between himself and other persons, and when they are recognized as separate from himself, tender feelings may be expressed toward them. Later, however, as he learns to know himself as a person, similar in kind to other persons that he recognizes about him, he may place on himself the same erotic feelings of value and tenderness and regard that he has already placed on others. However, the term "autoerotic" is not usually used to refer to the placement of tender feelings on the self as a separate individual, but only to a more limited self-stimulation of pleasure.

Tender feelings, admiration, regard, and affection directed toward others is usually called *object love.* For the turning of tender regard, admiration, and even feelings of affection to the self, we have the term *self-love.* These feelings are turned toward the self in part as a reflection or incorporation of the attitude of mother, nurse, and others. As a mother shows pleasure in and admires her child, so he learns to find pleasure in and admire himself. Normally in the process of development the feelings of satisfaction and pleasure are first turned to others when a clear conception of others is developed, and they are associated with these satisfactions. To give pleasure to another person, while not unnatural, is not a primitive behavior trend and represents motivation which is derived. To turn these positive feelings back on the self is usually a much later process. If narcissism is exaggerated it usually represents a throwing back on the self of love which, for some reason, is not permitted or appreciated when given to others; and it is an attempt to make up to one's self for love not received from others. It is well to distinguish here between active and passive love. Active love is the giving of one's love to another person; passive love is the doing of things to secure the love of someone else.

Directions That Hate May Take. While love is first directed toward the self but may later be directed toward another person, hate is first of all directed toward other persons but on occasions may be turned back to the self. Psychoanalysis has no fancy names to give to these two directions hate may take. That hate in the form of aggression and hostility is directed out toward other persons is only too well known. The management of these fundamental tendencies to hate constitutes one of the major problems of civilized life. The question as to whether war is inevitable has been a frequent topic for debate. One thing seems to be clear, namely, that tendencies toward hate are the common property of all persons. However, the degree to which these tendencies can be redirected in constructive channels has not as yet been fully explored, and in these unknown possibilities is the hope that civilization will reach stability and eliminate destructive war. Doing harm to oneself or having others do harm to one (which is the meaning of masochism) is not natural, and implies a turning of these impulses to do harm to others back onto the self. Why should anyone wish to do harm to himself? And yet the evidence of self-directed hate in disguised forms is plentiful. Every day we see persons who inflict hardships on themselves, belittle themselves, assume unnecessary tasks and obligations, and place burdens on themselves with feelings not unlike the stormy and aggressive feelings that are directed toward others. Doing things to bring hate or aggression (punishment) from another person onto the self is called passive aggression, as contrasted with active hate (aggression) which attempts to harm the other person.

To present a complete catalogue of psychogenic drives is an impossibility. To attempt to do so would incur the same error made by those who used to prepare lists of instincts. In the foregoing section certain fundamental drives and processes were distinguished. In the process of reducing any one of these fundamental drives, other subsidiary processes will be employed which also take on the nature of drives. These subdivisions can be extended indefinitely until they include such drives as to read the morning newspaper over a neighbor's shoulder, to exchange a shirt which is the wrong size, to entertain a friend who is visiting the city, to plan an interesting summer vacation, or to show contempt for a person who gives one a slight. The division and subdivisions multiply in a limitless manner, and one would never be satisfied with his task.

This book is largely concerned with a discussion of the motivation and development of the so-called psychogenic drives. So instead of listing them here as inevitable personality characteristics they will be introduced in the succeeding discussion as dynamic elements of personality, each with its own motivation and reason for existence.

HIERARCHY OF NEEDS

Maslow [39] has suggested that needs arrange themselves in a hierarchy going from the most elemental and physiological to those which represent the higher development of the individual. He would place needs on five levels: the first level would comprise the basic physiological needs of hunger, sex, and so on. The second level would comprise the needs of safety, that is, of avoiding external dangers that might result in harm

[39] A. H. Maslow, "Preface to Motivation Theory," *Psychosomatic Medicine*, 5 (1943), 85–92; A. H. Maslow, "A Theory of Human Motivation," *Psychological Review*, 50 (1943), 370–396.

to the individual from the outside. In the third level there is the need for love—that is, to be given love, warmth and affection by another person. On the fourth level is the need for esteem—that is, self-respect, self-esteem, and also the respect and esteem of others. Finally, there is the need for self-realization, of being able to accomplish and achieve—to paint a picture, to secure a position, to occupy a place in one's group. Maslow suggests that these represent a hierarchy of five levels. Gratification of needs on the first or more basic levels frees a person for the higher social needs; for instance, if a person's physical needs and his needs for safety and love are taken care of, he can turn his attention and devote his energies to the more distinctly ego needs and efforts toward self-realization on the higher levels. On the other hand, if these more basic needs are not met, they claim priority, and activities on the higher levels must be temporarily postponed.

In a stable society a man is able to cultivate his higher needs. On the other hand, in Europe during and after the Second World War, vast sections of the population were forced to direct their efforts to satisfying the basic needs of safety and hunger, and the higher needs had to be temporarily foregone. Maslow illustrates his principle by such aphorisms as: "Man lives not by bread alone except when his stomach is empty." "The search for love is not a main motivation except in rejected people." "Sex is not a fundamental motivation for those who are sexually satisfied." Those persons in whom a need has been satisfied are best equipped to deal with deprivations of that need in the future. It is the individual who has grown up in a secure and happy home, not deprived of his basic needs, who is best able to stand such privations in later life, while the individual who has suffered insecurities in childhood is the one who is first to succumb to difficulties and deprivations in later life. This principle was verified over and over during the war: the emotionally secure individual was the one able to stand the greatest shock of war conditions.

Maslow [40] uses this hierarchy principle as a criterion of normality and maladjustment. The healthy man is one whose basic needs have been met so that he is principally motivated by his needs to develop and actualize his highest potentialities. The maladjusted and neurotic person, on the other hand, is one who is dominated by his more basic needs. Since his previous insecurities have never made him feel entirely safe with regard to gratification of his more basic needs, he is never quite free to turn his attention to activities of self-realization and achievement. Carrying this a step further, one might say that a healthy civilization is one that provides the satisfaction of the needs on the lower levels, enabling men to turn their energies toward goals which will satisfy the needs on the higher levels.

[40] A. H. Maslow, "A Theory of Human Motivation," *Psychological Review*, 50 (1943), 370–396.

Maslow's hierarchy theory has its implications for psychotherapy. The *be aware of their needs* individual whose first-level needs have been met is the most stable and the least in need of therapy; while the individual who has to struggle to satisfy his primary needs is the most unstable and the most in need of therapy. For one whose basic needs have been met, short-term, superficial therapy will probably be profitable when he is temporarily disturbed; while the person whose basic needs have been frustrated requires deep, long-time therapy. The task of the therapist may be described as that of providing the basic satisfactions of safety, love, and esteem when the individual has been deprived of these, so that the higher needs of self-realization can have an opportunity to seek expression. It is for this reason that therapy consists essentially of a relationship in which the therapist gives his client security, support, and ego enhancement by being accepting and permissive. When an individual partakes of these, he, in a measure, makes up for deprivations along these lines suffered in infancy, childhood, and adolescence, and continues his growth toward characteristics and attitudes of greater maturity.

APPLICATIONS AND IMPLICATIONS

Social control of drives. All human effort is directed toward the gratification of basic drives. Therefore fundamentally, all of the basic drives, both physiological and psychogenic, are good. They have positive value, and their expression is to be encouraged and fostered. As we have seen, they arise in the interests of self-preservation and race perpetuation, and concerning these needs there can be no argument nor need for justication. What must be explained, however, is how these basic drives could ever have been considered unworthy or evil; and yet one of the ancient Greek philosophies, Stoicism, taught that man should be free from passion and should be indifferent to pleasure or pain. Undoubtedly this attitude has been an economic necessity forced on people in all ages and in all parts of the world in order to make the toleration of hardship acceptable. To us, it appears to be a species of rationalization: what one cannot have is not worth striving for.

Education should have as one of its aims, encouraging the expression of basic drives and helping the child to acquire effective and adequate methods for their expression. Unfortunately education has often seen its task as quite the opposite of this and has been concerned with teaching laws and rules and attempting to channel behavior into socially approved forms. So education aims to be principally social and moral. It has been considered, primarily, the servant of society in helping to inculcate in the child the controls that are necessary in our own culture. Consequently, major emphasis in education has been put on the matter of *control* and this, of necessity, results in the suppression of drives which are considered particularly dangerous or objectionable in civilized society. Education for individual happiness and adequacy, as well as for the protection of society, would do well to shift its aim toward effective and socially useful *expression* of basic drives.

Control of Sex. These principles can be illustrated by reference to society's attitude toward the control of sex. Sex has been thought of as something evil and vile, to be repressed in all its manifestations except within the institution of marriage itself. All expressions of sex particularly were to be suppressed in growing children. No one thinks of suppressing the drive to alleviate hunger. However, society feels it necessary to place hedges about the sex drive. One can understand the reason for this in that the family is recognized as perhaps the basic institution of civilization, and its sanctity and preservation is valued above everything else. It is through the family that personality and social control are developed. However, there is much evidence to indicate that society has overdone the stringency of its control, and much individual maladjustment with a train of social ills has resulted from too stringent suppression of the sex drive. Granting the necessity of control in the interests of social stability, this should be rather a matter of redirection than of suppression.

In dealing with adolescents, teachers commonly are on their guard lest sex raise its "ugly" head and find illicit expression. Teachers of adolescents would do better if they could shift their attitude to planning social and recreational activities in which boys and girls could find, under sympathetic supervision, wholesome and normal outlets for their growing interests. Instead of becoming horrified at any expression of sexual interests, teachers would have a more constructive influence if they provided club-rooms and planned parties at which boys and girls could have fun together.

Morals as Related to Social Regulation of Drives. Morals have been developed throughout the history of the race in the interests of the social regulation of drives. Naturally as one individual satisfies his drives, he may interfere with the satisfactions of another individual. Rules have grown up which tend to constrain a person from being too rapacious in his own interests, particularly where they would interfere with the interests of others. Also an individual may, in the long run, interfere with his own satisfactions if he indulges without restraint in the satisfaction of some one need. Morals, therefore, help to give balance and stability both in the individual economy and in the regulation of social affairs. The greatest happiness can be achieved when there is a fair balance in the satisfaction of the various drives. However, if too much control and suppression is exercised in the interests of morals, the result may be a breaking out of neurotic tendencies in the individual. It is possible to push morals too far and to destroy the optimum development of individuals by a too thoroughgoing damming up of individual expression. This is a problem that will have to be dealt with increasingly as society becomes more closely knit.

Regulation of Drives Through Institutions. Institutions help to regulate drives in the interests of the group. Instead of permitting the sex drive unbridled expression, the institution of the family has come into being in the interests of the growing child, and society takes pride in preserving the family against all encroachments because of its value in providing more adequate expression of individual development. Institutions have developed differently in different parts of the world in response to varying conditions. Some of these conditions will be briefly mentioned. The sex ratio between men and women has had a part to play in determining the nature of marriage and the family. Where there are an equal number of men and women the monogamic family has been found to be of most value. However, various kinds of polygamy are practiced in certain sections of the world, due partly to variations in the sex ratio. Education is a second social requirement which has helped to establish the institutions of the family and the school. The kind of subsistence that is available to a society helps to determine the institutions of work and economy. An agrarian society will establish different institutions from a nomadic or an industrial society. Property helps to determine the kinds of institutions that society will have. Where articles are scarce, or where they are in abundance, forms of communism may develop, whereas articles which are for individual use and which must be passed from one person to another by trade may lead to a capitalistic society. The control of love and sex is another force helping to determine marriage and the family. The control of aggression leads to the state and the law. Finally, the defense of the group against enemies influences the form of society. When Germany and Japan gave clear indications of world conquest, American society was rapidly transformed from one in which little attention had to be paid to national defense to one in which the presence of a large armed force seemed to be a necessity. Each of these institutions which has grown up in response to the conditions imposed on living has as its purpose the regulation of the basic drives of the individual.

The control, regulation, and direction of basic drives is the prerogative of parents and teachers in the first place. Eventually, however, each individual is expected to become self-directing and to carry within himself a set of habits that fit the mores which are the basis of order in a society and a legacy to be passed on to the next generation.

Inner Control of Drive. One major function of the ego is to manage the control of the drives which are turned over from external authority to internal authority. Every individual manages himself so as to adapt to the culture and institutions in which he grows up. The individual who fails to acquire this inner control is looked upon as being criminal or insane. One of the major purposes of education is to help the individual achieve this balanced control of the various drives which arise in the course of development. This does not mean, however, that these inner driving forces are to be repressed, but that the direction of their expression shall not interfere with equally satisfactory forms of expression in other persons. However, no child should be forced to accept uncritically the customs which are passed on to him by his elders, but as he matures he should make his own adaptations to the conditions surrounding him on the basis of intelligence. Freud [41] has enunciated a reality principle by which the ego adapts itself to its surroundings in the interest both of the expression and satisfaction of the fundamental drives and of the interests of the social group.

Knowledge of drives and conflicts an aid in understanding the individual. To understand an individual, it is necessary to discover what drives are operating and how these drives are in conflict. To be of assistance to an individual who is in need of working out more satisfactory adjustments, one needs three kinds of information: first the extent to which an individual has a drive for achievement, or for recognition, or for nurturance; and secondly, the more detailed ways in which these drives tend to be expressed, that is, in what situations they operate, toward what persons they are directed, and which more basic drives they serve. Thirdly, it is necessary to know with what conflicts between these drives an individual is struggling, and how these conflicts are directed with respect to situations and persons.

QUESTIONS FOR DISCUSSION

1. What kinds of disequilibrium take place within the body and what processes tend to restore the equilibrium? Are there disequilibriums in the personality? What steps does a person take to restore his mental or personality equilibrium?

2. Does the avoidance of discomfort and the search for pleasure as the basic motives for all behavior explain such acts as voluntarily submitting to pain in the dentist's chair, advancing in battle, submitting to hazing in joining a fraternity, obeying training rules during the football season?

3. Psychoanalysts continue to refer to "instincts" even though instinct theory has been generally discredited in psychology. To what do they have reference? What justification is there for speaking of a "sexual instinct," a "life instinct," and "death instinct"?

4. What is the relation between drive and learning?

5. What does it mean to say that the ego drives are more urgent than the libido drives? If the sexual drives are more flexible than the ego drives and are less urgent why are they so inaccessible to direct educational influence?

6. Speculate as to how the psychogenic drive "curiosity" could have developed out of more basic viscerogenic drives.

[41] Sigmund Freud, *op. cit.*, 1920; first published in German, 1916.

7. Give illustrations of the need for security in (a) the baby just after weaning (b) the baby when a brother or sister is born (c) the child when he first enters school (d) adolescence (e) the first year of marriage (f) old age.

8. Why is it said that hate comes before love?

9. How does the distinction between masculine and feminine differ from the distinction between active and passive?

10. What evidence is there that the psychological differences between men and women are cultural? biological?

11. What is the meaning of active love? passive love? of active hate? of passive hate?

12. It is said that the aim of society should be the direction and regulation of drives rather than their suppression. Illustrate this principle in the case of aggressive drives, sex drives.

13. How can a counselor use his knowledge of drives in psychotherapy?

RECOMMENDED READINGS

1. DASHIELL, J. F., *Fundamentals of General Psychology* (Boston: Houghton Mifflin Company, 1937).
2. HOLT, E. B., *Animal Drive and the Learning Process* (New York: Henry Holt and Company, 1931).
3. HORNEY, KAREN, *New Ways in Psychoanalysis* (New York: W. W. Norton and Company, Inc., 1939).
4. KLEIN, MELANIE, and RIVIERE, JOAN, *Love, Hate, and Reparation*, Psychoanalytical Epitomes, No. 2 (London: The Hogarth Press, 1937).
5. LANGER, W. C., *Psychology and Human Living* (New York: Appleton-Century-Crofts, Inc., 1943).
6. MASLOW, A. H., "A Theory of Human Motivation," *Psychological Review*, 50 (1943), 370–396.
7. MUNN, N. L., *Psychology* (Boston: Houghton Mifflin Company, 1946).
8. MURRAY, H. A., JR., and others, *Explorations in Personality* (New York: Oxford University Press, 1938).
9. PLANT, J. S., *Personality and the Cultural Pattern* (New York: The Commonwealth Fund, 1937).
10. SHAFFER, L. F., *Psychology of Adjustment* (Boston: Houghton Mifflin Company, 1936).
11. YOUNG, P. T., *The Motivation of Behavior* (New York: John Wiley & Sons, Inc., 1936).

III

Frustration

In this chapter the nature of frustration, the methods of meeting and overcoming it, and its implications for individual adjustment will be examined and analyzed. Frustration is an essential experience of all living matter. We have just been considering the needs and drives of an individual growing out of the conditions of maintenance and development of the organism. It is a well-known fact that these needs are not satisfied gratuitously but require adaptation on the part of the organism. This is to say that needs are practically never immediately satisfied but are frustrated. An exception to this is the oxygen need which is continuously met and satisfied by the reflexes of breathing. Frustration is not something that occurs rarely and which is to be considered a sign of misfortune. On the contrary, since the rhythm of metabolism continually throws the organism into disequilibrium, frustrations are being continually produced which require effort and activity to restore the equilibrium. Life is a series of needs and activities directed toward meeting them. Alexander [1] has made the point that pleasure is dependent on previous displeasure and that "gratification without some antecedent frustration is hardly conceivable."

DEFINITIONS OF FRUSTRATIONS

Accepted definition. The first condition for the presence of a frustration is that a need, or drive, or tendency toward action be aroused. Secondly, the satisfaction of this need is blocked, interfered with, or simply is not available. That is, there is a barrier or obstruction to its satisfaction. A baby's cry on entering the world might well be interpreted as a reaction to frustration occasioned by having lost its warm, comfortable security in the uterus. A boy's ball has gone over into the neighboring lot and is just out of reach beyond the pickets of the fence. The fence then is a barrier which frustrates the boy's efforts to regain possession of

[1] Franz Alexander, "A World Without Psychic Frustration," *American Journal of Sociology*, 49 (1944), 465–469.

his ball. Or a man has lost his way in the wilderness and his food supply runs out. As hunger develops, he is in a state of frustration because a need is aroused, but no means of satisfying it is at hand. The boy whose parents forbid him to go coasting on a winter's afternoon or the adolescent girl who is not permitted to go to the bowling alley with her friends in the evening is frustrated by restraining parents. So frustration may be defined as the blocking or interference of the satisfaction of an aroused need through some barrier or obstruction.

As learning develops, the individual acquires responses which lead to the ultimate satisfaction. There may be frustration at any of the stages of the progress toward the goal. Life is made up of a hierarchy of subsidiary accomplishments, each of which is a means toward a more basic goal or satisfaction. If the blocking occurs at any of these intermediate stages there is frustration at this point, and the ultimate goal is also frustrated. For instance, a child hears the bell of the passing ice-cream vendor, and the desire to have an ice-cream stick is aroused. In order to get the stick, the child must go through a somewhat complicated process of first finding his mother, asking her to let him have a nickel, finding his way out of the door and down the street to the wagon of the vendor, asking him for the flavor which he wants, and giving him the nickel. Frustration may take place at any stage of this series of events. The child may not be able to find his mother. She may not be willing to give him the nickel. He may not be able to find the vendor after he has finally persuaded his mother that he should have the ice-cream stick. The vendor may be out of the flavor on which he has set his heart.

In frustration, however, the blocking to the achievement of an anticipated goal may not be caused by an actual barrier but by some event which is a cue or signal that an obstruction may be anticipated. Here we may make a distinction between goal-attainment and reward-expectation. For instance, in the illustration just given, the boy may hear his mother scolding his younger brother before he asks for the nickel. He has already learned that when his mother's anger is aroused she is not apt to be in a very generous mood, and he begins to doubt whether she will give him the nickel that he wants. The sounds of her scolding become a cue to what he may expect when he asks her, so these sounds themselves take on the nature of a frustration. The boy's interpretation of these sounds determines the reward-expectation which anticipates the actual goal-attainment of success in getting the ice-cream. No immediate want is frustrated by the sounds of his mother scolding his brother, but he has learned that he can anticipate being frustrated when his mother is in this bad humor, and his heart already sinks in expectation of the refusal. His recognition of his mother's angry state is just as clearly a frustration as would be the later more vivid refusal by her.

CLASSIFICATION OF FRUSTRATION

The frustration barrier is always in the environment. However, the environment should be considered comprehensively and not be limited to the environment which is external to the indvidual. The distinction as to what is external and what is internal is difficult to make. Quite evidently a stone or a book is external, whereas a thought or a pain is internal. A tooth may be considered internal as long as it is part of the person, whereas it becomes external when it has been extracted, in which state however, it is not entirely external; it is still part of the self. One's clothing, one's room, one's desk, one's family, one's house and land, one's school, club, state, are in wider and wider circles, parts of the personality. A father whose son becomes mentally handicapped may receive a more severe threat to his personality than if his own hand had been cut off. The distinction between *personal* and *impersonal* may be more significant than the distinction between *internal* and *external*.

Rosenzweig [2] has made a valuable classification of the types of frustration. First of all he divides frustrations into two general classes, those which originated in the external environment, and those which originated in the internal environment.

External frustration. Rosenzweig mentions as his first type, external *privation* or *lack.* For instance, a farmer may be frustrated by a long-continued drought or by the barrenness of his soil which has deteriorated over a period of years. Poverty is an all-inclusive privation frustrating many individuals in modern society. The little child may suffer the frustration of privation when he feels that he does not have the toys, the clothing, the advantages, or the freedom other children possess.

A second type of external frustration is that caused by *deprivation* or *loss.* Deprivation is a general term to indicate separation of an individual either from people or things that he needs in order to round out his satisfactions. The most depressing privation at the beginning of life is that connected with failure or inadequacy of nourishment. Since this is often linked with the lack of support from parents, it may be closely connected with the threat of loss of love. However, as a child matures, he may find himself deprived in many ways, particularly when there are other children with whom he can compare himself. Perhaps the first and strongest danger for an infant is loss of love and protection. The little child feels this almost from the beginning when his mother fails to cuddle him, give him support, and look after his physical wants. Even the separation of mother and child may be a primitive form of frustration. Mothers know this in general, but perhaps do not realize to what extent even momen-

[2] Saul Rosenzweig, "Frustration as an Experimental Problem. VI. General Outline of Frustration," *Character and Personality,* 7 (1938), 151–160.

tary separations may be interpreted by the very small child as a threat of loss. Frustration also comes when means for satisfactions which were once in the individual's possession are no longer available. The property owner, for instance, may suffer deprivation or frustration through flood or fire or business depression. A child suffers loss and hence frustration when he loses his toys or ruins them by leaving them out in the rain, or when some playmate moves away to another town. Another child is frustrated when his mother stops making decisions for him and leaves him to make his own. Deprivation or loss is experienced by the child who for the first time is taken to school and left there by his mother.

A third type of external frustration is that in which there is a more obvious *obstruction* or *barrier*. First of all, there are those obvious frustrations or barriers which exist in the physical environment, as when a baby's activities are confined to the limits of a playpen and he has access only to toys that are inside the pen. Restraints are made by the will of parents, nurses, and teachers in denying freedom of movement and the satisfaction of certain wants.

A particular kind of frustration which is somewhere on the borderline between being external and internal is illustrated by those pains and discomforts which come from injuries to the surface of the body and which result in attacking or withdrawing behavior. The body has a sensitive network of sensory nerve endings, so that any injury done to the surface of the body is immediately transmitted as pain or discomfort. Every child learns what must be avoided in order to shun pain, and many objects are responded to as signals of a possible threat of danger.

As Lewin[3] has pointed out, some features of the environment may serve as barriers to positive valences or drives, whereas other features of the environment stimulate negative valences or tendencies to avoid danger. In this last category, when the stimulus which is recognized as having potentialities for harm or danger is a person, the threat is one that is recognized as having the significance of a punishment. So a punishment is a kind of frustration, one which stimulates attacking or withdrawing tendencies in order to escape the possibility of harm with its attendant pain and discomfort.

As has been noted, the obstacle in the environment may be physical, as when a spoon is just beyond the baby's reach, or it may be social, as when the mother has removed the spoon beyond the baby's reach. Or going one step further, the obstruction may be social in the sense that it requires knowledge of and adherence to the rules and laws which have been set up by a group of persons or a society, and which are generally accepted and maintained by them. When one finds several spoons laid at his place at the table, he may not know that he is expected to use them in order,

[3] Kurt Lewin, *A Dynamic Theory of Personality* (New York: McGraw-Hill Book Company, Inc., 1935), 81 ff.

taking first the one placed on the outside. The barrier may be the difficulty of a task as, for instance, the difficulty of an examination. Going still further, we may find moral barriers which seem to be supersocial, having their sanction in immutable, universal laws, although it is generally recognized that these moral restraints are extensions of social laws and regulations.

The variety of circumstances which can serve as external frustrations seems to be practically limitless. One may be frustrated, for instance, by the superiority of one's rivals which detracts from the praise and recognition that an individual himself may receive. One may be frustrated by duplicity of others, by dishonesty, unfairness, cheating, by the destruction of one's reputation. Human intercourse is filled with opportunities for frustration inasmuch as most of our needs have a social implication.

Maslow makes the point already noted that mere deprivation need not cause the bad effects attributed to frustration, but only when this deprivation carries with it loss of love, prestige, respect, or achievement. Deprivation hurts, because it symbolizes loss of these other things. Sex deprivation can be borne with relative ease and only becomes a frustration when it is interpreted as implying inferiority, lack of respect or worth, isolation and rejection by the opposite sex.

Internal frustration. Turning to the internal and personal frustrations, first of all, we may recognize *internal privation or defect*. Any sort of bodily deformity or disfigurement—inadequate physique, short stature, weak eyesight, deafness, or deficient intelligence—may cause frustration insofar as it handicaps a person in his achievements or makes it difficult for him to secure recognition from his fellows. The second type of internal frustration is *deprivation or loss*. Illness or injury may incapacitate a person for his work, for social intercourse, or for other satisfactions. Third, there may be *internal obstructions or barriers* of a psychological sort. To any drive or desire which has been initiated, there may be internal inhibitions preventing attainment of adequate satisfactions. For instance, a boy may want very much to help himself to all the kinds of cookies that are being passed around, but he feels that it would be improper or discourteous to do so. Fear of failure or fear of ridicule serve as barriers to discourage a person from undertaking tasks or engaging in certain activities.

Internal frustrations may be characterized in yet other ways as regards the nature of the drive which is frustrated. Four separate characteristics of internal frustration may be identified. First, there is strength of the impulses themselves. This probably is most clearly seen in adolescence. The adolescent, having lived for several years in a sort of equilibrium so far as his impulses and wishes go, may suddenly find himself overwhelmed with impulses. If these impulses have been made to seem in earlier life at all dangerous or bad, they become many times so as their strength increases at adolescence. The phenomenon of adolescence may be attributed in part to the anxiety which comes from the overwhelming surge of the impulses themselves. Some adolescents in our culture usually meet this new surge of impulses by exaggerated expressions of love or hate. In other cases we find that they build up various defenses against these overwhelming impulses and become religious, reticent, suspicious, studious, or inhibited.

Second, not only may the impulses themselves be recognized as dangerous, but the pain or other feelings that are associated with dangerous impulses may become the cause of anxiety. The young lady who has been disappointed in love may find amorous feelings too dangerous to admit and will scrupulously avoid in the future any experience which has the possibility of calling up romantic feelings. Many persons apparently cannot afford to permit themselves the luxury of pleasure because they are not willing to run the risk of frustration.

We have already pointed out a third kind of internal frustration: external dangers, restraints, prohibitions, deprivations, and threats may become internalized, and one's own conscience may become an additional frustrating threat.

Finally, as the fourth characteristic, one is afraid not merely of one's internal prohibitions but also of the feelings of guilt and suffering which arise from the loss of approval of the conscience. For example, one may remember that he failed to thank his hostess for a pleasant evening on leaving, and experience that form of discomfort which comes from having omitted something important. These feelings may be so intense and so painful that they add considerably to the barrier which the original prohibitions themselves have erected against the admission of certain forms of thought or behavior.

These last two groups of frustrations are also called *conflicts,* and since conflicts are to be discussed in a separate chapter at greater length, it is not necessary at this time to go into more detail concerning the variety of frustrations which are caused by internal barriers or inhibitions.

SOME GENERAL CHARACTERISTICS OF FRUSTRATION

Unpleasantness of frustration. Frustration is always accompanied by a feeling tone which is unpleasant, just as the overcoming of the frustration leading to satisfaction of the want or drive is pleasant. The unpleasantness associated with frustration gives driving force to the efforts made to overcome the frustration and surmount the barrier. If this irritation or discomfort were absent, the conditions necessary for doing something about frustration would not be present. When the frustration is intense, the feeling becomes intense and is recognized as pain or extreme discomfort. Pain is thought of most simply as being caused by injury to us or some bodily disturbance, but one recognizes many other frustrations as having a painful quality. Grief, for instance, can have the same anguish as intense pain. The most potent discomforts giving rise to frustration are those which imply some limitation in power, capacity, or prestige of the person.

On the other hand, as we shall see later, sometimes frustrations in the form of self-imposed withdrawals, deprivations, or even injuries yield greater satisfaction, in spite of the pain of loss that accompanies them, than gratification would yield because of the individual's need for safety from still greater threats of harm. A person will submit to grinding pain in the dentist's chair with the satisfaction of knowing that his tooth is being made sound again. A person eases his conscience for his sins or omissions by payment in the form of self-punishment.

Frustration equated with punishment. In infancy, frustration becomes equated with punishment, that is, is thought to be brought about as a punishment by some person, and this tendency to attribute all kinds of frustration to some personal origin is continued into adult life by the majority of people. This may account, in part, for the origin of religious beliefs of divine retribution and other anthropomorphic attitudes which are commonly held. Education must recognize the fact that science is needed not only to counteract superstition and prejudices which have been acquired early in life but also to overcome a natural tendency of everyone to equate the frustration from natural sources with frustration imposed by individuals. This confusion between frustration caused by people and frustration caused by external events arises because frustration is usually produced from the first days and weeks of life through the mediation of persons, particularly the mother. Feelings of discomfort arising from hunger and other unsatisfied and distressing inner states which are projected out onto the mother and which arouse hostility toward the mother as being a bad person, that is, one who is responsible for these unpleasant feelings, are expressed in behavior by crying. Crying by the infant tends to arouse in the mother feelings of pain and sympathy on the one hand, or annoyance on the other. The mother may run to administer comfort, or she may show her annoyance by frowns, harshness in her voice, or even by slaps and vigorous handling. These punishments the infant interprets as a direct response to his own bad feelings, and he tends to interpret all outer frustrations as being like these rebellious inner feelings. These outer frustrations are, in part, real and, in part, enlarged in fantasy to the same magnitude as his own overwhelming inner feelings. The child who is unable to tolerate early frustration and who reacts vigorously against it is the one who usually regards later frustration coming from the outside world as equivalent to frustration coming from persons, that is, to punishment, and such a child will tend to be badly adjusted to reality. This child will tend to confuse the obstacles in the real world with the difficulties which he has had or that he has fantasied, with people.

Frustration in infancy is an important determining factor of personality throughout life. There are reasons to believe that personality is formed through the frustrations experienced in infancy. As an infant reacts to his various deprivations and shocks, life-long patterns for reaction are established. Wolf [4] in a significant experiment, temporarily deprived rats of the use of their eyes or ears in infancy. Later when the use of these sense organs was restored the rats were put into competitive situations with rats who had not suffered these temporary deprivations. Those rats who had been deprived of vision when infants had difficulty in responding to visual stimuli, and those deprived of hearing were similarly handicapped. Deprivation in infancy handicapped these rats all through life. Hunt [5] has shown a similar persisting effect in connection with the hoarding tendencies of rats as related to their feeding frustration in infancy.

FACTORS DETERMINING THE RESPONSE TO FRUSTRATION

Strength of drive. The response to frustration depends on a number of factors. In the first place, response to frustration becomes more severe in proportion to the strength of the drive or want which is frustrated. As an illustration, the child whose desire for the ice-cream stick is intense, will show stronger frustration reactions than the child whose want is relatively weak. For instance, of two children, one having had ice-cream for lunch and the other not having had ice-cream for several weeks, the first can be expected to have only a feeble drive to get the ice-cream stick and to respond only slightly to any obstacle placed in his way, whereas the other child can be expected to respond more vigorously to any barrier thrust in his way.

Strength of barrier. In the second place, within limits, the stronger a barrier, the more intense the desire and efforts to overcome the barrier. This has been studied experimentally by Lewin.[6] Wright,[7] and others. This law is recognized in common folklore by such proverbs as, "Grass on the other side of the fence is greener," "Nothing so good as forbidden fruit," "A fence between makes love more keen," "Distance lends enchantment."

[4] Alexander Wolf, "The Dynamics of the Selective Inhibition of Specific Functions in Infancy," *Psychosomatic Medicine*, 5 (1943), 27–38.

[5] J. McV. Hunt, "The Effects of Infant Feeding Frustration upon Adult Hoarding in the Albino Rat," *Journal of Abnormal and Social Psychology*, 36 (1941), 338–360.

[6] Kurt Lewin, *A Dynamic Theory of Personality* (New York: McGraw-Hill Book Company, Inc., 1935).

[7] H. F. Wright, *The Influence of Barriers Upon Strength of Motivation*, Contributions to Psychological Theory, 1, No. 3 (Durham, N. C.: Duke University Press, 1937).

This same phenomenon has been observed many times in everyday life. For instance, experiments have shown that when mild interference or distractions are presented in doing any kind of work there is an increased energy devoted to the task and an increased output in the task itself.[8] To the surprise and distress of many parents, some children actually seem to study more efficiently with the radio going by their side than with it turned off. There is even evidence from experimental studies that learning is facilitated when an obstacle is placed between the point of choice and the goal.[9] A problem or puzzle of mild difficulty will stimulate a greater output of effort, but if it becomes too difficult discouragement and abandonment will ensue. Wright[10] found that if the obstruction became so great as to appear insurmountable, there was a sudden cessation of effort, and the child would tend to withdraw from the situation altogether.

(3) **Availability of substitutes.** A third factor which conditions the reaction to frustration is the possibility of achieving an equally attractive substitute. For instance—to go back to our illustration of the boy who wants the ice-cream stick—if when he goes to his mother for the nickel, he finds that his mother is planning a trip to the zoo that he has been wanting for a long time, the ice-cream may fade into insignificance and the anticipation of this other wish may fill his mental horizon. So the response to a frustration may change in relation to alternate methods of reaching the satisfaction desired or the relative strength of other wants and the ease with which they can be satisfied. The availability of two different modes of reaching a reward will have an effect similar to that of a frustration with increased indecision and delay.

(4) **Goal as end and as means.** A fourth factor which conditions the strength of a reaction to a frustration is whether the goal desired is an end rather than a means. If the goal desired is an end in itself, then the response to frustration tends to be relatively strong and pressing. On the other hand, if the goal is a means to an end, frustration placed in the way toward reaching the goal may elicit only a weak response toward overcoming it. For instance, in one of Wright's experiments, waitresses would reach over to a rear row of desserts to select a particularly plentiful dessert for their own consumption, but would take the dessert nearest at hand, even though not so carefully prepared, when it was for service to others in the dining room. The factor is not without its complications. In part, it depends on whether alternative means are available for the at-

step of end of line

---

[8] Such experiments are stock in courses in experimental psychology. For a classic example, see J. J. B. Morgan, "The Overcoming of Distraction and Other Resistances," *Archives of Psychology*, 5, No. 35 (1916).

[9] K. F. Muenzinger and D. O. Vine, "Motivation in Learning. IX. The Effect of Interposed Obstacles in Human Learning." *Journal of Experimental Psychology*, 29 (1941), 67–74.

[10] H. F. Wright, *op. cit.*

taining of the goal in question. If alternative means are available, then any one means may arouse relatively weak resistance, whereas if there are no other means the response to frustration may be more intense. Reactions to frustration can be relatively intense if they concern basic needs of hunger and sex and rest as well as those relating to security, safety, affection, recognition and the like, whereas those frustrations which arise at every turn in the day's activities as we pass people on the street, go up and down in elevators, drive to and from our work, may elicit relatively weak reactions toward overcoming them. However, one cannot always tell by the apparent trivialness of a frustration how deeply it goes in threatening one's security and adequacy.

Barrier immediately presented. A fifth factor which determines the reaction to frustration is whether a barrier is immediately presented or not. If a barrier is like the fence which prevents the boy from reaching his ball, it is physical and real and immediately presented, and the reaction to it is more intense. A boy attempting to row up a bay when the tide is going out will only put forth more effort if he is aware of the opposition he is encountering. McCord [11] in experimental work with rats has demonstrated that there is a greater frustration response when there is a barrier or obstruction in the way of gaining food than when there is deprivation or the absence of food.

Cumulative effect. The cumulative effect of a number of minor frustrations is a sixth factor which conditions the response to a frustration. This is particularly important if frustrations have not been drained off in immediate activity but have piled up in postural tensions. Where any one frustration may be so minor and immaterial that apparently it occasions very little reaction, a number of frustrations superimposed upon it may have a cumulative effect. A man driving to work in the morning, for example, is certain to experience a variety of frustrations, such as red traffic lights, cars getting ahead of him, cars ahead driving slowly, and the like. Ordinarily one takes such frustrations in his stride and adjusts to them easily and rapidly. However, if he is carrying with him the cumulative effect of a number of unresolved frustrations (which might be the case if there had been quarreling at home) he might react quite violently to any one of these simple frustrations in driving.

Emotional security. In general, a situation which provides the support of social comradeship and emotional security is going to have less disrupting effects when frustration occurs than when a person is isolated and emotionally insecure. Wright [12] found, for instance, that children would react to the frustration of being deprived of interesting toys much more

[11] Fletcher McCord, "The Effect of Frustration on Hoarding in Rats," *Journal of Comparative Psychology*, 32 (1941), 531–541.
[12] M. E. Wright, "Constructiveness of Play as Affected by Group Organization and Frustration," *Character and Personality*, 11 (1942), 40–49.

constructively and maturely when two chums shared the misfortune together than when they were alone.

Self involvement. G. W. Allport [18] believes that frustration responses are more or less intense as a greater or less amount of the self is involved. A man may not become very upset over the loss of a game of tennis but may experience a distinct emotional reaction at failure to pass an examination.

Momentum. Freud points out that once a particular method of meeting a frustration has been selected and embarked upon it acquires a peculiar momentum of its own. Once a person has committed himself to any particular method of gratification he becomes bound to follow through with that method. In this sense human adjustment lacks complete resiliency and adaptability.

Personality structure of the individual. The personality structure of the individual is a tenth factor which conditions the response to frustration. Freud, for instance, has made us aware of the extent to which unresolved frustrations are carried about unconsciously over a long period of years, some even from early childhood or infancy. The individual who has accumulated a number of these unrelieved frustrations is almost certain to respond to any new frustration less adequately than one who has worked them out satisfactorily as they arose. We recognize these individuals by their overaggressiveness, their feelings of inferiority, or by their neurotic behavior. Any fresh frustration imposed upon a neurotic individual is almost certain to be responded to less adequately than by the person who is well adjusted, that is, one who has taken care of his frustrations as they have arisen.

TYPICAL FRUSTRATIONS

Loss of love. Frustrations permeate human life so completely that it would be quite impossible to attempt to catalogue or classify the variety of frustrations. However, it may be of value to mention certain frustrations which present unusual barriers to infants and children as they develop, and which may cause adjustment difficulties in later years. Perhaps the most general frustration of all is loss of love. This is a frustration that is felt as a threat to security from birth onward, and one that is vigorously reacted to. Loss of love does not have the effect of certain other more immediately presented frustrations, but its consequences are far-reaching and underlie many of the other frustrations of infancy. Accordingly, most children become highly sensitive to cues and signs of love or its lack and tend to react with their whole personalities to frustrations

[18] G. W. Allport, "The Ego in Contemporary Psychology," *Psychological Review,* 50 (1943), 451-478.

or lacks in this area. Among these signs of love and support probably *separation* is paramount, and separation or threat of separation is responded to more acutely as a frustration than any other one incident in infancy. But here again a modification must be made, for the threat comes most acutely when the separation implies loss of love or disinterest on the part of the parent and is felt less acutely when the parent makes it clear that the separation is forced by circumstances and that attitudes and feelings are as warm and vital as ever.

Feeding frustration. Of the more manifest kinds of frustrations, one that is commonly recognized as being highly important in the first year of life relates to feeding. Illustrations of frustrations in feeding during the early weeks of life have been given already many times in this chapter. Taking in nourishment is among the most important activities when life begins, as well as throughout all subsequent ages, and the degree to which this need is satisfied or frustrated is important in personality development. On the whole, children who are brought to child-guidance clinics for study and treatment have had very unsatisfactory nursing experiences. Frequently they have been nursed by their mothers for only a few weeks and then shifted to the bottle because the mother's milk has been inadequate, or for some deeper psychological reason. In some cases, there seems to have been no attempt to nurse the child at the breast from the beginning. Psychological studies would indicate that bottle feeding never satisfactorily compensates for breast feeding. On the other hand, some normal children who seem to be making splendid adjustments in all phases of development have frequently been nursed by their mothers for a period of several months, sometimes over a year, and then have not been weaned from the bottle until several months later. The weaning process is one of the greatest frustration threats experienced by the young child and may be thought of as a prototype of all later frustrations. The degree to which a child is helped to make this new adaptation easily and without frustration seems to have an important bearing on the degree to which this same individual is able to meet many of life's later frustrations.

Exploration restriction. Another frustration experienced by young children concerns their tendency to explore. Children first explore their environment by bringing objects to their mouths and later by grasping, touching, pulling, and manipulating. Later, when the child learns to get about, he explores in a more wholesale fashion. Parents find it necessary to limit these activities in their children. This is done in the interests of safety for the children, as a precaution against disease, and injury from falls, playing with matches, and the like. Then, too, parents find it necessary to prevent their children from destroying furniture and books, or getting things in too much disorder. This means that the activities of children must be curtailed and sometimes rather sharply directed, and naturally this restriction and redirection is an immediate and direct frustration which may have widespread implications.

Cleanliness training. Cleanliness or toilet training is recognized as an important frustration in early childhood. Children have to learn the time and place for their toilet functions. This learning does not come naturally and requires considerable patience and tolerance on the part of mother and nurse and must be carried out over a period of several months. It is easy to make this learning highly frustrating to the young child if it is attempted too early in life, if there is an attempt to perfect the learning in too short a time, or if it is carried out by methods which are restricting and unsympathetic. The difficulties attendant on toilet training may have far-reaching influences on character development, causing the child to be overly clean and orderly on the one hand, or rebellious on the other.

Rivalries within the family. The entrance of another child into the family usually brings with it a series of frustrations to the child or children already present. A child, used to receiving all of his mother's interest and attention, finds that he is suddenly being neglected for a newcomer who monopolizes the mother. This means not only that he feels he is being neglected in attention to his wants, but that he feels a more serious frustration in no longer occupying the central place in his mother's regard. These frustrations produce well-known kinds of behavior varying from disguised hostility and aggression toward the new child to regressive behavior and a return to infantile ways.

Lessening dependence. With the growing-up process and the young child's increasing ability to get about, he finds that he is expected to do more things for himself and to require less attention and waiting on from his elders. He is expected to learn to feed himself according to the accepted custom of his family, to keep himself clean, to attend to his clothing, to be responsible for its care, to keep himself looking neat, and to take responsibility for certain chores around the home. Under wise management and encouragement this lessened dependency and increased responsibility comes easily and naturally with a minimum of frustration, but even under the most skilful guidance there is some frustration as adult care is withdrawn. As in all other situations, the child who has had most secure relations with his parents is the one who feels the least frustration with increased maturity. The wise parent will make lessening dependence seem a very positive and valuable development— something to arouse pride rather than anger or fear.

Restrictions on early sex experiences. As the infant begins to explore his world he becomes acquainted with various parts of his body and finds his genital organs particularly sensitive and manipulation of them yielding an exquisite pleasure. However, in our culture, gratification from manipulation of these areas is strongly forbidden and the majority of parents are alert and vigorous in thwarting expression of autoerotism. This perhaps is one of the most serious frustrations that the young child experiences both because the pleasure is so marked and because opposition to it is so determined. The frustrations centering around masturbation are reacted to by the most extreme emotional reactions, fantasies, and repression.

Sex patterning. Children are, at an early age, forced to adopt a sex rôle following the conventional patterns of the culture into which they are born. Boys are made to look and act rough, vigorous, and boisterous; girls to look and act sweet, coy, and passive, despite whatever natural inclinations they may actually have. Boys are made to be ashamed at playing with dolls; girls are forbidden to be tomboys. This "sex typing" requires a certain amount of domination and restriction by the parents with consequent frustrations for the growing boy or girl who has identified with a person of the opposite sex.

Age patterning. Similarly, children are expected to look and act their age, and there are standards of clothing and conduct appropriate to each age. Children are impelled by ridicule or shame to desist from acting younger than they are, and are frequently urged to adopt behavior of the next age level. This forces children into somewhat restricted behavior patterns which must be continually modified, with consequent frustrations as they pass from year to year. The child who departs from these norms will be looked upon as infantile and will suffer the taunts and ridicule that are designed to force him into the stereotype.

School frustration. With increasing age there is increasing demand for learning. Even before school, parents may insist on their children acquiring certain skills, perhaps the rudiments of reading and arithmetic, and hours of practice may be set apart. When the school age is reached, this channeling of the middle hours of every day into certain forms of learning activities becomes routinized. Every child encounters severe frustrations on first going to school when he has to learn to regiment himself into the school situation. He has to learn to sit still, to refrain from speaking or even whispering except when permission is given, to refrain from childish expression of temper or quarreling, and he must learn care and order with materials. This channeling proceeds at a rapid rate so that within a year or so the majority of children have adopted the uniform pattern of behavior of the school child, and those few whose earlier insecurity makes it difficult for them to tolerate frustrations stand out as "unadjusted" and "problem" children.

Of particular significance in schools are the frustrations which arise when there is disharmony between a child's capacity and provision for proper outlets for that capacity. This shows itself with peculiarly unfortunate outcomes in the case of bright children for whom the school does not provide experiences that are sufficiently challenging or stimulating.

Adolescent frustrations. It will be seen that each one of these frustrations represents the acquisition of patterns of thought and behavior which mold the growing child gradually into the adult in a given culture so that eventually he can take his place and manage himself acceptably in the social group. Adolescence, when childhood is finally left behind and adult responsibility develops, provides another set of frustrations. In this period there is the well-known frustration connected with assuming responsibility for self-management in all aspects. In particular, the growing boy and girl must acquire skills and attitudes that will enable him to find his place in the world of work, and he must adjust himself to members of the opposite sex so that he can establish satisfying and happy sex relationships and family responsibilities. Unfortunately, the adolescent must also overcome the resistance to this maturing process shown by his parents, who themselves are frustrated by his final acquisition of independence, and who attempt to keep him in some respects still a child. All of these problems constitute frustration for the adolescent, barriers which he must find his way around in order to achieve adult maturity.

Adult frustrations. However, frustrations are not eliminated when the processes of development are completed. The adult is continually beset by difficulties to be faced and solved. There are the problems of economic life—earning a living, saving for a rainy day, adjusting to the ever recurring cycles of unemployment and prosperity. There are the uncertainties of maintaining a place within one's social group—the family, the church, club, and the community, as well as within the larger state and national groups. There are problems of accident and illness constantly threatening and sometimes overtaking the adult.

A man's work has its own peculiar frustrations. Ichheiser [14] has pointed out four types of frustration in connection with work. First, there is the frustration of *function*. A vigorous, athletic person may be forced to do sedentary office work, or a person inclined to be irritated by small details may find himself in a position where great accuracy and precision are required. A second type Ichheiser has classified as frustrations of *conviction*. There is the worker with socialistic beliefs who works in a factory making luxuries to be purchased only by the very wealthy, or the physician, obliged to practice in a hospital whose professional standards are below those that he would like to observe in his own practice. A third group includes frustrations of *ambition*. A man may find himself working at a lower level than he would like to, as in the case of a well-trained musician of classical tastes who is forced to play in a jazz band. A fourth group Ichheiser has termed frustrations of *response*, that

[14] G. Ichheiser, "On Certain Conflicts in Occupational Life," *Occupational Psychology*, 14 (1940), 107–111.

is, the frustrations which arise in conflict over the use of tools or materials or in feeling that one's superior officers are unjust and unfair in requirements or in evaluations.

Deprivation arising from death. There are certain shocks and hazards which must be faced by everyone at some time or other during life. Death of relatives or friends constitutes a loss which, in cases where the ties of affection are close, becomes a severe type of deprivation. Frustrations occasioned by the death of some loved person are so cruel that they frequently produce profound melancholia. Death is a distinct traumatic event even for the young child. Children may appear to relinquish quickly the memory of a loved person, but deeper study indicates that most respond to such a loss for years afterward.

Cmmon **Failure.** Failure is a frustration which everyone meets at one time or another whether it be in games, in school, or in later vocational endeavor. Our present culture is organized on a highly competitive basis so that in all fields of activity there must be both winners and losers. To lose in any contest is a distinct form of deprivation, resulting in frustrations that are difficult for many people to handle.

Frustrations from life experiences. This survey of typical frustrations could be expanded indefinitely, but only a few further illustrations will be given. Disappointment follows when the response of other persons does not come up to our expectations. We have to meet all kinds of persons in the world, some who aid in gaining satisfactions and others who hinder. The child who grows up with good parents in an atmosphere of security tends to expect that everyone whom he meets in life will contribute to his satisfactions. It is a distinct shock for such a child to learn later that there are mean, untrustworthy, deceitful, overambitious persons who are ruthless in causing him harm and loss. Many persons offer their friendship and love in generous fashion to others, only to be rebuffed and to have their love unrequited. Then there is the discrepancy between ideals and their fulfilment. When life is ahead, we plan a vocational career, establishment of a family and home, winning a respected place in our community, making some contribution through our endeavors. However, it is the exceptional individual who lives such a favored existence that everything goes according to plan and schedule. For most persons, unfortunate choices, accidents, and calamities manage to frustrate the complete accomplishment of their ideals. These are only a few of life's frustrations.

HOW FRUSTRATION IS REVEALED

The clinical worker and the teacher should be alert to the earmarks of frustration. Probably the best evidence of its presence is a large output of energy directed toward some task. The stronger the drive, the greater the frustration, other things being equal. One may assume that the person who burns the most energy in some enterprise is the person most frustrated. Another indication of the presence of frustration is hesitation at one's task—faltering, loitering, giving it up, postponing it. The child who flags and loses interest in his school work is giving evidence of frustration. Even to a more marked degree, the child who is tardy or who plays truant is probably still more frustrated. A third criterion is a reluctance to resume one's task. A fourth indication of frustration is the presence of meaningless responses, that is, behavior which apparently serves no immediate or apparent purpose. This kind of behavior represents, in all probability, some substitute response in the face of frustration which, because of its inappropriateness, carries little obvious meaning with it. The response that is meaningless characterizes neurotic behavior. Likewise, the meaningless repetition of responses—doing the same thing over and over—is another sign of severe frustration. Usually the person who succeeds in surmounting his frustrations is the one whose behavior is adaptive, that is behavior which has been modified in the search for a better method of overcoming these frustrations. But if the frustration becomes too intense, then adaptiveness may be lost, and stereotypy in behavior results. The presence of strong unpleasant emotion is also a rather sure sign of frustration. One might say that emotion is a universal concomitant of frustration for which there is no immediate and adequate solution. Philip [15] has listed anger, disappointment, despair, resentment, excitement, impleasure, and negative self-feeling as feelings accompanying frustration. Frustrated persons become supersensitive to criticism and ridicule.

RESPONSE TO FRUSTRATION

In considering the responses to frustration, two elements must be kept in mind: (1) the goal toward which the drive is directed; (2) the barrier blocking the way toward that goal. In general, the following are methods of meeting frustration:

1. Removing the obstacle
2. Getting around or surmounting the obstacle
3. Modifying or abandoning the goal, or accepting a substitute goal

The precise reaction to be selected always involves a conflict and compromise between the urge toward obtaining the acquired goal and the urge toward avoiding the barrier.

Aggression and rage. It is generally recognized that the most primitive form of response to frustration is aggression accompanied by rage and

---

[15] H. L. Philip, "An Experimental Study of the Frustration of Will-Acts and Conation," *British Journal of Psychology Monograph Supplement*, 7, No. 21 (1936).

anger. Dollard and others [16] postulate the thesis and present evidence that "the existence of frustration always leads to some form of aggression." This thesis is developed in great detail.[17] In aggression the goal is retained and the individual attempts to remove or surmount the obstacle and to reach the goal by a greater outlay of energy.

Aggressive responses to frustration tend to become disintegrating and disorganizing. The disorganizing effects of anger are well known. Everyone has observed the paralysis and confusion engendered by a state of hurry. One who uses aggression to overcome obstacles has committed himself to a course of action from which he finds it difficult to be deflected.

Zander [18] has demonstrated that emotionally unstable persons react aggressively to a smaller degree of frustration and interference than stable persons; and conversely, emotionally stable persons can tolerate larger degrees of frustration without responding aggressively than unstable persons. The aggressiveness of a person, therefore, is a function of his stability in the face of frustration. However, Zander believes that aggression is a healthy and normal adjustment to frustration, particularly when it is justified by circumstances, and he found that children who react aggressively to frustration show fewer neurotic manifestations than children who meet frustration in other ways. Indeed, the person who responds to frustration most aggressively is the person who has the greatest self-confidence in himself and in his abilities.

Learned motor response. With developing motor coördination and skill, the infant gradually acquires new and more effective methods of meeting frustrations. Little by little he acquires control over objects and persons and in that way learns to overcome situations that frustrate him. If an infant, when very tiny, pushes his toy over the edge of his high-chair beyond his reach, he has no other recourse than to show anger, annoyance, or indifference. Later when he can crawl or run about, he can retrieve objects and by thus gaining command over the situation can overcome directly his own frustrations. He may also learn how to manage people so as to get them to do his bidding and help him satisfy

[16] John Dollard, L. W. Doob, N. E. Miller, O. H. Mowrer, R. R. Sears, *Frustration and Aggression* (New Haven: Yale University Press, 1939).

[17] Although these authors have, in their own words, attempted to "push the frustration-aggression hypothesis as far as it will go with reference to either individual or to social facts that are relevant to it," they also recognize that they have failed to do full justice to a consideration of other outcomes that are related to frustration (p. 18). For instance, they say, "Various consequences of frustration other than aggression will be largely ignored. *Substitute responses* and *rational problem-solving* both involve extensive theoretical formulations in their own right and to examine them in detail here would be impossible."—John Dollard and others, *Frustration and Aggression*, 19.

[18] A. F. Zander, "A Study of Experimental Frustration," *Psychological Monograph*, 56, No. 3, Whole No. 256 (1944).

his wants. One might even say that the somewhat blind and impulsive forms of aggression which show themselves by thrashing about, kicking, and writhing later become channeled into meaningful and skilful behavior which yields a more direct method of overcoming many barriers. One may think of motor development and the acquisition of skills as growing out of the earlier undifferentiated emotional behavior. But this latter is also the prototype of behavior that is later recognized as being truly aggressive.

It would appear as though there were two rather distinct and dissimilar methods of meeting frustration. One method leads more or less directly to an adequate solution of the problem and satisfaction of the wants that have been raised. The other method, accompanied by marked output of emotion, is relatively blind and plunging and only by chance leads to a satisfaction of the need that is aroused. The first type of response to frustration is predominantly intellectual and manipulative, the second predominantly emotional. Of course in actual life, both kinds of response are made in varying degrees and combinations.

There is some evidence that strong emotion and adaptive learning are naturally antagonistic. Learning takes place most effectively in the absence of strong emotion because strong emotion produces disorganization of adaptive behavior. Such a study as Patrick's [19] indicates that there is a tendency for frustration to be met by trial and error or rational learning *or* by disorganized regressive emotional behavior, but not by both.

In general, frustration that leads to adaptive response is relatively mild. Such a frustration is also one in which the person feels *challenged* rather than *blocked;* in which he feels adequate rather than inadequate. This motor response may be first characterized by the presence of motor or muscular tension, particularly of the potential sort that is poised and ready for action. Naturally the tensions that are aroused are directed toward one kind of response rather than another, as determined by previous learning in situations that bear a close similarity to the one that causes the present frustration. In its main primitive form this type of response leads to restless behavior and random activity; it arouses what has been called trial-and-error activity. The cat in the cage in Thorndike's early learning experiments is a good illustration of this type of response. The animal tries whatever behavior is in his repertoire of reactions, going from one to another in an apparently random fashion (although undoubtedly were one able to know precisely what is going on in the nervous system, it would by no means be random), gaining, and not with too much difficulty or after too long a time, satisfaction of the

19 J. R. Patrick, "Studies in Rational Behavior and Emotional Excitement. II. The Effect of Emotional Excitement on Rational Behavior in Human Subjects," *Journal of Comparative Psychology,* 18 (1939), 153-195.

want. Repetition of this same frustrating situation leads eventually to learning according to the law of effect as Thorndike [20] has so conclusively demonstrated.

On a higher level, this response to frustration takes on the character of rational problem-solving. Here there must be a possibility of concept formation through the use of language and other symbols. When there is concept formation, the trial-and-error process can be carried on by implicit and symbolic muscular movements rather than by gross muscular movements in the actual situation. Mild and not too extreme frustration is a necessary condition for all learning, and the presence of such frustrations must be a necessary condition for education.

Not on test

Substitute methods of meeting frustration. *Withdrawing—Resignation.* We have discussed the direct method of meeting frustration through aggression, and the so-called progressive or constructive method through learning to solve the problem. Let us now see what happens to these basic methods of meeting frustration when the frustration is severe, or when no adequate solution seems to be forthcoming. If the aggression becomes too intense, or if it brings with it still greater frustration in the form of counter-attacks by some person, which may be recognized as punishment, the aggression may be repressed. Doob and Sears [21] have formulated the following "law": "the frequency of substitute responses to aggression varies positively with the strength of anticipatory responses to punishment for being aggressive." These authors also believe that the stronger the strength of instigation to the frustrated goal-response the greater the tendency to make direct aggressive responses, and the less the tendency to make substitute response; and the greater the anticipated punishment, the less overt the aggressive response (and consequently the more disguised and repressed the substitute response). There are two possibilities of adjustment when aggression is repressed—one is to continue the same goal and find some substitute method of reaching the goal; the other is to abandon the goal in favor of some goal more easily and surely reached or to modify the goal so that part of its values can be achieved. Zander [22] believes that in our culture these substitute responses occur more frequently than aggressive responses.

Fantasy. The first of these substitute responses can best be illustrated by *fantasy.* In fantasy the motor response is shifted to words or images, and satisfaction in fantasy takes the place of the satisfaction which is

[20] E. L. Thorndike, *Human Learning* (New York: Appleton-Century-Crofts, Inc., 1931).

[21] L. W. Doob, and R. R. Sears, "Factors Determinating Substitute Behavior and Overt Expression of Aggression," *Journal of Abnormal and Social Psychology*, 34 (1939), 293–313.

[22] A. F. Zander, "A Study of Experimental Frustration," *Psychological Monograph*, 56, No. 3, Whole No. 256 (1944).

denied in reality. Through fantasy one can, with little effort, achieve methods of overcoming his frustrations, but in a way entirely divorced from the reality of the outside world. This leads to an unbalanced state in the individual. In the real world of events and people, he continues to be frustrated. In the imaginary land of his mind's eye, he is enjoying satisfactions far beyond any that he has ever been able to experience in reality, but it is all a will-o'-wisp to be blown away when reality which has not been satisfied comes pressing back on him in its inexorable demands.

Repeating Behavior. Another method of meeting frustration which avoids open aggression is that of repeating behavior. This has been demonstrated by Maier and others [23] in animal experiments. In human behavior we recognize this type of response in what has been called by Hamilton [24] "persistent non-adjustive reactions." We see this in some of the nervous responses called "tics" in which a person endlessly repeats a jerky nervous movement or twitches some small muscle, or we see it in the compulsive movements of washing the hands, opening or shutting drawers, trying locks on doors, opening and closing faucets. Stereotyped behavior of this kind has been found, in many instances, to represent a symbol or abbreviation of some more overt attempt to overcome the frustration. In this type of behavior it would seem as though there were a permanent fixation on a given method of overcoming the obstacle. As an example, a boy may strive so desperately and unsuccessfully to compete with his father for his mother's love and attention as a little fellow that he may become fixated on this struggle to compete with men as a life pattern.

Abandoning the Goal. As frustrations increase in intensity there is a greater tendency to abandon the goal. When the goal is abandoned or modified there are a number of possible alternative modes of adjustment available. One of these is withdrawing and giving up the attempt (temporarily, perhaps) to reach the goal. Lewin [25] who has studied responses to frustration experimentally, presents in his book a picture of a little child who is crouched forward so that its head is between its legs. This picture illustrates an extreme form of withdrawing as though the infant wished to put his head in the sand or to build a shell around himself against the situation which he finds so intolerable. This withdrawing form of response to frustration is characterized by more or less ex-

---

[23] N. R. F. Maier, N. M. Glaser, and J. B. Klee, "Studies in Abnormal Behavior in the Rat. III. The Development of Behavior Fixations Through Frustration," *Journal of Experimental Psychology*, 26 (1940), 521–546.

[24] G. V. Hamilton, "A Study of Perseverance Reaction in Primates and Rodents," *Behavior Characteristics*, 3, Serial No. 13 (Baltimore: The Johns Hopkins Press, 1916).

[25] Kurt Lewin, "Environmental Forces in Child Behavior and Development," in Carl Murchison, editor, *Handbook of Child Psychology* (Worcester, Mass.: Clark University Press, 1931), Ch. XIV, 590–625.

treme inhibition. It is accompanied by fear and at later ages by persistent fear in the form of anxiety or worry. It may also be characterized as loss of interest, as when a child in school who is severely frustrated, finds that the display of aggression will lead to still more severe frustration, and responds by losing interest, becoming passive, indifferent, and so forth. Children who were required to repeat the drawing of a man tended to spend less and less time on each succeeding drawing, and there was increasing complaint about continuing the activity. French [26] describes this method of meeting frustration in terms of the "contraction of the integrative field" in order to bring it within the limits of the ego's integrative capacity, whereas the confident individual reaches out for new responsibilities.

Once there was a boy who was accused in elementary school of having destroyed a picture made by a classmate. When he tried to explain his innocence to the teacher, she ridiculed him by calling him "Rosamund," who was always ready with excuses. The nickname "Rosamund" clung to him throughout life. Later he never attempted to excuse himself or clear himself of guilt in any connection. When he was accused of a serious crime, he made no attempt to defend himself but remained silent.

However, as Thorndike and Woodyard [27] have demonstrated, this type of response to frustration is not accompanied by loss of power, so that even if a person loses interest in the face of frustration, he still has at his command the same amount of mental power to apply to the prosecution of tasks. But the *quality* of work may go down when a person is required to do what he does not want to do.

The character and degree of disintegration which results in abandoning a goal will depend not only on the intensity and suddenness of the frustration but also on the relation of the frustration to the activity. If the frustration arises when the activity is being planned or has barely been initiated, it may be abandoned with little disruption. But if the person has already invested a great deal of time and energy in advancing his goal, the disruption may be more severe.

Substitute Response. Another method of responding to a frustration is to adopt a *substitute response,* which perhaps does not contain all of the satisfaction in the goal originally aimed at but, at the same time, reduces the strength or potency of the want or need to some degree. Substitute responses, therefore, represent partial solutions or satisfactions. The Yale group have formulated this as a "law" as follows: "The greater the degree of inhibition to a more direct act of aggression, the more probable

26 T. M. French, "An Analysis of the Goal Concept Based upon Study of Reaction to Frustration," *Psychoanalytic Review,* 28 (1941), 61–71.

27 E. L. Thorndike, and Ella Woodyard, "The Influence of the Relative Frequency of Successes and Frustrations upon Intellectual Achievement," *Journal of Educational Psychology,* 25 (1934), 241–250.

will be the occurrence of less direct acts of aggression." [28] A number of types of substitute responses will be discussed in subsequent chapters under the heading of the mechanisms whose functions seem to be to provide alternate methods of meeting the basic demands of the organism. For instance, sublimation represents a response which is substituted for complete gratification of an original want or impulse. An adolescent girl whose close, strict family supervision has prevented her from making normal social contacts, derives great satisfaction in developing talent as a portrait painter. Since sublimation is also a response that fits in with the demands of society, it has its compensations and hence is quite tolerable to the individual even though through sublimation the individual is not winning entire satisfaction of the need that has been aroused. Rosenzweig and Sarason [29] have demonstrated that there is a greater tendency to resort to mechanisms when there is a forgetting or repression of past failures, but that remembering past failures is associated with a more open type of aggressive response.

Regression. In the face of severe frustration in which the possibilities of overcoming the barrier directly or surmounting it indirectly seem to be impossible, there may be a *regression* to a form of response which was to a degree effective at an earlier stage of development and which seems to be the next most promising form of response to attempt. Usually this regression may be recognized because it is a reaction accompanied by emotion on a primitive level. The child who regresses may bite, sulk, whine, or have a temper tantrum, indicating that progressive methods of meeting the frustration have failed, leaving as the only recourse a retreat into infantile methods more highly charged with emotion.

Miscellaneous. Allport, Bruner, and Jandorf [30] in their biographical study of the reactions of victims of the Nazi revolution, point out other modes of response to conditions of extreme frustration and disorganization of life patterns. Some individuals attempted to maintain self-stability by adopting such temporary frames of security as faith in the underground movement, hope of emigration, official conformity with the régime, occupational conformity, or adoption of routine duties and modes of living. Others met the situation by heightened in-group feeling and sought refuge in a closer union with family, ethnic groups, societies, and the like. Still others met the situation by changes in their philosophy of life. Some became more religious, others put their hope on supersti-

[28] John Dollard, L. W. Doob, N. E. Miller, O. H. Mowrer, R. R. Sears, *Frustration and Aggression* (New Haven: Yale University Press, 1939), 210.

[29] Saul Rosenzweig, and Seymour Sarason, "An Experimental Study of the Triadic Hypothesis: Reaction to Frustration, Ego-Defense, and Hypnotizability," *Character and Personality*, 11 (1942), 1–19, 150–165.

[30] G. W. Allport, J. S. Bruner, and E. M. Jandorf, "Personality Under Social Catastrophe—Ninety Life-Histories of the Nazi Revolution," *Character and Personality*, 10 (1941), 1–22.

tions, charms, fetishes, or philosophical systems. An interesting adaptation was the lowering of levels of aspiration and the willingness to accept a lowered standard of living. Under extreme provocation there was a lowering of moral standards and of standards of usual cleanliness and appearance. This latter could well be explained as a form of regression.

Personality Disorganization. Finally, when the inner pressure is great, and the outer barrier is also strong, frustration may lead to emotional excess or to exaggerated, confused, disorganized behavior or to personality breakdown. The artist may destroy his work, as Rodin destroyed the statue with which he was displeased, as Tschaikowsky tore up a score, or as Shelley misplaced his manuscripts. There may be confusion, conflict, and oscillation between the excitatory and inhibitory stimuli. A frustrated person may become more active and exhibit his tension by nervousness and restlessness.

Social Outcomes. Wright [31] has discovered that frustration has certain social as well as individual outcomes. When a group of children are subjected to a common frustration the cohesiveness of the group is increased. There is a greater tendency to work coöperatively in overcoming the barrier, there is greater friendliness between the members of the group, and conflict behavior within the group is decreased. On the other hand, hostility to an outsider is increased, and group destructiveness is enhanced. These phenomena have been observed to hold between nations as well as in smaller groups where they have been experimentally studied.

In an earlier illustration the little boy who wanted the ice-cream stick and whose mother was unwilling to give him the nickel had various alternatives of meeting this frustrating situation. First of all, he could attempt to work out another way of gaining his end, perhaps by remembering a nickel in one of his trouser pockets or by attempting to borrow the nickel from his younger brother. If his frustration was more intense, he may have responded more immediately and vigorously by striking at his mother or calling her a name and exhibiting anger while doing so. If, however, his mother was severe in denying him the nickel he could respond by retreating and inhibiting further attempts to get the ice-cream stick, perhaps accompanying his actions at the same time by evidences of anxiety. If this is the type of response made, he could substitute for actually getting the ice-cream stick some sort of fantasy in which he manages to secure a mountain of ice-cream for himself. Another alternative would be to find some satisfactory alternative, such as looking for ice-cream in the refrigerator or taking some candy. Another substitute response, instead of speaking angrily to his mother, would be to beat up his younger brother in a quite uncalled-for attack.

[31] M. E. Wright, "The Influence of Frustration upon the Social Relations of Young Children," *Character and Personality*, 12 (1943), 111–122.

Finally, he might adopt various childish appeals: whining, teasing his mother for the nickel, or developing a temper tantrum of such violence that the mother would be frightened into giving him the nickel to alleviate her own fears.

Just which method of meeting frustration will be adopted in a given situation by a given individual cannot at present be stated. The factors influencing choice of response to frustration are only dimly known, and much clinical and experimental work must be done before these relationships are established.[32]

CRITERIA OF ADEQUATE REACTIONS TO FRUSTRATION

Adequacy of satisfaction. Naturally, the only really appropriate criterion of the adequacy of a reaction to frustration is whether the want or need which is thwarted is eventually satisfied. This, of course, is the goal of the whole process of adjustment, namely, to reduce the degree of disequilibrium which is reflected by the mental state recognized by us as a need. The adequacy of response to frustration by this criterion is always a matter of degree. Needs are always more or less completely satisfied. The situation in which all barriers are overcome or circumvented and the goal is fully achieved is by no means the universal outcome. Often one may have to take a second-best choice, and accept the leftovers or some less satisfactory substitute because his first choice has been sold out. To have to withdraw from the particular want which has been aroused, and to be satisfied with achieving it in grandiloquent fantasy, is certainly less adequate than to find one's way around the barrier. To become fixated in a vain attempt to overcome the barrier or to select an unsatisfactory (neurotic) substitute for the original goal, must both be classed as unsuccessful reactions to frustration. But to find some way of getting around the obstacle or to modify one's goal are both successful methods of meeting frustration.

Economics of satisfaction. A single frustration cannot be taken by itself, however. One may have to tolerate certain frustrations in order to gain other ends that one considers more important. As Kitty Foyle phrases it, "Lots of times you have to pretend to join a parade in which you're not really interested, in order to get where you're going." There is an economy in the satisfaction of the large variety of wants which are at any time operative in the individual. By no means can all be satisfied. Any individual must weigh the different values he places on his satisfactions and, accordingly, be willing to forego certain pleasures in order to achieve deeper and more lasting satisfactions. Even this algebraic summation of values is an imperfect solution of the problem when a

[32] R. R. Sears, "II. Non-Aggressive Reactions to Frustration," *Psychological Review*, 48 (1941), 343–346.

society is being considered. In this situation one must think in terms of the optimum satisfactions of all individuals in the society. This may mean that in order to achieve this maximum satisfaction of wants in the social group, the satisfactions of certain individuals may have to be ruthlessly sacrificed. In such instances, individuals may have to suffer for the good of the group. This happens not infrequently in condemnation proceedings. Sometimes whole communities, containing the homesteads of several generations, have to be removed if it seems to be in the general interest to flood the area for a reservoir for the purposes of flood control. To make life tolerable for these individuals and to help them eke out what satisfactions there may be left for them is one of the tasks of mental hygiene.

Increasing maturity. Another criterion of the adequacy of reactions to frustrations can be stated in terms of the *progression* or *regression* of these reactions. As has already been pointed out, certain reactions to frustration lead to exploratory behavior, learning, and problem solving and, in general, more adequate mastery of the external environment. Where learning takes place we see evidences of growth and greater adaptability. This is a sign of increasing maturity. On the other hand, if the frustration is intense, the individual retreats from exploration and more adequate command of and adjustment to the situation in favor of more infantile and emotional reactions, and we say that the reaction to frustration is less adequate.

EDUCATIONAL IMPLICATIONS

Frustration is needed for growth and reform. Frustration, instead of being something to be avoided, should be recognized as an absolutely necessary stimulus for growth, development, and learning. No child has ever grown from infancy to childhood except through the mediation of mild frustration. Learning takes place in the face of frustration as a necessary process in the solution of problems. Frustration is necessary in order to make us aware of our environment. It is only through having to orient himself to the outside world that the infant learns to discriminate objects that he finds there and to respond to them in appropriate fashion. Our awareness of the outside world is only at the behest of our needs. We lay hands on our environment in order to wrest from it satisfaction to our needs. This means that these facts have certain implications for parents and teachers. On the one hand, children should certainly not be protected against all frustration. They should be given certain gentle and easy opportunities to explore, discover things for themselves, and work out their own problems. As an example, the father who gives his son an Erector Set for Christmas and then proceeds to take charge of it and help his son make all the models, is denying his son an opportunity of learning how to manipulate these materials constructively. Maier [33] believes that the values of frustration extend not only to learning but also to reform. His observations lead him to conclude that no great or effective social movement or reform is possible except when it rests upon previous frustration and even suffering.

But frustration should not be too severe. On the other hand, children should be removed or protected from too serious frustration. Modern parents may err more often in burdening their children with frustrations that are too difficult rather than too easy—at least, this is true for children who are making a poor adjustment in the process of growing up. The essential criterion should be the ability of the child to take it. So many of these parents feel that they are babying and coddling their children, when just the opposite is probably true. A child who presents behavior problems needs, first of all, to have the frustrations removed with which he has not been able to cope and to be given easier tasks to do. If the child is unsuccessful in school, the remedy is not to put pressure on him to try to make him learn, but to remove the frustrations so that he can proceed to be successful on the level of his abilities. If a child in school is having difficulty with the teacher, the wise principal will first try to help the teacher understand and accept the child, but if this is not effective, then he will not hesitate to remove the child from that room and place him in charge of another teacher. When practical, the first thing to do in cases of difficulties in adjustment is to change the situation producing frustrations that the child is not able to surmount and place him where his responses can be adequate. From such a situation he can proceed to develop in an optimum manner. The amount of frustration with which a child should be confronted is an important factor in determining the education to which he is best suited. This same principle applies equally in the world of adults. A workman might make a much better adjustment to his job under a different foreman, or a teacher under a different supervisor, and it is no sign of weakness or indulgence to make such changes readily.

QUESTIONS FOR DISCUSSION

1. Give illustrations of the statement "frustration in infancy is an important determining factor of personality throughout life." (P. 49.)

2. Give illustrations of the principle that frustrations are more intense the more the ego is involved.

3. What are the implications of the statement that mild frustration is necessary for development and learning? What are the criteria of mildness? Are there dangers that this statement will be misinterpreted?

4. When an infant learns to meet frustrations by his own learned efforts,

[33] N. R. F. Maier, "The Role of Frustration in Social Movements," *Psychological Review*, 49 (1942), 586–599.

what becomes of the aroused aggression? Does this suggest a direction for the control of aggression?

5. Can you provide illustrations of situations where strong emotion interfered with adaptive learning and effective adjustment?

6. Speculate on the factors which govern the choice of one or another response to frustration.

RECOMMENDED READINGS

1. DOLLARD, JOHN; DOOB, L. W.; MILLER, N. E.; MOWRER, O. H., and SEARS, R. R., *Frustration and Aggression* (New Haven: Yale University Press, 1939) .

2. LEWIN, KURT, *A Dynamic Theory of Personality* (New York: McGraw-Hill Book Company, Inc., 1935).

3. MASLOW, A. H., "VII. Deprivation, Threat and Frustration," *Psychological Review*, 48 (1941), 364–366.

4. MASLOW, A. H., & MITTELMAN, BELA, *Principles of Abnormal Psychology* (New York: Harper and Brothers, 1941).

5. MILLER, N. E., and others, "I. The Frustration-Aggression Hypothesis," *Psychological Review*, 48 (1941), 337–342.

6. ROSENZWEIG, SAUL, "An Outline of Frustration," in J. McV. Hunt, editor, *Personality and the Behavior Disorders* (New York: The Ronald Press Company, 1944), Vol. I, Ch. XI, 379–388.

7. ROSENZWEIG, SAUL, "I. The Significance of Frustration as a Problem in Research," *Character and Personality*, 7 (1938), 126–128.

8. ROSENZWEIG, SAUL, "VI. A General Outline of Frustration," *Character and Personality*, 7 (1938) , 151–160.

9. SEARS, R. R., "II. Non-Aggressive Reactions to Frustration," *Psychological Review*, 48 (1941), 343–346.

10. WRIGHT, M. E., "The Influence of Frustration upon the Social Relations of Young Children," *Character and Personality*, 12 (1943), 111–122.

11. ZANDER, A. F., "A Study of Experimental Frustration," *Psychological Monographs*, 56, No. 3, Whole No. 256 (1944).

IV

Aggression

possitive &
negative
aspect

Living in the midst of the amenities of civilization, modern man forgets that *homo sapiens* is one among the animals. Man must satisfy his needs by wresting his food from a hostile and unwilling environment. He must be ready to protect himself from dangerous enemies. He must learn to survive fire and flood. Aggression is a prime human characteristic necessary for survival in the struggle for existence. Aggression is normal, not pathological. One would not, even if he could, eliminate aggression from the world. Yet, necessary as aggression is, man also finds it to be the cause of his greatest social evils. We know this today as no generation has ever known it before, immersed as we have been in a total world war.

Civilized man has erected laws, restraints, and prohibitions for keeping aggression within bounds, making it possible for a peaceful organization of society to develop. Parents and teachers, recognizing the danger to society that constantly threatens when aggression breaks over its bounds, teach children from the beginning that aggression is bad and must not be expressed. In this chapter the origins of aggression will be set forth, and the different modes of expressing it described. Aggression has its values, both positive and negative, and these must be seen clearly. Methods of controlling aggression will be reviewed and consideration will be given to the therapy of aggression.

DEFINITIONS

Aggression. There are four meanings to the term aggression. In its first sense, aggression means *self-assertiveness, vigorous activity*. The term will not be used in this sense in this book, for there is no particular dynamic significance in this general meaning.

The second meaning is to *gain possession,* either of another person or of an object. The term aggression used in this sense refers particularly to an act of appropriation when it meets opposition, as when a person forcibly takes possession of another person, takes an object away from another person, and, in general, uses considerable energy in acquisition.

Aggression in its third meaning signifies an act of *hostility, attack,* and *destruction.* The essence of this meaning is the act which *injures* another person, either directly or indirectly, either his person or his possessions. In this meaning, aggression arises as resistance to control by others and represents all that is violent and destructive.

The fourth meaning of aggression refers to the act of *control, dominance,* or *management* of another person or groups of persons, organization, and affairs in general. We speak of a person as being aggressive when he shows capacity for leadership, exhibits tendencies to organize and run things, or attempts to bend others to yield to his wishes and to do his bidding.

The trend of self-assertiveness, particularly when expressed in a violent, energetic way, runs through the last three of these definitions. The act of gaining possession and the act of control do not necessarily involve injury or destruction, and may have constructive outcomes. Aggression as used in this chapter will refer primarily, but not exclusively, to aggression in the third sense, that is, as an act of hostility aimed at injuring another person. It should not be forgotten, however, that aggression as an act of gaining possession and as dominance are important meanings which must also be reckoned with.

Hostility. Hostility may be defined as a state of enmity and ill-will, and as such is related to the third meaning of aggression. Hostility, then, refers to the attitude, meaning, or intent of a person which is expressed in action by aggression. Lowrey [1] points out that one may be hostile yet not aggressive, and contrariwise, much aggression (as in its second meaning) does not express hostility.

Hate. Hate refers to a feeling of aversion or dislike. It is the emotion which accompanies aggressiveness in its third meaning, that is, when it is an act of hostility. Hate involves the whole person, and indicates the relation of the ego to its object. Anger may be an isolated emotional response, but hate is the attitude of the person. When one says, "I hate," it is the whole self which hates, and not some isolated drive within the person.

GENERAL FACTS REGARDING AGGRESSION

Aggression a function of general activity. of life Aggression has been the subject of study by observational methods in child psychology. Several interesting relationships have come out of these studies. It has been found, for instance, that children who are the most aggressive are also the ones who are most likely to receive aggression from others. It has also

[1] L. G. Lowrey, *Problems of Aggression and Hostility in the Exceptional Child,* Proceedings of Fifth Institute on the Exceptional Child, under the auspices of the Child Research Clinic of the Woods School (Langhorne, Pa.: 1938), 22–30.

been noted that children who are most aggressive in their play with other children are also most aggressive toward adults.[2]

It would seem from these studies that aggression is a function of the general activity of a child; at least, this is the way in which these findings have been interpreted. The additional observation that the most aggressive children are also the most sympathetic adds plausibility to this interpretation.[3] However, such a simple explanation probably does not include all there is to these phenomena. It is quite possible, for instance, that children who show aggression toward their playmates are displacing toward them some of the hostility which they feel toward their parents, but which is not permitted open expression. Children who are most aggressive toward others may actually invite aggression toward themselves as a kind of punishment, or they may even attempt to do reparation for the damage which they have caused by their display of sympathy. The meaning of these dynamic factors will be set forth more clearly in the following discussion. Suffice it to say here, however, that aggression cannot be looked on merely as good spirits and healthful activity, but that it also has dynamic significance for the adjustment of the individual.

It is believed that tendencies toward *aggressiveness* are constitutional and inherited, corresponding in some way with capacities to be active and vigorous rather than passive and quiescent.[4] However, aggression as it occurs in specific acts would require some sort of dynamic explanation in terms of the adjustments which the individual makes to the conditions of life.

Aggression accompanied by emotion. Aggression is normally accompanied by the emotion of anger or rage, and by physiological changes which place the organism in a condition of readiness for immediate and intense physical activity. These are all mediated by the sympathetic division of the autonomic nervous system. Strong emotion, such as anger or rage, is in part an awareness of the particular muscular responses that are made when aggressive behavior is stimulated, and in part, it is an awareness of the physiological changes which accompany these muscular responses.

FUNCTION OF AGGRESSION

Aggression has two main functions: first, to wrest satisfaction from the outside world; and, second, to destroy the source of pain. Both functions

[2] A. T. Jersild, and F. V. Markey, *Conflicts Between Preschool Children*, Child Development Monograph, No. 21 (New York: Bureau of Publications, Teachers College, Columbia University, 1935).

[3] L. B. Murphy, *Social Behavior and Child Personality* (New York: Columbia University Press, 1937).

[4] C. S. Hall, and S. J. Klein, "Individual Differences in Aggressiveness in Rats," *Journal of Comparative Psychology*, 33 (1942), 371–383.

are related to the need of the organism to maintain itself in an environment where the process of nourishment requires effort, and to protect itself from harm or destruction in an environment full of potential dangers or enemies.

To gain satisfaction. When an internal need is aroused, uncomfortable stimuli set the organism into action in search for means of alleviation.[5] This act of searching and appropriating what is needed in order to allay distressing internal stimuli corresponds to aggression in the second meaning as given above. Not only does one have to appease internal cravings, but also seek sources of pleasure. The infant during the first year will reach for objects and bring them to his mouth for the obvious pleasure that he gains from the contact. Later his aggressive activity is devoted, in part, to gaining pleasure through sight, sound, taste, smell, and touch. A child will adopt aggressive tactics in order to hold or to win back an aggressively rejecting mother. Sometimes a child will be naughty or will do poor work in school in order (in part) to force his parents to notice him, to punish him if necessary, to attend to him at least— anything to prevent them from neglecting or rejecting him completely. To meet the threat of loss such a child may develop possessive tendencies and may hold on to his toys against anyone who attempts to dispossess him. David Levy [6] says that such children become the reactionaries in society. As an individual, a person makes aggressive efforts to gain ego satisfaction. He must count for something with his fellows. He must surpass them in his efforts. He must beat them in the race to gain the coveted object or prize. This leads to rivalry, competition, and dominance—all forms of aggression in the fourth meaning of the term.

To avoid pain. An individual finds it is necessary not only to gain satisfaction and pleasure, but also to destroy the source of pain. He not only learns to attack and threaten with destruction persons who attempt to hurt him, but he anticipates dangers and fights off situations which, by past experience, promise to carry harm with them. So we find that children are sometimes aggressive in order to test their fantasies in which harm or punishment follow if they are bad, and to test whether they will be able to survive it. Children, for this reason, are sometimes disorderly in school without apparent reason. Looking on the teacher as a possible enemy, and anticipating harm or punishment that has come to them in the past, they actually seem to invite it as a way of testing their ability to survive.

Over and beyond these two basic functions of aggression is the fact that aggression helps an individual to demonstrate his superiority over others. Aggression, then, serves to enhance the ego as well as to manage

[5] Cf. Ch. II, "Drive," for an elaboration of this point.
[6] D. M. Levy, "Hate as a Disease," *Journal of Educational Sociology*, 16 (1943). 354-358.

specific dangerous situations. Indeed, it would appear that the major part of the aggression in the world has as its function the enhancement of individual superiority.

CONDITIONS PRODUCING AGGRESSION

Biological factors. It is the thesis of this book that, by and large, aggression is functional, that is, is learned as a response to experience and grows out of simple reflexes. However, it is possible that there is an organic or biological basis to aggression. Of two infants it is commonly observed that one will be more active, aggressive, and energetic than the other. This difference is usually ascribed to biological inheritance, to better nutrition, and to less fatigue. Some cases of aggression may possibly have an organic or glandular basis. For instance, children recovering from encephalitis are usually restless and hyperkinetic. This may mean that they become boisterous, unruly, violent, destructive, disobedient. They frequently are noted for quarreling, fighting, temper tantrums, pyromania. There is a connection in these cases between the inflammation of the nervous tissue and later aggressive behavior. This difference in the aggressiveness of children can be explained in part by differences in the organic condition, but the actual meaning and intent, as well as the amount of aggressiveness, rests on the child's responses to experience and his attempts to work out methods of adjustment. Deutsch [7] states that aggressive drives are intensified during menstruation. It is well known that the drinking of alcohol tends to be accompanied by a release of both aggressive and sexual impulses.

Frustration. *Types of Frustration.* The general explanation of aggression may be summed up in the statement, "Aggression is a response to frustration." Frustration leading to aggression may be divided into three major types. In the first place, frustration in the sense of *deprivation* or *unfulfilled desire* leads to aggression. Aggression is a response to the organic tension which is set up when some organic need remains unsatisfied. In the second place, aggression follows *interference* or *restriction*. Hold down the arms of an infant who has been accustomed to freedom of activity, and he will immediately become tense and struggle for release, his body will suffuse with blood, and he will wail. Dennis,[8] who has made experimental observations on his own children and on Indian children, believes that infants do not respond aggressively to mere restraint of movement except when (1) there is intense and enduring stimulation, and (2) when some customary sequence of events is inter-

---

[7] Helene Deutsch, *The Psychology of Women* (New York: Grune & Stratton, Inc., 1944), Vol. I, p. 168.

[8] Wayne Dennis, "Infant Reaction to Restraint: An Evaluation of Watson's Theory," *Transactions of the New York Academy of Sciences*, New Series, 2 (1940), 202–218.

fered with. He points to the Indian papoose who placidly submits to being bound to a board and carried on its mother's back for long periods as an example of restraint that does not arouse protesting responses. Someone has commented, however, that this same Indian child is free to explore with his eyes. Nevertheless, a white child, not accustomed to such confinement, would protest vigorously against it.

Lewin [9] points out that restriction of space increases aggression. However, frustration is due primarily to the change in the space. A child who is used to playing in the yard and is later confined to a small pen will respond with clear-cut aggression. A family of six attempting to live in one room will have more quarrels than if its members were spread out over six rooms.

One important restriction in modern life is the over-long work hours in school and factory. The violence with which children rush from school at the end of the day is testimony to the long hours of enforced restraint. Such long hours of confining work are responsible, in part, for disciplinary problems in school and labor unrest in industry. Parents may arouse aggressive trends in a child by the imposition of high standards of conduct and by requiring high levels of achievement.

The third type of frustration leading to aggression is *attack from the outside* which causes *pain* or *discomfort*. A child will respond with aggression not only to kicks and punches from another, but to attempts to take away his toys, deprive him of pleasure, or injure his name or reputation.

Aggression is a response not only to actual frustration, but also to the *anticipation* of frustration. Frequently children are resistant or destructive not because they are denied some wish, but because they fear that they will be denied it. The little child who fears that his mother will leave him to go to the movies after he has gone to bed will use every device possible to postpone going to bed.

Insecurity. In a more general sense, aggression will arise from emotional insecurity, from parental rejection, and from the loss of love. This aggression, which is a result of insecurity, is of a more general sort than the specific sadisms just described, growing out of specific frustrations. The child who is neglected by his mother or who, through cruelty, harshness, or punishment, has tangible evidence of the lack or loss of the mother's love, is driven to win back these evidences of love and affection by aggressive means. If love and security are not forthcoming, attention is a second best substitute, and the attention-getting activities of children, which are aggressive in nature, are an attempt to win immediately the attention of the other person with the hope and wish that this attention will actually indicate interest and love. A child attracts attention to

[9] Kurt Lewin, *A Dynamic Theory of Personality* (New York: McGraw-Hill Book Company, Inc., 1935).

himself in school by disorderly conduct or by making himself ridiculous for no other purpose than to command the teacher's attention, with the underlying hope that he will bring her to acceptance of him. Children whose parents are incompatible with each other and inconsistent with regard to their demands are frequently aggressive. The broken home, not necessarily, but usually, represents abnormal love relationships; and the child suffers by virtue of this insecurity. His natural response is an aggressive one. Adolescents with a greater need for love react to their insecurity by sporadic outbursts of aggression. The college boy who has left home and feels lonely and bewildered may amaze his elders by joining in a rowdy game and destroying furniture and breaking windows, something he would never think of doing at home. The extent to which hostility develops into overt aggression depends in large part on the extent to which emotional security is denied in infantile affectional relations.

Aggression and hostility are inevitable concomitants of the process of growing up. No emotional tie with a member of the family is ever relinquished without engendering hostility, and in the struggle for independence both in infancy and in adolescence, hostility is aroused as a means of achieving this liberation.

In both boys and girls this struggle for independence is directed primarily toward the mother, so that there is a natural tendency to turn toward the father for support.

There is an interesting connection between the more immediate frustrations and the deeper underlying insecurity which children whose parents are hostile or immersed in their own affairs, deeply feel. The child who is accepted and secure can, without undue aggressive tendencies, tolerate frustrations which the less secure child cannot. Aggression, therefore, does not come necessarily from those who have suffered physical punishment. It comes primarily from children who have not been loved, whose siblings have been preferred, who have been insecure in their emotional relationships. Such children are most likely to react to punishment by retaliatory aggressiveness. The accepted child, however, whose frustrations are lenitive and who can depend upon his parents for support does not have to meet his frustrations in so aggressive a manner.

Sibling rivalry, which shows itself by all sorts of aggressive acts between children in the same family, is increased by insecurity of the child with his parents. If the child feels perfectly secure in his parents' regard, then there will be a minimum of rivalry and aggressiveness between him and other members of the family. If, on the other hand, he is not sure how he stands with his parents, or if he is sure that they tend to criticize and dislike him, and that other children in the family are preferred, then his tendencies toward rivalry and aggressiveness are increased.

Insecurity also arises from a feeling of strangeness or difference from other persons. A little child may be startled by someone wearing a strange dress or speaking in a strange language. Everyone feels more secure with persons who think, dress, act, talk as he does. One may even go further and observe that there are tendencies to feel hostile and show aggression toward the person who is strange. Mountain folk are extremely suspicious of strangers. Most persons are suspicious of and hostile toward the foreigner. Without doubt, one important cause of war is this insecurity that we all feel toward people who differ from ourselves in inner or outer characteristics.

Feelings of inferiority. A fourth condition which produces aggression is a feeling of inferiority. It should be recognized that this is a derived condition. In the first place, one would have to explain how feelings of inferiority develop, and if they could be traced back it would be found that they grow out of early frustration and insecurity. However, in later years these feelings of inferiority have an independent existence in an individual apart from his earlier experiences; and an individual tries to manage inferiority feelings by aggressive tendencies. We all recognize the person who, feeling inferior, tends to put on a show of self-confidence, bluster, bravado, and overbearingness. This is his method of attempting to establish a status of his own and of working out peace with his own inner feeling of inadequacy. Some persons who feel inferior develop a will to power in order to anticipate and control potentially frustrating and painful conditions. One never knows the extent to which the brilliant achievements accomplished only by aggressively overcoming obstacles have been motivated by the need to reduce inner feelings of inferiority. These feelings of inferiority follow a person even after his efforts have won him high achievements. The captain of industry, the scholar, the politician who has achieved fame and success, may still be struggling with inner feelings of unworthiness and failure. The present misery in which the world is plunged may be due in part to the attempts of little men to disprove the reality of their littleness to themselves.

Then there are those children who are afraid of growing up and of taking on more mature responsibilities. They compensate for these fears by exaggerated strivings to appear grown up. The fundamentally insecure child will attempt to bolster his feelings of inferiority by identifying with the strong and mature, by wearing mature clothes, or by adopting the gestures and bravado of those who are older and more successful than he.

Excessive love—overindulgence—lack of parental control. We have discussed how emotional insecurity following lack of love helps to produce aggressive tendencies. It is interesting that excessive love and overindulgence can arouse aggressive tendencies by quite a different route. The overindulged child tends to suffer from a lack of parental control. In every family early frustrations have produced their aggressive reactions. In the normal child, these aggressive responses are subdued by parental pressure and the normal and good parent will not permit a child to show unbridled hostility toward others. The overindulgent parent, however, puts no restrictions on the child's behavior, and aggressive tendencies run their course without check. Such a child fails to develop frustration tolerance and in later years when someone, for instance a teacher, attempts to control him, aggression becomes violent and unmanageable. There is another mechanism at work in overindulged children. Even though they have not been disciplined at home, they soon learn that certain things are acceptable and others unacceptable, certain things are right and others wrong in the world about them. Every child feels a need for punishment of his offenses; and if punishment is not readily forthcoming from parents, then the child may have to become bad enough and disagreeable enough so that in exasperation punishment will follow. So it has been found that the overindulged child, toward whom excessive love and little control have been exercised, may become overly aggressive in order to receive the punishment which he feels is his due in order to relieve the increasingly painful guilt. Queerly enough, children who apparently are the most obtuse to social demands frequently are the ones who may have the sharpest pangs of conscience.

Lack of skill. In a much simpler sense, aggressive tendencies may arise simply because the child lacks skilful methods of otherwise achieving his ends. The infant is helpless. He has not learned to get about and do things for himself. He is dependent on the good-will and devotion of his parents. His only method of satisfying his wants is the sadistic one. Fantasy and feeling come before skill; and in the early years, while skill is undeveloped, fantasies may be overpowering and destructive. As a reality sense increases, as he learns to know himself as an individual separate from other individuals, as his powers of discrimination increase, as he gains skill and confidence in the world around him, the unreal, magnified, and frightening images that he has adopted recede and sadistic impulses diminish. Of particular importance are skills in social relations. The child who is fortunate in having many playmates learns how to adjust his aggressive impulses to social demands. The solitary child who has no opportunity to learn these skills may show his aggressive tendencies crudely and explosively. There may be a slight resurgence of aggressive impulses at adolescence as the inner strivings tend to get out of hand, but normally skill in social relations quickly helps to put these impulses under control.

A word should be said here of the relation between aggression and dominance. Dominance of one individual over another, as may be shown by greater skill in competitive situations, may be considered a condition of security for the dominant individual. The dominant individual need not necessarily be aggressive—he may be paternal or patronizing. Aggression occurs, however, when an individual is dethroned from a dominant rôle with its accompanying frustration, insecurity, and feelings of inferiority.

Finally, a child may show aggression because it is the only pattern of response which he has learned—he has never had an opportunity to learn to express coöperation or sympathy.

UNIVERSALITY OF AGGRESSION

As one surveys the conditions by which aggression is produced, one dismisses the possibility that it can be eliminated from human affairs. When a mother asks, "Is it necessary for my child to be aggressive, to be impolite to other children, to insist on having his own way?" one can only answer that these tendencies are not only common and universal, but, in fact, necessary and inherent. The raw material for war lies inevitably in human nature. Frustration is universal. It is impossible to bring up a child without forcing him at some time to endure waiting, to share, to give up something for others. Even in the best of homes, a child cannot constantly have his wants satisfied without delay. And so far as frustration is necessary, aggression as response to it is equally necessary.

On the other hand, it is not necessary to posit aggression as an instinct. To say that there is an instinct of aggression makes a mystery of it. We have seen how aggression arises from frustration and insecurity. To be sure, the reflexes out of which aggression is constituted are given at birth. The vocal cords to produce the cry, the vascular system to produce the flushing, the muscular system to produce the tensing and thrashing are all present and ready to be called into action at the appropriate stimuli. How these primitive reflexes are coördinated to produce the forms of aggression which we know in later life is the story of development and learning.

Social nature of aggression. One is tempted to speculate on the differences in aggressiveness in various societies. Margaret Mead [10] describes the Arapesh tribe of New Guinea, among whom aggressiveness as a social form was practically non-existent. Neighboring tribes, on the other hand, were very war-like and fierce. Those who have studied the matter believe that aggressiveness grows out of social conventions and restrictions, that there is no natural social pattern of aggressiveness, but that it is a function of the conditions of life.

In general, anthropologists tell us that aggressiveness increases in a system in which there is scarcity, and hence insecurity. The recent world war undoubtedly was stimulated in part because of the unequal distribu-

[10] Margaret Mead, *Sex and Temperament in Three Primitive Societies* (New York: William Morrow and Company, Inc., 1935).

tion of natural resources, and certain proud nations felt that they were deprived of a chance of establishing a high standard of living.

A second factor leading to aggressiveness has been traced to social conventions and restrictions, of which, in our own culture, sexual taboos are among the strictest. This leads to a certain amount of unsatisfied tension making men and women more than ordinarily ready to be aggressive. In Samoa, for instance, Margaret Mead found a society with considerable sexual freedom and a remarkable lack of tension. In our own society, the restlessness of youth is due, in part, to the fact that they are expected to postpone their sexual gratifications. The aggressiveness of some unmarried women again may be attributed to their increased tensions growing out of lack of satisfaction, and it is also probable that in some instances the reverse is true—aggressive trends acquired in childhood block the person from gratifying sexual experience.

A third factor leading to aggressiveness in this social system is the rigidity of its structure which prevents a person from leaving a frustrating condition. In a frontier system, when antagonisms become too tense, it is possible for the younger member of the family to pack up and seek his living elsewhere, but in a static society, where it is difficult for a young person to leave home, personal tensions increase within the home, giving rise to frictions and animosities.

Every social system tends to control certain forms of aggression and encourage others. We marvel at the barbarism of certain primitive societies, but find difficulty in recognizing that our own culture permits, indeed encourages, certain forms of aggression. In our own culture, for example, aggressiveness leading to the destruction of life and property is strongly prohibited by our code of laws and penal system. On the other hand, rivalry and competition are encouraged, and have become the accepted pattern of our culture.

In another way, society authorizes and makes arrangements for certain kinds of aggressive expression. For example, there are certain group sanctions toward hatred in individuals. In college life such hatreds are fanned into an open blaze during a football season when college and team spirit runs high, and college songs abound in such expressions as "On to victory," "Do or die," and "Make the enemy bite the dust." Hatred has been institutionalized in churches, parties, schools, social classes and nations; and through these institutions the individual is permitted to release aggression which inner scruples would make impossible for him as an individual. The Christian is distinctly militant, as may be seen in such hymns as "Onward Christian Soldiers" and "Fight the Good Fight." Christianity makes war on paganism, and its missionary activities are aggressive. Different sects may war with each other within the Christian fold. We speak of class struggle with Capital pitted against Labor for

the control of production and the benefits of its output. The party system, said to be essential to an adequate functioning of democracy in government, very definitely represents a conflict and struggle at election
time. The conflict between nations does not need further comment. Its
fury and horror in the Second World War is still poignant in the memories of everyone.

In each of these institutionalized forms of aggression, the common pattern is for the members of any one group or institution to band themselves together for coöperative action. They constitute the in-group, between whose members aggression is minimized. The out-group, the rivals
or the enemy, are those toward whom the aggressive trends of the group
are directed, and each member of the hostile party or group is considered an enemy by virtue of membership in his group. In this way hostility and aggression become depersonalized. Hostility is no longer directed
toward a single individual who has harmed someone in one's own group,
but against any representative of the opposing group. For example, an
aviator may drop bombs on cities with impunity for the purpose of causing widespread suffering on individuals, no matter what individuals, as
long as they are of the enemy. Before a war there may be more hostility
felt between groups within a country than toward its possible enemies
outside. War often helps to externalize aggression, and to reduce animosities within. Alexander [11] believes that hostility toward the out-group
is the condition for internal peace. One must attack the evils without in
order to have peace within.

Durbin and Bowlby [12] in their book, *Personal Aggressiveness and War*,
have analyzed the causes of war. They follow very closely along the lines
of this analysis. According to these writers, there are three main causes:
one, the *possessiveness* of nations who are not satisfied with their present
wealth and territory and cast envious eyes on that which is possessed by
their neighbors. This possessiveness leads to overt action in the form of
war. Already we have seen that the infant's possessive tendencies are the
forerunners of later aggressiveness. The second factor mentioned by these
authors as the cause of war is *economic insecurity*. The starved nation
will prey upon its rich neighbors. The Scottish Highlanders will raid
their richer neighbors, the Lowlanders. Germany will cast envious eyes
on the territory and natural resources of the Soviet Union and the British
Empire, and will strike out toward the grain of the Ukraine and the oil
of the Caucasus. *Strangeness* is mentioned as the third cause of war. As
has already been noted, there is a tendency to feel hostile toward people

11 Franz Alexander, "Peace Aims," *American Journal of Orthopsychiatry*, 13
(1943), 571–581.
12 E. F. M. Durbin and John Bowlby, *Personal Aggressiveness and War* (New York:
Columbia University Press, 1939).

whose customs, language, and ideals differ from our own. And to this it may be added that in some primitive cultures men acquire their wives by force.

DEVELOPMENT OF HATE

Hate commonly refers to the attitude of dislike of one person for another, and the wish to hurt or to get away from the other person. But hate in a more general sense is the denial of value. In this sense hate is the opposite of love, which will be later spoken of as the affirmation of value.

So far this discussion has been kept on a simple level of the reactions of a person and of society to frustration and insecurity. Nothing has been said of the responses of the recipient of aggression to the aggressor and, in turn, the counter-responses that the aggressor makes to the responses which his aggressiveness invokes in others. It is here again that our language becomes inadequate because the same behavior may have different meanings in adult life and in infancy.

When the little child meets his frustrations by aggressiveness, he finds that such behavior is not acceptable to his elders and tends to provoke preventive or retaliatory measures. This is commonly called *punishment* or is so interpreted by the infant. Punishment receives more extended treatment in the chapter of that title. Here, we are concerned with the fact that the child responds to this punishment in various ways, outstanding of which is the intensification of his aggression. It is at this point that *hate* apparently enters. The original aggression, at the beginning at any rate, is not directed so clearly toward an individual but is merely a response to the frustration. However, the response to punishment is clearly directed toward the punishing person. The child wishes to do the punisher harm, to rid himself of restraint, and the feelings accompanying these tendencies to action may rightfully be called hate. Actually, the distinction between aggression caused by frustration and aggression in response to parental restraint or punishment is difficult to maintain. Consequently, it is probably correct to say that there is an element of hate in all aggression which is of a hostile nature and which aims at destruction.

Hate is related to the attempts that a person may make to lessen pain and to destroy the object producing the pain. We have already spoken of punishment as one form of outer pain. Hate may also be stimulated by inner pain, such as frustrated physiological needs, which in the infant, at least, may be as distinctly distressful as any form of injury to the surface of the body.

Opposite orientation of aggression and hate. It should be noted that in the beginning at least, aggression and hate are oriented in precisely opposite directions. Aggression is directed toward the object with the intention of possessing it. The healthy infant is aggressive in its desire to nurse at its mother's breast, and to partake of the nourishment it so eagerly craves. Aggression originally means approach, union, coming together. Hate, on the other hand, is directed away from the object and instead of portending eagerness and pleasure, signifies separation and getting away from. It is more closely allied to fear, and vents itself in acts of destruction. But, even in the act of sucking from the mother's breast, the eagerness may be akin to a tendency toward destruction, and later aggression and hate may join each other in seeking to cause the annihilation of the object causing inner pain.

METHODS OF EXPRESSING AGGRESSION

The counselor, the teacher, the parent, the foreman, or anyone having to deal with other persons should recognize the signs of aggression. In modern society overt aggression is suppressed and its expression is dispersed; therefore it assumes a variety of forms of expression. In this chapter there will be no effort to describe the ways in which aggression is distorted by the various defenses against it. These will be described in Chapters VIII–XVIII dealing with the mechanisms.

Infantile. Various infantile forms of aggression have already been described. Many of these persist throughout life and may easily be recognized. The mouth is probably the first aggressive instrument and is used for aggressive purposes throughout life by biting, spitting, pouting, vomiting, or making noises of contempt. As already noted, the excretory products—feces and urine—have their aggressive significance. The eyes may also be used aggressively. We speak of "a killing glance," "his eyes shot out fire," the Ancient Mariner held the wedding guest with his "glittering eye." The dominance and submission of two persons can be readily determined by the way in which they return the gaze or avert the eyes.

As the child matures and acquires motor skill, he acquires methods of hurting other people by hitting, pushing, and kicking, and after he acquires the use of weapons and tools, he learns to hurt by throwing and shooting. One learns not only to cause bodily harm but to hurt by destroying property, by breaking, cutting, spoiling the work of others, and stealing. Or one harms another in less direct ways by using his time, diverting his interests, and interfering in various ways with his pursuits. A child can hurt his parents by his failure, by his untidiness, by speaking slang, or disregarding his personal appearance or a mother can show aggression toward a child by denying it pleasures.

Verbal. Then there are the verbal forms of aggression which are a direct outgrowth of oral aggression, such as shouting, screaming, calling names, scolding, or using threats, profanity, or obscenity. A person can use "biting" words with a "sharp" tongue. Swearing and cursing may serve as a substitute for more active forms of aggression and may, in many instances, serve more as a form of release of accumulated tension than as a direct attack on an individual. Invoking a deity is a common phenomenon whereby fantasy is considerably more extravagant than actual behavior. In a less direct but perhaps still more potent way, one can hurt another person by making attacks on his ego, by showing contempt, by disparaging and discrediting him to others, by disagreeing with his ideas, by showing him insolence and disrespect before others. There may be no more severe method of hurting another person than by neglect—"cutting" or snubbing him, or forgetting his name. Teasing is a specially interesting type of ego attack because it is playfully linked with erotic stimulation at the same time. In many instances there is an element of jealousy in teasing. When an older person "teases" a boy about his girl friend there is envy along with disparagement; while discourteous remarks about clothing or successful accomplishment undoubtedly reflect envy. Teasing frequently expects a retort in the same vein for if genuine anger is evinced the attacker retreats by saying "I was only teasing." The methods of hurting another person by attacking his self-esteem are too numerous to mention.

Resistance. Aggression can also be shown by various forms of resistance. A little child, for instance, will show his tendencies toward aggression by disobedience, negativism, and defiance. At about the age of two, when children are beginning to realize the significance of themselves as independent persons, they will attempt to demonstrate this independence by a flare of negativism. Frederickson [13] has demonstrated experimentally in a significant study that negativism and resistance in young children of two and three are definitely correlated with the increased frustration that training requires. The insecure child who suffers much frustration from his parents may show counter-aggression by disturbances in eating, such as refusing to eat, holding food in the mouth, refusing to swallow, or by indulging in unreasonable food fads. In later childhood and in adolescence, these same tendencies may show themselves by resistance to authority and by attempts to evade regulations. Sometimes aggressiveness in the form of resistance will show itself in the enjoyment of secret, forbidden pleasures—smoking behind the barn or stealing out without permission at night. In children aggression may show itself either by intrusion or rejection of companionship. A group of children may cruelly keep another child from their circle; one child may try to crash into the game of others. These same attempts at joining

[13] Norman Frederickson, "The Effect of Frustration on Negativistic Behavior of Young Children," *Journal of Genetic Psychology*, 61 (1942), 203–226.

groups or excluding from groups may find aggressive expression throughout life.

The delinquent shows aggression by attacks on persons and property in defiance of laws and customs.

Rivalry and competition. Rivalry and competition represent another form of aggressiveness—one that is not only condoned but actually encouraged in our society. Entering into competition either in sports, in school, or in business is sometimes thought to be a worthy sublimation of aggressive tendencies. This form of aggression occurs frequently between siblings who strive for first place in parental regard. The desire to be first or important stimulates aggressive striving throughout life. One may also show aggression by taking sides or by alternating preferences, thereby wounding the unpreferred individual. A mother can show her hostility to one child by preferring another child.

Sometimes aggression is shown by attempting to win others to one's cause, which naturally increases power over the enemy.

Administering punishment. Administering punishment is another form of socially acceptable aggression. A parent is supposed not "to spare the rod and thus to spoil the child." To be sure, teachers are no longer permitted to use corporal punishment; but this privilege has not been withdrawn from parents. Actually teachers have at their command sarcasm, ridicule, and other forms of punishment even more devastating than direct attacks on the body.

not always aggression

Aggressive feelings and attitudes. There are many *feelings* and *attitudes* of an aggressive nature which reach expression by less distinct routes than those already mentioned. *Intolerance* of another person's beliefs or behavior will lead to attempts to get rid of the person or to suppress his utterances or behavior. *Envy* and *jealousy* lead to hostile acts in attempts to harm the other person, to destroy his prestige or his property, and to degrade him in the eyes of others. *Resentment,* the smoldering afterglow of repressed aggression, will frequently lead to hostile attacks either to the person concerned or to others, perhaps after a considerable interval of time.

VALUES OF AGGRESSION *possition aggression*

Positive values. Aggression has both positive and negative aspects. Parents may strive to eliminate expressions of overt aggression in a youngster, but at the same time they do not want to stifle it entirely. The man who has the energy and spunk to stand up for himself and protect himself against insults and injury is admired by everyone. Aggression is necessary for self-preservation. Man would not be able to exist on this planet without asserting himself against his enemies and winning for himself food and shelter. Aggression is necessary as a protection against loss of freedom. If we are not to become the slaves of another, we must assert our own rights. An infant should be permitted to get enough satisfaction through aggression from his infantile, sadistic sources to permit him to carry on the struggle for existence in mature life. For it is on the basis of aggression learned during infancy that the adult maintains himself when he is grown up.

Aggression is a necessary adjunct of growth and differentiation. Only as a child asserts himself will he be able to grow and became adequate to meet new situations. Rebellion against parents is a necessary part of the growing-up process. As we have already seen, this may first show itself in the negativism of a two-year-old. Rebellion crops out again in self-assertiveness at each stage of childhood. It becomes particularly strong, and highly so, in adolescence when the youth is endeavoring to break away from his family ties and establish himself as an independent person. To us, birds seem cruel when they peck at their fledglings and force them to leave their nest to venture forth on their wings. Perhaps the parents of adolescents are overprotective in attempting to hold on to their growing sons and daughters when they should be encouraging them to independent enterprise. The parent who overprotects the child is hindering his growth toward maturity.

The aggressive play of children should be looked upon as a safety-valve which permits them to try out in reality the aggressive fantasies which, if suppressed, would remain magnified and troublesome in later years.

tennis

The third positive value of aggression is that it is pleasurable, and certainly this is no reason why it should be stamped out. However, the pleasurable nature of aggression is one thing that makes it difficult to control. One remembers in *Gone with the Wind* how restless and eager Southern boys were to take up the Rebel cause and join the Rebel Army.

The discussion of the management of aggression by turning it in on the self has been reserved for discussion in Chapter XV. It can be mentioned here, however, that this is another positive value of aggression. One of the potent controlling forces in human life is the use of inward aggression to curb desires. At times we may pity the person who feels it necessary to punish himself by restrictions and puritanical living. However, this inward turning of aggression may also be looked on as a desirable form of social control. Turning one's aggression inward and controlling one's impulses and desires enables one to continue to love, a result which might be difficult to accomplish if love were mixed with too much unbridled outgoing hostility and hate. Aggression turned on the self restricts life and causes unnecessary suffering, but when one considers that man must live as a social being with regard for the rights of others, such suffering also has positive value.

It should be emphasized here that aggression has great positive value which present civilization could ill afford to be without. Through the development of aggressive trends man is able to turn his energies to constructive tasks and enterprises. Without an aggressive component, man would not be able to tame the forces of nature, to improve his ways of living, to battle against the forces of evil rampant in the world. When aggression is fused with love it is possible for a person to work for the betterment of others, for the improvement of their ways of life, for the general happiness, and toward overcoming diseases, poverty, intolerance, and slavery. Zander [14] found that aggressiveness and good-will were not incompatible, for his friendliest subjects were also the most aggressive. In the modern world aggressiveness is directed more toward mastery than toward destructiveness. In more primitive societies a man's impulses expressed themselves by overcoming others and destroying them. The remnants of this tendency may still be seen in the two world wars; but in a stable society man expresses his aggressive tendencies by his attempts at mastery, at achieving a position of leadership and control, and in excelling his fellow-men.

NB (margin annotation)

Negative values. The negative aspects of aggression need not be dwelt on too long as they are well known. Hate turned outward can be used to cover up love and to increase misery and unhappiness in human affairs. Hate and hostility are destructive to human relations. Where these are permitted open expression within the family, they lead to a most unhappy and wretched form of living. Freud [15] has said that aggressiveness is the most powerful obstacle to culture. Civilization could have reached a much higher level were it not for the recurring wars which destroy not only material possessions but human institutions.

Hate is also disruptive because it cannot be turned against the person or persons who stimulated it and, consequently, has to be repressed. This goes back to the cycle of aggression, punishment, and hate. As we have seen, aggression stirs up counter-aggression in the form of punishment, and punishment leads to fear, hate, and retaliation or repression. A little child does not dare to tell his father what he thinks of him or how revengeful he feels toward him. In the clinic he will express these feelings freely on some play-object or doll which he stabs full of holes, or whose head he cuts off, or suspends helplessly in mid-air. The repression of hate builds up tensions which make a person nervous, anxious, and fearful. It is the release of these tensions that was indicated when aggressive play was mentioned as having positive value. Aggression turned inward has been shown to have its positive value in putting controls on social impulses, but aggression turned inward also has its negative values in so

[14] A. F. Zander, "A Study of Experimental Frustration," *Psychological Monograph*, 56, No. 3, Whole No. 256 (1944).

[15] Sigmund Freud, *Civilization and Its Discontents*, International Psychoanalytical Library, No. 17 (London: The Hogarth Press, 1929), 102.

far as it limits expression and denies pleasure, and enforces self-denial and forebearance in gratifying one's own desires.

CONTROL OF AGGRESSION *negative aggression*

Reduce frustration—provide security. It has already been said that aggression is universal and necessary. There is no possibility, therefore, of stamping it out even if this were desirable, which it is not. It is necessary, however, to control aggression by turning it away from destructive ends and by directing it into constructive and productive channels. It should be reëmphasized that no one would desire to see aggressiveness eliminated or stamped out of human nature. Indeed, some children need more, not less aggressiveness, and they should be encouraged and taught how to defend themselves in rough and tumble play and give-and-take between each other. Parents and teachers should exercise restraint and not intervene too much or too frequently in settling children's disputes. The point at which to begin reducing tendencies toward aggressiveness is to *reduce frustration* and *provide security* since these are the conditions which produce aggression. The time to begin in the control of aggression is in early infancy. The most important single factor is that the parents should accept the child and give it emotional security. The child's wants should be attended to regularly and without too long a period of frustrated waiting. Children should be given more freedom to express themselves naturally and should have fewer restrictions placed on them. Frustration cannot be wholly eliminated, however, and this is as it should be, for, as has already been mentioned, growth itself depends on a certain amount of mild frustration, and this is merely repeating that the development of aggression is both inevitable and, to a degree, desirable. Aggressiveness can be reduced by helping individuals feel greater pride and satisfaction in themselves, greater self-esteem, and more opportunity to identify with socially constructive enterprise.

Parents, however, can avoid causing certain forms of insecurity in their children. For instance, it is possible to minimize arousing jealousy. When a new baby comes into the family, the mother can remember that she must not devote all her interests to the newcomer but must plan to show her older child that he still has a warm place in her affections. Parents can help a great deal by avoiding all forms of exclusiveness and cliquishness within the family. Where circumstances permit, it is often wise to keep relatives apart rather than to run the risk of permitting situations which breed jealousy, frustration, and aggression. Although it is not always possible, particularly when times are hard, arrangements for grandparents or aunts and uncles to live outside the family group may be desirable.

Provide controls. As a second general method of controlling aggression, society has adopted external controls by its institutions, laws, customs, and regulations. Every stable society has settled down to a fixed order of social arrangements which provide for the control of aggression. If a child is born into a family group where law and order prevail, he grows up to find that his tendencies toward aggression are channeled into behavior which is acceptable to the group. Society has erected its structure of law in order to regulate aggression by forbidding certain of its expressions.

Aggression may also be lessened by eliminating some of its causes in group living. To the extent that society can guarantee social and economic security, one cause of hostile aggression can be removed. An equitable distribution of wealth reduces envy. A democratic organization of society and social institutions helps in the control of aggression by giving each individual a share in determining his freedom to express his satisfaction or dissatisfaction with arrangements and forms of government. Then it is believed that the relaxation of sexual taboos would remove certain important frustrations in this area and thereby remove another important cause of aggression. If society is to eliminate destructive and brutal aggression of wars in the future, some form of international organization must be provided which will outlaw war and at the same time provide other constructive modes by which aggression can be expressed. In such a world order there would be social and economic security, some kind of equable distribution of wealth, and a democratic organization which would give all nations, groups and individuals a chance to express their wishes and grievances.

External controls, however, cannot be relied upon solely for the control of aggression. This control must be built up within the psychological structure of each individual. The individual must not behave solely because he fears a policeman but because within himself he has standards of right and wrong and good and bad. The control of aggression depends, therefore, on the strengthening of the ego. This means that there must be a greater respect for persons and personality, that every individual shall have a right to be respected as an individual, and that through education individual controls shall be built. This education must start with the family but should be continued in all the character-building agencies of society, including the school and the church.

One need not be too concerned about the powerful aggressions of infancy and early childhood, for these tend of themselves to disappear with increasing maturity as the ego of the child gathers about it greater strength. The little child builds enlarged aggressive fantasies because he is so close to his parents and is not able to see them with true perspective. To the extent that a child is separated from his parents when he goes to school and plays with other children, he no longer considers his father as a terrifying ogre or giant but as another man among men. Just as the elm tree in the front yard seems by no means so towering when one returns to visit the homestead in later years, so one loses the awe-inspiring fantasy concepts of parents as experience is broadened and a better perspective gained. One sure method of reducing dangerous aggression is to enlarge experience through education.

Control of Aggression Through Education. Education has an important task to play in directing and controlling aggression in several ways. In the first place, the parent or teacher would be unwise to disregard aggression and permit it free expression without control or direction. While it is admitted that aggression is necessary, certain *forms* of aggression are by no means necessary; and one task of the parent or teacher is to help the child inhibit certain forms of expression and channel his aggressive tendencies into constructive activities. If the aggression is disregarded, the child will not be helped to master it.

Education can assist in reducing the intensity of aggression by eliminating competition as a method of learning and by not placing too great emphasis on the ambition to excel in physical strength, mentality, or possessions. Competition and the desire to excel are ingrained in our culture but are by no means universal to the same degree in all cultures. This tendency to want to excel others is a man-made product and can be toned down, as well as fostered. While competition is recognized as an incentive to learning, other incentives should be used which do not make the same use of aggressive tendencies. One very special attitude which in the broad sense is within the province of education concerns the attitudes toward femininity and its equation with inferiority. This attitude is a feature of western civilization but, by no means, a necessary one. While it is true that men and women differ in their physical strength and stamina, there is no evidence to indicate that women are in any way inferior to men in mental capacity and other personality and character qualities. The inferiority of women is a fiction which has had pronounced, but unfortunate influence in causing strivings toward masculinity and dissatisfaction with the feminine rôle.

Another way in which education can cope with the tide of aggressiveness is by providing ample play facilities by means of which children can work off their aggressive tendencies in harmless ways. Parents may become perturbed at the rough and boisterous play of children and at their rudeness to each other. Many parents have raised the question as to whether playing war with toy soldiers, airplanes, and guns will not produce war-like tendencies in their sons and daughters when they grow up, and whether playing "cops and robbers" and other games of attack may not be making young gangsters out of their children. The consensus of opinion today is that far from producing a war-like race, these games have just the opposite effect by providing a release of aggressive tendencies. Observers report that there is no marked increase in either aggressiveness or anxiety as a result of the war. In these harmless ways, the aggressive fantasies of children become dissipated and lose their violence. It is natural and healthful for boys and girls to play vigorously and even roughly.

Parents and teachers should avoid harsh and severe methods of training. Violence produces counter-violence, and brutality breeds brutality. While it is by no means true that a child who has received corporal punishment is necessarily a sadistic child, in general, one would expect more aggressiveness from children whose parents are harsh and tyrannical.

Finally, education has as one of its great responsibilities helping every boy and girl to develop socially acceptable outlets for aggression. This can be done, in the first place, by teaching children good habits of work and constructive skills. The man or woman who can employ his talents constructively has available outlets for his aggressive tendencies which are of greatest social value. Our forefathers expended their aggressive impulses in subduing a continent. Now everyone should devote his energies to contributing in some constructive way to the satisfaction of human needs and reduction of human ills.

THERAPY OF AGGRESSION

If a child has had unfortunate experiences and becomes what Pearson [16] calls chronically aggressive, then these educational procedures must be modified to help the child reduce and redirect his needs to be aggressive. The aim in therapy is to reduce fear and anxiety, which arise when a child's aggressive tendencies overpower him. The entering wedge must break up the mutual reinforcement between hatred and fear; that is, fearing the parents' hostility and meeting it by hatred. The group of scientists from Yale [17] who have studied the problem of aggression have enunciated as a basic principle that "The occurrence of any act of aggression is assumed to reduce the instigation to aggression." Just as eating a good meal reduces the demand of hunger, so giving vent to hostile tendencies reduces the need to be aggressive. The individual who can explode in a temper usually carries no grudges, for the storm clears the atmosphere, and calm follows. The individual, on the other hand, whose aggressive impulses are inhibited accumulates tension which, mounting by slow degrees, may explode at a later date with unaccountable fury.

Therapeutic methods in the reduction of aggression. Therapeutic methods designed to reduce aggressiveness encourage the symbolic or

[16] G. H. J. Pearson, "The Chronically Aggressive Child," *Psychoanalytic Review*, 26 (1939), 485–525.

[17] John Dollard, L. W. Doob, N. E. Miller, O. H. Mowrer, R. R. Sears, *Frustration and Aggression* (New Haven: Yale University Press, 1939).

play therapy

fantasy expression of aggression. In little children this may be done by means of play. The little child may mold an image out of clay and then proceed to dismember it, stamp on it, bat it around, and vent on it the full strength of his hostile feelings. An older child or an adult can be encouraged to express the full depth of his feelings by talking about them. Such therapy, of course, requires special qualifications in the therapist, who must not be discouraged by the violent display of aggressiveness and who can "take it" without feeling the need to show counter-aggression or to suppress these hostile and destructive impulses which children may display. This release of expression of aggressive tendencies is the first step in the corrective process.

However, aggressiveness is not reduced merely by encouraging freer expression of it. One must go back to the factors which caused the aggressiveness in the first place and modify or eliminate them. As has been previously stated on pp. 74 f., aggression arises from frustration and deprivation. In particular, aggression frequently becomes overpowering when the child feels neglected, unloved, and unwanted. Aggression is a protest against these feelings and an attempt to win emotional security by force. Accordingly, the therapist must first of all take steps to establish a strong and secure relationship with the child and give the child every assurance that he is liked and wanted and that he will not be rejected or punished by the therapist for his aggressive behavior. The client needs to be assured that his aggressive impulses are natural and that his response is no different from one made by others under similar provocation. Of special importance in the reduction of aggressive tendencies is to help the individual gain his self-respect by getting rid of ideas that he is bad, unworthy, and unlovable. The aggressive child must be relieved of his burden of guilt and made to feel that he is accepted in spite of his aggressive behavior.

Finally, it is important that the individual be helped to understand the basis for his aggression. This insight cannot be achieved when the child is in a state of panic or when he loses control over his aggressive tendencies. When the temper tantrum or destructive tendencies mount in fury, the wise therapist will bring the counseling session to a close, recognizing that the individual can be helped only when he is able to express his feelings symbolically (by play or by telling how he feels) and calmly and with less pressure and urgency. It is generally recognized that the treatment of hyperaggressiveness is more difficult than states of fear and inhibition.

Difficulties in the therapy of aggression. There are certain difficulties in therapy directed toward the amelioration of aggressive tendencies. For instance, we have already seen that aggression is pleasurable, and what is pleasurable is usually difficult to relinquish. If a child finds pleasure in tormenting others, no amount of release in expression is likely to reduce

1.

the need for it. Perhaps the corrective here is the fact that we live in a world of reality and that either the child is going to meet resistance and reprisal at the hands of others whom he annoys, or he is going to suffer himself when he breaks his own toys and damages his own projects.

Another difficulty with therapy is that parents are often unable to tolerate the release of aggression. If the parents bring a difficult child to the clinic and the therapist proceeds by giving the child permission to express some of his inhibited, aggressive tendencies, this aggression is likely not to be confined to the clinic, but will be carried over to home and school. To the parents, the child appears to be getting worse. He becomes more unruly, disobedient, and negativistic. An increase in the child's aggression becomes a threat to the parents in two ways. For the therapist to accept the child's aggression apparently puts the blame and responsibility on the parent and this will arouse guilt in him; and if a child shows increased aggression, the parents fear criticism and censure from the community. Parents usually attempt to suppress aggression in their children as a protest against their own fears and anxieties. This means, of course, that as a child is being treated for aggressiveness the parents would profit by therapeutic treatment also. If parents can be told that as the treatment of their child proceeds he may become more aggressive as a stage he must pass through, then perhaps they will be able to accept it more willingly. What is true as concerns the parents is also true of the school and community at large. In general, people have difficulty in understanding the aims and processes of therapy inasmuch as they seem to go against the goals which it is their aim to achieve. Aggression in a child arouses aggressive impulses in his parents. It is because he fears that he may be unable to control his own impulses and that he may do harm to the child that most parents find it difficult to tolerate aggression and feel that they must suppress it.

Another handicap to therapeutic treatment may be found in those situations in which the child's aggressive tendency grows out of an unhealthful home situation. If this home situation is not changed, there is constant reinfection. Just as the physician is defeated at the outset if he is attempting to cure a patient who is constantly reinfected, so the therapist's efforts are likely to result in failure if the family relations of the child offer continued frustration. In such cases it might be necessary either to carry on therapeutic work with the parents at the same time that the child is being treated, or to treat the child in an institutional or foster-home setting.

QUESTIONS FOR DISCUSSION

1. Speculate on the genetic origin of hostility and destructiveness.
2. Why should the rejected child show aggressive traits?

3. Why should the overindulged child be aggressive?

4. What suggestions can you glean from this chapter as to steps which might be taken to reduce (a) industrial conflict (b) war between nations.

5. Discuss aggression within the family. What causes it? How is it expressed? Should it be suppressed? How can it best be utilized?

6. What does it mean to say that self-aggression is a valuable form of social control?

7. To what extent do you believe that heredity is responsible for making some persons "aggressive." To what extent does a person become aggressive because of his experiences? How could experiences in infancy make a person aggressive as an adult?

8. Discuss methods for "preventing" aggressiveness in young children. Relate this discussion to your previous discussion of the origins of the aggressive personality.

9. Are there exceptions to the therapeutic method of reducing aggressiveness in children by encouraging the symbolic or fantasy experience of aggression? (P. 91.)

RECOMMENDED READINGS

1. APPEL, M. H., "Aggressive Behavior of Nursery-School Children and Adult Procedures in Dealing with Such Behavior," *Journal of Experimental Education,* 11 (1942), 185–1999.

2. BLOS, PETER, "Aggression in Children," *Child Study,* 15 (1938), 228–230.

3. DOLLARD, JOHN, DOOB, L. W., MILLER, N. E., MOWRER, O. H., and SEARS, R. R., *Frustration and Aggression* (New Haven: Yale University Press, 1939).

4. DURBIN, E. F. M., and BOWLBY, JOHN, *Personal Aggressiveness and War* (New York, Columbia University Press, 1939).

5. FITE, M. D., "Aggressive Behavior in Young Children and Children's Attitudes Toward Aggression," *Genetic Psychology Monographs,* 22 (1940), 151–319.

6. FLÜGEL, J. C., *Psychoanalytic Study of the Family,* International Psychoanalytical Library, No. 3 (London: Hogarth Press, 1921).

7. ISAACS, SUSAN, *Social Development in Young Children* (New York: Harcourt Brace and Company, 1937).

8. JERSILD, A. T., and MARKEY, F. V., *Conflicts Between Preschool Children,* Child Development Monograph, No. 21 (New York: Bureau of Publications, Teachers College, Columbia University, 1935).

9. LEVY, D. M., "Hostility Patterns in Sibling Rivalry Experiments," *American Journal of Orthopsychiatry* 6 (1936), 183–257.

10. PEARSON, G. H. J., "The Chronically Aggressive Child," *Psychoanalytic Review:* 26 (1939), 485–525.

11. WOLBERG, L. R., "A Note on the Treatment of Aggression in Emotionally Disturbed Children," *Psychiatric Quarterly* 18 (1944), 667–673.

V

Punishment

Punishment is a universal method of control and is used in all societies, both primitive and civilized, as a method for child-rearing. In its simplest terms, punishment is the infliction of pain or loss on another in order to prevent certain behavior. For instance, if a child is too aggressive in his nursing or reaches out his hand for some forbidden object, his mother may push him away or slap his hand. At first, this may be wholly unplanned and impulsive on the part of the mother; later, her punishment may be planned to a greater degree so that she may guide the child in the ways she wishes him to go.

Whether punishment is administered with or without plan, it is always *intended* in the sense that it is the infliction of pain or some privation in order to produce a certain result. From the very beginning the child recognizes this intention on the part of his parents and responds accordingly, both by modifying his aggressive tendencies and by developing attitudes of hate toward his parents. Later a child may interpret any pain or loss as punishment, whether this pain or loss be intended as punishment by some person, or whether it comes from impersonal sources. For instance, if a child falls down and bangs his forehead, or catches his hand in the door, he may have the feeling that these accidents did not merely happen but were intended by some unseen power. In later years he may respond to any pain or privation as though it were a punishment, and may modify his original aggressive behavior accordingly.

Punishment not synonymous with discipline. In this chapter it should be understood that punishment is not considered to be synonymous with discipline. Discipline refers to *any* method used to guide or control behavior. Frequently, disciplinary measures are encouraging rather than punitive and repressing. It is indeed unfortunate that punishment has been interpreted by many parents and teachers as the only method possible in controlling a child's behavior.

Punishment is aggressive. Punishment is aggressive behavior on the part of the person who is administering it. Aggression, in one sense, was defined in Chapter IV as an act of hostility or attack, and certainly pun-

95

ishment would be an illustration of this variety of aggressive behavior. To the person administering the punishment, it is a response to frustration; that is, the frustration caused by the child who in his own physical exuberance hurts the parent or damages something that the parent values. Since aggression is the normal response to frustration, the parent who is frustrated by the child who hurts or annoys him responds by counter-aggression—that is, by punishment.

Punishment is preventive. A parent does not always administer punishment because what the child does *actually* hurts or damages, but in order to *prevent* hurt or damage which would be threatening; that is, the parent feels threatened that he may be judged a bad parent if his child has uncouth manners or is sickly. All punishment is preventive in this sense. Some punishment may be for disciplinary and therefore educational purposes, but its severity is still based on and in proportion to the fears experienced by or threats to the punisher's security, prestige or status. Without fear of pain to the punisher there would be no punishment, either for disciplinary or other reasons. When the punisher is threatened severely, the punishment is severe. When the threat to the punisher is severe, the counter-aggression may have as its purpose in extreme cases, annihilation, and in less extreme degrees, crippling or rendering less effective or adequate the behavior of the offender.

Mrs. M., who never wanted her baby, worked nights as a nurse during her pregnancy, bore it prematurely, refused to nurse it, later refused to feed it, left it alone day after day, gave it frequent doses of phenobarbital, refused to allow the father to touch the child, kept it confined to its crib, permitted no social stimulation, and just barely kept the child alive in a jaundiced condition until it was placed in an institution, was trying to annihilate what represented to her her own sinful behavior.

Mrs. B., whose husband has left her and who finds great difficulty in supporting her children, nags them constantly and holds them to impossible standards of school work. By her constant nagging she makes the children so unhappy they cannot concentrate in school. Mrs. B. does not annihilate her children, but her aggressive behavior makes them moody, rebellious, they tend to have few friends, and consequently are not adequate either scholastically or socially. Such behavior results from a fear that unless her children do well in school they will not be able to get jobs, and hence she will be without support.

Punishment as a frustration to the recipient. To the child, punishment itself is a frustration, but it is a derived or secondary frustration which will reinforce his aggressive behavior that was stimulated by the original frustration. Here then, we see frustration in the child used in two senses: the original frustration, whatever its source, and the later and secondary frustration, which is punishment. And aggression in the child is also used in two senses: that which is stimulated by the original frustration or deprivation, and that which is a response to punishment.

Universality of punishment. Every parent punishes his child in one form or another. This is true not only of bad parents, but also of even the most mild and tolerant of parents. Parents may never inflict sharp pain, and they may attend as well as any parents can to the child's needs, but a child's aggressive tendencies must be curbed; he must be guided and controlled in his comings and goings, and he must be restrained from endangering his life or from harming property. Despite the necessity of this preventing and directing behavior, it will be interpreted by the child as punishment.

PURPOSE OF PUNISHMENT

The purpose of punishment discussed here should not be confused with the motivation of the punisher to be discussed in a later section. (See pp. 106–108.) Here we are only concerned with the effect which the punisher *intends* on the person being punished. Punishment is inflicted in the first instance as a means of restraining in a child behavior which is annoying to the person who punishes. Later, what is annoying may be generalized and conceptualized, and any act which is judged to be bad, sinful, wrong, or harmful will be punished. A parent will attempt to steer a child away from dangerous and harmful experiences. He will also want to prevent the child from doing what is bad or wrong or sinful according to the moral code and social standards of his group. Consequently, punishment is used not only to restrain a child from behavior which is annoying to his elders or dangerous to himself but is also used formally as an educational device.

Typically, punishment is administered to prevent aggressive behavior on the part of the child. The parent will use forceful means to protect himself from bodily injury. He will also prevent his child from hurting other people. Most parents feel very strongly about such matters, and considerable anxiety is aroused in a parent by a child who shows harmful or sadistic tendencies toward other children. Punishment is used, too, to prevent or correct injury to self-esteem, as for instance, calling names or insulting another person. Again, punishment is used to prevent a child from destroying property—for breaking a window, marring walls, or for forgetting to fill the radiator in an automobile. Punishment is frequently used as a means of preventing the child from getting hurt, as for instance, to prevent him from running into the street where he may be struck by a passing automobile.

In a more general sense, punishment is used to prevent any transgression of the moral or cultural code. It is a method that parents use to stamp out behavior which is unacceptable, and to direct the child into acceptable behavior patterns.

KINDS OF PUNISHMENT

Infliction of pain. The most primitive form of punishment is the infliction of pain in the form of physical contact or injury. Punishment is given by the hand in the form of a slap or a blow, or by some extension of the hand as a switch or a whip. In extreme cases punishment may result in an actual physical injury, as when a whip raises welts on the body. The little child, perhaps more in fantasy than in actuality, is afraid of all sorts of violence as forms of punishment. For instance, he is afraid of being eaten up, as may be seen in the fairy-tales in which the ugly witch throws the children into an oven for the purpose of devouring them. Or he fears such violence as being dropped, drowned, suffocated, or poisoned. For a child, death itself is the ultimate in punishment.

Questionable

Injury to loved object. Another form of punishment is the infliction of injury or harm on some loved object or person. The illness or death of some loved person is looked upon as an act of divine vengeance. A little child will consider the harm that may come to his possessions—the breaking or destruction of a doll or other favorite toy—a most grievous form of punishment to him.

Forced labor. Being forced to undertake hard tasks or difficult labor under threat of physical pain is a common form of punishment. A child may be required to perform some monotonous task at home, or at school where he is made to write meaningless sentences scores of times, and in the adult world criminals are sentenced to years of hard labor.

Physical restraint. Physical constraint is another form of punishment, perhaps the most common method used by society. Its enemies are incarcerated in prisons, jails, and penitentiaries; an ill-behaved pupil is sentenced to stay after school or is prevented from going out to play with the other children at recess time. This may be physical constraint, but it may also be sociological or ideological. For instance, a boy is blocked from attaining a coveted book not only because it is out of reach (physical barrier), but also because his parents forbid him from climbing on a chair to get it (sociological barrier); or an appeal is made to some standard of value: "You are a good boy, and good boys do not do what will displease their parents" (ideological barrier).

Deprivation as punishment. Deprivation is another favorite form of punishment. The little child is sent to bed without his supper, or he is denied some favorite dessert. The prisoner may be forced to subsist on a fare of thin soup and poor bread. Deprivation of shelter is still a more drastic form of punishment. A newspaper story recounts an instance in which a child was punished by being made to stand for an hour alone outside the home in pitch darkness.

Sometimes punishment takes the form of deprivation of pleasures. The boy scout may be excluded from the group that goes on the over-night hike, or the college student may not be permitted to play in the game because he has broken some training rule. Sometimes the punishment takes the form of deprivation of special privileges, as when a child is told that he cannot have the use of some favorite toy for a period of time. In this connection the unequal treatment of children in the family may serve as a punishment. When one child is discriminated against and is not given what the other members of the family receive, this is a most severe form of punishment, because he is made to feel that he is unloved or unworthy, and also because he suffers a loss of self-esteem when compared unfavorably with someone else.

Exclusion from group. One ordinarily thinks of physical pain as being the most severe kind of punishment, but this is not necessarily true. Probably the most severe forms of punishment are the loss of love and exclusion from the group or unfavorable comparison in the group. This may be accomplished in the family by sending a child to his room or by locking him away in a dark closet or cellar. Schools recognize the effectiveness of this kind of punishment by requiring the child to stand by himself in the corner apart from the rest of the group or by sending him to a closet or cloak-room. Parents may punish a child by committing him to an institution, by placing him in a foster home, by sending him away to school or camp, often with the excuse that it is in the child's best interests. A. Freud and Burlingham[1] state that children know only one main punishment for anybody who offends them: that this person should go away and not return. In adult society banishment from society to the dungeon or to the convict colony is recognized as the most drastic form of punishment which can be conceived apart from death itself.

Depreciation as punishment. Another form of punishment which also has severe effects on a child's security is expressed in depreciation of him; for example, making him feel inferior or unworthy by heaping ridicule, scorn, criticism, or disapproval on him. Since teachers in many states have been prevented by law from inflicting corporal punishment, they have discovered ways of inflicting still more exquisite forms of mental torture by subtle sarcasm or irony.

A Swiss schoolmaster, W. Schohaus, has collected a number of anecdotes of school experiences which vividly portray unfortunate and destructive incidents in the classroom:[2]

In the elementary school I was considered one of the best pupils, and my speech was never objected to there. Then I went to the Gymnasium at Z. "You

---

[1] Anna Freud and D. T. Burlingham, *Young Children in War-Time* (London: George Allen & Unwin, 1942), and *War and Children* (New York: International Universities Press, 1943).

[2] Willi Schohaus, *The Dark Places of Education* (New York: Henry Holt and Company, 1932), 325.

have a potato in your mouth!" was one of the first things my German mastei said to me. Derisive laughter followed on the part of my school-fellows, and a deep wound to my pride. My little defect in speech was never attended to, but neglected, and therefore it became worse. . . . Anyone who has ever been made a laughing-stock before others remains permanently a victim of the defect.

Threats as punishment. The student of human nature should be aware not only of these overt forms of punishment, but also of the cues that indicate their approach. Threats and scoldings are well-known examples of these. Almost any sign of disapproval, ranging from outspoken criticism to a frown, scowl, or tut-tut, may be recognized by the child as punishment, or at least as an anticipation of punishment. Children usually become extremely sensitive to their parents' feelings and attitudes, and many children do not wait for overt punishment, but respond with alacrity to the slightest sign of parental displeasure or annoyance. In psychological experiments, merely to inform a subject that his response is "wrong" has been spoken of as a punishment—and probably rightly so. Any reference to the wishes, beliefs, attitudes, or standards of another beloved or respected person may be as effective in controlling behavior as more overt forms of punishment. As a matter of fact, many children are more afraid of the frown of displeasure than they are of the switch itself, for in their fantasies they can magnify the severity of the pain far beyond what it would be in reality.

Threats to the ego are particularly traumatic and damaging. Frequently one hears parents or nursemaids exercise control over an unruly child by threatening to call the police, "I will tell your father," or to send a note to the teacher. Threats to the sex rôle of a child may also be peculiarly damaging to personality. The teacher who refused to have an adolescent boy with a beard in her class, or the mother who objects to her daughter's "dates" or choice of clothes is threatening the masculinity or femininity of these adolescents.

Neglect. Perhaps we should not close this recital of the different forms punishment takes without mentioning neglect. The good child who is not noticed is actually punished by the neglect, and is made to feel that his acts are not worthy, for no other reason than that no one has thought to comment on them. It is essentially a form of deprivation. Neglect of a child's health, his cleanliness, and routines essential to good child development, failure to provide educational and social opportunities or suitable living accommodations commensurate with his needs, are all forms of neglect, and as a child compares himself with other children not so neglected, he may sense these forms of neglect as rejection of himself. This intensifies his feeling of guilt since he fears that in some way he has provoked the neglect. Similar forms of punishment are employed by husbands and wives as measures of hostility and counter-aggression.

RESPONSE TO PUNISHMENT

Before the various modes of response are considered, it is worthwhile to note that the response may be to punishment itself or to the anticipation of punishment. One may respond not only to punishment, but also to slight evidences of displeasure or annoyance on the part of the parent or teacher, indicating that punishment is forthcoming. One may even learn what behavior is subject to punishment and may respond to his own aggressive behavior or destructiveness or autoerotic pleasure or wrong-doing as though he had already been punished. A little child, for instance, stepping out into the street after having been cautioned not to, ran and struck another child who was playing with his velocipede, saying "You're a naughty boy, you can't play with this." It is as though the aggressive bad behavior was the cue to punishment that was to follow, and a person may respond to this aggressive or wrong behavior as though punishment has already been meted. Sometimes a child will attempt to avoid punishment following some misdeed by denying that he had any connection with it or by hiding the damage that was done.

Inhibition and repression. The first and normal response to punishment is the inhibition of the action toward which the punishment is directed. If a little child reaches out for the gas cock and receives a slap on his hand from his mother, he will likely withdraw his hand and cease from his attempts to reach the cock. There are certain mathematical relationships between the response to punishment, the amount or intensity of punishment, and the strength of the drive. In general, the stronger the drive to any action, the less intense the response to punishment. Again, the stronger the punishment, the more intense the degree of response to it. So the response to any punishment is in direct ratio to the intensity of the punishment and indirect ratio to the strength of the drive.

Whether punishment reduces the amount of criminality in the state is frequently debated. Is there a falling off in crime following the passage of a more stringent legal code with more severe punishment? There can be no doubt that harsher laws act as a deterrent to crime. However, stringent and punitive laws do not reduce the causes of crime. The incentives to crime remain even after laws are made more severe, and consequently they do not have a reconstructive and healing function.

Punishment is the basis of all repression. Repression of thoughts and fantasies in the unconscious part of the mental life is a consequence of early punishment experiences. What is punished seems to be bad, dangerous, disgusting, vile, or dirty and hence to be avoided and put out of mind. Material which has been repressed can be traced by analysis back to early childhood for which punishment was received in one form or another.

Influence of punishment on learning. Thorndike,[3] in his experiments on learning, believes that punishment does not directly affect the strength of the learned connections between stimulus and response. In earlier theories, there was a belief that punishment helped the individual to unlearn things that he had previously learned—as though by punishing a child, one could help him forget. If there seems to be a diminution of learning following punishment, it would probably be found to be in the nature of an inhibiting or repressive tendency. If this be so, these tendencies stamped out by punishment could be made to reappear at a later time when the individual is released from the inhibition.

Actually, punishment has been found to be an effective agent in the learning process, but not in influencing the strength of connections directly. The value of punishment lies in its influence in directing the behavior of the individual and in helping him to select or eliminate the behavior that he will practice and learn. Punishment induces a person to shift to another response. In the laboratory it has been shown that the rat which finds his way to a cul-de-sac in a maze blocked by an electric shock quickly learns to avoid that entrance and to select some other entrance that will not "punish." Punishment, then, serves in the process of learning by shunting an individual away from the wrong or useless response. In certain situations punishment may actually induce an individual to adopt the right response, and through practicing it, thereby to learn it. For instance, if there are only two alternative responses, and a person is warned that one of these is wrong, he will naturally turn to the other one, which will be the right one. If a given response is pointed out as being the right one, and every other response is pointed out as being wrong, this too, will lead the individual to practice the correct activity, and its learning will thus be facilitated. This would happen in helping a child to learn the execution of a command. He is told plainly what the command is. He is told that failure to execute the command will be punished. This leaves two alternatives—to execute the command, or not to execute the command. If the punishment is distasteful enough, he is driven to the only alternative open to him, namely, to execute the command.

Punishment also facilitates learning in other ways. In the first place, at the same time that punishment or any one of its substitutes annoys, it also stimulates and incites the individual to speed up the search for the correct response so that he will not be punished. Mild punishment leads to greater accuracy of response. Since punishment blocks the way to unde-

[3] E. L. Thorndike, *Human Learning* (New York: Appleton-Century-Crofts, Inc., 1931). Lecture 3

sirable and unacceptable responses, it confines behavior to what is correct and hence facilitates accuracy. Crafts and Gilbert [4] find that punishment promotes retention of learning as well as the original learning itself.

Acceptance and tolerance of punishment. There are several other possible forms of response to punishment or to its anticipation. Punishment may be expected, even tolerated and welcomed. Punishment is aimed as much at wounding the ego and self-respect as at causing physical pain, and a child may respond by efforts to defend and bolster his ego as well as to minimize the pain. A child who was sent to his room was found later enjoying himself in fitting wings to his model airplane, and he said that this was just the thing that he wanted to do at that particular time. A boy may welcome being sent from the classroom as a punishment if a girl in whom he is interested is sent out at the same time. Another child laughed at the blows which he received, saying that they only hurt a little. For a child to respond in this way to punishment is usually extremely exasperating to parents and teachers, because they feel as though the purpose of the punishment was being defeated. This is an interesting commentary on the motives for punishment, which would seem to be not only to stop the person from exhibiting certain behavior but also to make him feel uncomfortable or to hurt him in the process. Actually, the meaning of the acceptance of punishment goes deeper than these surface manifestations. And, as we shall see later (see pp. 284–292), one way in which a person responds to his own misdeeds is by feeling a need for punishment and actually seeking punishment for them.

Punishment is also welcomed because it is a sign of the parent's love for a child, even though painfully expressed. A parent must see some value in a child to be willing to punish him. In most children's eyes neglect is a more serious indication that they mean little to their parents than punishment. Children can differentiate between the punishment which signifies hostility, dislike, and disgust, and the punishment which signifies care and correction. A child often accepts punishment because by so doing he can keep the esteem of the person who punishes rather than alienate him altogether.

Responding to punishment by rationalization. Another method of reacting to punishment is by attempting to justify the behavior that is being punished. Children will seize upon all sorts of rationalizations. They will say that they meant no harm, that they were only trying to protect another child, that they had actually meant to do their lessons, but that they had been sent on some special errand at the time which they usually set aside to do their homework.

Aggressive response to punishment. Another frequent and important

[4] L. W. Crafts, and R. W. Gilbert, "The Effect of Punishment During Learning Upon Retention," *Journal of Experimental Psychology*, 17 (1934), 73–84.

response to punishment is the feeling of strong emotion such as anger, hatred, animosity, and resentment. Here we see the sequence continuing. Frustration leads to aggression. Aggression injures or interferes with another person and arouses retaliation in the form of punishment, which arouses in the person receiving it even stronger feelings of resentment and hate. Sometimes punishment is reacted to by attempts at retaliation, or getting even. The child being struck will attempt to strike back. The teacher who uses a sharp tongue in trying to control a pupil may receive a sarcastic reply. Sometimes the retaliation is not shown immediately, but will come out in later sabotage, violations of prohibitions, or even unconscious accidents and injuries. Cruelty is frequently born of punishment. The child who has been punished perhaps not too justly, but who dares no retaliation on father or mother, may take it out on the pet dog or rabbit, or may vent his spleen on his playmate. Punishment leads to intolerance, to stubbornness, and to a number of similar variations of the expression of strong hostile feelings aroused by punishment.

Feelings of inferiority aroused by punishment. Punishment also breeds feelings of inferiority. A little child's feelings of omnipotence, that is, his feelings of being able to accomplish whatever he wishes, are rudely dashed. Punishment destroys these feelings, and as the little child rages against a stronger force which inflicts pain on him and enforces constraint and deprivation and withdraws love, he is made to feel his inadequacy and ineffectiveness.

Fear and anxiety aroused by punishment. Punishment breeds fear and anxiety. This is particularly true when the seriousness of anticipated punishment is magnified in fantasy. Feelings of dread in the anticipation of punishment are usually as severe, or even more severe, than feelings stimulated by the punishment itself. This anxiety comes to one not only in the tension aroused from the anticipation of punishment, but also from the feeling that others are against him, that, "I am criticized and not appreciated," that, "I suffer the loss of my parents' love." Going still further, there is fear of retaliation from the hostile fantasies which the punishment arouses. When a supervisor makes a suggestion to a teacher this may be interpreted as criticism—a form of punishment. The hostility aroused in the teacher gives rise to dread and anxiety. We have just shown that punishment arouses feelings of resentment and hostility. Even when these feelings are not openly expressed, they are usually present in fantasy. These fantasies may become so real that the child may dread the retaliation which he anticipates from those toward whom the fantasies are directed. In games where this fear has a play value, punishment in the form of penalties or forfeits adds to the excitement. The writer recently played a game called "Oh Hell" in which those playing objected to having bonuses given for making a "bid" and insisted on having penalties given for failing to make a bid, as this made the game more exciting.

Feelings of guilt frequently attend punishment although punishment sometimes relieves guilt. Guilt accompanies the feeling that punishment is due, particularly when this need for punishment has been assimilated and introjected by the person himself, as well as when it has been aroused by a threat from some outside authority. Shame apparently arises more from punishment for illicit pleasures than from punishment for aggressive tendencies, but the feeling tones of guilt and shame are much alike, and there is overlapping between them. Similar feelings are expressed by such terms as remorse, sorrow, repentance, and regret. Punishment that is introjected is felt as a wrong-doing and unworthiness, and the need for punishment is commonly recognized as conscience. These feelings receive outward expression through acts of repentance, restitution, offering apologies, and the like.

Withdrawal caused by punishment. Another major method of response to punishment is withdrawal, which involves inhibition and repression. As the impulses to react aggressively to punishment are inhibited, they are turned in other directions. The individual who has been punished considerably, or who suffers greatly from the threat of punishment, instead of responding by counter-aggression and resentment, may respond in exactly the opposite way—by withdrawing and becoming distant, restrained, shy, and isolated. When a child comes to the playroom in the clinic and is withdrawn and unfriendly, one can guess that this child has been subjected to severe criticism or punishment. Accompanying this tendency to withdraw would be the arousal of vivid fantasies of violence and destruction. The normal response to punishment of anger and resentment, which is repressed in the withdrawn individual, finds expression in his day-dreams and unconscious fantasies in which he evens his score by the most sadistic and cruel acts. These fantasies may turn inward, not only because he fears retaliation of those toward whom his hostile fantasies are directed, but also because of the tendency to turn punishment inward so that the fantasies may be of his own annihilation and destruction.

Disorganization of behavior caused by severe punishment. One more response to punishment to be mentioned is disorganization of behavior. In experiments with animals it has been found that when too close or sharp a discrimination is required, responses tend to become disorganized. An animal will develop highly excited movements, many of them quite meaningless so far as their value for adjustment is concerned. The child who is punished often, severely, inconsistently, and without reason may develop similar kinds of disorganized behavior. Under severe punishment there is a loss of accuracy in learning, nervousness is increased, and there is a tendency to spread of nervous discharge. Tics, nervous grimaces, and motor incoördination can frequently result from severe and unjust punishment. Harsh punishment may also lead to emotional outbursts and uncontrolled temper.

SOME FACTORS DETERMINING THE EFFECT OF PUNISHMENT

In general, punishments are more effective at earlier ages than at later ones. In the first place, the emotional effects of punishment and the fantasies with regard to them are greatly enlarged and magnified during the first years of life. The extent to which small and mild punishment may produce severe repercussions in a child is not usually recognized. One writer, Farrow,[5] reports how he was able to recall during psychoanalysis the dramatic effect of even mild punishment administered by his parents. He speaks of "taps," meaning light blows, and how these were magnified, both in feeling and in their significance, in early childhood. The light tap signifies the possible devastation of the sharp blow. Later, as a child's experience broadens, and he gains perspective with regard to people around him, he discovers that the original punishment experiences are by no means as terrifying as he earlier believed. In later childhood a boy or girl may laugh at the punishment which, at an earlier age, would have terrified him, and adolescents may even glory in their ability to "take" punishment with Spartan fortitude.

Punishment is also more effective when administered by a person to whom one is emotionally tied than when it is administered by a person with less emotional attachment. It is for this reason that punishments within the family are usually of far greater significance than those given outside the family. Punishments administered in the home leave serious repercussions on the growing child. A teacher may inflict similar punishment, but the child may respond in quite a matter-of-fact way. To be sure, children may pale at the thought of what the policeman might do, but in general, the sharp word or the frown coming from father or mother is going to have an influence far exceeding similar expressions from strangers. Apparently the ties of love and affection in the home, and the threat of loss of love make the punishment within the family so much more drastic because of the emotional insecurity threatened.

MOTIVATION OF PUNISHMENT

Outlet for aggression and hostility. The question may be raised, "Why do parents and teachers punish?" The definition of punishment given at

[5] E. P. Farrow, *Analyze Yourself* (New York: International University Press, 1945) 2nd edition, reprinted of *A Practical Method of Self-Analysis* (New York: W. W. Norton and Co., 1943)

the beginning of this chapter, implying that punishment is intended in order to produce a certain result in child behavior, by no means gets to the root of the matter so far as motives of the person who punishes are concerned. In the first place, punishment is an acceptable outlet for aggression and hostility to the parent. It is true that the parent who punishes is generally applauded. He is felt to be doing his duty in the upbringing of his children. Likewise, the stereotype of a teacher is a stern individual who metes out punishment. It is well known that teachers frequently give expression to their hostility by punishment in the name of discipline of the pupils.

Enjoyment in administering punishment. One may go a step further *sadistic people* than this and say that administering punishment is sometimes actually enjoyed. This goes back to the childhood pleasure of being aggressive. A parent does not carefully plan to have a good time punishing his children, but unconsciously he finds pleasure in releasing inhibited aggressive tendencies in this way.

Need to assert dominance. The parent who has to resort to frequent punishment as a method of control may be recognized as an individual with his own adjustment difficulties. Often punishment is a cover for feelings of inferiority, because it provides an opportunity for the demonstration of superiority and dominance. The more inferior a person feels, the more need he has to assert himself forcefully. The teacher who has to resort to threats of punishment in order to control her class is fundamentally an insecure person, attempting by these methods to compensate for her own limitations.

Punishment as retaliation. Punishment may also be a form of retaliation or of getting even. This does not mean that a parent is inflicting cruelty and injustice on his own child for indignity suffered by punishment in the present, but he may be retaliating for punishment received many years before, perhaps in his own childhood. In some instances, the hatred and resentment against unfair punishment in childhood may be openly expressed only years afterward when the situation is reversed. Girls may have illicit sex relations and bear illegitimate children as a source of retaliatory punishment against their own neglectful parents— disappointing the parents because the parents have disappointed them.

Projecting a need for punishment. Sometimes punishments represent a projection of the need for punishment within the person. Moral training may have left the parent with unconscious feelings of sin and unworthiness, and he may feel that he deserves punishment for his shortcomings. It is easy in such circumstances for a parent to project these feelings of unworthiness and the need for punishment on his children. We see this, for instance, in a mother who holds impossibly high standards for her children and resorts to a continuous series of small punishments in order to try to force them to her impossible standards of attainment.

(6) **Punishment may assist in <u>releasing tension</u>.** Punishments also serve as release for emotional tensions. The mother whose own love life is not satisfied and whose sexual needs are not met may release her tensions by sharp, frequent scoldings and punishment of her children.

(7) **Punishment used in <u>ignorance of better methods of control</u>.** One must recognize that punishment is sometimes due in part to ignorance of more progressive methods of control and guidance. Many parents cannot imagine any other way of bringing up a child than by forcing him to adopt their own standards of behavior. Not infrequently a parent welcomes suggestions as to other methods of handling his children and without difficulty is able to substitute positive methods of guidance for punitive ones. To observe methods used by nursery and kindergarten teachers is sometimes helpful to a parent, who is thereby enabled to substitute these methods for her own. However, it should be recognized that a child does not have the same emotional relationship to his teacher as to his parents, and the parent may find that methods which seem to work miracles in school fail in their effectiveness at home.

VALUES OF PUNISHMENT

Positive values. Although punishment as a means of control is finding less and less support in child guidance, it must be recognized that punishment has undeniable positive values. Punishment is by no means a cure-all, and in fact, does not cure anything, but there are occasions when punishment has its merited place. First of all, punishment serves as a deterrent, and may be used by a parent in order to guard a child against impending danger. Whiting and Mowrer [6] have demonstrated that punishment is more effective in breaking a habit than as a barrier to the activity or non-reward of the activity. There are positive methods which a parent may adopt in teaching a child not to play in a dangerous street. But a critical situation may arise in which there is no time to work through these positive methods, and a child must be forcibly prevented from playing in dangerous places.

Punishment may be thought of as having importance in social control. The child who is punished by loving parents takes unto himself the prohibitions and restraints that his parents intend and makes them his own. (This will be elaborated in the chapter, "Introjection and the Superego.") Persons without these inner controls based on punishment

[6] J. W. M. Whiting, and O. H. Mowrer, "Habit Progression and Regression—A Laboratory Study of Some Factors Relevant to Human Socialization," *Journal of Comparative Psychology*, 36 (1943), 229–253.

(it may be mild parental restraint) become psychopathic and may require the external control of an institution such as a prison in order to keep their impulses within bounds.

Even so, it should be recognized that in these critical situations punishment is only a deterrent and is not a remedy. One can stop a child from any form of undesirable behavior by proper punishment, but this does not help the child to find a more acceptable method of satisfying the need leading to the undesirable behavior in the first place. In this sense then, punishment is like a cough drop—it will momentarily soothe the inflamed membrane and deny the impulse to cough, but the inflammation is still there, and the relief is only temporary.

Punishment also provides a person with information concerning the consequences of wrong behavior. Here we are thinking, probably, of so-called natural punishment, which is the inevitable consequence of ill-considered action. The child who touches the hot radiator will be burned, and the pain will act as a deterrent from touching the radiator on a future occasion. Cattle are now confined in the pasture by a single strand of electrified wire. They early learn that to touch the wire means to receive an electric shock, and they avoid it. Even in cases where the pain is not so intense, a person who wishes to learn may profit greatly by punishment. The typist who strikes the wrong key is forced to stop and erase the error. This slight annoyance in itself is an incentive to learn. Indeed, there is no education without the fear of punishment. Those who are eager to master some skill willingly accept a learning situation in which errors receive mild punishment. A society can well afford to tolerate a few breakers of its rules for it is by means of the punishment of infractions that the knowledge of the rules is kept alive.

Punishment also has value in reducing guilt. In Chapter XV we shall see that guilt is related to the fear of impending punishment. A tension is created which can only be relieved by the punishment itself.

The fourth positive value of punishment accrues to the person who gives rather than receives the punishment. The annoyed parent may be helped by giving his son or daughter an immediate thump instead of inhibiting his annoyance and anger and storing it up as continuing resentment over a period of time. Most tense situations would be aided if parents could express their feelings on the spot. It is sometimes said that punishment should not be given in anger, yet there may be more value in the immediate release of the emotion aroused by the child's naughtiness than in long, subdued warfare. Children know whether the punishment is deserved or not and when it is for their own good or for the pleasure of the person giving it. In general, there is less to be feared from deserved punishment, intended primarily for the child's good than from undeserved punishment, indicating primarily the release of a pent-up need by the person giving it. Certainly children should not be punished by a parent as an outlet for annoyances which the parent has received from some other quarter.

Negative values. On the whole, however, more can be said against punishment than for it. It is true that punishment may be used to remove symptoms of maladjustments, but in doing so, no attention is being paid to the child's needs, impulses, motives, and fantasies. Whatever the frustration that has caused the child to be naughty and aggressive, these frustrations are not removed by punishing the child. Many times the very frustrations that made a child naughty are actually intensified by punishment. For instance, if a child causes a disturbance in the classroom and is sent into the cloak-room as punishment, this separation from the class may intensify the feeling of isolation and insecurity, which may have had a large share in producing the annoying behavior in the first place. One frequently hears of punishment being used to demonstrate to the child that his behavior is not acceptable, but this is assuming that everything that a child does is the result of conscious planning on his part. Most misdeeds that a parent feels should be punished represent the unconscious solution which a child has attempted to make to the difficult situations confronting him.

Unfortunately, the effects of punishment are not confined to the deed itself, but tend to spread to the child's self-esteem and value based on the self. When used to deter a child from certain behavior, punishment may cripple initiative in many directions. Frequently, a child who lacks spontaneity and is described as being stolid will be found to be the child who has received more than his share of punishment. Punishment may also destroy interest. One rule with regard to the use of punishment is that one should never select as a punishment an activity one wishes the child to like and enjoy. Keeping a child after school certainly is not calculated to make the child like school better. Giving the child tedious and annoying tasks is not calculated to make the child like these tasks. For instance, if a child has to copy a poem or meaningless sentences as punishment, he cannot be expected to form an interest in poetry or in writing. In general, one should avoid using as a punishment activities which on another occasion the child is encouraged to foster.

A fourth reason why punishment is bad is that its effects spread in still other directions. In particular, a child who is punished may feel that this means that he is not liked or appreciated as an individual. A parent should be most careful to associate punishment with the specific act, and to realize that the child is not helped when he believes that he is not well thought of, and that his efforts, in general, are not appreciated. The halo effect of punishment can account for a number of feelings of inadequacy and insecurity in later life.

EDUCATIONAL IMPLICATIONS OF PUNISHMENT

Distinction between firmness and punishment. We shall decide that punishment on the whole is unnecessary and undesirable as an educational method, and that other and more positive methods of guidance and control should be used. This, however, should not be interpreted to mean that parents should not hold firm requirements and standards. Firmness and punishment are by no means identical. One can be firm in directing children where there is a tendency to deviate from desired behavior without necessarily having to resort to punishment to see that it is carried out. Because punishment is in disrepute is not the same as saying that children should not be directed or supported when there is a tendency for them to deviate from desired behavior.

Use persuasion or other educational means before resorting to punishment. It is a general rule that wherever possible an attempt should be made to get a child to substitute desirable behavior for the undesirable by persuasion and by other similar means before resorting to punishment. Parents should make very clear to a child what is expected and correct him so there can be no misunderstanding or doubt. Children should be given *quiet* encouragement to do that which is expected of them. The quietness of this encouragement is emphasized as a protest against stormy, blustery methods of shouting and issuing sharp commands. The successful parent may speak in a low voice, but its decisiveness and the strength of will behind it cannot be misunderstood by the child. A parent should have a relative unconcern about the outcome. He should act as though he expected the child to do the right thing. To show anxiety over the results in teaching a child habits of cleanliness is going to arouse anxiety in the child's mind, and make it difficult for him to do the thing that is expected of him. A parent should not only be unconcerned over the child's behavior, but should have serene confidence of the results of this method of discipline.

When a child has committed a fault or a misdemeanor, it is most important to try to understand the meaning of the behavior and how it fits into the child's mental economy. If teachers and parents could put their efforts into trying to understand what a child is expressing by his naughtiness, there would be less pressing need to punish him. Children should have an opportunity of telling what their behavior means to them and of offering an explanation for it. Frequently, these explanations will be an attempt at self-justification, and the child will be able to give the naughty behavior very little meaning. However, if the adult appears interested in what the child is thinking and feeling and gives him an opportunity of telling how he feels without retaliatory blame or censure, the expression of deeper motivations will be facilitated.

In general, it would appear unwise to punish a child for slowness in learning toilet habits. To use punishment for this purpose is only likely to make the child more anxious and make it still more difficult for him to establish regular habits of cleanliness. A parent may wisely begin in establishing such habits by quiet encouragement rather than with blame and punishment. Even if one wished to break up habits of thumb-sucking or masturbation, it would be unwise to do this by punishment, and much more sensible to pay attention to the causes of these needs to secure pleasure from his own body. A parent, perhaps, cannot disguise from the child his own feeling of disgust and annoyance at the child's attempts at autoerotic pleasure, but to attempt to stop these practices by drastic punishments does not help matters any. If the case is severe, it is much better to attempt to eliminate the cause in faulty parent-child relationships than to stamp out the practice.

Forms of punishment. Assuming that punishment will sometimes be necessary in emergency situations, some general rules governing the wise selection and use of punishment are presented.

It has already been mentioned above that one should not use as punishment something that one wants the child later to like.

There has been considerable controversy over the place of corporal punishment. Some feel that corporal punishment is more of a disgrace and humiliation than are other forms. Perhaps there is also some vague feeling that receiving physical blows may result in masochistic pleasure. It is commonly believed that corporal punishment arouses greater hate than other forms, and Barbour [7] suggests that corporal punishment should not be administered by anyone whom the child is expected to love (a parent or teacher) but by someone the child can continue to hate. But the fact that corporal punishment arouses hate is one of the strongest arguments against it. On the other hand, there is no doubt that other forms of punishment are perhaps even more of a threat psychologically than the infliction of physical pain. As a matter of fact, if punishment has a place at all, there is also a place for physical punishment. A mother, for instance, who wishes to prevent her son from playing with the cocks on the gas stove may find a few smart slaps on the hand more effective than any form of repression or rebuke.

Punishment that arouses a high degree of fear should be avoided. This would include any punishment involving a severe physical threat to the child or throwing it into a state of panic. The barbs and stings of sarcasm and ridicule may do more psychological damage than would be done by several smart blows.

[7] Richmond Barbour, "What's Wrong with Corporal Punishment?" *Nation's Schools,* 33, No. 6 (1944), 25–26.

In general, punishment should be light. In the main, punishments have token value—it is the idea behind the punishment rather than its severity. Also, a mild punishment is merely a foretaste of the possibility of severer punishments. Even the frown or mild statement of disapproval may be more effective than a severe beating.

When a punishment is given after an offense, it usually represents revenge and retaliation on the part of the punisher. Punishments should not be given primarily to inflict pain or make the person uncomfortable, but to shunt a person off from undesirable behavior. So far as possible, wrong or bad behavior should be anticipated and forestalled. This is an extremely important principle in learning and applies not only to the learning in the classroom, but to any habit or skill. Wrong acts should be preceded by warning. In general, an act which has not been forewarned should not be punished. A child should certainly not be punished for an accident or for some offense that he did not know at the time was wrong.

It is foolish to issue idle threats of punishment, particularly if they are not carried out. Many parents try to control their children by frightening them with threats: "If you play with matches, I will have the policeman come and get you." "If you use that bad word again, the ugly witch will come and lock you up in a dark room." The traumatic effect of these fantastic threats is by no means commonly appreciated. They arouse attitudes of hate and rebellion to authority instead of helping children to judge the merits of the situation.

A child should know why he is being punished, the reason being made very clear in language he can understand. Certainly, children should not be punished for mistakes, explanations for which are beyond their comprehension. Explanations should imply respect for personality, permitting the child to retain his self-respect and mitigating the traumatic effect of the punishment.

Punishment should be reasonable and planned, not impulsive. There should be some connection between the punishment given and the nature of the offense. Punishments should be administered promptly rather than postponed. It is very important that the child see a connection between the act which he is to avoid and the punishment which is given to deter him on another occasion.

A child being punished should not be made to feel unloved. A punishment for some misdemeanor is not misconstrued by the child to mean that he is generally unwanted and unappreciated. Along this same line, punishment once administered should be forgotten, not brought to the child's attention at a later time either as a threat or as a reminder. The atmosphere should be cleared, and relationships allowed to assume their normal state.

Parents should be careful not to permit the occasion for punishment to develop into a struggle. It is unwise to carry on an argument or debate over the circumstances surrounding a misdeed which eventually leads to punishment.

Punishment should not be retaliatory or revengeful. It should be given because it is in the best interest of the child, and not because the parent has a need to hurt the child in retaliation for some harm done to him or to his possessions. Neither should a child feel that the only time he is sure that his parents are interested in and care for him at all is when they take the trouble to punish him. He should receive much more positive evidence of his parents' love.

The person who punishes should be helped to understand its effects. Somewhere along the line education should help every child to know the harmful results which grow out of the unwise use of punishment.

In conclusion, let it be emphasized again that punishment does not represent the most constructive form of child control and guidance. Children learn more by positive encouragement and direction based on love than they do through the deterrent and destructive influence of punishment.

QUESTIONS FOR DISCUSSION

1. Distinguish between punishment which is administered without feeling and punishment accompanied by anger. What different effects will it have in a child? What different responses will elicit from a child?

2. A group of Toronto psychologists in mapping out a program of training for the Dionne quintuplets proposed exclusion from the group as a form of punishment when necessary. What are the relative merits of different forms of punishment? How might exclusion from the group have influenced the personalities of those experiencing it as a punishment?

3. Discuss corporal punishment. Why is there so much popular opposition to its use? Compare it with other forms of punishment as to its dangers, influence, and effectiveness.

4. It has been asserted that punishment leads to repression rather than to a weakening of the connection between stimulus and response. Discuss the significance of this distinction.

5. Under what circumstances would a child ever welcome and tolerate punishment?

6. Why is punishment administered by a parent more effective than when given by a teacher?

7. Why is punishment not generally recommended as a procedure to be used in education?

8. Discuss the spreading effect of punishment. What spreads and to what does it spread?

9. Can a parent or teacher be firm (effectively) without resorting to punishment?

10. Why is it important that a child who is punished should not be made to feel unloved?

RECOMMENDED READINGS

1. ESTES, W. K., "An Experimental Study of Punishment," *Psychological Monographs* 57 (1944). No. 3, Whole No. 263.
2. ISAACS, SUSAN, *Social Development in Young Children* (New York: Harcourt Brace & Co., 1937).
3. LEWIN, KURT, *A Dynamic Theory of Personality* (New York: McGraw-Hill Book Company, Inc., 1935).
4. MORGAN, J. J. B., *Child Psychology* (New York: Farrar & Rinehart, Inc., 1931, 1934, third edition, 1942).
5. MORGAN, J. J. B., *The Psychology of the Unadjusted School Child* (New York: The Macmillan Company, 1926, revised edition, 1936).
6. POWDERMAKER, FLORENCE, and GRIMES, L. I., *Children in the Family* (New York: Farrar and Rhinehart, Inc., 1940).
7. STAGNER, ROSS, *Psychology of Personality* (New York: McGraw-Hill Book Company, Inc., 1937).
8. THORNDIKE, E. L., *Human Learning* (New York: Appleton-Century-Crofts, Inc., 1931).

VI

Anxiety

Anxiety occupies a focal position in the dynamics of human behavior. It is a common reaction to frustration. Since anxiety is highly distressing, indeed one of the most intolerable psychic states with which the human organism has to deal, it demands some sort of adjustment which will afford relief. A large part of human adjustment is concerned with avoiding or relieving anxiety. Growing out of many frustrating situations, anxiety serves as the driving force for a large number of subsequent adjustments.

The mental distress of anxiety is the well-known state of dread or apprehension, which may range all the way from very acute terror or anguish, approximating pain in intensity, to mild states of vague apprehension or being ill at ease. When anxiety relates to a challenge to the personality of the individual, we speak of such states as embarrassment, confusion, feelings of inferiority, and in a more special sense, guilt or shame. Probably all of these various anxious states may be thought of as outgrowths of a more primitive startle reaction or fear.

better

a chronic complex emotional state, c̄ apprehension or dread as its most
not good — fear c̄ absence of danger   DEFINITION *prominent component*

good Anxiety may be defined as *mental distress with respect to some antici-pated frustration.* In this sense, it is to be distinguished from the immediate response to frustration itself, which is reacted to with aggression, or the danger which is reacted to with fear. Whatever the frustrating situation is, it is recognized as dangerous because it will result in either pain or loss. The essence of human learning is that the individual shall acquire the capacity for recognizing by certain signs or cues, situations which promise to satisfy his needs or cause him harm so that he can anticipate them on some future occasion and thereby make ready to accept and use those that satisfy and avoid those which promise to frustrate. For example, a child may have his finger caught in the closing door. This produces a sharp pain which is reacted to by crying and feelings of rage. The child associates his pain with the door, and particularly with its closing. On another occasion, he observes the door as it is closing, be-

Tillich — anxiety strives to become fear
because fear can be met by courage
3 types of anxiety
1. of death
2. of meaninglessness
3. of condemnation

116

comes afraid and is careful to see that his hand is not on the door's edge. If he has put his hand on the door's edge in order to close it, there is momentary anxiety which is the reaction to the sign or signal of danger, that is, the possibility or probability of a future pain (or loss).

In the face of anticipated danger, there is not only recognition of the dangerous potentialities in the situation, but also an estimation of the person's strength or ability to adjust in comparison with the threat confronting him. When a person feels confident of his ability to cope with danger, anxiety is reduced to a minimum. A boy who has learned how to handle a sailboat and who feels confident of his ability to swim, would feel little or no anxiety in his first experience in handling a sailing canoe. On the other hand, if an individual feels incompetent or helpless in a situation, anxiety mounts to great heights. Another boy who has had little experience in managing a sailboat or who cannot swim might experience extreme anxiety in being called upon to take charge of a sailing canoe.

Anxiety is also a function of the extent to which the person, himself, is involved in the danger. If the anticipated danger is the bite of an insect, a scratch on the skin by a cat, or the loss of one's hat on a windy day, the anxiety, while real, will not be so intense as when the existence or safety of the person is threatened. Here, too, the threat that causes the most severe anxiety may not necessarily be one that involves physical danger. The most acute anxiety arises when the individual feels that his personal adequacy or his existence in the group is threatened. He may fear the loss of his status as the only child in the family, or the loss of his job and means of livelihood, or he may be threatened with failure in school. It should be recognized that behind the anxiety over a trivial frustration due to some minor loss, such as breaking a dish or failing in an examination, lies the far greater threat to one's security in his relationships with other persons.

Probably the greatest threat to any individual is that of extinction or separation from the world. We shall see later that the fear of separation causes the most pronounced anxiety in the infant, and fear of social ostracism, losing one's standing with others, losing one's power and capacity to enjoy, give rise to the most profound anxieties to most individuals throughout life.

ANXIETY AND FEAR DIFFERENTIATED

As has already been said, *anxiety* and *fear* have much in common. Both are responses to a danger situation; the physiological reactions are similar, if not identical, and the individual's emotional tone is much the same. However, anxiety may be differentiated from fear in a number of ways. Fear is an *immediate* response to the present danger situation.

The little child expresses fear of the large dog that suddenly appears around the corner by running to his mother. Anxiety on the other hand, as has already been mentioned, is fearful *anticipation* of dangerous situations to be encountered in the future. Fear relates to a specific object. One fears snakes, a clap of thunder, a threatening fire.[1] In anxiety, on the other hand, the object is more vague and less well defined. Since anxiety points to the future, the object to be feared, which has not yet presented itself, may be magnified in fantasy. In anxiety there is usually disproportion between the object to be feared and the emotional reaction. One may show profound anxiety at the possibility of having offended another person by some slight, derogatory remark. Where this disproportion exists it points to the probability that the anxiety is not only a response to the anticipated danger but also to some previous situation, the overt response to which has been repressed. For instance, the person toward whom the critical remark was made might be a surrogate of someone else whose love and praise one esteems highly.

Fear is concentrated. The emotional reaction rises rapidly and comes to a climax in a short space of time. Anxiety, on the other hand, is more diffuse. It tends to be spread over a longer period of time and usually never reaches the same intensity as the fear reaction to an immediate strong stimulus.

In fear there is a tendency to find an escape from the immediate dangerous situation. Anxiety is characterized by helplessness and impotence in the danger situation. The anxious person feels that there is actually nothing that he can do immediately to facilitate escape or to avoid the approaching danger. Anxiety implies that the person is incapable of taking precautionary measures.

Finally, anxiety has been said to have the function of protecting a person from fear. No situation is ever hopeless, and an anxious person might set about to avoid the oncoming danger, or to negate its power or influence. If by learning, a person anticipates a situation which might arouse fear, and inaugurates defense measures before the danger actually arises, then fear itself is actually prevented from arising. However, to the extent that the anxious person attempts defense measures, he reduces the degree of anxiety. In the next chapter a number of defense measures for the reduction of anxiety will be considered.

FUNDAMENTAL CONSIDERATIONS

Anxiety a drive. Anxiety is usually recognized as an unendurable form of suffering. Almost as poignant as pain itself, it is a distressing state of

---

[1] To be sure, it is common to speak of fearing death, hunger, injury, poverty, or unemployment, meaning to fear their possible future occurrence, so that fear is the more generic term and can be held to refer to what is more strictly anxiety.

affairs which demands relief. It would surprise most persons to realize how much behavior is motivated by a desire to escape anxiety by either reducing it or disguising it in one way or another. Anxiety spoils pleasure and takes the edge off enjoyment of the common affairs of life. Most persons will go to any length, not excluding self-destruction, to gain relief from anxiety.

Zinn [2] tells the story (not verified as true) of a mountain climber who felt uneasy in treacherous places because of his inexperience. All members of his party had traversed a narrow ledge along the side of a high cliff. This man held back because of his anxiety, and finally, when it became his turn to edge along the narrow footing, his anxiety became so acute, that to escape from the dilemma, he leaped to his death.

The search for relief from anxiety, then, drives a person to take extreme measures, if need be.

Reduction of anxiety—reward. As in the case of all drives, reduction of the drive through experience serves as a reward. Just as hunger, as a drive, is reduced by the ingestion of food, so the reduction of anxiety serves as a reward and hence as a reinforcing factor in learning, as defined by the law of effect. If the anticipation of any punishment is thought of as arousing a small bit of anxiety, then escape from punishment serves to reduce anxiety and hence serves as a reward. On this basis can be explained the acquisition of various forms of inhibition, withdrawal, and repression. When an individual withdraws or inhibits some behavior for which punishment is anticipated, the anxiety over the anticipated punishment is reduced, and this serves as a reward, which results in learning, so that the next time this same situation arises, the inhibition is more surely and readily made. In this same connection, anxiety is the force behind repression, as has already been mentioned in the previous chapter, "Punishment." The force which brings about repression is the need to escape from anticipated punishment, and this need is recognized as anxiety.

Anxiety is learned. Anxiety is not an instinctive or natural response, although the physiological reactions underlying anxiety is part of man's hereditary legacy. Since anxiety is a response to the anticipation of danger, it must have been learned from the actual experience of danger situations, the recognition of cues to signal their approach on subsequent occasions, and the transfer of the emergency reaction to these signals rather than to the events themselves. Anxiety is acquired to a large extent through identification or simple imitation. A child may find that it pays him to be afraid of the same things that other people are afraid

[2] E. Zinn, *Anxiety-Clinically Viewed,* Paper presented before the Monday Night Group, 1939–1940 (New Haven: Institute of Human Relations, Yale University, mimeographed, 1940).

of, and this applies not only to fear of the immediate danger but also to anxiety at its anticipation. Anxiety can be passed on from parent to child. Anxiety in a parent breeds anxiety in children. An anxious mother is almost certain to have tense, worried, nervous children. The anxious child will usually be found to have come from an insecure home.

Anxiety a psychosomatic event. The precise relation between the motor response, the physiological response, and the felt emotion has stimulated much speculation among physiologists and psychologists. The naïve point of view is that we run because we are afraid. According to the James-Lange theory,[3] we are afraid because we run. Actually, the process is a single psychosomatic event resulting from the danger situation and can only be separated into parts by our analysis of it. When danger presents itself or threatens, the organism prepares itself for an emergency reaction. Our felt emotion is probably, in large measure, our awareness of this internal readjustment. These inner adjustments are followed closely by the motor response or the continued postural tension. Anxiety, therefore, is not an epiphenomenon attached to a response to danger as something supererogatory, but is the awareness of the inner preparations for the responses that one makes to the anticipated danger. However, anxiety cannot be defined solely in terms of the physiological. Anxiety is a psychological phenomenon and must be discussed in terms of the dangerous situation and the availability of adequate methods for coping with it.

Capacity to tolerate anxiety. Capacity to tolerate anxiety varies in different individuals. Some persons have low tolerance and must resort in an emergency to defensive measures to protect themselves against the anxiety. Yet other persons seem to be able to tolerate considerable amounts of anxiety. These differences are sometimes spoken of as being constitutional. However, constitutional differences may mean those arising out of early experience rather than those coming from biological inheritance. As we shall see later, the rudiments of anxiety find expression very early in life, perhaps even before birth, and it is in these first shock experiences that the capacity to tolerate anxiety is probably first developed.

Normal persons and infantile anxiety. Those who have studied the behavior of infants recognize that in infancy anxiety wells up in large quantities. One has only to observe the frantic wailing of a baby to recognize the intensity of these disturbances. Even the normal person in adult life is unable to separate himself entirely from the influence of early infantile anxiety. As we shall see, the situations that cause anxiety to the little baby serve as the roots of anxiety all through life. The dangers which are threatening in infancy still remain for most people fan-

---

[3] William James, *Psychology* (New York: Henry Holt and Company, 1890), Vol. I, 449; Carl Lange, *Om Sind sbevaegelsen, et psko-fysiologisk studie* (Kjø benhavn, 1885).

tastic bugaboos forever. Every person, however normal, carries with him the traces of original fear. These are readily observed in dreams and crop up in unaccountable disturbances of behavior such as speech disturbances, motor incoördination, paralysis, and the like, in periods of stress. The individual who as an infant was forced to find many avenues for the discharge of accumulated tension, is the individual who has heightened irritability for nervous discharge of anxiety throughout life. Freud and Burlingham,[4] and Despert [5] have found that children who became anxious about the war previously showed anxiety reactions.

ANXIETY SITUATIONS

Birth: the first traumatic situation. Anxiety puts in its first appearance at birth and is evidenced by the infant's spasmodic efforts to catch its breath and to utter its first wail. Considerable mystery surrounds the so-called "birth trauma." This concept was first brought forward by Otto Rank,[6] who developed its implications in a monograph. Many persons find it difficult to conceive how any personality trend in later life could have found its origin at the time of birth. This difficulty is due to a common belief that experiences in later life must have come down from early experiences through a process of memory. According to this naïve point of view, fears and anxieties could only find their origin in events accessible to memory. Actually, however, development, at least in the early years, is as much physiological and organic as it is strictly mental. Birth is an experience requiring extensive adjustment. The organism contains the requisite mechanism for making this unprecedented adjustment, and this same mechanism can be called upon at later occasions when equally serious traumatic situations arise. It is in this sense that birth becomes the prototype of later anxiety reactions. In birth there are such threats as the danger of asphyxia and the necessity for taking the first breath, the danger of hemorrhage to the lining of the nervous tissues, dangers coming from special difficulties of birth and its possible long duration, those coming from hypothetical glandular difficulties, and those arising from carbohydrate metabolism and its utilization by the brain.

Birth is a *separation* from the mother and, as such, serves as a prototype of corresponding threats of separation that repeat themselves through life. The process of growing up may be thought of as a series of separations. There is a separation implied in the weaning, later in leav-

---

[4] Anna Freud and D. T. Burlingham, *Young Children in War-Time* (London: George Allen & Unwin, 1942), and *War and Children* (New York: International Universities Press, 1944).

[5] J. L. Despert, "School Children in Wartime," *Journal of Educational Sociology,* 16 (1942), 219–230.

[6] Otto Rank, *The Trauma of Birth* (New York: Harcourt, Brace and Company, 1929).

ing the mother and taking the first step, and still later leaving the home to go to school.

Birth is an *emergency* and requires an emergency reaction involving the action of the sympathetic nervous system. For the first time, characteristic signs of sympathetic action are to be observed. There is evidence of the flush of blood to the exterior portions of the frame. There is the muscular tension and activity as seen by small thrashing reactions. There is the adjustment of breathing and the use of the vocal cords.

Birth necessitates *new* adjustments. New situations call forth new reactions which have never been made before. Similarly, throughout life, where new situations are faced for which previous adjustments are not effective, there is the necessity of trying from among the repertory of reactions that which would seem most helpful in the new emergency. At the beginning of life the infant calls on its reflexes for these emergency adjustments. In later situations one has to depend on the reactions made available by learning. Where learned responses do not seem to be adequate one falls back by regression to more primitive forms of behavior.

The neonate is *helpless,* and he is dependent on his own innate reflexes for establishing these adjustments. This condition of helplessness also characterizes anxiety states throughout life, and, in this way again, birth serves as a prototype for later anxiety. To the extent that an individual feels adequate in the situation, his anxiety is reduced or even absent. It is probably true that an infant coming into the world without difficulty and with good physical equipment shows less anxiety, whereas premature babies and those whose birth is difficult show more signs of anxiety in later years.[7]

Danger resulting from failure to have internal needs satisfied. A baby's first need, arising shortly after birth, is nourishment. Postponement of nursing increases the inner tension and augments the hunger drive. The longer nursing is delayed, the more intense the inner disturbance becomes. The infant gives a signal of its inner pain by a sharp piercing wail. A *trauma* is an external stimulus which requires an abrupt change in previous adaptation and the response may be a *panic*. The degree to which a given situation is traumatic depends on the magnitude of the excitation it arouses. The greater the dread of repeating the experience, the more traumatic it has been. As learning develops, the infant comes to recognize signs that his hunger needs are going to be met, usually by the presence of the mother, and indications that she is preparing to give him the breast. He also learns to recognize signs that the

[7] Phyllis Greenacre, "The Predisposition to Anxiety," *Psychoanalytic Quarterly,* 10 (1941), 66–94, 610–638; J. H. Hess, G. J. Mohr, and P. F. Bartelme, *The Physical and Mental Growth of Prematurely Born Children* (Chicago: University of Chicago Press, 1934); Mary Shirley, "A Behavior Syndrome Characterizing Prematurely Born Children," *Child Development,* 10 (1939), 115–128.

means for stilling his inner disturbance are not at hand. The reaction to these signs indicating that he must tolerate his inner needs still longer we call anxiety. Anxiety, then, is the anticipatory warning that inner needs are not on the way to being met, and serves to protect against the more powerful fear or startle reaction that is likely to follow.

Absence of the Mother. The most obvious of such cues is the absence of the mother, as was stated in the discussion of birth separation. Separation from the mother becomes the prime cue of the threat that inner needs are not likely to be immediately met. Separation from the mother, therefore, serves as the principal danger situation and the stimulus for the arousal of anxiety, and anxiety depends on the perception of the loss or absence of the mother. Most parents fail to realize how important their presence is to the young baby and how great a threat even a brief withdrawal is. Some infants become alarmed when the mother steps out of sight or momentarily leaves the room. The little baby's excitement in playing peek-a-boo is testimony of the importance to him of the presence and absence of the other person. This response to the presence or absence of the mother is one of the first learned reactions, and a connection is established between the inner danger or distress of hunger and the outer signal of "mother is not here." Anxiety arising from longing for the absent mother becomes a prototype of all subsequent anxiety which is due to libidinal or sexual longing. Traumatic situations of separation come in a series of episodes throughout infancy and childhood. First, there is loss of the breast and the necessity of weaning resulting in anxiety that food will not be forthcoming. Many children become alarmed when they find a strange person in the place of a familiar one. The fear here, however, is not so much of the strange person as it is in the absence of the familiar person. This anxiety at separation also may serve as an explanation for fear of the dark when the mother cannot be seen even though close by, and fantasies of separation become magnified. The birth of a sibling in the family necessitates the mother's withdrawal of some of her attention to her first child, and this absence becomes the signal for anxiety. Anxiety over competition which involves separateness may be far more acute than a more serious threat which is shared with another person.

The overprotected child whose mother has given him more than ordinary attention becomes particularly anxious at the threat of separation. And it is not uncommon to find even overprotected adolescents or adults becoming highly anxious when there is a threat of separation from the person on whom they depend. This anxiety spreads and becomes the need to be a member of a gang, a team, or a club. Death, itself, is seen as a separation from one's family and loved ones, and the fear of death is, perhaps, as much a fear of this separation as it is of physical pain. During the Second World War the statement was made that all neuroses, including war neuroses are due to separation anxiety,[8] but Rosenberg in her article on war neuroses [9] disputes this, and believes that this does not take into account the anxiety that arises from actual fear of external harm.

It should be noted that anxiety arises more from *loss* of love than from *lack* of love. Indeed, the psychopathic child who has never known love is curiously deficient in expressions of anxiety.

Anxiety Contains Recognition of Anticipated Helplessness. In all of these situations there is also implicit the recognition of anticipated helplessness in a situation. The infant senses that if its parents do not come to meet his needs he is helpless in a situation. Anxiety, then, has been called a rediscovery of helplessness, and the feeling of helplessness or inadequacy almost always accompanies an anxiety attack.

Intensity of Anxiety Related to Degree of Deprivation. The intensity of anxiety is related to the degree of the deprivation or its threat. The longer the mother is absent or the more frequently these episodes of neglect occur, the more intense the anxiety that is aroused. However, there may not be too close a connection between the actual carelessness on the part of the parent and the degree of anxiety shown by the child, for anxiety is more a product of the child's fantasy of being neglected than of the actual neglect itself. The younger and more helpless the child, the greater his separation anxiety. Anxiety and grief are practically identical at the beginning of life, for grief is the emotional reaction at loss or separation, and this is also the condition for the initial anxiety states.

Danger from external harm. To turn to external conditions, it is found that anxiety may also arise from threats of danger from the outside as well as from threats of privation. For example, the threat of being trapped by fire is a well-known stimulus for intense panic. In panic there is first the fear that arises from actual pain. Then there is the fear that comes from a pain inflicted by others in the form of punishment or its mental equivalent of scorn and belittlement. In attacks on personality and personal adequacy, the threat is, perhaps, as much a fear of loss of love related to the fear of withdrawal as it is a fear of actual harm or damage to the person.

Anxiety from Pain Signals. Anxiety comes when there are signals that pain and other forms of external danger are anticipated. At first the child burns his hand on the hot stove, gets a sharp pain, and is thrown into a panic characterized by crying and general emotional disturbance. By learning, he recognizes the stove as a stimulus for pain and avoids contact

[8] W. R. D. Fairbairn, "The War Neuroses: Their Nature and Significance," *British Medical Journal*, 4284 (Feb. 13, 1943), 183–186.

[9] Elizabeth Rosenberg, "A Clinical Contribution to the Psychopathology of the War Neuroses," *International Journal of Psychoanalysis*, 24 (1943), 32–41.

with it in the future. So signals of danger are typically responded to by avoidance. Anxiety is aroused particularly by the threat of punishment. Originally the punishment that is feared is physical. From direct threats of physical punishment grow the fears of disapproval, condemnation, or humiliation.

Anxiety from Anticipated Punishment. Anxiety is felt at the possibility of punishment for *actual* behavior. When a child has done something for which it has been punished in the past, a repetition of this act is a cue that punishment may be expected in the future, and this is sufficient stimulus for the arousal of anxiety.

Little Arthur has been punished by his mother for teasing his baby brother. On a later occasion when Arthur could not resist the temptation to take away one of his brother's toys, it was noticed that this was followed by distinct signs of anxiety. He went running to his mother and nestled up to her as though to say, "I have done something for which you will punish me. Please don't do it."

This anxiety comes, not only when the aggressive or destructive behavior is intended, but also when it is accidental. Most persons will show signs of anxiety when they have broken a dish or offended someone quite accidentally or unintentionally. A destructive child suffers from severe anxiety, and conversely, the anxious child is usually aggressively difficult. Hate arouses anxiety and anxiety breeds hate as a defense against it.

Anxiety from Fantasied Behavior Which Might Occasion Punishment. Anxiety may arise, however, not only from the threat of punishment for actual behavior, but also for *fantasy* behavior, which may never result in actual overt behavior at all. Here we are coming to the heart of the anxiety problem. As is well known, many children feel hostile tendencies toward their brothers or sisters or their parents, but fear to express the full extent of their feeling because they know they would be punished for so doing. However, the hostile feelings are present in fantasy, and not uncommonly the fantasies of the kind of harm they would like to do to a brother or sister or father or mother become widespread and extreme in intensity. In play with dolls representing parental figures, for instance, the child will stamp on the doll, stick it with scissors, pull it apart, or throw it around violently. These fantasies, however, are not always clearly distinguished from the actual deed itself, and there frequently is a fear that the parent will retaliate because of these unexpressed hostile impulses. Because there is fear of this retaliation, hostile impulses and fantasies themselves become the occasion for anxiety even though they have never reached open expression. It is as though the child who feels aggressively toward another person becomes afraid of the other person whom he suspects of hostile tendencies toward him.

Anxiety from threat to ego status. This analysis of anxiety, as arising from threats to the gratification of inner needs or from outer harm, fails to indicate the synthesis of these two in the threat to the status of the self as personality develops. Probably the most serious of all the sources of anxiety are these threats to adequacy, self-esteem, and social status. In modern life one fears more deeply than anything the possibility of losing one's reputation and standing in the community and becoming an outcast; or one fears loss of social adequacy, intellectual capacity, or social grace. The woman who fears the loss and destruction of her femininity will strive to make herself loved and admired by the opposite sex by keeping her youth and good looks. The man who fears he will not measure up in competition with other men will select a dangerous occupation, work overtime, or wear sporty clothes.

Anxiety arising from threat to defenses built up against basic dangers. As will be shown later in Chapter VII, an individual builds up various defenses against his anxiety because he finds the anxiety so intolerable. However, these defenses are continually being threatened and, if there is danger that the defenses will be broken down, there is liability that the anxiety will be exposed and will become acute again. Horney [10] calls this the threat of being unmasked. Where these defenses are punctured and tend to crumble, anxiety rushes through the gap and threatens to engulf the person.

One defense that is commonly raised against anxiety, as we have seen, is repression, and where there is danger that repressed material may come up into consciousness, there is a possibility of a recrudescence of anxiety. This means that when someone attempts to show a person the true nature of some of his unconscious tendencies, he raises the barriers of repression even higher in order to avoid the threat of the return of anxiety. The uncanny and the eerie, as seen in mystery stories, represents a partial return of the unconscious, and the creepiness associated with these experiences is a mild form of anxiety. Where a symptom has been set up as a substitute for some repressed tendency, the abolishment of this symptom is usually followed by a further arousal of anxiety. The person who tries to suppress some tic or nervous grimace finds that his efforts are accompanied by anxiety, which means that, as his defense is taken away, the support against repressed material is weakened and anxiety is the result.

Immediate situations which may give rise to anxiety. The situations causing anxiety which have been thus far described are those which arise in infancy; however, it is recognized that situations eliciting anxiety daily present themselves. Close inspection of these situations indicates that they resemble in one way or another the infantile anxiety-provoking situations, and that where the anxiety is out of proportion to the immediate danger threatened, the response is both to the immediate situa-

[10] Karen Horney, *Self Analysis* (New York: W. W. Norton & Company, Inc., 1942).

tion and to repressed material from the past. A person is more susceptible to anxiety when he is hungry, thirsty, fatigued, or has unrelieved sexual tensions, also when he is ignorant of the plans of others which involve him, or is held in suspense or idleness.

Immediate Situations Which Threaten Satisfaction of Inner Need. Studies of the worries of boys and girls show that the most pronounced worries concern success—whether in school or in work.[11] During the recent depression, anxiety over financial security was widespread, and probably throughout the world today there is more anxiety concerning the food supply and ability to maintain even a minimum level of subsistence than over any other single concern. The accumulation of debts is a cause of anxiety for most persons, and anyone who takes his debts lightly requires special understanding. Delinquency in the payment of mortgage interest and insurance premiums threatens the stability of living and is usually a grave threat. The possibility of losing one's job and facing unemployment is always anxiety-provoking. Crowded living conditions, with personal rivalries and jealousies easily aroused, do not lead to peaceful living. Many adolescents worry over the possibility of being unable to support themselves or their parents in later years. All of these economic anxieties are outgrowths of the early infantile anxieties over the possible dangers to the satisfaction of internal needs, particularly hunger.

Separation has been seen to be a prime signal of privation. This social anxiety based on separation from the group and criticism is particularly poignant in later years. The possibility of ostracism, exclusion from the group, or the loss of popularity, is always anxiety-provoking. A man dreads being excluded from the party, being snubbed at his club, or excommunicated from the Church; while a wife dreads the possible loss of her husband's regard. Since personal acceptability is conditioned to such a large extent by the impression one makes on others, most persons are considerably concerned over their personal appearance. Here the standard seems to be the average or the fashion of the day, and most individuals feel uncomfortable when they deviate too much from the practices around them. The tall and the short, the thin and the fat, and those marked with blemishes or scars, easily make these defects the focus of anxiety. The adolescent may concentrate his anxiety on pimples. Shabby, dirty, or old clothing causes the young person much mental distress.

Any threat to a love or affectional relationship is almost certain to arouse considerable anxiety. The distress of marital unfaithfulness has been portrayed in uncounted novels and plays. Abnormal parental attachment, on the other hand, may be equally the cause of anxiety, in

---

[11] Rudolph Pintner, and Joseph Lev, "Worries of School Children," *Journal of Genetic Psychology*, 56 (1940), 67–76.

that the more dependent a person becomes on another, the greater the
threat of loss were the relationship in any way to be broken.

Sex difficulties have long been recognized as a potent cause of anxiety.
When Freud announced that in his professional practice most states of
morbid anxiety had a sexual origin, he focused attention on this not uncommon cause, which stirred a storm of protest at the same time that
the truth of this finding was being verified by the experience of countless
other psychoanalysts. However, later researchers did indicate that
anxiety over sex is only a phase of anxiety over more basic privations and
dangers, and indeed, sexual anxiety may be another of the focal points
on which earlier anxiety has been settled.

Situations Which Threaten External Danger. The second large group
of immediate situations which may arouse anxiety consists of those which
threaten external danger. This is too obvious to warrant extended discussion. Everyone feels unnerved at the possibility of getting hurt or
meeting accidental injury. The news of any major catastrophe, such as
sudden death, a serious accident, the spread of war, the threat of a disastrous fire, the rising of threatening flood waters, is almost certain to
arouse dread. Most persons become anxious at the possibility of becoming ill or contracting some serious disease, whether this threat is to themselves or to others who are close to them. If this anxiety over ill health
becomes exaggerated, it may approach hypochondriasis, which is a morbid concern over health and soundness of the body. Such hypochondria-
cal anxiety may grow out of fear of danger from without, as, for instance,
the invasion of bacteria, or fear of some inner disturbance, as anemia or
failure of eyesight.

Experience concerning anxiety in the civilian population has accumulated during the Second World War. There was less evidence of anxiety
or neurotic difficulties following the bombing of London in 1941 than
was anticipated. Apparently realistic immediate danger arouses less anxiety (although more fear) than a less imminent danger which can be magnified in fantasy. Then, too, the bombing was something to be reacted
to, whereas anxiety is sometimes more intense when a person feels helpless and impotent to cope with the situation. As far as the children were
concerned, if they had the security of being with their parents, instead of
becoming anxious, they even thrilled to the noise and excitement of a
bombing attack.

Fear of external danger generalizes into fear of hostility or criticism
from others, however expressed. With children, this frequently focuses
on school work. Examination anxiety arises from the criticism which a
child receives from parents or teachers for a poor examination paper or
from their anxious exhortation to the child to do well. School marks and
the bringing home of the quarterly report card are difficult situations for

most children to face. Failure in work of any kind is a threat that hangs over many like the sword of Damocles, and rivalry, whether in school or at work, carries with it the threat of possible defeat and loss of status. In this connection it is interesting to note that there is almost no relation between anxiety concerning examinations and success with them. In fact, cases have been studied by the author in which persons who have intense anxiety prior to the taking of an examination are consistently successful with them.

Hallowell [12] would have us distinguish between cultural and individual anxiety. Some situations arouse anxiety pretty generally throughout a whole culture—these may be considered normal. But the anxiety which deviates from the normal cultural patterns marks off the individual possessing it as neurotic.

Sex differences in anxiety. Three recent studies [13] have pointed out certain characteristic differences in the worries between the two sexes. Zelig's study indicates that girls are more anxious than boys and have a larger number of worries. Boys on the whole seem to be more afraid of external harm and worry about their adequacy. Such worries as financial security for themselves and those they must support, success in work, being ill and underweight, and having to wear glasses, occur more frequently among boys than girls. Girls, on the other hand, are more concerned over their social relationships. They worry lest they shall not be considered pretty and popular, and they fear lest no one should care for them. They are concerned over school marks. They are afraid of being robbed. They dread having to give a talk before a group at school. And they fear lest harm should befall some member of their family.

It becomes very difficult to trace the source of anxiety in any given individual because of the displacement that anxiety commonly undergoes. Due to ambivalence, it is often difficult to admit the fear engendered by the very person whom one at the same time loves and who remains highly important. Consequently, fears are often shifted to less immediate objectives and persons. One frequently is anxious over hostile tendencies directed toward immediate members of the family or over secret impulses of longing for closer relationships. Usually such impulses are unsuspected, are difficult to believe, and would give rise to most intense anxiety if an individual were to become aware of them. However, these impulses, even though unconscious, may be very real, strong and pressing, but they seek expression in distorted forms and various transplantations

[12] A. I. Hallowell, "Fear and Anxiety as Cultural and Individual Variables in a Primitive Society," *Journal of Social Psychology*, 9 (1938), 25–47.

[13] Ruth Lunger, and J. D. Page, "Worries of College Freshmen," *Journal of Genetic Psychology*, 54 (1939), 457–460; Rudolph Pintner, and Joseph Lev, "Worries of School Children," *Journal of Genetic Psychology*, 56 (1940), 67–76; Rose Zeligs, "Children's Worries," *Sociology and Social Research*, 24 (1939), 22–32.

and displacements, because the individual cannot afford to recognize
them directly. To fathom the cause of anxiety may never be easy and may
require an extended period of analysis.

HOW ANXIETY IS EXPRESSED

Physical symptoms. Anxiety shows itself by a number of well-defined
physical symptoms. When these are tabulated, it seems clear that they
represent the physiological reactions characterizing the activity of the
sympathetic nervous system. Most frequently these symptoms indicate
that the sympathetic reaction has been *stimulated,* but sometimes the
reverse behavior indicates a *collapse* of sympathetic response. In the first
place, there are the cardiac disturbances, such as palpitation of the heart,
a rapid heartbeat, or, on the other hand, a feeble pulse. Sometimes pain
around the heart has a functional origin related to anxiety states. In the
second place, there is a close connection between anxiety and respiratory
disturbances. Some have seen a close connection between this relationship and the fact that at birth one of the major adjustments has to be the
initiation of breathing. In anxiety one may observe rapid breathing or
the heaving of deep sighs. Sometimes anxiety is characterized by a feeling
of suffocation or by choking sensations, or in extreme fright by the cessation of breathing itself. In the third place, there are alimentary disturbances in anxiety. Hunger frequently alternates with loss of appetite. Indications that the digestive process is reversed may be found in nausea or
vomiting on the one hand, or in diarrhea on the other. Fermentation,
which frequently results when digestive processes are retarded, may show
itself by belching or by colitis.

There are other well-known physical manifestations of anxious states.
Among these are a number of motor disturbances, such as shaking, trembling, or shuddering—all indicative of the motor tension and pressure
for release in situations of great danger. Clearing the throat or wrinkling
the forehead may be telltale signs of this motor tension. A reversal and
collapse of motor tension may be shown by sudden weakness—slowing
down of movements and the like. Increased sensory sensitivity may show
itself by various paresthesias. There may be a creeping feeling or a tin-
gling of the skin. Hyperesthesia—increased sensory sensibility—or its opposite, anesthesia, are other symptoms. Irritability to noise, even to faint
sounds, or sensitivity to bright lights may be indicative of anxiety. Glandular disturbances are most noticeably indicated by profuse sweating
without adequate cause. On the other hand, there may also be coldness
in the extremities, and the clammy hand is sometimes a telltale indication of the tension which the individual is undergoing. Headaches are
not uncommon accompaniments of anxious states, and while migraine
cannot by any means always be explained so simply, it should always be

suspected as having a possible partial cause in anxiety. Anxiety is frequently shown by insomnia, and fatigue is a condition not uncommonly aroused by anxiety. Dizziness may also be a phenomenon closely related to these nervous disturbances. The anxious person may be lacking in energy, show inability to concentrate, or possess a poor memory.

Homesickness, an expression of anxiety due to separation, may become a real illness, the individual showing some of the same symptoms that have already been described. Homesickness usually wears off after the strangeness of the situation subsides, but if the separation is a real threat to security it may persist stubbornly.

Sleep disturbances. Anxiety shows itself with particular force during the night and expresses itself in various forms of sleep disturbances. Insomnia is a frequent sign of anxiety. The anxious child may toss for hours unable to go to sleep, or the sleep may be restless and fitful. Anxiety may also show itself in sleep-walking, talking, or in nightmares. Children may scream out in their sleep or partially wake with heavy sobs. On a simple level these sleep disturbances may represent fear of being deserted by the mother or of losing the parents' love.

Anxiety attack. When anxiety becomes intense and gives rise to exaggerated signs of physiological disturbances, it is called an anxiety attack. In the infant, this may be shown by the screaming fit in which crying becomes violent and prolonged, accompanied by flushing of the skin and motor discharge. In an older child, the anxiety attack is commonly known as a temper tantrum. Here the child may cry violently in rage, throw himself on the floor, or act in other vehement and destructive ways. This same anxiety attack may show itself in adults by a pronounced form of any of the physical symptoms above catalogued, with possible loud and angry speech or violent behavior. Crimes may be committed as part of an anxiety attack.

Confusion and doubt. Another direct expression of anxiety is to be found in confusion in thought or speech. It is a telltale sign that a sensitive area has been struck when a person becomes confused and illogical in his trend of thought or argument. Errors, blunders, and mistakes all testify to an underlying nervousness and confusion, which are certain signs of the presence of anxiety. Doubt is a certain indication of the presence of competing trends within the individual that prevents him from taking a certain position on either side, and the state of doubt indicates the anxiety which this conflict has aroused. In more extreme cases a feeling of unreality may develop.

Enhanced need for security and affection. Another way in which a child gives evidence of anxiety is his tendency to cling to his parents and to refuse to be separated from them. In the clinic this child shows obvious signs of terror at any indication that he is to be left alone with a strange person, and frequently the examination can only be carried out when the mother remains in the room. A request for gifts, even mere tokens, is a sign that the child feels uncertain about his relationships and is, to some extent, anxious concerning them.

Feeling. Manifestations of anxiety which have been described so far are in terms of *physical* symptoms and behavior. Anxiety also expresses itself by a wide variety of *feeling* states. Indeed, anxiety growing as it does out of primitive startle and fear states, is perhaps first and foremost a feeling which subsequently is transformed into action of some sort. The behavioral manifestations of anxiety have been described first because these can be observed by an onlooker, whereas feeling states can only be known to the person who experiences them. By definition, anxiety is a state of dread or apprehension. In a mild state, it is known as uneasiness. The point has already been made that anxiety is usually accompanied by a feeling of helplessness. In a more general sense, it is related to pessimism, a tendency to look on the dark side of things, always to be anticipating the worst. There are a number of recurring fears which are typical anxieties. For instance, there is the fear of dying, either from sudden causes or from long-continued illness. There is a fear of going insane, which haunts numbers of people. Occasionally a mother will have anxiety lest a son or daughter become delinquent. These fears may be either for oneself or for others who are close, and toward whom one has strong affectional ties. Sometimes anxiety shows itself by feelings of strain, exhaustion, or fatigue. Unreasonable and violent hates and rages are probably in many instances tinctured with anxiety and become intensified because of the underlying fear behind them. Lonesomeness, a feeling of isolation, and a feeling of being rejected by others, are other forms that anxiety takes. Then there are a number of states in which anxiety is much more diffused and does not have a specific direction or pertain to a specific object. Depressive states and gloomy moods probably, in most cases, represent a diffused form of anxiety. Feelings of inadequacy and inferiority which beset so many persons are akin to these feelings. Many disturbances of sex life, either by the exaggeration of feeling or by the drying up of feeling, would represent the direction that anxiety has taken.

Fantasy. Anxiety also exhibits itself through fantasies. These are legion, and cannot be described in detail here, but their main direction can be pointed out. One important group concerns anxiety over health —hypochondriasis. Many persons are beset by fears of possible illness which they might contract, or over the seriousness of illness which they are already suffering. It is not uncommon for persons to worry over possible heart disease, tuberculosis, cancer, or venereal disease. These concerns over physical health can become so exaggerated as to occupy almost all of one's waking hours. Some persons are obsessed with the necessity of consulting their pulse often, or taking their temperature;

others show their anxiety by picking scabs which are not allowed to heal fully.

Another set of fantasies have to do with fears concerning moral scrupulousness. An individual becomes disturbed over possible infractions of rules, offenses to other persons, a dread lest the law catch up with him for some possible offense.

The fantasies of some persons relate to fear over loss of property and of possible catastrophe that may destroy their wealth or cause loss of position. Others fear some loss of capacity, that their skill or talent may become ineffective, or that sexual potency may be lost. Still others dread loss of caste and the position which they occupy in society or some social group.

A number of fantasies of dread concern a possible criticism by others or blame for one's faults or shortcomings. Sometimes the fear of failure and the dread that one will not measure up to the expectations of others becomes a besetting preoccupation. Or some persons may actually fear success as though becoming successful would arouse the hostility of others who might be envious. Anxiety fantasies are well-known dream phenomena, and it is not uncommon for an unacceptable wish or impulse to be expressed as an anxiety dream. MacKinnon [14] believes that under anxiety a person sees things better and worse than they are—he has unduly elevated hopes and unduly severe fears that he will not be able to accomplish his goals.

EVALUATION OF ANXIETY *Positive*

Anxiety, notwithstanding its unpleasantness and its disorganizing tendencies, has positive values. Anxiety is the basis of much creative effort, for it is at the behest of anxiety that man looks ahead in order to avoid danger. Anxiety thus becomes a stimulus and spur to progress. It is the main incentive impelling man to seek security. Inventors are stimulated by the drive of anxiety: the lightning rod was invented as a way of eliminating the dread of fire. Anxiety is the force that moves men to sublimate the natural expression of their basic desires, which seem so full of danger, and thus it lays the basis for all constructive and civilized efforts.

Anxiety and ego development. Anxiety is a necessary condition for personal development, for every individual passes through anxiety situations in the process of growing up. In order to master the anxiety that is aroused, the young child has to learn to adjust. One ordinarily thinks of adjustment in response to inner needs and outer promptings. A considerable part of adjustment, however, is in relation to situations which are fear-provoking. The uniqueness of personality is, to a large degree, determined by the methods employed by a child in mastering or defending

[14] D. W. MacKinnon, "A Topological Analysis of Anxiety," *Character and Personality*, 12 (1944), 163–176.

~~itself against anxiety.~~ Even small amounts of anxiety, aroused in response to minor frustrations and momentary irritations, require their own particular adjustment. An excess of anxiety impels an individual to attempt to overcome it. However, the more that anxiety is restricted to the mere signal or sign that danger is present, the more constructive the defensive acts which a young child can adopt. When the anxiety is so intense that strong hostility is aroused, ego development is hindered rather than furthered, because strong defensive measures have to be adopted which prevent the child from giving its attention to interests round about.

Those who have studied emotional reactions in early childhood point to the extravagance of anxiety and reactions to it. As perception develops, and the child learns to understand and control people and situations, the threat of separation and of helplessness becomes less exaggerated in fantasy, and hence the defenses against it can become more reasonable and objective. However, if the young child is in an actually rejecting and hostile environment, any anxiety that is aroused can become a destructive rather than a constructive force.

A healthy individual is one who is intent on reaching his goals: he can devote his attention to the situation that confronts him, and can put his abilities to work in mastering it. The anxious individual, however, becomes mainly concerned in relieving his anxiety, and this interferes with the main task at hand. It is as though an individual were beset by a cloud of mosquitoes. He must drop his work wherever he is and devote himself to beating off the pests that surround him. To the extent that he has to drop his tools to slap the mosquitoes, the work on which he is engaged suffers. The anxious individual then becomes egocentric, and must concern himself first of all with his own affairs and his relations with others before he can clear his attention to devote himself to the task at hand.

Anxiety also has social value in that it helps to uphold social institutions. It is commonly recognized that individuals follow many cultural patterns through fear—fear of retaliation and punishment for being different. A college community with all its freedom and informality is bound by strict canons of taste and propriety beyond which the individual does not trespass lest he be subject to scorn and ridicule.

EDUCATIONAL IMPLICATIONS

The English school of psychoanalysts has made much of the origin from inner organic processes of most of the dynamic psychological processes described here. However much one is impressed by the possibility that psychological processes are responses to inner demands, it is also true that these same processes can be reinforced or diminished by the attitudes of the parents. A good mother who is kind, protective, and supporting helps to minimize anxiety in a child. On the other hand, a mother who is rejecting and punitive tends to augment anxiety. The good mother hesitates to appeal to fear as a mode of discipline. She will avoid the tactics employed by ignorant nurses who threaten to call the policeman or invoke imaginary bogies in order to wield power over the helpless child. It is curious how many parents wish their children to fear them under the guise of authority. The good mother, since she is not anxious herself, does not feel a threat from the immature behavior of her offspring.

The good parent is also a *strong* parent, one who helps a child to control his inner fears. The good parent is in command of his own impulses and offers calm, but firm, control, even in the face of tempestuous desires shown by a child. The weak parent who cannot say "no," who vacillates between yielding and sudden anger, and who fails to give the child support against his inner impulses that frighten him because of their dangerous propensities, tends to raise the level of anxiety in the child. Such a child may show considerable amounts of aggression, which represent a projection of these anxious states.

A spoiled child intensely fears loss of the mother or separation from her. The spoiled child is really made defenseless against anxiety because the possibility of losing the parent becomes more of a threat in view of his dependence. The child who has learned to depend upon his own initiative and resourcefulness is never quite as susceptible to anxiety as the child who has been overprotected. This does not mean, of course, that the wise parent is one who thrusts his child out to become self-contained and independent before he is mature enough. Independence is not something that can be given to a child, but it may be fostered by providing conditions for its development.

It is interesting that many parents cannot bring themselves to permit their children to be openly afraid of them. To be afraid of a parent is only natural inasmuch as the parent is bigger, stronger, and more powerful. The parent also can control and direct. Consequently, anxiety is natural, even with respect to the kindest and mildest parents. Yet for a child to show anxiety by crying, displays of temper, evil looks, and negativism, throws a parent into confusion. They cannot understand this resistant and uncoöperative behavior, and tend to mitigate it so far as possible. It would be much better if parents could openly accept expressions of anxiety from their children as natural. In the first place, when these feelings receive open expression, they tend to reduce in amount. In the second place, repressed anxiety tends to spread, and if it can receive immediate and open expression, there will be less repression of it.

This does not mean that parents should encourage crying, fretfulness, or temper displays. On the contrary, these should not be permitted to become prolonged and to extend into anxiety spells over a considerable period. There is nothing educative about leaving a child to cry itself out. On the other hand, parents should not become unduly alarmed at these emotional displays and attempt to hush them up without giving them any release in immediate expression. The other side of this picture is represented by the child who shows intense anxiety, and needs reassurance. There is no value in forcing a child to go into the surf when the waves give rise to a paroxysm of terror, nor to force him to eat certain foods, or to join in games which are obviously extremely distasteful. The child in a panic, either caused by its own inner fears or outer dangers, needs the affectionate reassurance of a comforting individual.

METHODS OF OVERCOMING ANXIETY

There are two main schools of thought with regard to the overcoming of fears. One looks on fear as an isolated phenomenon, akin to any other habit or skill, which has arisen from a rather immediate situation and which results in an isolated response. Those who see fear in this light propose to overcome it by direct methods of manipulation and reconditioning. The other group sees anxiety as having a deeper dynamic significance and as penetrating to the heart of one's adjustment problems. Those who see anxiety in this latter light believe that it can be overcome only by methods which penetrate beneath the surface, make inquiry into the deeper origins of anxiety, and propose more thoroughgoing personality transformations as a way of overcoming it.

 Direct methods of overcoming fear in another. Psychologists have proposed a number of somewhat direct methods for overcoming fear. These have been reviewed and summarized by Jersild and Holmes.[15] It cannot be denied that in isolated instances each of these methods has in its own way been successful. It is probably true that most fears can be dissolved by appropriate direct measures, although there may be at the same time deeper repercussions on the personality. One of these direct methods is the use of verbal explanations and reassurances. The child who is afraid is told how groundless are his fears and is urged to attempt to overcome them. This is a natural and common-sense method which every parent employs in dealing with minor anxieties. Sometimes an example of fearlessness in others is held up to a child. He is told that Jimmy, who lives next door, is not afraid of the big boys living further down the street; or Arthur is helped to see how foolish is his fear of the dark by referring to how unconcerned his sister is in going to sleep in a dark room. (Making such comparisons in the same family will un-

[15] A. T. Jersild, and F. B. Holmes, *Children's Fears*, Child Development Monograph No. 20 (New York: Bureau of Publications, Teachers College, Columbia University, 1935).

doubtedly intensify the rivalry, even though it may lessen the immediate fear.)

A third method is that of passive conditioning. The feared object is *associated* with some pleasant or unfeared stimulus or reward, but no attempt is made directly to work on the child's fear. A child who fears dogs may be taken to a playground where he can use the swings and slides, for which he has a passion, but where there is also to be found an occasional stray dog or two. The pleasure on the swing or slides may help to diminish the fear of the dog.

Going one step further, as a third method, *pressure* may be put on the child to enter into the feared situation. He may be held up to contempt or ridicule. He may be called a sissy or a scared cat, and therefore forced to meet the lesser of two evils—the greater evil being the criticism.

A fifth method consists in providing opportunities to become acquainted with the feared object—at first, at a safe distance, but nearer as familiarity breeds contempt, a procedure whose effectiveness was proved in the experiments of Mary Cover Jones.[16]

The sixth method is somewhat related to the last method and is that of gradually lessening the distance or grading the presentation of the fear stimulus. The dog who is feared is first held on the other side of the room. When the fear at that distance wears off, the dog is brought somewhat closer. By gradually narcotizing the fear, the intensity of the stimulus can be gradually increased. Sometimes this can be done by presenting only a small part of the feared object and gradually increasing its amount, as when a child is given a taste of nasty medicine and the amount is increased as the tolerance is increased.

A seventh method of overcoming anxiety is by promoting skills. This is an effective and altogether sound method, since it strikes at one of the basic causes of anxiety—namely, a feeling of helplessness. To the degree that a child increases his skill in swimming, he will lose his dread of the water until the fear apparently vanishes.

An eighth method of overcoming fear is that of ignoring it—hoping that it will pass away naturally. Parents who adopt this method will change the subject when some fearsome topic is being discussed, hoping that with the passage of time increasing development will take care of the fear.

A ninth method is similar to the previous one; namely, removing the cause of the fear, steering the child away from anxiety-producing situations, and helping him when he is afraid. By giving the child security, helping him to manage his fear, and giving him support when afraid, it is believed that he will gradually have less occasion to be afraid. It should be mentioned that giving sympathy to an anxious person has not

16 M. C. Jones, "The Elimination of Children's Fears," *Journal of Experimental Psychology*, 7 (1924), 383-390.

been found efficacious in reducing the anxiety except temporarily. Sympathy acts in a manner similar to an anesthetic—it may lower anxiety temporarily, but when the effect of the sympathy wears away, which may be soon, the anxiety returns with full force. Sympathy may be thought of as more valuable in allaying anxiety in the person who gives the sympathy than in the anxious person toward whom it is directed. All of these direct methods fail, perhaps, to recognize the underlying meaning of anxiety.

Direct methods of overcoming anxiety in self. Writing books on how to rid oneself of fear is a popular pastime of physicians and psychologists. It is not to be wondered at inasmuch as anxiety is such a distressing state that persons are eager to find ways of eliminating it. Following are some of the suggestions that are frequently given.

Since one contains within himself the conditions for the arousal of anxiety persisting from his infantile response to traumatic situations, it is not possible for most individuals to avoid a certain amount of anxiety. However, after one becomes mature it is possible to exercise a certain degree of self-control in this matter. Becoming informed is a method of ridding oneself of vague fears. The individual who learns to recognize the different varieties of mushrooms no longer need feel anxious at any and every mushroom. He who informs himself about tuberculosis can reduce his vague terror at this dread disease. The radio, by keeping the public informed of the progress of battles, helps to mitigate anxiety during war.

Secondly, we can reduce anxiety by preparing for the emergency. Those who live in war regions are less anxious if they have prepared themselves a shelter to use in the event of an air raid. A person insures his life or his property in order to reduce anxiety over the possibility of accident or catastrophe.

Thirdly, individuals avoid anxiety by keeping busy and putting forth effort to accomplish their ends. Vague anxieties may strike terror in the dead of night, but they dissipate in the light of day. The closer one gets to his difficulties and the more energy he turns into surmounting them the less anxiety he will experience concerning them.

Davidson [17] reports that conditions aboard a war vessel tend to mitigate anxiety more than in land fighting in the army. He mentions such factors: every man has a job to do; news of the progress of the battle is broadcast to every man on the ship by a public-address system; men can see what is happening; there is thought and hope of retaliation; there is a distinct relief when the ship is not hit by torpedo or bomb; and since most sea battles are fought at day rather than at night there is less terror. Suspense and uncertainty are the greatest causes of anxiety.

[17] S. M. Davidson, "Anxiety States Arising in Naval Personnel—Afloat and Ashore," *New York State Journal of Medicine*, 42 (1942), 1654–1656.

more important

Psychotherapeutic treatment of anxiety. Methods of meeting anxiety that go into the problems more fundamentally can be discussed under the general heading of psychotherapy.

It has been proposed that one set aside a time for the consideration of one's problems, and an effort be made to face them without flinching. If one faces one's own problems with confused and disorderly thinking, the results may not prove beneficial. If, however, one attempts to evaluate the cause of the worry, and, particularly, relates present concerns with past experiences, the outcome may be a healthy reëvaluation of the concerns which seem at the present time so forbidding. In addition to thinking about one's problems, the advice is also given to do something about the cause of the worry, to seek a new way of living, to change something that will break into the vicious circle. This might be a change in one's work, making new living arrangements, or seeking new friends and recreations. Another suggestion is to develop balancing factors—positive outlets for one's energies that will counteract the fears which otherwise might engulf one.

Another suggestion with some merit is that the person confide in someone who will be willing to listen to the problems which are presented so that they may be talked out. It is generally recognized that talking over one's problems reduces their sharp edge and helps to dissipate anxiety. It is frequently suggested that an anxious person by all means seek advice and assistance from someone else. There is a natural tendency to be reticent with regard to one's own problems—particularly the more perplexing they are. This is not only to hide them from the inquisitive eyes of others, but also to avoid arousing too much anxiety in oneself. However, it is generally recognized that one must go through a period of facing one's problems directly, even at the expense of arousing anxiety, if one is to free oneself from them.

Children have discovered that they can abreact and hence reduce their anxiety through play. Children reduce their anxieties about the war by playing war games; or their anxieties about gangsters or "mugging" by playing out these activities. Oldsters could take a lesson from children and reduce anxiety by playing out the situations which give rise to fear. Indeed, reading detective and mystery stories, or attending gruesome movies or movies of war scenes may serve just this purpose.

These are all bootstrap methods of dispersing anxiety. To be sure, they are straightforward and rational and appeal to most persons as dictates of common sense. However, they fail to take into account that the roots of anxiety, particularly neurotic anxiety, are not all in the immediate present, but are forces continuing unconsciously from previous shocks and frustrations.

Reassurance. Reassurance in its various forms tends to allay anxiety, but does not pretend to root it out or disestablish it. Reassurance is like an anesthetic applied to pain. The pain is deadened temporarily, but the condition that is the source of the pain is not corrected. As in the case of physical pain, when the effect of the anesthetic wears off the pain returns, so when the effect of reassurance fades out the anxiety will return—particularly if the anxiety-producing situation persists. Reassurance consists of direct assurances on the part of the counselor that worry is needless, and the client can have confidence through the prestige and authority of the counselor; or more indirect methods can be used, such as pointing out that many other persons are threatened with equally serious problems. Reassurance is a convenient temporary device for dispelling anxiety over a short period of time but should not be confused with more fundamental methods.

Transference. Psychotherapy can be discussed under the three headings of *transference, release,* and *interpretation.* Transference refers to the positive and negative feelings and attitudes that a client develops toward a counselor during a period of treatment. It is normal to find that the first effect of a growing transference is a reduction in anxiety. Insofar as the relationship promises security and removes the threat of separation and lack of support, it counteracts the anxiety that the client brings to the treatment process. However, transference, itself, may later increase anxiety. As the counselor begins to assume greater value in the eyes of the client, he will wish to be well thought of and to hold himself high in the counselor's regard. Consequently, to explore into the past and present problems, which may not be altogether too creditable, would be a threat to the counselor's continued acceptance, and the patient may justifiably dread the loss of his counselor's high regard. This is an inevitable outcome of the counseling process, and must be handled by talking the matter over openly and facing the threat directly.

Release. Another phase of the treatment process is encouragement of open expression which provides *release* of repressed tendencies. This is done through the support and acceptance and permissiveness of the counselor, who makes it possible for the individual to express things without fear of consequence which have previously been anxiety-provoking. As these new expressions find release and, at the same time, are not condemned or criticized by the counselor, the fear of them tends to evaporate, and anxiety is lessened. Anxiety is regularly reduced (although temporarily increased) when hidden fears are brought out into the open, either by talking about them, or by experiencing the fearful situations directly but safely.

Interpretation. The main tool of psychoanalytic therapy is *interpretation,* which is essentially a relating of material brought in during the hour, either through play or free association, to other experiences of the individual, either during the hour itself, or to events and feelings which are more remote. These interpretations have as their purpose the uncovering of unconscious material, and as this material is faced by the subject, it tends to arouse more active anxiety. It is only through this arousal of anxiety that the anxiety-provoking situations lose their terror-inspiring qualities, and the cause of anxiety is eliminated. A bungling counselor can easily make premature interpretations before the client has been prepared for them and arouse anxiety in doses too large to handle. As a result of such premature interpretation, the client is frightened from the psychotherapeutic experience altogether, or his resistance is raised so high that the interpretative process is retarded. Correct psychotherapy proceeds slowly on the foundation laid by the developing transference. This means that as the client feels greater trust and value in the counselor, ties are forged which enable him to withstand the later shocks produced by the uncovering of unconscious material. It is important to interpret hostility as it appears by revealing its true nature and intent, but at the same time with the reassurance that it will not be met by retaliation. A large part of psychotherapy comes about through expression of hostility to the counselor which, since it is not met by punishment but is tolerated by the therapist, can also be accepted without anxiety by the client. Anxiety is relieved when the infantile and fantasy nature of the dreaded object is finally revealed, although basic anxiety will persist even after thorough analysis. It is a frequent experience for those who have been aided therapeutically to lose entirely the feeling of awe and terror with which they previously held their own impulses, and this freedom gives them new courage and incentive to grapple with interest, enthusiasm, and spontaneity, the real experiences of life that lay before them. It is in this sense that everyone must pass through early anxiety into the larger and more complete experiences of living, whether in the normal process of development in infancy, or in a therapeutic expression in later life. Psychotherapy is merely the working through of experiences which should have been accomplished normally many years before.

QUESTIONS FOR DISCUSSION

1. Miller and Dollard in their *Social Learning and Imitation* refer to anxiety as a drive. What characteristics does anxiety possess which would permit us to ascribe to it the qualities of a drive?

2. Answer the criticism frequently made of the "birth trauma" that it is not possible to remember incidents and experiences accompanying birth.

3. Give illustrations of the threat to a baby or child of separation from its parents.

4. What is the relation between punishment and anxiety?

5. How is it possible for a person to carry residual anxiety within himself over large periods of time, that is, to be an anxious person?

6. Why is anxiety sometimes reduced, as in a bombing episode, when the immediate danger is intense and real?

7. Why should some of the most intense anxieties be concern over fantasies?

8. Direct methods of overcoming anxiety either in the self or in another person are called superficial as compared with the more fundamental method of psychotherapy. What are the grounds for reaching such a conclusion?

9. Why does reassurance only allay and not eliminate anxiety?

10. The physiological expressions of anger and fear are much the same—what differentiates these two emotions?

RECOMMENDED READINGS

1. CAMERON, D. E., "Observations on the Patterns of Anxiety," *American Journal of Psychiatry* 101 (1944), 36–41.

2. DOLLARD, JOHN, and HARTEN, DONALD, *Fear in Battle* (Washington: The Infantry Journal, 1944).

3. ENGLISH, O. S., and PEARSON, G. H. J., *Emotional Problems of Living* (New York: W. W. Norton & Company, Inc., 1945).

4. FREUD, SIGMUND, *The Problems of Anxiety* (New York: W. W. Norton & Company, Inc., 1936).

5. GREENACRE, PHYLLIS, "The Predisposition to Anxiety," *Psychoanalytic Quarterly* 10 (1941), 66–94, 610–638.

6. HORNEY, KAREN, *New Ways in Psychoanalysis* (New York: W. W. Norton and Company, Inc., 1939).

7. ISAACS, SUSAN, *Social Development in Young Children* (New York: Harcourt, Brace and Company, 1937).

8. JERSILD, A. T., *Child Psychology* (New York: Prentice-Hall, 1933, 1940; third revised edition, 1947).

9. LANGER, W. C., *Psychology and Human Living* (New York: Appleton-Century Crofts, Inc., 1943).

10. MASLOW, A. H., & MITTELMANN, BELA, *Principles of Abnormal Psychology* (New York: Harper and Brothers, 1941).

11. MORGAN, J. J. B., *The Psychology of the Unadjusted School Child* (New York: The Macmillan Company, 1936; revised edition, 1936).

12. PINTNER, RUDOLPH, and LEV, JOSEPH, "Worries of School Children," *Journal of Genetic Psychology*, 56 (1940), 67–76.

In the psychology of motivation a number of processes or methods of adjustment have been recognized, and names have been given by which to identify them. This chapter proposes to orient the reader with respect to these mechanisms, to show what function they have in the process of adjustment, to give a rough classification of them, and to indicate how they are related to each other. In succeeding chapters some of the mechanisms will be discussed in detail. They describe not only the *structure* of personality but also its *operation*—personality in action. These mechanisms are part of the process of adjustment and should be thought of as dynamic forces having motivating power rather than existing as static structures.

In the chapter on frustration it was pointed out that man has developed a number of methods for meeting situations which are frustrating to his needs. These methods, to be expounded in subsequent chapters under the general term "mechanisms," are primitive processes by which an individual adapts to frustrating circumstances. These mechanisms are primary, and they constitute the methods of adjustment used by everyone—by normal individuals as well as by those who are maladjusted. A traditional way of looking at human behavior is to think of it as essentially intelligent and to believe that the typical human method of adjustment is by intelligently and consciously mediating between impulses, and inner and outer obstacles to their expression. According to this point of view, if the conscious and intelligent part of a man were sufficient, he would never have to resort to unconscious mechanisms. When some frustration arises he would consider it as a problem to be solved, and when the problem was solved intellectually, then without emotion the individual would proceed to put the solution into operation. This, however, is not the true picture of man. To react to frustrating situations intelligently represents a high degree of maturity, and is the end stage of a long process of development. An intelligent and suc-

cessful adjustment must be built upon a substructure of more fundamental and primitive means of adjustment: mechanisms. Everyone,
normal and abnormal alike, adjusts to situations in infancy and, indeed,
throughout life according to the dynamic processes which are now to be
described.

FUNCTION OF THE MECHANISMS

The mechanisms are frequently spoken of as defenses against anxiety.
A person must bow to reality. The prohibitions and restraints of one's
parents, as well as the limitations and frustrations forced on one by external circumstances, are a kind of reality. These prohibitions and frustrations are real and are usually not to be brooked or avoided; it is
necessary to manage and control in some way one's impulses and wishes.
This management is the function of the mechanisms. Freud [1] in one
of his last books took up the concept of defense, one of the first concepts
which he used in his early formulations, and stated that he thought it
would be advantageous to use it again as a concept "provided we employ
it explicitly as a general designation for all the techniques which the
ego makes use of in conflicts." So the mechanisms are concerned with
managing in some way the impulses whose direct and natural expression
gives rise to anxiety. Mechanisms are not only defenses *against* anxiety,
but also indicate methods by which the impulses giving rise to anxiety
are redirected.

CLASSIFICATION OF THE MECHANISMS

There is an impressive variety of methods which are used as defenses
against anxiety. This chapter attempts to review them. Indeed, Deutsch [2]
stated that any aspect of personality may be used as a defense mechanism
against anxiety—intelligence as well as stupidity, acting in reality as well
as in fantasy. Aggressiveness can be used as a defense against weakness
and passivity, and vice versa; masculinity can be used as a defense
against femininity and vice versa; and maturity can be used as a defense
against the danger of immaturity and vice versa. The classification of
the mechanisms has presented considerable difficulty, and no classification scheme is wholly satisfactory. In the following summary these defense mechanisms are grouped under the following headings:

1. *Repression*—the exclusion of an impulse from consciousness, and *inhibition*—the blocking of discharge or expression of an impulse
2. *Escape* from conditions which might arouse expression of the impulse
(also withdrawl)

[1] Sigmund Freud, *The Problem of Anxiety* (New York: W. W. Norton & Company,
Inc., 1936).
[2] Helene Deutsch, *The Psychology of Women* (New York: Grune & Stratton, Inc.,
1944), Vol. 1. p. 23.

3. *Disguise* of the true meaning and significance of the uninhibited expression of the impulse
4. *Modification* of the expression of the impulse
5. *Payment of a penalty* for the interdicted expression
6. *Autoerotism*

Many of the mechanisms will have features which would justify placing them in more than one of the foregoing groups.

Repression and inhibition. The most primitive mechanism is *repression* and the *inhibition* of the impulses against which a person must defend himself. In infancy repression may be a vague, undifferentiated kind of blocking, and similar generalized repressions may be recognized in later life in the form of fainting and sleep. We see it in the infant who lacks spontaneity, is timid and bashful with strangers, and is limited in his capacity to play. However, as development proceeds, the repression applies more and more specifically to the actual situation, so that in children or adults we find that isolated experiences can be repressed and blocked from consciousness, lifted from their context as it were. It is through the action of repression that the so-called unconscious springs of behavior are formed, so that repression becomes operative as a mechanism in the action of all other mechanisms insofar as their operation is unconscious. However, there is a question as to the extent to which there ever can be complete repression. It would seem as though no impulse is ever completely dammed up, and every impulse manages to secure some sort of modified or substitute expression. Repression is discussed more fully in Chapter X devoted to that topic.

Escape or flight from anxiety-arousing situations. A second general method of defending oneself against impulses which might arouse anxiety is to *avoid situations* in which these impulses might be aroused to action. This second group of defenses can be summed up under the general heading of *escape* or *flight reactions.*

Regression. Escape to the *past* may be a way of avoiding present activities and the anxiety which they may arouse. Much pleasure-seeking, particularly those forms that involve gratification of the senses and those of an autoerotic nature, fall into this category. A child's urgent desire for sweets or for much noise and excitement may be a way of conquering fear tendencies. But anxiety can never be relieved by regressive means. (Regression is discussed more fully in Chapter IX.)

Flight to Fantasy. Thirdly, among the methods of escape, which is also of the nature of withdrawal, is the *flight to fantasy.* This is sometimes accomplished by resorting to drugs or alcohol. The alcoholic is a person who wishes to escape from his anxieties or feelings of inferiority. By relaxing his inhibitions he finds it possible temporarily to escape from the feelings of insufficiency and the littleness which beset him, and for a brief time can enjoy a lulling sense of security. The flight to unreality is only temporary, and must be repeated with increasing frequency if it is to continue to be effective. Horton [3] presents evidence to support his thesis that the amount of drinking in any society varies with the level of anxiety in that culture. He points out that alcohol may arouse anxiety as well as reduce it by making the person helpless through impairment of his physiological functions, by the antagonisms which may be aroused by his release of aggressive or sexual impulses, and by the painful sequels (hangovers) to the narcotic state. Children frequently attempt to escape anxiety through play. A child who has an obsessional need to play is probably meeting anxieties by this method. Children's play is a prototype of similar creative activities throughout life, and much of the artist's work could be thought of as a method of meeting pressing anxieties.

Another method that we find in young children is the desire for knowledge. The questioning stage which normally comes to a maximum at the age of four, in most instances has an obvious relationship to the child's concern over many problems related to his position in the world and relationship to others. Children's curiosity and desire to make collections are other expressions of this same method of defense. This desire for knowledge may carry on throughout life, and may be the driving force in the life of the scholar and scientist.

Hyperactivity. A person may try to defend himself against anxiety by hyperactivity, restlessness, constant agitation and moving about. A child who comes into the playroom and runs aimlessly about from toy to toy, presents telltale signs of anxiety. In an older person irritable moods and unreasonable impatience indicates that all is not well. The ambitious individual, ever striving to get ahead, is probably using this as a method of managing his anxiety. Anxiety also shows itself in disturbances of attention, in flitting from one thing to another, or going off into spells of wool-gathering during the course of a conversation.

Flight to Reality. Quite the opposite method of meeting anxiety is the *flight to reality.* This is seen in the individual who immerses himself in business. Some individuals accomplish this by means of their work. They willingly accept a heavy load of responsibility and keep the lines taut day and night, in season and out of season, permitting no opportunity for disturbing concerns to penetrate their daily round of affairs. It is interesting to note what tortures such an individual suffers during vacation periods when he comes face to face with his own affairs. Others use a similar method by immersing themselves in social activities. The social butterfly who runs from tea to ball in a continuous round is likewise using this as a method of running away from personal anxieties. Some attempt to escape from anxiety via sex. Indeed, in a large number of

[3] Donald Horton, "The Function of Alcoholism in Primitive Societies: A Cross Cultural Study," *Quarterly Journal of Study of Alcohol,* 4 (1943), 199–220.

cases sex actually is fostered as a way of escape from distressing realities concerning the self. Others attempt to escape anxiety by adopting prudent or cautious courses of action. These individuals are constantly on the lookout for possible dangers. They take out large amounts of insurance, heap their bins full of coal, and attempt to anticipate every emergency. This method requires constant vigilance, and usually leaves the person still unsatisfied that he has not taken care of all contingencies. Some attempt to meet anxieties on the realistic level—by an intelligent appraisal of alternatives and conscious attempt to choose the lesser evil. This method has its merits, and while it may not fully take care of all the emotional contingencies, it at least faces situations of which the individual can be consciously aware. Even counting ten, which has been advocated as a method of reducing anger, serves its purpose at the same time as a defense against anxiety. Some persons avoid anxiety by prolonged rest or vacation periods in which they withdraw from active work and throw off responsibilities.

Disguising the source of anxiety. Repression represents the exclusion of an impulse from consciousness. In general a more successful defense against anxiety is to permit the expression of the impulse in relatively unmodified fashion, but to *disguise* its source or its true nature.

Introjection. Two very common forms of disguise are known as *introjection* and *projection*. Both these processes originate early in life, when distinction between the self and the non-self is not clearly comprehended. Introjection is taking another person into the self or making him part of the self, a process common with infants who find it easy to treat persons with whom they come into close contact, particularly the mother, as part of themselves.

By introjection the individual adopts some more specific mode of behavior or feeling of another person. The result of introjection is called *identification,* evidenced, for instance, by the boy who identifies with his father by introjecting his characteristics, or by the individual who adopts (introjects) his attitudes toward politics, religion, or morals from another person. If a girl should produce an hysterical symptom due to a disappointment in love, and this same symptom should be taken up by her dormitory mates, this latter process would be called introjection.

Projection. Projection is a protection against having to recognize the bad within. As has already been mentioned, it can be considered a form of displacement—displacing attitudes or feelings from the self onto another person. Projections and identifications have many facets of comparison: in many senses they are opposites. For instance, identification represents an enlargement of the self, whereas projection represents a diminution of the self. One identifies himself with the good characteristics in others but one projects the bad characteristics of the self on others.

more Cate *Aggression.* Another defense against anxiety, using projection, is to attack. Hate sometimes serves as a cover for fear. "Those whom the Gods fear they would destroy." It is as though the person who is to be feared and who has hostile tendencies toward one, but who cannot be placated, either because his hostile feelings are too intense or because one feels weak and inadequate, must be put away. For this reason the very persons who fundamentally feel the most timid and afraid are those who are sometimes stimulated to take the boldest measures, to enter the most hazardous undertakings, to become leaders of the most polemic movements. It is popularly thought that by adopting these strenuous rôles a person is attempting to whip up his own courage, but a more correct way of looking at the matter is to perceive that the individual is adopting aggressive measures as a defense against his own underlying insecurity.

The dynamics of this defense is somewhat as follows. Through frustration one feels hostile toward another person. This hostility, however, if openly expressed, would invoke counter-hostility of the person toward whom the feeling is directed. The fear of this counter-hostility makes a person passive. By projecting one's own hostility out onto the other person, he is made to appear dangerous. Sometimes one's fear of another person can best be managed and controlled by open hostility toward that person. Aggression which is based on fear is the most dangerous variety, because it is the most inaccessible to reason. Anxious aggressiveness shows itself in such unreasonable and destructive acts, as a child cutting its own clothing or wantonly destroying furniture or other prized possessions without apparent reason. In very little children this may show itself in the purposeless banging and slapping of toys, and in older children in their bullying. Defiance and stubbornness of adults is the product of anxious aggression, and vacuous threats may be a weakened form. Unprovoked personal attacks, bad thoughts and obscene language, and attempts to control another person arising from fear of being controlled are further expressions of anxious aggression.

more Cate *Character Defense.* Horney [4] has contributed to our understanding of these defenses against anxiety by pointing out how certain character traits are apparently built up in order to control underlying feelings of insecurity or dangerous aggressive tendencies. She mentions three of these: *narcissism*, *masochism*, and *perfectionism*.

(conceited) NARCISSISM—A FAÇADE OF STRENGTH. The first of these—*narcissism*—
self-centered in which the person builds a façade of strength, presenting to the world and also to himself a picture of a strong, confident, dominant individual, relates to the fear of losing caste and not being appreciated. Such an individual seeks power by running for office and endeavoring to gain

[4] Karen Horney, *New Ways in Psychoanalysis* (New York: W. W. Norton & Company, Inc., 1939).

control over enterprises and organizations. He parades the strength of his intellect and his capacity to master difficult fields of concentration, demonstrating to others that he has abilities which must not be belittled. He may attempt to persuade the world of the dominance of his will and the fact that he can ride over obstacles and activities and come through successfully. He is a person who becomes a slave-driver, exploits others, and employs them for long hours and small wages. By getting the jump on others, they never have a chance to come back or do not dare to raise their voices in protest. This individual seeks prestige and magnifies his titles, his position, and his authority. Those who wish to build this façade of strength seek admiration openly. Some attempt to prove themselves by winning social recognition for their achievements. Some make definite bids for admiration by grooming, taking on fine manners, building themselves splendid edifices. Others attempt to stave off hostility by their achievements and are possessed with high ambitions. Still others strive to become self-sufficient and independent, disdaining the need for leaning on others, hesitating to ask others for advice, and insisting on making their own decisions. These personality tendencies may have been taken on as protections against the dangers of becoming alone and helpless, and, hence, they become barricades against this form of anxiety. The mechanism of compensation is frequently employed by the narcissistic individual, who attempts to cover weakness with strength in other directions. There are several factors which encourage a person to seek this method of defending himself against basic anxieties. His own increasing incompetency may drive him to seek for substitute methods of enhancing himself in his own eyes and in the eyes of others. Some are driven in this direction by false expectations of what the world owes them. In most cases these tendencies are fostered by impaired human relations and a feeling that they have been neglected or deserted.

MASOCHISM—A TENDENCY TO HUMBLE ONESELF. The second of these character trends—*masochism*—takes exactly the opposite direction. Here we find the individual who tends to humble and lower himself. He renounces claims of greatness and power. He willingly assumes dependent relationships on others, and seeks to find others who will dominate and exercise mastery over him. For instance, one individual enters marriage with every expectation that her husband will provide for her, take care of all her needs, and make her difficult decisions. The masochistic individual has a need to please others and to be liked. He dreads self-assertion. He will ingratiate himself with others and attempt to win their affection and approval by his gifts, his helpfulness and friendliness. He avoids the hostility of others by self-effacement, by making no demands, by humbling himself so that, by no stretch of the imagination, would another person feel threatened by him. He avoids the danger of hostility, exploitation, and criticism of others, which are, in reality, as

[handwritten margin notes: basic roots — enjoy sex in pain]

[handwritten margin notes: secondly — enjoy being pushed around]

[handwritten notes at bottom: opposite - sadism - enjoys hurting others]

we have already seen, the dangers of one's own hostile impulses which are liable to counter-attack and punishment. The masochistic person seeks to escape harm and alienation of the regard of others by doing nothing which might arouse their antagonism and hostility. Negroes have adopted servility as a common racial pattern, not because they inwardly feel humble and inferior, but as an unconscious defense against hostility which the treatment they have received has aroused.

PERFECTIONISM: FROM FEAR OF CRITICISM. The third character defense mentioned by Horney is *perfectionism,* which is related to the fear of criticism and the loss of love. This individual adopts a high level of aspiration and extravagant goals and insists on attention to the perfection of minute details in the accomplishment of these goals. The perfectionist is one who would escape criticism by leaving nothing behind which could be criticized. He also attempts to place himself on a lofty pedestal from which he can cast disparaging looks on others who have failed to attain equal heights.

Rationalization. A process by which impulses are disguised or masked is that of *rationalization,* which has as its function the excusing or interpreting of behavior by an individual so that its unconscious motivation will not be recognized, and so that the behavior can be accepted as consonant with the other activities of the self. In a sense rationalization depends on the existence of repression and utilizes a variety of mechanisms to disguise the impulse, feeling, or idea which is repressed. However, it is a process which is sufficiently distinct to receive independent discussion in the chapter, "Rationalization."

Modifying expression of impulse. We have now mentioned repression or the blocking of discharge of the impulse, escape from situations which might arouse the impulse, and keeping the response but disguising its significance, as methods of defending the self against anxiety. A fourth method is that of modifying the response, removing some of its objectionable qualities, and also using it as a bolster and bulwark against the dangerous impulse in its pristine form of response. The first of these mechanisms by which the impulse is modified so that it acts itself out in behavior in a more socially acceptable form of expression is *sublimation.*

Sublimation. In sublimation the expression of the impulses is de-emotionalized and socialized. Sublimation is recognized as a more or less successful method of meeting frustration when it is not exaggerated or carried to an extreme. In sublimation the activity is consonant with the original impulse but is modified so as to be harmonious with the demands and interests of society. Adolescent interests in art, religion, poetry, social service, athletics, and nature are all illustrations of the sublimation of more primitive childish tendencies.

Obsessional Trends. Obsessional traits, including tendencies toward system, orderliness, neatness, cleanliness, and the like, represent another set of defenses. These traits represent defenses against one's own hostile tendencies, for by regularizing life one keeps unruly tendencies in curb. A man may develop very precise speech to avoid his unconscious tendency to criticize or attack. Also, unacceptable wishes and desires can be kept in leash by distorting their expression to fit into some kind of system. The slogan or fixed idea is obsessional in character. Fixed beliefs about God, property or government neutralize and channelize the emotional pressure of aggressive drives, and help a man to master anxiety. It is said that in the Second World War less neuroticism appeared in Russian soldiers than in soldiers of other nations because anxieties were held in suspense by the ideologies and beliefs in the Soviet program and way of life.

Laughter. There are a number of miscellaneous well-defined forms of expression which may serve as substitute releases for anxiety. The best known of these is laughter, which is obviously a release from previous states of tension. It is not uncommon to observe that when anxious and tense situations find sudden release, they are accompanied by a peal of nervous laughter. Sometimes the laughter itself motivates the release. All sorts of humor represent the working off of aggressive and exhibitionistic tendencies in a harmless and disguised fashion to serve as an acceptable mode of escape from tense states. If a bit of aggression can be interpreted as a joke, its sharp edge is blunted as it is made to seem trivial. Much of the aggression at Hallowe'en time is passed off by children in the name of fun.[5] Nervous reactions, such as tics, nervous gestures, facial grimaces, clearing the throat, sucking the lips, and meaningless repetitive movements, may also serve as substitute releases. Fingering a cigarette is a well-known mode of easing the tension when in a state of excitement.

Compensation. Another mechanism that represents a method of modifying a primitive tendency is *compensation*. Compensation refers more to the threats to ability and prestige than to reactions to danger and threats to the expression of wishes. When one's status or prestige is threatened, measures are taken to find some alternative skill or achievement which can serve as a substitute for the prestige which is threatened.

Strauss, the builder of the George Washington and the Golden Gate bridges, was a very small man.

A little boy caught in the evacuation of Belgium was found with a big bandage on his toe. He said that he had not been wounded, but his little sister had a machine-gun bullet wound, and he could not afford to let her get ahead of him so he bound his toe with a larger bandage than his sister had.

[5] For a case illustration of aggression as a substitute release see R. F. Creegan, "A Symbolic Action During Bereavement," *Journal of Abnormal and Social Psychology,* 37 (1942), 403–435.

Compensation is a defense against limitation or a handicap in the person. It has to do with the status of an individual and his need to protect his status in his group. In this sense compensation stands alone in that it is the only mechanism which seems to refer specifically to status and not to the conflicts arising over the satisfaction of needs.

Paying a penalty. Finally anxiety may be reduced by paying a penalty for expressing or even fantasying the dangerous impulses. Various forms of self-punishment, to be described in detail later, serve as still another defense against anxiety. Self-injury and mutilation, for instance, not only help to reduce the anxiety by the payment of a penalty, but also limit the person's freedom in expression and protect him from the danger of uncontrolled expression. One may defend himself against anxiety by restricting his needs, by living frugally and economically, and going without many of the pleasures and even the necessities of life. By thus restricting the satisfaction of his needs he is protecting himself against the guilt which self-gratification might arouse.

Restitution. Tendencies toward restitution and constructive activities in general represent another method of meeting anxiety. Almost any form of constructive or positive self-expression may take on this significance. It shows itself very clearly in the need to care for, supervise, direct, or even possess another person—particularly a child. Such constructive activities contain the possible need to make up for or atone for hostile tendencies on a previous occasion. The boy who feels protective toward a younger brother, or who warns his sister to be cautious in crossing the street, may be balancing the books in order to even up for earlier feelings of hate toward these or other individuals. Frequently the tendency to take, as in asking for gifts, or even stealing, is in order to be able to give— the giving signifying a tendency to make restitution for earlier destructive impulses.

Autoerotism. Finally, when all other defenses against anxiety fail, an individual may be thrown back on to attempts to stimulate pleasure in himself as an antidote. But autoerotic practices are treacherous because they withdraw the person from contacts with the outside world and instead of helping him to adjust leave him at the mercy of outer influences.

COMPLEXITY AND INTERRELATIONSHIPS OF THE MECHANISMS

The classification of the mechanisms is unsatisfactory to most persons. It does not represent the clean-cut, logical type of classification such as is found in botany, representing coördinate and subordinate categories. Many students would like to be able to take an item of behavior and find one label by which to classify it among the mechanisms. Unfortunately the matter is not so simple as this. We have, in the first place human personality adjustment and behavior in all of its complexity. The mind searches for some order in this huge, complex mass. What it finds in the present state of analysis is a number of characteristics to which names have been given. Certain of these names are described under the headings of mechanisms in this book. However, they are by no means exclusive of one another but represent much overlapping. It is possible to find certain behaviors that can be described in terms of two or more of the mechanisms. For instance, a boy of five who adopts lisping may be said to have *regressed* by *identifying* himself with his two-year-old brother. Here two mechanisms are used to describe the one bit of behavior. The one tells us that the behavior is that of an earlier level of adjustment, and at the same time the other tells that it resembles the behavior of a younger brother. Both can be used to describe the lisping. Or to take another example, a father gives his son an unnecessarily harsh punishment for bringing home an unsatisfactory school report. He not only thrashed him, but sent him to his room and forced him to go to bed with only bread and water for his evening meal. In this case one might say that the father in *identifying* himself with the boy *projected* his own fault upon him. That is, this father had been made to feel in his own childhood that the reports that he brought home from school were of utmost importance—a good report was worthy of the highest honor; a bad report brought shame and dishonor. Even as a man he still carried about within him these same feelings, and when his young son started going to school it was natural that he should have identified himself with him and projected onto him his own shame toward poor work in school. An understanding of the mechanisms should help in understanding the fundamental motivations of behavior. However, anyone who requires a logical and clean-cut classification which would permit a simple pinning of labels on different expressions of personality is doomed to disappointment. To classify behavior into exclusive categories forces us to simplify behavior in a way not in accordance with the facts. The mechanisms are concerned with behavior in terms of its dynamic significance.

UNCONSCIOUS NATURE OF THE MECHANISMS

The question is frequently raised whether a mechanism must be unconscious in order to be a mechanism. For instance, in rationalization is it not possible for a person to be aware of the fact that the reason he gives for his behavior is not the true reason? If a person excuses himself with full awareness of what he is doing, can this, then, be called rationalization and classified as a mechanism? While this is in large part a matter of definition and as such one can let terms he uses apply to whatever he wishes, the confusion points to a failure to grasp the essential nature of a mechanism. A mechanism is essentially a defense against one's own impulses which are difficult to accept. A rationalization may be thought of, first of all, not as an excuse which protects one's reputation but primarily as an excuse which helps a person make peace with himself, that is, with his own dangerous and unacceptable impulses. The question has been raised, for instance, whether, if the nature of a rationalization is explained to a person so that he becomes aware of the motives of his behavior, it can then be called a rationalization. However, if a rationalization has been explained to and has been accepted by a person, the issue is whether the next time the same situation arises he will resort to the same kind of excuse. If he does so consciously, knowing what he is doing and why he is doing it in order that he may still keep in the good graces of his family or employer, the excuse has lost its essential quality as a mechanism, and it perhaps becomes more in the nature of a falsehood. If a person really understands the basic motivation behind his rationalization and is willing to face it and accept it, it would seem as though the need for rationalizing has disappeared and he can speak out the truth. If he still finds it difficult to accept the truth of his own underlying motives or to permit other persons to know that he possesses these motives, it may mean that he has not fully assimilated the reality of his unconscious motives, and there may still be the need for covering them up by rationalization.

Naturally, in any mechanism the person is fully aware of what he is *doing*. He knows, for instance, that he is attributing hatred or evil to another person when he is projecting or that he is creating an art product or worshiping in a church when he is sublimating. What he is not aware of, however, is the *underlying motivation for this behavior*. Behavior is not unconscious. The motivation for the behavior may be partly unconscious and that is what makes the behavior truly a mechanism.

EVALUATION OF THE MECHANISMS

At the end of each of the following chapters in which the mechanisms are discussed there is an attempt to evaluate them and to state whether, on the whole, they may be considered to be constructive or destructive for individual adjustment. In a strict sense this is attempting the impossible. The mechanisms represent defenses which a person puts up against his own impulses. Actually they are not either good or bad, constructive or destructive, to be approved or disapproved. They are necessary and neutral. As was mentioned earlier, mechanisms are universal and found in every individual so that they cannot be rejected as undesirable in a wholesale fashion. Indeed, Nunberg[6] points to the

[6] Herman Nunberg, "Ego Strength and Ego Weakness," *American Imago*, 3, No. 3 (August, 1942), 25–40.

mechanisms as evidences of the strength of the ego. The ego is doing something about its anxieties, and the mechanisms represent an attempt to nullify the discomfort of the anxiety and to adjust to the situation. The value which may be attributed to any mechanism depends on the outcome of the operation of that mechanism rather than on any absolute judgment which may be placed on the mechanism itself. The same mechanism can be judged as good or bad according to the use to which it is put and the social value of the outcome. If, for instance, some of Beethoven's creations represent a regression to a childhood pattern or mood, one would say that this regression was worth more than the mature adjustment of a million men. Bisch [7] has written a book called *Be Glad You're Neurotic,* piling illustration on illustration of the contributions of famous men whose genius has, in reality, been an expression of their neurotic tendencies. Most persons, however, whose mechanisms lead to such distinctive and neurotic kinds of behavior as to be bizarre or peculiar, can offer little in the way of social justification of their peculiarities. The mechanisms are to be judged by their social outcomes rather than by any absolute standard. One author [8] has stated that defense systems against anxiety (and he probably has in mind in particular the sublimations) are the stuff culture is made of. In general, sublimations which have been deëmotionalized and socialized are recognized as the most valuable kinds of adjustment, while those that involve the greatest amount of repression carry with them the greatest emotional loading and are recognized as less acceptable solutions to conflicts. Perhaps the evaluation of a mechanism involves quantity as well as quality. Most mechanisms involve an output of energy. For instance, one might say that there must be a continued output of energy in order to maintain a reaction formation, that is, behavior which goes exactly contrary to the actual impulse and feelings. Where too much of the available energy is absorbed in creating disguises and masks for original impulses, not enough is available for individual development along constructive lines.

The question is sometimes raised whether one is not making the interpretation of behavior unnecessarily difficult and complicated by assuming that there is always an unconscious motive to explain it. There is nothing in this treatment of the mechanisms that assumes that behavior *must* have only a hidden and unconscious motivation. Each of the illustrations given could be explained simply and straightforwardly as well as in terms of unconscious motivation. There is no must or

---

[7] L. E. Bisch, *Be Glad You're Neurotic* (New York: McGraw-Hill Book Company, Inc., 1936).

[8] Geza Roheim, *Origin and Function of Culture,* Nervous and Mental Disease Monograph Series, No. 69 (New York: Nervous and Mental Disease Publishing Company, 1943).

necessity about the explanation given. The point is, however, that there are times when behavior is motivated unconsciously, and the illustrations selected are those for which the mechanisms can furnish an explanation. Most socialized behavior can and should be taken at its face value. However, when such behavior seems extreme, exaggerated, and uncalled for by the situation, one must search for a hidden explanation since the obvious one does not suffice. Mechanisms are indicated when the obvious and straightforward explanation is not sufficient.

QUESTIONS FOR DISCUSSION

1. In what way can a person's character be called a defense against anxiety?
2. In the light of the discussions in this chapter why does the direct attempt to overcome an undesirable trait of personality (symptom treatment) result in the formation of other undesirable behavior?
3. Must a mechanism always be unconscious?

RECOMMENDED READINGS

1. FRENKEL-BRUNSWIK, ELSE, "Mechanisms of Self-Deception," *Journal of Social Psychology,* 10 (1939), 490–520.
2. FREUD, ANNA, *The Ego and the Mechanisms of Defense,* International Psychoanalytical Library, No. 30 (London: The Hogarth Press, 1937; also New York: International Universities Press, 1946; first published in German, 1936).
3. HORNEY, KAREN, *New Ways in Psychoanalysis* (New York: W. W. Norton and Company, Inc., 1939).
4. LANGER, W. C., *Psychology and Human Living* (New York: Appleton-Century-Crofts, Inc., 1943).
5. MENNINGER, K. A., *The Human Mind* (New York: Alfred A. Knopf, 1930; 1937; third edition, 1945).
6. SHAFFER, L. F., *The Psychology of Adjustment* (Boston: Houghton Mifflin Company, 1936).
7. STRECKER, E. A., and APPEL, K. E., *Discovering Ourselves* (New York: The Macmillan Company, 1931; second edition, 1943).

VIII

Fixation

Fixation is a mechanism that operates as a defense against anxiety by stopping the process of development. In general, one knows what is meant by fixation, namely a pause in the process of development which may extend over a shorter or longer time. If one thinks of development as being held up at any stage so that the patterns at that stage become more or less fixed and inflexible when they ought to become more adaptive and flexible to meet the demands of responsibility in maturity, one can see that in fixation one has a concept with considerable significance. Fixation helps to explain, in part, the variations in character and personality from person to person. Some persons simply stop growing at a certain stage, and their personalities take on as permanent structures the behavior patterns operating at that stage.

DEFINITION

Fixation is used in common language in a general sense, but in psychoanalytic usage it has a somewhat more precise meaning. In general parlance, fixation means an arrest of development at any stage. One, for instance, speaks of the perpetual sophomore meaning a person who is rough and ready, boisterous, awkward, and who has never learned ordinary self-control. A college graduate may be fixated on the college level and keep for years his interest in college sports and activities, may wear the college emblem, and attend college activities. The youth who, when he graduates from high school, is forced to enter some monotonous occupation, may cling to high-school activities and points of view as his only lease on a stimulating and varied existence. The dependent adult who must seek the help, advice, guidance, and counsel of others whom he believes to be stronger and wiser than he may still be reacting to the situation when as an infant he depended on others for his nourishment. Fixation is well illustrated in its common meaning by grief or mourning. In mourning one clings in memory to the departed person. Life still revolves around the activities which related to the person who has gone, and memories still dominate the thoughts. The person in mourning is unable to make new friendships, to take on new obligations, or to adopt new interests. Mourning, however, unless pathological, persists for only a limited time until the person is able to adapt himself afresh to the life about him. A person who is disappointed in love may live "fixatedly" for years in much the same way as a person who is in mourning.

During the Civil War a beautiful girl in Charlotte, N. C. was engaged to marry a soldier. Her people had a very fine house, she had lovely clothes and was popular with her friends. After he was killed in action, she was never known to leave her house. She lost interest in everything. For years she wore the same dresses he had seen her wear. After the death of her parents she lived alone with her servants. Nothing was allowed to be changed in the house. She existed in this state for years.

In its psychoanalytic meaning, fixation is used to denote the arrest of a component of the pleasure urge at some infantile stage of development. For instance, a child who is never entirely satisfied in his demands for nourishment in the first year of life and whose nursing or feeding activities were considerably thwarted may never outgrow his inordinate need for food on the one hand, for being given things on the other, or for using the mouth as a pleasure organ. If one is sensitive to expressions of oral cravings one can see them in many adults. This has been found to be at the root of some cases of the excessive use of alcohol.

In particular, the psychoanalytic meaning of fixation refers to the excessive attachment of desire to some persons or object. Probably the most striking illustration of this is parent-fixation, or, in the case of a boy, mother-fixation, the tie which binds a boy or youth or even man to his mother, so that he is prevented from experiencing other normal relationships in friendship or marriage.

FUNDAMENTAL CONSIDERATIONS

Motivation. *Insecurity.* The concept of fixation is somewhat muddled by lack of clarity as to its motivation. It is evident that infantile fixations take place because of some aberration in the child's relationships to those who are responsible for its care and protection, especially the parents, or because of some extraordinary traumatic experience which the child has had. Most clearly, fixation is motivated by some threat of insecurity which causes an individual to cling to present adjustments and to fear to attempt some new mode of adjustment. We are all familiar with the tendency to hold on to what one has when the situation looks doubtful and insecure. Not only do we cling to our possessions but also to methods of behavior and to our thoughts and feelings in the face of overwhelming threats of insecurity. We do not dare to let go of the adjustments which have served us in the past and to try some new way with all of the danger which it entails. A teacher may cling to her method of teaching year after year for fear of losing classroom discipline or efficiency in results.

Traumatic Experience. There is no doubt but that some fixations are caused by traumatic experiences, such as injuries or severe frights. A child who has been injured hesitates to venture in the direction of the situation in which the injury was caused, a fact well illustrated by the adage, "A burnt child fears the fire." Insofar as this happens, the child is limited in his exploration and is forced to forego trying out new experiences. For the little child perhaps no situation is more frightening than one in which he feels that he is being left alone and that support is withdrawn.

Parental Neglect. So the threat of insecurity which leads to fixation may in many cases be caused by parental neglect which may come at any time in infancy, and the behavior patterns which are operating at that time will be those which, according to this theory, will be the ones to be fixated. Not only will neglect by the parents bring on fixation, but severe punishment has the same effect. Punishment, which operates in a similar fashion as a traumatic experience, has as its outcome the prevention of the child from exploring in the future in a certain direction. It is much like the electric grid in the maze which, in giving the rat a shock, helps the rat to learn to avoid that particular alley in the future. Insofar as a child is prevented from exploring in any alley in his growing experiences, he is fixated on his present patterns of adjustment.

Threat of Danger in New Experience. Fixation may be motivated by a threat of danger on entering into a new phase of development. The child, for instance, who is frightened by his first visit to the seashore by being submerged in a wave which surprises him may become panic-stricken whenever he is near the water for some time thereafter, and his opportunities for learning to swim are considerably postponed. The child who finds school an unhappy experience on the first day for any one of a multitude of reasons, such as his fear of losing his mother, rivalry with other children, or the severity of the teacher, may develop a distaste for school that will be difficult to overcome. Some unpleasant or terrifying experience when trying something new is often a block to further activity in that direction. Every abandonment of a tried stage for an untried in development is a threat to security and contains an element of pain. If this pain is too intense, the venture into the new will be abandoned, and there will be a retreat to the safety of the tried and familiar.

Overprotection. Fixation can also be motivated by overprotection by adults. The mother who in her own fear for the safety and proper development of her child hedges it around with too many restrictions and safeguards is preventing the child from venturing out to try new experiences. Overprotection by adults leads to too great dependence on the part of the child and instills in him a fear of adventure. On the one hand, if parents attempt to throw their children out into experiences too early they cause insecurity, while, on the other, if they coddle and nurse their children too long into childhood, they also create an insecurity which comes from too great dependence. Here again the primary motivating force which causes fixation is inability to tolerate frustration, for the spoiled child who is denied no satisfaction is less able on a later occasion to tolerate frustration than the child who has learned through experience to wait for its satisfactions.

Experiences Which Are Excessively Stimulating. Fixation may also be caused by premature experiences with certain situations or by experiences which are too strong in their stimulation. In these cases the reaction becomes unduly strong, dominating, pleasure-giving, and hence hard to relinquish. The child who is thwarted in securing nourishment may not be the only child who in later life has strong oral characteristics. The child who gets his nourishment easily and often may also be the child who becomes fixated on these activities. An environment which gives opportunity for encouraging and tolerating indulgence may create fixations at these levels. The child who has strong preoccupations in sexual matters may be suspected of having had early exaggerated experiences of a sexual nature. The child whose sexual experiences have been stifled for lack of stimulation will be found in later years to be the child who has little interest along sexual lines. The law of compensation apparently does not work in this area. David Levy,[1] on the other hand, in experiments with infants and also on the weaning of puppies finds that those who sucked from nipples with large openings so that the process of securing nourishment was easy were those with tendencies toward having the need for continuing to suck much more than those who got their nourishment through nipples with small openings. His explanation is that those who received their nourishment easily did not spend much time in the sucking process, hence there was left a residual oral tension which led to the need for further sucking. It is as though this oral tension is released only by a certain amount of sucking, and if there is a discrepancy between nutritional and sucking satisfactions so that the nutritional satisfactions come before the sucking satisfactions are completed, there will be a tendency to continue sucking on whatever is convenient. Whatever the reason in Levy's experiment, there was what may be called a fixation of the process which came easily and had insufficient exercise. Lewin, in one of his early experiments with Ovsiankina,[2] showed that there is a tendency to return to unfinished tasks at the earliest oppor-

[1] D. M. Levy, "Finger-Sucking and Accessory Movements in Early Infancy (An Etiologic Study)," *American Journal of Psychiatry,* 7 (1928), 881–918.

"Experiments on the Sucking Reflex and Social Behavior of Dogs," *American Journal of Orthopsychiatry,* 4 (1934), 203–224.

[2] Kurt Lewin, and M. Ovsiankina, "Untersuchungen zur Handlungs und Affektpsychologie, VI: Die Wiederaufnahme unterbrochener Handlungen," *Psychologische Forschung,* 11 (1928), 302–379.

tunity in order to attempt to complete them. This need for making a satisfactory completion of one activity before leaving it to turn to other activities is related to the need to work out adequate adjustments at one level before going on *to attempt adjustments at another level.

The development of tendencies toward fixation has been explained on the basis of strong impulses as contrasted with the weak ego, for example, the young lady in *Oklahoma* who "cain't say no." Just why some impulses become strong and why the ego organization in these same cases is weak is not explained. Probably the explanation lies in one of the kinds of motivation mentioned above.

Self-Punishment. Fixation may have a revenge or self-punishment function. A girl who has been jilted in love may forego all serious love expressions and in place of giving love seek to humiliate men. Such a "reaction to the scar" represents a halt in normal outgoing expression. There may also be a masochistic pleasure in repeating dangers, even needlessly, as though to prove that the danger can be surmounted and will not actually overwhelm.

It will be seen that the exact forces which lead to retardation or acceleration of development are not clearly indicated. Fixation apparently results from some disturbance in the child's security in parent-child relations. It clearly is a result of the influence of traumatic experiences and of severe neglect or harsh treatment by the parents. On the other hand, fixation occurs when there is overprotection by the parents. As an attempt at generalization it would seem as though fixation develops at those points where satisfactions are adequate and which are at the same time at the threshold of frustrations toward which the child is not prepared to adjust. A fixation point, then, is another defense against anxiety and against frustration intolerance.

Unconscious nature of fixation. In fixations, particularly those which take place in infancy, the original experience is practically always repressed and hence becomes unconscious. When a person finally reaches the stage of self-awareness in later life, he simply finds himself the possessor of certain tendencies which mark him off as a person. He may be optimistic or pessimistic, generous or stingy, orderly or disorderly. Where these tendencies have come from he is not aware. Most persons would resent it were they to be told that tendencies within themselves whose origin is unknown to them are fixations from infantile modes of behavior. Naturally experiences in adult life are considerably modified from the kinds of expression from which they grew in infancy. These later expressions, one might say, have developed by the long process of learning. However, the interesting thing is that there is still a core of the original infantile tendency which persists even into adult life in a recognizable form, indicating that during all of the years there is a continuing drive for expression. Using the terminology of the mechanisms expressed in this book, one might say that in adult life these early trends are sub-limated. One only becomes aware that these fixations exist in the indi-vidual on rare instances, when, under their instigation, an individual is forced to adopt patterns of thought and behavior which characterized him in infancy, but which he was thought to have cast off as he matured. In the next chapter it will be shown that in situations of frustration there actually may be a regression or return to some of the more primitive forms of expression which usually have been fixation points in the process of development.

Because fixations are unconscious they are not susceptible to conscious modification on the part of the individual. No matter how hard he tries the individual with fixated character trends is unable by his own force of will to modify them. Their springs are out of reach and inaccessible. Sometimes a person with strong trends toward anger, or drink, or sexual appetites feels as though he was possessed with forces within, not under his control. Modification becomes possible only as these unconscious and repressed trends are brought into the individual's conscious awareness.

Fixation as basis of character development. Fixation is a convenient concept for understanding the development of character. From this point of view every individual's character is a residue of a number of fixations which determine his attitude toward people and situations in maturity. Every person has fixations which he carries with him from each stage of early development. An infant, for instance, responds in one way on an-other to the early experience of nursing. Some will become inordinately greedy as a result of frustration, whereas some will become placid and satisfied and optimistic as the result of an abundance of nourishment whenever needed. Whatever the early nursing situations, they determine the pattern of response to food and to oral pleasure which sets into character patterns in later life. Similarly, at each subsequent stage of development, attitudes are adopted which carry on for the rest of life.

Fixation and maturity level. Fixations determine to what level an individual will advance. If an individual becomes fixated at one level and is prevented from making adequate adjustment at the next stage, he becomes permanently immature. This concept becomes particularly im-portant in considering normal sexual development of the adult. The man or woman who becomes fixated at one of the earlier infantile stages becomes permanently infantile in his sexual life and is unable to achieve normal potency as an adult.

One should not get the idea, however, that fixations are irrevocable and represent necessarily permanent distortions to development. Every human being has the capacity to develop. However, one must begin where one left off, perhaps with infantile trends.

ILLUSTRATION OF FIXATION

Fixation on parents. Most typically this is fixation on the mother by the boy and on the father by the girl. Parent-fixations occur when parents have been more than ordinarily firm in discipline and are protective or possessive of the children. All of the conditions for parent-fixation are not entirely clear. Fixation of parent love may result from excessive tenderness as well as excessive control on the part of the parents. The parent who selfishly uses a child for his own pleasure may make this attention overimportant to the child. The child does not dare to turn away from his parents because of the danger of loss. Fixation of parental love may also occur when it has been repressed, for once parental love is repressed it may be chained. The child who is made to feel ashamed of the strength of his feelings toward father or mother may be unconsciously held to them and find himself unable to form other attachments. Parent-fixation is shown by a number of signs. In the first place, it shows itself through friendly esteem, veneration, and affection. In this sense, there is a modicum of parent fixation in everyone insofar as everyone has tender feelings toward his parents. However, it fully deserves the name when it shows itself in later years by dependence on the parents and continued looking to the parents for support and protection. The middle-aged man who runs to his parents at any difficulty, expecting them to get him out of trouble and to give him the same support that he received as a little child is suffering from a parent-fixation. The youth who in adolescence is content in his parents' home, who likes to stay at home evenings, and who wants to go with his parents on picnics and excursions instead of seeking the companionship of those of his own age is showing tendencies toward fixation. It is normal for an adolescent to become dissatisfied with the parental home, to find it intolerably stodgy and dull, to want to go out and mix with boys and girls of his own age, and to wish to spend his week-ends and holidays with his peers. Fixation is also shown by lack of interest in persons and things outside the home. The fixated person, when forced to leave the home, becomes violently homesick and very unhappy in making his new adjustments.

Fixation on a parental figure is almost certain to lead to difficulty in later object choices. The boy or girl who is fixated on a parent will find it difficult to select a suitable love partner. The girl cannot find a man who compares with her father. No one can come up to him in gallantry, tenderness, or virility. The girl who goes through high school and college and never finds boys attractive will be usually found to have a strong father-fixation or a strong mother-fixation although this would be difficult for her to admit on first thought. A fixated person commonly will find companionship with others much older than the self, thus accomplishing an easy displacement from the parent on whom the fixation rests. It is typical for the young adolescent to have crushes on some much older person of the opposite sex. This would seem to be a transition process in breaking away from the family ties to finding relationships among others of his own age. Where there is strong parent-fixation, relationship with a marriageable person becomes dangerous, and various substitutes are sought. Some find pleasure by seeking a relationship with married persons in whom there is safety. Others find the safety in relationship or companionship with their own sex. Some indicate their fixation by a curious split in their love life. With these persons the inhibition and protest against incestuous relations is so strong that when they marry they actually have difficulty in having natural sexual relations, while their sexual feeling is given toward someone else outside the family, perhaps a prostitute.

The gifted musician, Johannes Brahms (as is also true of many geniuses) was subject to a mother-fixation. He failed to consummate marriage with the respectable women with whom he had affairs. His love for Clara Schumann is believed due to his identification of her with his mother. Over his mother's grave he said, "I no longer have a mother, I must marry." But he never did. He assured Professor Robert Kahn that "the most beautiful thing in the world is to possess a mother." [3]

VALUES OF FIXATION

Parent love and, hence, fixation has the approval of the community. Mother's Day seems to be an established institution, and the mercantile community has also set a Father's Day. The fourth commandment demands that one honor his father and mother, so that this attitude toward parents is of long standing in our own culture. In general, if erotic energy is tied up in fixation there is less available for disposal in forming new attachments. Every fixation point, therefore, makes it less easy for a child to advance and make normal development in subsequent stages. It is for this reason that fixations interfere with the love life. Energies are drawn off to other forms of expression leaving inadequate energies for normal potency and the relationships that go with it. Fixations, therefore, interfere with happy marriage. Fixation may also diminish the plasticity in dynamic qualities of an adult's desire. The adult becomes early set in his ways. He is less adaptable to people and events and his character is inflexible. Fixation will constantly interfere with the normal forms of sexual expression and tend to divert the person off into one or another of the common forms of perversion.

It will be seen from these remarks and generalizations that too broad a

[3] R. H. Schauffler, *The Unknown Brahms* (New York: Dodd, Mead & Company, 1933), p. 225.

fixation represents a handicap to a person's maximum mature development. Important fixations, of course, are determined in infancy, that is, before the age of five or six, and are, so far as we know, the outcome of experiences and relationships in infancy. The person who goes into adult life with a fixation is like the tree which, hindered in its early growth by an obstacle which bends it in one direction or another, is prevented from growing to full perfection.

EDUCATIONAL IMPLICATIONS OF FIXATION

Parents can encourage fixation by being overprotective of their children. The parent who stresses babyish behavior as being cute, calling it to the attention of friends and neighbors, is helping the child to feel satisfied at not growing up. Likewise the parent who condones infantile behavior and finds excuses for temper tantrums, destructiveness, sulking, expressions of rivalry, and the like, is encouraging children to find an infantile way of meeting their difficulties rather than a more mature way. The parent who is fearful of letting the child have independence is likewise forcing the child to continue childish methods. A mother who continues to dress, to feed, even to sleep with her child long after he passes his fifth year, is making it very difficult for the child to learn to be independent and resourceful. The wise parent encourages independence, in such matters as selection of clothing, handling money, making Christmas purchases, choosing friends and courses of study, and in countless other decisions.

In order to avoid fixation in their children, parents must avoid either of two extremes. On the one hand, they must be careful not to give too exclusive love to their children since it will tend to warp them to excessive dependence. Stating on the one hand that parents cannot give their children too much affection and emotional security, and, on the other hand, that they can harm them by demanding too great an attachment is not inconsistent. Children need all of the security that they can be given in early life, without at the same time having dependence and fixation demanded of them in return. The wise parent will avoid fixing the child's affection on himself. The good parent is one who gives without stint, but does not expect to receive love in return. He will see to it that opportunities for the arousal of love and interest in other directions are provided. The wise mother will encourage her child to play with other children and to go to school, instead of limiting the child's social contacts and forbidding him to associate with certain boys and girls. Instead of keeping too close a watch on the son or daughter in the evening, this same wise mother will encourage her adolescent children to form friendships with boys and girls of the same age. This comes hard to many parents who find that they are about to lose the important position of being the person to whom their children turn in need or in danger. A parent, however, should recognize that his own children will achieve only their maximum development when their interests burst the home roof, and they seek to establish a home of their own.

It is also possible to fixate self-love and to find the self so important that it becomes difficult to establish a mature object relationship in later years. A person may be driven to a fixation on himself because he is afraid of his relationship with others. This is the "burnt child" tendency. Not being sure of his relationship with others, he does not venture forth and encourage or pursue them but retires to himself as the surest repository of his love impulses. Such a person finds that his pride is easily wounded. Rather than suffer the ignominy of a rebuff, he does not seek relationships with others. The person whose self-love is fixated will choose love objects on a selfish basis; that is, for what they can contribute to his own self-pride and conceit.

QUESTIONS FOR DISCUSSION

1. Give illustrations of fixation in a child just entering school, a young adolescent, a college graduate.

2. What is meant by "mother fixation"? How does it arise? Why is it considered undesirable?

3. The expression is sometimes used in describing an immature person that he has failed to "work through" some of his early experiences. What does this mean in terms of fixation?

4. How can a person be helped to outgrow a fixation? What are the conditions for attaining maturity?

5. Discuss psychotherapy in relation to fixation.

RECOMMENDED READINGS

1. FLÜGEL, J. C., *The Psychoanalytic Study of the Family,* International Psychoanalytical Library, No. 3 (London: Hogarth Press, 1921).

2. FREUD, SIGMUND, *A General Introduction to Psychoanalysis* (New York: Liveright Publishing Corporation, 1920; 1935; first published in German in 1916).

3. SEARS, R. R., "Experimental Analyses of Psychoanalytical Phenomenon" in J. McV. Hunt, editor, *Personality and the Behavior Disorders* (New York: The Ronald Press Company, 1944), Vol. I, Chapter IX, 306–322.

4. SEARS, R. R., *Survey of Objective Studies of Psychoanalytic Concepts.* Social Science Research Council Bulletin, No. 51 (New York: Social Science Research Council, 1943).

IX

Regression

Regression is a well-known phenomenon obvious every day in grown-ups who act like babies. Regression may be classed as a mechanism in the sense that it is the step taken by an individual in order to avoid meeting and solving some difficult and frustrating present situation. It is an escape from reality. On the other hand, regression is also linked with fixation as having to do with the processes of development. Regression represents a <u>backward step in</u> development, a returning to older modes of thought, feeling, and behavior which were of service at an earlier time and are being retried in the hope that by some miracle they can be equally serviceable in the present.

DEFINITION

Regression is a term commonly used to signify a retreat to more child-ish ways of thinking, acting, and feeling, but technically it has two distinct meanings. In its *first* meaning, regression is used to refer by reversion to a pattern of behavior which was the individual's at an earlier age. Barker, Dembo, and Lewin [1] have called this variety of regression "retro-gression." A clear illustration of this first meaning is seen in the reversion to infantile speech as, for instance, baby-talk or lisping, or use of the same speech forms which he himself used earlier as a baby. One may find, to use another illustration, that a little child who is threatened by the arrival of a rival newcomer to the family may regress to more infantile forms of behavior and will wet or soil himself, will adopt child-ish speech, and will become fussy and whiny. In the second meaning a person may *not* be repeating his own earlier patterns of behavior. Barker, Dembo, and Lewin call this "regression proper," which of course may include retrogression. This meaning of regression refers to a surrender of sublimation in favor of a more primitive and natural form of expression.

[1] R. G. Barker, Tamara Dembo, and Kurt Lewin, *Frustration and Regression: An Experiment with Young Children*, Studies in Topological and Vector Psychology. II. University of Iowa Studies in Child Welfare, Vol. 18, No. 1, University of Iowa Studies, No. 386 (Iowa City: University of Iowa Press, 1941).

With this meaning regression is used to refer to any kind of immature behavior. For instance, when a person becomes angry he may discard his more civilized and adult methods of showing anger and aggression by scorn or ridicule, in favor of the more primitive method of hitting the other person with his fist.

Fundamental considerations. *Variations in Way Regression Is Expressed.* Regression may be a return to behavior or action of a rather clear-cut and specific nature, or it may be a change in the kind or quality of behavior or personality which is more primitive and less highly organized. Barker, Dembo, and Lewin have made an analysis of the variations in behavior in development, which would also apply to the process of regression. As behavior develops there is a change in its *kind* or *quality*. One expects a little child to be dependent but, as he grows older, to depend less upon others and to take care of himself to a larger extent. Behavior varies in *organization*. The mature person has many goals and purposes. In regression one has fewer and simpler goals. The mature person's multiplicity of goals is lost. Development also means more *hierarchical organization*. One is willing to aim at sub-goals which serve the purpose of helping to accomplish more distinct and long-time goals. The mature person, for instance, is more willing to work at relatively meaningless and uninteresting tasks which contribute to some larger end which he is striving to attain. In regression there is a return to a striving for other basic and fundamental goals immediately. Maturity also means a more *complicated organization*.

In maturity there is an *extension* of the *area* of *activities* and *interests*. As the child develops he is able to take on a greater variety of interests. When frustrated, however, he may retract some of these interests and channel his energies in the direction of overcoming some obstacle to his basic drives. This extension of the area of activities may exhibit itself in more widespread activities, or it may lead to a greater time perspective. That is, the person may be able and willing to plan farther ahead. The mature person can lay plans far in the future and think far ahead with regard to his education or career. In regression, however, one has to retract and make plans to meet the more immediate situation. As one becomes more mature, there is a greater *differentiation* and *specialization* of *behavior*. One gives his attention to finer and finer details. In regression, on the other hand, attention to the details is lost, and one responds more to the gross situation with less differentiated activity.

Finally, maturity implies a *greater degree of realism*. In regression, on the other hand, one looses contact with immediate problems and responds more in a spirit of play or fantasy with less regard to the realistic conditions imposed by such problems.

Object Regression versus Drive Regression. Barker, Dembo, and

Lewin make a distinction between "object regression" and "drive regression." By object regression they mean regression to an object or person toward which one responded in the past, as when a child picks up a discarded toy which he played with when he was younger. An adolescent girl, for instance, who is disappointed in her relationship with some friend may turn temporarily to her dolls as a solace. Drive regression, on the other hand, refers to the kind or quality of behavior, as when a child continues to play with the same toy but plays with it in a more violent manner, throwing it about or breaking it instead of playing with it constructively.

Motivation of regression. *Regression and response to frustration.* Regression is one mode of response to frustration. Almost any frustration which presents a person with a difficult problem to solve, or a threat he is unable to meet, may lead to regression. The man, faced with the apparently unsolvable frustrations thrust upon him by some catastrophe, may begin to implore divine intervention in much the same way that he ran to father or mother for help when he was small.

Regression is a moving away from reality, and the person who adopts regression as a way of meeting his frustrations is using a form of escape from the solution of the problems with which he is confronted. He regresses back to the form of adjustment used at an earlier stage, one which was in a way satisfactory, but which he has grown out of as he has taken on more mature independence and self-reliance. Sears [2] believes that when frustration makes a change in response necessary, the response adopted is the one next strongest in order to the situation.

Regression Due to a Failure of Energy. Wells [3] makes the point that regression may be due to a failure of energy to cope with the demands of the present situation—the "straw that breaks the camel's back." He likens the frustrating situation which leads to regression to "load" as it is used in engineering or physics and points out that when the load or difficulty exceeds the energy available, there is likely to be a retreat to a form of adjustment which demands less energy. For instance, a wife who finds it too difficult to think of standing up to her ferocious husband manages him by devices she used as a child with her own parents. This concept, while lacking experimental or clinical verification, may be of some value as a hypothesis for deciding in which cases regression will be the form of adjustment used.

Regression Resulting from Conflict. Frequently, inner frustrations

2 R. R. Sears, "Experimental Analyses of Psychoanalytical Phenomena," in J. McV. Hunt, editor, *Personality and the Behavior Disorders* (New York: The Ronald Press Company, 1944), Vol. 1, pp. 306–332.

3 F. L. Wells, "Social Maladjustments: Adaptive Regression," in Carl Murchison, editor, *Handbook of Social Psychology* (Worcester, Mass.: Clark University Press, 1935), Ch. XVIII, 845–915.

and conflicts are stronger motives for regression than outer frustrations. The person may find that his own standards and scruples make it difficult for him to face the emergency. For instance, when a boy is goaded on to strong aggressive feelings toward a teacher but is held back by his own inhibitions toward showing aggression, he may manage his conflict by some defense mechanism such as identification in which he becomes very docile and helpful, or takes his aggression out by bullying younger children. This response to inner frustration may be noticed particularly in adolescents who, unable to go out and find satisfactions in social intercourse with their contemporaries, may be driven back to earlier forms of adjustment. For instance, the adolescent will frequently fall back on ritualistic and obsessional acts as a way of managing his overwhelming, yet dangerous impulses.

Alan in early adolescence became very untidy and distressed his whole family by refusing to wash his face and hands or give any attention to the neatness of his attire. In so doing he regressed to a very early infantile stage. But later he became very particular about his choice of ties, the cut of his shoes, and sleeked his hair down daily. In this way he was managing his earlier disorderly tendencies by the very same steps which he took when he was very young (about three) when he placated his parents by his neatness and cleanliness.

Regression appears with particular clarity in the aged who seem to find more and more pleasure in living in the past.

   Regression a Reaction to Lack of Security. Regression may also be caused by lack of security—that is, emotional security. An individual who does not feel secure will retreat to a more restricted and simplified range of interests. He will be more concerned with himself and his problems. A person who does not feel secure in his work or marriage cannot make plans for the future or establish a home; he must adapt himself to a restricted and simplified time perspective and strive to achieve the more immediate goals. Children who have not been mothered will either develop negativistic and aggressive tendencies or regressive tendencies, or both.

   One may justly ask why some persons use regression as a way out of a difficult situation, while others find some compensation or sublimation. It has been said that an individual is held back from making new adjustments by virtue of the strength of older, firmly entrenched modes of adjustment. In other words, where there have been fixations in the process of development, it would be easy for a person to regress to these earlier stopping points when he is confronted with a difficult problem. The simile that Freud used is that of an army making an excursion into enemy territory. It will have its base camps and its foraging parties. If the advance parties have to retreat, they will fall back on the entrenched positions set up along the way. The stronger the fixations at any point of development, the easier it would be to regress them. The nature of one's regressions is an index to the nature of the process of early development itself.

The extent to which infantile dispositions remain intact is a subject for controversy. Psychologists, as a rule, would be inclined to doubt whether there are traces of infantile behavior which would ever have strength enough to be potent in determining adult behavior. They would point to our knowledge of the psychology of forgetting, which would indicate that unused behavior tends to be forgotten rapidly at first and later approaches extinction over a period of time. However, there are two kinds of fairly convincing evidence indicating that certain infantile patterns are not really effaced but are still present somewhere in the nervous system to be revived at later periods of life as needed.

One of these evidences is in the observation of mentally disordered patients. Dieterle and Koch [4] report a regression of two hysterical patients to the earliest oral stage. These young women in their psychoses went back to a stage where they became like babies, adopting the most infantile patterns of crying and nursing from a bottle. These are common observations to be made in patients in any mental hospital.

The other evidence comes from certain experiments with hypnosis. Platonow,[5] a Russian psychologist, for instance, by giving suggestions to persons under hypnosis, has been able to get them to act as though they were little children in a variety of realistic and convincing ways. However, P. C. Young,[6] who has experimented with this phenomenon under hypnosis, believes that this is not true regression but is a stimulation of regression in the hypnotic state. He believes that under hypnosis regression cannot take place to a state earlier than five or six, which is about the age at which a child is able to control his behavior by language patterns.

However, more recent work done during the war indicates that the regression effect under hypnosis may be real rather than an artifact. Erickson and Kubie think that there may be two kinds of hypnotic regression, one in which a person simulates his behavior, thoughts and feelings in a vivid and realistic way as he imagines them to have been in childhood; and the other a genuine revival of past patterns of ideation and behavior. Some rather remarkable results have been obtained recently in regressing individuals under hypnosis to stages of early infancy in which the individual behaves realistically in ways that he could not possibly know about either through his observation of infants or his reading about them, or his own memory. Under hypnotic regression

4 R. R. Dieterle and E. J. Koch, "Experimental Induction of Infantile Behavior in Major Hysteria," *Journal of Nervous and Mental Diseases*, 86 (1937), 688–710.

5 K. L. Platonow, "On the Objective Proof of the Experimental Personality Age Regression," *Journal of General Psychology*, 9 (1933), 190–209.

6 P. C. Young, "Hypnotic Regression—Fact or Artifact," *Journal of Abnormal and Social Psychology*, 35 (1940), 273–278.

individuals have given answers to mental tests which reproduce faithfully responses expected from young children.[7]

The experiment of H. E. Burtt [8] on his own son is also pertinent here. Beginning at the age of fifteen months, Burtt daily read to his son passages from Sophocles' *Oedipus Tyrannus* in the original Greek for a period of three months. Other selections were then introduced, and the daily readings were continued until the child was three years old. Later at ages 8½, fourteen and eighteen, certain of these passages were relearned. At age 8½, 30 per cent fewer repetitions were needed to learn this Greek than to learn new material. At age fourteen, the saving was 14 per cent. At the age eighteen there was no advantage to the material experienced in infancy. This experiment demonstrates that infantile experiences do persist in the nervous system into later years, but become increasingly less effective.

Regression in Behavior and Fantasy. Regression can be accomplished either by behavior or by fantasy and memory. When regression is accomplished by behavior, we speak of the behavior as a *symptom.* We recognize it as a regression because it seems to be strangely out of place and nonadaptive. It strikes one by its very peculiarity as being singularly inappropriate to the frustration which the person is facing. A child, for instance, who wets the bed at night, apparently is doing nothing to work out a solution to any of the problems faced by him and certainly makes it difficult for others in his family. Yet it is clearly recognized that enuresis, in some cases, is a return to the stage of irresponsibility in sphincter control which characterizes the very young baby. Thumb-sucking is another well-known kind of regressive behavior. However, regression can also be accomplished in fantasy, as when one lets his thoughts go back to the past and dwell upon it. The person who lives in the past, who thinks only of the triumphs and successes which he won at that time, who bemoans the happy times now long since departed, is indulging in a form of regression. Morgan has called this "the old oaken bucket delusion." If one will recall the words of this song, he will immediately recognize the appropriateness of the allusion. In the song the person returns to his childhood, has forgotten for the moment the irksomeness and boredom of the chores which were thrust upon him, and now sees them through the rose-tinted glasses of sentiment and fancy. "Backward, turn backward, O time in your flight, make me a child again just for tonight." [9]

[7] M. H. Erickson and L. S. Kubie. "The Successful Treatment of a Case of Acute Depression by a Return Under Hypnosis to a Critical Phase of Childhood," *Psychoanalytic Quarterly*, 10:583–609, 1941. L. R. Wolberg. *Hypnoanalysis.* New York: Grune and Stratton, 1945.

[8] H. E. Burtt, "An Experimental Study of Early Childhood Memory: Final Report," *Journal of Genetic Psychology*, 58 (1941), 435–439.

[9] From a poem by Will Carlton.

Degree of Regression. Regression varies in its completeness and thoroughness. On the one hand, there are many momentary and isolated expressions of childlike behavior which can be found in every individual. Everyone occasionally likes to turn back the hands of time and become a child again. A parent, in buying toys for his child, frequently buys those toys that he cares for himself. We recognize this tendency particularly at vacation times and on holidays. The old "grad," returning for his college reunion, throws off his cares and responsibilities and for a brief season adopts the undergraduate irresponsibility. In many dreams there are frequently infantile elements to be found. Symptomatic acts: tics and mannerisms, which apparently have little reference to the main stream of personality, can be recognized as a persistence of infantile trends. Much eccentric behavior is infantile in character.

The other extreme occurs when the whole personality is involved in retreat to infantile levels of response. In such instances the individual becomes less adapted to the world of reality and becomes more and more queer, isolated, childish, and irresponsible.

Regression also varies in amount or degree of retreat. The middle-aged woman may retreat to the days of her girlhood or to her maidenhood affairs. A man may retreat to the immaturity and irresponsibility of his college or high-school days. Such retreats represent a degree of immaturity but are seldom serious. When the regression is to some infantile level, then greater problems are introduced. There is a belief that regression increases in severity the further back into infancy one goes for his patterns of behavior and the greater the split with the present situation. The degree of retreat is a function, in part, of the severity of the superego and its archaic or infantile character. The person whose superego is realistic and is in harmony with ego strivings is not liable to pronounced regressions; but the person whose superego is harsh, tyrannical, demanding, and is based on fantastic and exaggerated concepts is liable to deeper regression when frustrations arise.

Temporary and permanent regression. Regression may be either of a temporary nature or represent a more permanent transformation of the personality. If, for instance, an individual, unable to have his way, develops a temper tantrum in order to frighten another person and force him to yield, this would be thought of as a temporary form of regression. On the other hand, if an individual, through misfortune or illness, becomes more generally dependent on others and less able to take care of his own affairs, this would be more in the nature of a personality change and would have a relatively more permanent character.

Situational and established regression. Sometimes regression takes place only in certain situations. Some children take on childish ways when with their parents and become much more self-reliant and responsible in school. Most boys and girls recognize that there are times when they can be untidy and careless with their clothing, but that there are other times when they wish to do things neatly and to be fastidious in their appearance. On the other hand, regression may fasten itself to a person so as to become a personality characteristic. Some individuals become chronically and notoriously untidy, dependent, or quarrelsome wherever they are or whatever the occasion. In the situational regression the frustration is more likely to be an isolated frustration, whereas established regression would be caused by a continuing and pervasive frustrating state of affairs.

Regression accompanied by decrease in guilt and anxiety. Regression is generally accompanied by a decrease in guilt or anxiety because the conflict situation is left behind, and the retreat is to an infantile level where the conflicts were not so intense. This is one of the significant characteristics of regression. Naturally, one of the purposes of adjustment is to help to relieve the individual of some of his distresses. If a person has failed in his present situation and is in conflict over the demands of his superego and his method of meeting reality, he perhaps can dodge his difficulties by regression to a time when other persons took most of the responsibility of caring for him and managing his affairs.

Common

Regression to helplessness. All forms of helplessness or desire for protection and attention so as to be treated like a helpless child can be listed as regression. A person, for instance, who adopts such methods of attracting attention as bitter weeping, crying at failure, loud talking, exaggerated demonstrations of glee, calling for help, whining, fussing, and liking to be begged or coaxed to do things, is exhibiting regression. Along the same line, a person who is not only ill but seems to enjoy his illness and finds ways of prolonging it may be suspected of having adopted a regression. The motivation in these cases may be readily understood. When one is ill, one is helpless and has to be cared for and waited upon, and if one has met some unusual frustration, to become ill is a reputable way out. The hysterical woman is adopting regression as a method of getting her way.

In A. J. Cronin's novel, *The Citadel,* Dr. Manson is called upon to treat an hysterical woman who goes into violent tantrums, much as a little child might do, whenever she is unable to have her own way. She is brought out of her spell by a couple of vigorous slaps on the face and is suddenly confronted with a person who, not being afraid of her, forces her to stop and face the situation with which she is confronted.

Similarly, the woman who early in marriage leaves her husband and returns to her mother for comfort and sympathy when she is crossed or frustrated in some way is showing a kind of regression. Anyone who prefers to be helpless and cared for by others instead of independent and self-reliant has adopted childish modes of adjustment.

A young man had to have treatment in a sanatorium following a severe illness just after he graduated from high school and before he had learned a trade. He refused work, and he also refused nursing supervision which might have helped him to find himself. Instead he exposed himself to bad weather and refused food until it was necessary for him to return to the sanatorium in a precarious condition. To get back into the hospital where he had constant care and attention and no responsibilities was the purpose of his behavior.

Regression by retreat in constructiveness and differentiation. Regression may take place by a retreat in the variety and constructiveness of behavior. When there is a restriction and simplification in the field due to tension, the finer cues and signals on which less thoroughly learned reactions depend disappear, and there is a return to a more fixed and habituated behavior. This regression by a retreat in constructiveness is best illustrated by the experiment of Barker, Dembo, and Lewin.[10] These investigators set up a playroom which was divided by a screen. In the first part of the experiment this screen was made opaque, and the child was given some extraordinarily fine and interesting toys with which to play. These toys gave the child an opportunity of drawing on his imagination and participating in highly constructive play activities. In second session, after the child had been allowed to play for a certain time in this section of the room, the screen was lifted, and he was taken into the other chamber where there were toys which were much simpler and less interesting. A transparent screen was let down so that the other more enticing toys could be seen but not reached. It was found that when children were placed in this frustrating situation, there was a regression in the constructiveness of their play. By means of a seven-point scale of constructiveness these investigators were able to estimate that there was the equivalent of about 17.3 months average regression. The child who reacted strongly to the frustration showed regression equivalent to twenty-four months, whereas the child who seemed to mind the deprivation less was able to continue play with the simpler and less interesting toys in a constructive fashion, and the regression was equivalent to an average of four months. This historic experiment makes vivid the meaning of regression and provides an experimental demonstration of its existence.

Regression in responsibility. The tramp or the hobo is often a person who has regressed to the level of irresponsibility. There is a danger that, if the government carries too many persons over difficulties by relief measures, regression by irresponsibility may become a dangerously widespread form of adjustment. However, one must recognize the realities of our faulty economic system, and admit that in many cases it is

[10] R. G. Barker, Tamara Dembo, and Kurt Lewin, *Frustration and Regression: An Experiment with Young Children,* Studies in Topological and Vector Psychology. II. University of Iowa Studies in Child Welfare, Vol. 18, No. 1, University of Iowa Studies. No. 386 (Iowa City: University of Iowa Press, 1941).

better to have eaten and regressed than not to have eaten at all. Regression in responsibility is not as much regression to helplessness as it is regression to being cared for and protected by others.

Regression in speech and fears. Regression shows itself early in speech as seen in baby-talk, in lisping, in crying, and in prattling. A person may show his regression by the adoption of primitive fears of a fantastic nature such as fears of spirits, of cosmic catastrophes, and similar fears based on childish fantasies which could not be maintained by a mature, intelligent person. Many times children adopt a sing-song expression or regress to repetitions or nonsense syllables as a way of disguising hostile tendencies. Not daring to express feelings openly, there is regression to these more primitive forms of expression. The jingles and chants of childhood often have this disguised significance.

Regression through identification. One may also say that identifications which are extreme will apparently resemble the kinds of identifications made by little children and hence are regressive. Children carry their hero-worship to an excess. They take great pleasure in trying to be like someone else in their play. They will strut around and try to take the part of the mailman, the postman, the policeman, the engineer, the teacher, and other figures who impress them by having power and authority. So the grown-up who always wants to be someone other than he is takes on patterns that are in essence childish. Someone has suggested that the popularity of certain night-club singers who have a childish quality of voice might be caused by the opportunity they provide others to enjoy a regression through identification.

Regression in aggression. Probably the most outstanding illustrations of regression may be found in primitive modes of showing aggression. Aggression is one primitive tendency which is considerably modified by educational training to fit the patterns demanded by our culture. When these refined and modified methods of showing aggression are dropped in favor of the more primitive methods, this usually represents a movement in behavior back to a very early level. Little children will hit, bite, scratch, tear, throw things about, spit, and so forth. A little child is also destructive. To him there is as yet no meaning to the *lares* and *penates* of the ordinary household. He has no reverence for them because he is not yet inducted into feeling for their usefulness and their traditions. The little child will tear pages in books, write on the wallpaper, spill ink on the carpet, cut the furniture with his jack-knife without any of the feeling of the horror his elders possess. So a person who wreaks destruction may be said to have regressed to an infantile level. The person, for instance, who in a rage destroys his examination paper or his notes, when he is considerably thwarted, is showing this trend. There are many childish ways of showing aggression. Playing practical jokes, an institution of Hallowe'en and April Fool's Day, is a typical example of childish play. Laughing at others' misfortune, particularly where one is unable to take it when the joke is on oneself, resembles the behavior of a child. The attitude of complaining and fault-finding also resembles the little habits that children will fall into when they are continually frustrated by dominating parents. Instead of flaring up with one vengeful destructive act, they settle down into a manifest whining and complaining, and one can see similar patterns of behavior in adults who are chained to hapless lives. For instance, a common complaint is that of being misunderstood and of feeling that one's achievements are not fully appreciated by one's peers.

Miss U., an excellent history teacher in a senior high school, alienates most of the members of the faculty by complaining about how hard she works and how no one appreciates her efforts.

Regression by rivalry. Regression also shows itself in rivalry situations. Rivalry goes back to relations to siblings or even to parents in their early life. In many instances, rivalry between brothers and sisters in the same family is extremely intense, and there is continual striving for preference. When similar behavior shows itself in later life in intense competition, one may suspect a continuance of or going back to early patterns of aggressive behavior.

Regression by anger. Parallel with aggressive behavior are feelings of anger and hatred. Where these feelings are expressed in a primitive way by adults, we find a regression to the kinds of expression which characterize infancy. One may show anger in this primitive fashion by the temper tantrum, which consists of raging and raving, in creating a disturbance, making a fuss, raising the voice, stamping the foot, throwing oneself on the floor, or by extreme negativism. Where open expression of anger has not been permitted, we get such substitute forms as in sulking, being put out, feeling sore and pouting, holding one's breath. The adult is showing regressive tendencies when he gets angry when someone interferes with his plans, or when someone does not agree with and praise his pet idea, and the angry person tends to overcondemn the person or thing which causes him to lose his temper.

Regression by negativism. Similar to this are tendencies toward negativism. We see negativism as a trend in most children at the age of two and three when they learn to say "I won't" and will resist any suggestions made by their elders. So the adult who insists on having his own way, in throwing off restraints, in indulging in a bout of drinking, resembles the little child. Such a person will not play unless he can be captain. He resigns as president or secretary of his class when things do not go smoothly with him. He refuses to continue his work in arithmetic when he is corrected by the teacher. He does things because others do not want them done, or he refuses to do them when it is clear that others wish it.

He refuses to coöperate until he is given complete control of the situation. All of these are varieties of negativism, and when they are done by the adult they resemble the behavior of the two- and three-year-old child.

Regression by nostalgia. Still another variety of regression may be found in homesickness and memories. Nostalgia is a going back in thought to the "good old days" which become enshrined in the memory when the more disagreeable and irritable features of the situation are being brushed off and not brought to mind. The mature person adjusts himself to the new situation, finds new friends, new activities, and new interests. The childish person becomes sick when he is thrown into a new situation. He develops nausea and headaches, and is incapacitated in various ways as a sign of his rebellion against the new and his desire to go back to the old, familiar, and secure. The Garden of Eden or the Happy Hunting Ground are institutionalizations of regression in folklore.

VALUES OF REGRESSION

Negative values. Regression is generally recognized as an unsatisfactory mode of adjustment. Nothing good can be said about regression, as it is the negation of adjustment to the world of persons and events with which everyone has to learn to get along. Regression is a retreat from the reality of the present situation. The problems of the present are ignored and are left unsettled. The person attempts to work his way through his thwartings and frustrations and conflicts by resorting to more infantile modes of adjustment, which in themselves represent a more dependent and more helpless kind of adjustment. A person who adopts regression as a method of adjustment is forced to continue it in order to prevent present emotional crises from arising. The pressing problem is never really solved but is always dodged or avoided. The regressed person is less capable of meeting present frustrations.

Positive values. Regression may have an apparent temporary value insofar as it is a release from the present difficulties of life. Vacations and holidays represent temporary escapes from the toil and problems of everyday life. The need for vacations and holidays is a good indication of the strain and artificiality of modern civilization. The Shriners or the American Legion Convention or the college class reunion show childish or infantile characteristics in an attempt to escape from reality. Indeed, one might go further and suggest that all play on the part of mature people is, to a certain extent, regressive, but as a brief relief from the pressing problems of everyday life, is valuable. Adults frequently amuse themselves by retreating to an appreciation of children's humor, curiosity and wonder. Writers of children's stories frequently are regressing in their own adjustments as an escape from adult problems with which they are not mature enough to grapple. In primitive societies these escapes may be institutionalized in the ceremonial or the orgy, which permits a group relaxation of convention and a temporary return to more primitive kinds of behavior. Alcoholism represents one such escape in contemporary life and is an escape generally recognized to be temporary. The danger in alcoholism is that it may become a general habit of escape that progressively makes a person less competent to face the real problems of existence and causes that person to use an escape with increasing frequency.

EDUCATIONAL IMPLICATIONS

Parents can force their children to regression by putting too much pressure on them and holding for them standards which are too severe and ambitions which are too high. Likewise a parent can force a child to regress by being so dominating that any show of independence or initiative is crushed, and the child is forced to become docile and dependent. The child who has the best chance to mature so as to become emotionally stable, independent, and self-reliant is the child who receives the greatest security from his parents. Feeling secure in themselves, these parents take life confidently. They are not anxious about their child's growing up or about his finding a place in the world, and consequently the child, in identifying himself with his parents, feels this security in himself and dares to venture out to try new things and to take his place among other children without showing timidity or dominance. If, in addition, the child is given generous support when he is frustrated and praise and recognition when he is successful, he will learn to tackle his problems and to master them.

QUESTIONS FOR DISCUSSION

1. Horney discusses such concepts as fixation, regression or repetition compulsion (See *New Ways in Psychoanalysis*, chapter on "The Emphasis on Childhood") in terms of the repetition of infantile tendencies. She believes that personality is the result of a developmental process and not of simple repetition. Elaborate this point of view.

2. Discuss alcoholism from the point of view of regression.

3. How can a person be helped to overcome tendencies toward regression?

4. How does rivalry within the family sometimes result in regression?

5. To what extent and under what conditions does regression lead to an increase in anxiety? To a reduction of anxiety?

RECOMMENDED READING

1. BARKER, R. G., DEMBO, TAMARA, and LEWIN, KURT, *Frustration and Regression: An Experiment with Young Children*, Studies in Topological and Vector Psychology,

II, University of Iowa Studies in Child Welfare, Vol. 18, No. 1, University of Iowa Studies, No. 386 (Iowa City: University of Iowa Press, 1941).

2. FLÜGEL, J. C., *The Psychoanalytic Study of the Family*, International Psychoanalytical Library, No. 3 (London: Hogarth Press, 1921).

3 FREUD, SIGMUND, *A General Introduction to Psychoanalysis* (Liveright Publishing Corporation, 1920; 1935; first published in German in 1916).

4. MORGAN, J. J. B., *Psychology of the Unadjusted School Child* (New York: The Macmillan Company, 1926; revised edition, 1936).

5. SEARS, R. R. "Experimental Analyses of Psychoanalytical Phenomenon" in J. McV. Hunt, editor, *Personality and the Behavior Disorders* (New York: The Ronald Press Company, 1944), Vol. I, Chapter IX, 306–322.

6. SHERMAN, MANDEL, *Mental Conflicts and Personality* (New York: Longmans, Green & Co., 1938).

7. VAN OPHUIJSEN, J. H. W., "The Theory of Regression in Clinical Psychiatry," *Psychiatric Quarterly*, 4 (1930), 620–630.

X

Repression and the Unconscious

Repression and the unconscious have had diverse treatment in the various psychologies. Repression is the focal point in psychoanalytic theory and a discussion of repression and the unconscious appears in many places in Freud's writings. Psychoanalysis has been called "depth" psychology because it deals with processes which not only are out of reach of conscious awareness, but also go far back in the life history of the individual.

guilt
pain (& death)

Academic and experimental psychology, until recently, have given the unconscious superficial treatment. The unconscious has merely been recognized descriptively as absence of conscious awareness. As a matter of fact, the unconscious has had its most thorough treatment outside of psychoanalysis by the philosophers who have speculated at length on the significance of consciousness and the possible implications of the unconscious. Influential American psychologists have even ridiculed the Freudian point of view that there exist dynamic unconscious motivating forces within the individual.[1] It is only within the past few years that there has been an attempt to demonstrate the process of repression and the existence of unconscious motivating forces experimentally. There seems to be clear evidence that unconscious forces within the personality play a major rôle in directing behavior.[2]

[1] Knight Dunlap, *Mysticism, Freudianism, and Scientific Psychology* (St. Louis: C. V. Mosby Company, 1920).

J. B. Watson, "The Myth of the Unconscious," *Harper's*, 155 (1927), 502–508.

R. S. Woodworth, "Some Criticisms of Freudian Psychology," *Journal of Abnormal Psychology*, 12 (1917), 174–194.

[2] Numerous studies have attempted to relate forgetting to the pleasantness or un pleasantness of the material forgotten as a way of securing experimental evidence on the process of repression. The majority of these studies indicate that material which is pleasant is remembered only slightly better than material which is unpleasant, but that both of these kinds of material are remembered better than that to which the subject is indifferent.

All of the earlier studies, however, are based on hypotheses that do not permit the study of the phenomenon of repression, which relates to the protection of personality rather than to the avoidance of momentary pleasantness or unpleasantness. It is not possible to discover the presence of repression merely by finding out whether a person forgets unpleasant words. It is not unpleasantness in general that counts but the

There has been considerable confusion over the place that consciousness plays in mental life. Because each individual knows about his mind
only that of which he is aware, he is inclined to make mind identical with
consciousness. However, studies and observations of individuals demonstrate clearly that much behavior is governed by mental processes of
which an individual is not aware. The surprising way in which problems
seem to be solved during sleep or in periods of relaxation and the manner in which we surprise ourselves by unexpected feelings and attitudes
toward people make it seem an inevitable conclusion that many mental
processes take place below the level of conscious awareness. One sees the
mind as a tree which, because of the sap running to the branches from
the root through the trunk, begins to put out its leaves long before this
leafing process is visible to the eye.

LEVELS OF CONSCIOUSNESS

The conscious level. The mind can be divided into three levels: the
conscious, the preconscious, and the unconscious. Take, for instance, my
friend's name. As I think of it, it fills my mind. I am aware of it. It is the
focus of my attention. My friend's name is now conscious and belongs
to the group of conscious phenomena. Fifteen minutes ago I was not
thinking of my friend's name. It belonged to the class of mental phenomena that we would call preconscious. I could have thought of it had the
need arisen, and if someone had asked me who the person was with
whom he saw me on the street yesterday, I immediately could have mentioned my friend's name. It was ready and available to be brought into
consciousness. At a given moment there is only a small amount of material in consciousness. William James spoke of it as being in the focus
of consciousness,[3] but surrounding this conscious focus is a large amount
of material that could be brought into consciousness were it needed—

---

specific kind of unpleasantness for the individual. In later studies by Rosenzweig (Saul
Rosenzweig, and Gwendolyn Mason, "An Experimental Study of Memory in Relation
to the Theory of Repression," *British Journal of Psychology*, 24 (1934), 247–265), and
Sears (R. R. Sears, "Initiation of the Repression Sequence by Experienced Failure,"
Journal of Experimental Psychology, 20 (1937) 570–580), failure was included experi-
mentally as the frustration or threat to the personality, and in these two studies the
repression phenomenon was clearly demonstrated, although Rosenzweig used very
coarse measurements. Dan L. Adler (D. L. Adler, "Evidence for Repression and
Rationalization in the Solution of Moral Conflicts," *Psychological Bulletin*, 38 (1941),
600, 601), McGranahan (D. V. McGranahan, "A Critical and Experimental Study of
Repression," *Journal of Abnormal and Social Psychology*, 35 (1940), 212–225), and
Gould (Rosalind Gould, "Repression Experimentally Analyzed," *Character and Personality*, 10 (1942, 259–288) have more recently been able to demonstrate the process of
repression experimentally by improved techniques.

[3] William James, *Talks to Teachers on Psychology* (New York: Henry Holt and
Company, 1899).

memories of names, dates, experiences, images of places, people, and events, concepts, and words of all kinds.

It is also possible, however, that I could not have recalled my companion's name. I might have snapped my fingers and said, "His name has escaped me for the moment. I can't remember it. Wait a bit and perhaps it will come." I knew very well what his name was, but I could not produce it at the moment. It was unconscious. This amnesia or loss of memory may last only a moment or two. However, I may be unable to recall his name all day and perhaps for a longer period. The unconscious has its variations in depth. There are some unconscious memories which are so deeply buried that they are never to be recalled in the ordinary course of living—for months and years, perhaps for the duration of life.

Consciousness consists of two sorts of phenomena. On the one hand, it includes ideas, thoughts, images. Part of what is conscious is the immediate sensory presentation. Part of it is the image of such presentation, and part of it is indirect representation of experience as, for example, spoken, heard, or read words. The other part of consciousness consists of feelings and emotions. Consciousness is a proportionately infinitesimal part of our mental life. G. Stanley Hall likened consciousness to the ninth part of a submerged iceberg, the other eight-ninths corresponding to the unconscious. Even this is probably a very generous estimate of the proportion of mental activity which is conscious. For instance, as one reviews the day's activities, he realizes that he was not aware of the act of getting out of bed, shutting the window, turning on the bath water, pulling on his clothes, closing the door, turning to the right, looking for an approaching car before crossing the street. All of these were done automatically and unconsciously. While he was doing all of these things his mind was absorbed in thoughts about the fact that the newspaper was not in its accustomed place, that the bombing raid over England was frightful, that he must not forget to do an errand for his daughter.

What is conscious is constantly changing. Everyone knows how difficult it is to focus one's attention on any one thought for a long time. James called it the "stream of consciousness." [4] Consciousness arises when new adjustments are needed and when choices must be made. However, even very complex operations can be carried on without the coöperation of conscious awareness.

The unconscious level. The unconscious, on the other hand, consists of all mental activity and processes which are not conscious. In order to be straight on the matter we shall arbitrarily use the term *unconscious* in this chapter to mean active mental processes rather than the latent and passive memory traces. All drives belong in the unconscious. As a matter

not aware of it

[4] William James, *Psychology* (New York: Henry Holt and Company, 1890), Vol. I, p. 239.

of fact, drives themselves never can become conscious, only their representations in the shape of ideas and images. We know our drives only through the feelings that may accompany them or the verbal or ideational images representing them.

Repressed Ideas. Much (but not all) of what is unconscious consists of repressed material in the shape of concrete ideas. Only actual ideas can be repressed and hence exist in the unconscious. These may be the representation of inner drives. For example, it may be possible to repress thoughts of being hungry, the hostility that we feel toward a competitor, the attraction of a person of the opposite sex. In the unconscious an idea is not verbalized but is presented only in terms of sensory imagery. This we know from our dreams. Dreams which represent in part a surging up of the unconscious into the dream experience are in terms of sensory imagery, usually visual imagery. Less frequently in a dream, the experience is auditory or perhaps involves another sense. Seldom does a dream present itself to us in the form of a verbally expressed story but usually in terms of a sensorily presented experience.

REPRESSION

It was said earlier that part of the unconscious material consists of repressed ideas. This discussion turns abruptly to a consideration of the process of repression, which will permit us to understand how material becomes unconscious. Repression represents a flight of the ego from danger. It represents an endeavor on the part of a person to escape from tendencies within himself that he finds dangerous and untenable. Freud has likened repression to the process in the body of building up a wall of protective tissue, which will isolate the tumor or diseased part from the rest of the organism. Repression has a comparable function of isolating from the conscious part of the mental life that which is not acceptable because it is dangerous or repulsive or bad. Repression takes its place as one of the measures that the ego can adopt in defending itself against unacceptable and dangerous tendencies within. It is probably the most important defense against unacceptable impulses. Mechanisms which are to be described in succeeding chapters indicate other methods of defense against these same dangerous tendencies.

Distinction between repression and inhibition. It is important to make a sharp distinction between *repression* and *inhibition*. By repression will be meant the exclusion from *consciousness* of thoughts, feelings and wishes. Repression refers to the *thoughts* a person does not permit himself to think, to the *feeling* of hatred or scorn that does not find a place in his waking thoughts, to the *wish* to be dirty and untidy, which is stamped out through rigid suppression in our culture. Inhibition will be used to mean the blocking of impulses from *motor* expression. In inhibition there is a restraint of the impulses such that it does not find expression in behavior. One may repress his curiosity and inhibit making an inquiry concerning a person's health, or rummaging through a person's correspondence or the drawers of his desk. One may repress his tendency to love and inhibit meeting a person with cordial greeting and expressions of affection. One may repress his tendency to anger and inhibit the blow.

It will be seen that there is a close connection between repression and inhibition. In general they are parallel, but they do not necessarily coincide. It is possible, for instance, to inhibit behavior without repressing the corresponding mental process. One may withhold the blow, yet at the same time feel hatred toward an enemy. It is possible to withhold terms of endearment and expressions of affection and yet feel a strong love toward another person. It is possible, on the other hand, for tendencies to express themselves in behavior without parallel recognition in consciousness. For instance, little slips of the tongue or boisterous laughter at the ridiculous plight of a rival may betray the unconscious process which would be stoutly denied in thought and conversation. It is to these instances, where the meaning or intent of an expressed action is withheld from consciousness, that the term *repression* applies with particular force. By and large, however, the exclusion of a thought from consciousness by repression is paralleled by a corresponding inhibition in behavior and vice versa. Much of the understanding of the unconscious is gained through the medium of language; consequently the repression of the mental process, which reveals itself verbally, yields more complete and adequate knowledge of unconscious processes than does the inhibition of behavior, which is not verbally expressed.

The distinction between repression and inhibition, however, is not always as sharp as it has been made in the foregoing paragraphs. Thoughts and feelings are closely related to wishes and have their impulsive and driving components out of which behavior springs. There is a point at which the impulse is translated into behavior, at which repression and inhibition come together. When one says, for instance, that he represses a wish and inhibits the activity which would fulfil it, one is referring to one and the same process.

Repression and forgetting. In a recent study Gould [5] proposes to make a distinction between repression and forgetting. This distinction, however, is very difficult to carry through. It is well known that much of what is supposedly forgotten can be recalled under appropriate conditions so that much of forgetting is really repression. One could generalize and hypothecate that all forgetting is a process of repression, or to put it more forcibly, all forgetting is intentional (at least, unconsciously).

[5] Rosalind Gould, "Repression Experimentally Analyzed," *Character and Personality*, 10 (1942), 259–288.

This, however, would be impossible to demonstrate because it is in the nature of a universal negative. There is no doubt but that forgetting in part is an erasure of traces of experience in the nervous system which takes place with the passage of time. Light and transient experiences are quickly forgotten. Even intense experiences become less vivid with the passing of time. One could hardly deny that the manifold impressions of sight and sound, experienced in a long automobile ride, do not become permanent impressions in the nervous system. On the other hand, a considerable amount of what is usually thought of as forgetting is actually erased by a process of repression, as may be demonstrated by the vast amount of earlier experiences that can be recalled through the process of free association or by means of hypnotism.

A number of studies have shown a relation between forgetting and the nature of the material forgotten, giving additional evidence that there are dynamic factors in forgetting. Some years ago Lewin and Zeigarnik [6] demonstrated experimentally that completed tasks were forgotten more quickly than incompleted tasks. They also showed that it was the non-completion rather than the interruption, because tasks with a sharply defined terminus were remembered better than tasks which had no definite point of termination. More recently, Gould [7] has found that tasks, accepted by the individual as his own, were remembered better than tasks which he rejected. And Rosenzweig [8] has generalized that all these experiments were carried out with tasks and under conditions in which the need was to please the examiner (need-persistence tasks, he calls them). When the task is one the completion of which is especially important for the prestige of the individual (as in an examination—called "ego-defense tasks") Rosenzweig found that finished tasks were remembered better than unfinished ones. Gould [9] mentions three types of repression. In *direct* repression the traumatic incident itself is forgotten. In *substitute* repression there is a forgetting of events related to the traumatic event which itself is not forgotten. In *incidental* repression there is a forgetting of items and material temporally but not significantly related to the source of the anxiety.

Distinction between suppression and repression. Suppression is used when a second person restrains the activity of another. We say, for instance, that a mother attempts to suppress obstinacy in her child. Repression, however, takes place without such an overt and open act of

[6] Kurt Lewin and Bluma Zeigarnik, "Untersuchungen zur Handlungs und Affektpsychologie, III: Das Behaltenerledigter und unerledigter Handlungen," *Psychologische Forschung*, 9 (1927), 1–85.

[7] Rosalind Gould, op. cit.

[8] Saul Rosenzweig, "An Experimental Study of 'Repression' with Special Reference to Need—Persistence and Ego-defensive Reactions to Frustration," *Journal of Experimental Psychology*, 32 (1943), 67–74.

[9] Rosalind Gould, op. cit.

control. When a child, for instance, comes into a room filled with attractive toys and stands with his hands behind his back, the chances
are that he has not surveyed the situation and then made a conscious
decision that he should not touch what he sees. Actually, of course, the
process of repression has been initiated before, and now it occurs as
a more or less automatic response to a situation in which it would have
been dangerous for him to play spontaneously with the toys because he
then would have been soundly punished or criticized. There appears
in this distinction between repression and suppression another kind of
unconscious. It is spoken of as the *unconscious ego* and is the repressing force, rather than the impulse which is repressed. These two kinds
of unconscious will be discussed again later.

Motivation of repression. *Pain.* Repression is motivated by pain. Anything that causes pain is avoided. Behavior which in the past has led to
pain is inhibited, and painful ideas may be excluded from consciousness.
Pain, however, is used here in a very general sense. The process of repression would be more clearly described by saying that whatever is
unpleasant may be repressed.

Anxiety. One kind of discomfort which is closely related to repression
is anxiety. Freud in his latest statement has said that anxiety is one of
the kinds of pain leading to and causing repression. He earlier theorized
that anxiety was one of the outcomes of repression, principally because,
in his experience, anxiety frequently accompanied repression, and when
the repression was dissolved the aroused anxiety disappeared too.
His latest theory, however, rings truer to observation and fits in more
consistently with the general theory of the motivation of repression.
Anxiety, instead of following repression, precedes it. Anxiety, which, in
a sense, is a painful reaction to the disturbing and the unpleasant, may
be followed by repression. Repression, by holding in check unacceptable
impulses, eliminates anxiety about them. If repression is not complete
and water-tight, anxiety may still persist, so that the presence of anxiety
is a good indication that repression is incomplete or is threatened.

The simplest anxiety which causes repression arises from the fear of
being hurt. As has been expounded in previous chapters, this fear of
being hurt is interpreted by the child as fear of punishment, since he
tends to place a personal interpretation on any threat to him. Fear of
criticism, to which most persons are extremely sensitive, makes its appearance as a person develops a fear of being snubbed, neglected, or
ostracized. One may generalize and say that any drive endangering another drive or feeling may be repressed. As the fears of punishment and
retaliation from the outside become introjected, they give rise to the
fears of conscience. It is well known that we repress many of our activities because of our own inner standards and prohibitions as well as those
which come from the outside. Aggression, as mentioned many times in

this book, is an impulse which arouses such intense anxiety that it is particularly subject to repression.

Threat to the Personality. One may go a step further with Horney [10] to say that whatever is a threat to the success, recognition and security of personality, particularly those forces and tendencies and drives within that might undermine it, may be repressed. This formula would seem to be the most helpful of any in arriving at an understanding of how repression is motivated. In this connection Dan Adler found that 16 per cent of activities involved in selfish choices were not recalled in his experiment on repression; whereas only 4 per cent of activities involved in generous choices were not recalled, indicating a more severe repression of activities socially condemned.

Mr. R. is a gentleman who is liked by everyone in his community because of his forbearance, courtesy, thoughtfulness, and fairness. These characteristics represent an almost complete inhibition, at least in social relationships, of tendencies toward taking advantage of another person and outdoing another person in a business deal. The origin of these tendencies can be traced back to early childhood when Mr. R.'s mother and father would show their displeasure when he showed normal masculine aggressiveness. They were horrified when he came home with a bloody nose after a fight and made him feel that to be self-effacing was good and to assert oneself against another person was bad. Now when Mr. R. opposes another person as, of course, he is forced to do on occasion, he feels as though he had committed some sin, and a sense of unworthiness comes over him.

FEAR OF FAILURE. A particularly serious threat to the personality is the fear of failure. In some cases fear of failure serves as a challenge and spur to heightened activity, but in other instances fear of failure leads directly to repression. The individual does not dare to attempt something he might fail because the failure would be such a threat to his personal integrity and esteem. This fear of failure in every case has its origin in the high expectations held for the individual, probably when a child, by others. These high standards have been accepted by the individual as his own in later years. The writer once challenged a gentleman to a simple game of ping-pong. Although it was evident that he would have liked to play very much, he finally refused, and it was obvious that he could not expose himself to a possible defeat. It seems incredible that defeat in such an inconsequential activity as ping-pong should constitute a threat to a person's self-esteem, but such was the case.

To Escape Desire. Sometimes repression is used to escape desire. As persons get older and life denies them vital experiences, they may repress their earlier desires and become cold, unresponsive, and unemotional. The characteristic drabness and unexpressiveness of persons in middle life as contrasted with that of adolescence may often be due not so much

[10] Karen Horney, *New Ways in Psychoanalysis* (New York: W. W. Norton & Company, Inc., 1939).

to the aging process as to the repression of disappointed and unfulfilled desires. As a matter of fact, repression of incestuous impulses toward parents and other members of the family helps to establish a personality pattern of reserve in human relationships that is universal in our culture.

Repression Caused by Overprotection. Repression may also be caused by early learning as a result of overprotection by the parents. A mother whose anxiety causes her to surround a child by restrictions and who waits on the child and does things which the child ought to be learning to do for himself is making the child ineffectual and helpless in many situations. Such a child is more than ordinarily liable to meet difficulties by withdrawal and to repress his normal adventuresomeness.

The process of repression. Repression may grow directly out of experience. We may repress that which causes us actual pain, discomfort and unpleasantness, as experience teaches us what to avoid. The child withdrawing his hand from the flame is the prototype of all later repression. Or the child who has been ridiculed for not singing in tune with the others in the chorus may withdraw altogether and repress singing activities. Not only actual painful experience, but any frustrating experience may lead to repression.

A considerable part of repression grows out of early social situations. Children are extremely sensitive to expressions of approval or disapproval by their parents, particularly when such disapproval is accompanied and enforced by punishment. Parents, in the first place, suppress in their children what they consider bad. Most parents will spend effort in trying to prevent their children from sucking their thumbs or masturbating. They will stop their children forcibly from breaking things, from annoying other people, and from hurting or annoying themselves. They have certain standards of behavior and manners and morals which they enforce vigorously. Parents also strive to keep their children clean and to teach them to keep themselves clean. This applies with particular force to the toilet processes which children are, at an early age, taught to think of as being nasty and vulgar. Children are also criticized, or even punished, for failure and disobedience, and are at an early age made to feel shame at not carrying through a task or at doing it poorly. So a child represses his thoughts and inhibits his behavior because he is afraid of punishment and because he is afraid of losing his parents' love and continued interest and protection if he offends them by his unacceptable behavior.

These early injunctions, prohibitions, and suppressions are maintained by the larger society. Children soon learn that not only their parents but also their brothers and sisters, their friends and relatives, neighbors and fellow-citizens expect them to be courteous and clean, and to refrain from annoying others, from destroying property, and from taking what does not belong to them. Eventually these prohibitions, restraints, and social requirements are accepted by the growing child, and he submits to them. They become part of this outlook on life. When he begins slowly to take responsibility for his own behavior and thought life, these prohibited matters have already been firmly thrust out of mind. Eventually an individual resorts to repression as one method of protecting himself against disturbing conflicts or the possibility of conflict. He represses thoughts and actions because they have come to seem bad to him. The English school of psychoanalysis does not wholly subscribe to this view, but believes that there is an internal dynamics which accounts for repression phenomena. According to members of this group, repression arises not only from behavioral trends which have been punished, but also from burning, scalding feelings within the child, such as would occur in screaming fits and other strong emotional responses to frustration. Whether such intense inner feelings ever arise apart from external punishment or from frustrations which are interpreted as punishments by the child is a debatable question.

What may be repressed. There is an unreality about repression and the unconscious for the ordinary person which makes it very difficult to render them plausible through reading. If a person has repressed certain fantasies or feelings, and he is unconscious of them, naturally he does not know about them. If in addition there are things which seem bad or ignoble to him and about which he would feel shame or guilt, he not only does not know about them but moreover would resist knowing about them and would resent believing them true about himself. It is for this reason that much of psychoanalytic theory becomes repulsive, absurd, and implausible to the ordinary reader. These theories may have a certain attractiveness because they arouse a reverberation from the unconscious within, and yet since they are unconscious, most persons would find it difficult to believe that these repressions could possibly apply to them.

One may repress things that one may do either in act, in thought, or in fantasy. For instance, one may repress a tendency to ask questions or to think ignoble thoughts, or to fantasy how pleasant it would be to wallow in dirt. Little Margaret in the motion picture, *Journey for Margaret*, repressed her desire to cry. Sometimes children do not dare to cry because they fear they will be thought to be afraid. It is not going to be possible to enumerate here the variety of things that may be repressed. The inventory would be as miscellaneous as acts, thoughts, and fantasies themselves.

However, there are certain important tendencies which are so universally repressed and which are the basis of neurotic disturbances that these will be specifically mentioned.

Repression of Sexual Expression. It is possible to repress tendencies to

Same emotions affected in repressions

sexual behavior and love. It is well known that in certain individuals sex is very much repressed. Talk about platonic love is common enough because many persons find it painful, disgusting, and unpleasant to consider anything which pertains to sex. While this is true to a pronounced degree for certain exceptional persons, it is also true to a degree of every one in our culture. It is well known that sex is not a subject for general conversation, and expressions of sex are not for public display. The degree to which sex is repressed may also be seen in the degree of fear, shame, and disgust which accompanies much sexual behavior. Even the person who is normally adjusted sexually finds perverted sexual practices difficult to accept. In a slightly different but not unrelated category, expressions of love are frequently repressed. It is considered bad taste, for instance, to make too public a display of affection. Indeed, ordinary relationships, both business and social, are characterized by a marked restraint and objectivity and coldness, all of which represents the repression of the normal erotic forms of expression that might characterize intercourse between human beings.

Repression of Aggression. In like manner, expression of aggression and of hate are, to a very considerable degree, repressed in human affairs. Parents not only take great pains to repress all open expression of erotic impulses but vigorously suppress aggressive tendencies in their children which may annoy or harm themselves or others. Consequently, civilized society is characterized by a marked restraint in aggression. People have to resort to all sorts of subtle and covert means for showing their aggression through such channels as criticism, sarcasm, fault-finding, name-calling, even by ignoring others, or by innuendoes. The most deeply repressed aggression is frequently that which is directed toward other persons to whom one is closest. It is difficult for most persons to be aware of their unconscious tendencies of aggression toward father or mother, or even brother or sister. However, the first expressions of aggression were directed toward father or mother, and these were the first to be repressed —in many cases the most deeply and the most strongly repressed. It is strange that one can think of times when he felt envious of or annoyed at a brother or sister and yet can fail to recognize or admit the strength of these feelings. Almost by necessity, intense feelings of anger and hatred were originally present, and if a person does not recognize them or admit them it will have to be assumed that they are repressed.

One may go so far as to say that in our conscious and civilized relations to one another, repression of aggressive impulses is always present. In primitive society men banded together in small family or community groups, and all outsiders were considered enemies. Were it not for the repressions which an upbringing has provided us, we might all fall on each other and rend each other to pieces in the frustrations and discomforts of a subway rush.

Repression of Fantasy. Many of the fantasies of childhood are deeply repressed and show themselves only in behavior which has been altered by considerable displacement from its original form.

Partial Inhibition. A very common defense against anxiety is partial inhibition whereby through some kind of restraint or diminished activity an individual is able to protect himself against the danger of a situation and perhaps, at the same time, work out in a compromise or abbreviated form the wishes which are seeking expression. There are various ways in which this inhibition is translated into passivity and inactivity. The boy or girl whose teacher thinks of him as lazy, indifferent, inept, insufficient and as having learned the trick of passing the buck and avoiding obligations is really repressing his impulses in order to defend himself against the anxiety which their unrestrained expression would arouse. This passivity may also show itself in silence, in speaking with a low voice or in failure to participate in actual sports and games, or in backwardness in taking part in social affairs. His parents may worry because he seems to lack initiative and fails to exert himself along any constructive line. He may appear to have lost interest and ambition. An individual may show his inhibition by failure to complete some task or enterprise which has been initiated. He may become forgetful or distracted. It is difficult for parents and teachers to recognize that the languid, indifferent boy or girl is the one in whom desires are strongest but who has hidden them behind an impenetrable wall.

There are many physical methods of withdrawal and defense against anxiety. Illness can serve as a method of retreat from active concerns in life and force the person to adopt an inactive rôle. Forms of personal rigidity either in gesture or posture or in stereotyped movements or thoughts again represent methods of defense against active impulses and hence anxiety. Overt acts of aggression or of passion may be reduced to mere gestures. Tics are sometimes but not always abbreviated acts, and if they can be analyzed, they will be found to represent the miniature expressions of more forceful impulses. One finds these physical protections against danger in the form of paralyses and other physical incapacities—what was known in the First World War as shell shock. Davidson [11] reports that naval aviators in whom flying arouses anxiety develop night blindness or vertigo (as hysterical symptoms and not as malingering) as an unconscious protest against submitting themselves to danger. Sexual impotence and frigidity are still other forms of physical withdrawal and protection against the anxiety which sexual expression would arouse.

Disturbed Social Relations. Another telltale sign of the presence of

[11] S. M. Davidson, "Anxiety States Arising in Naval Personnel Afloat and Ashore," *New York State Journal of Medicine,* 42 (1942), 1654–1656.

anxiety is a disturbance in social relations. The person who withdraws from others, or the child who finds it difficult to enjoy playing with others of his own age is using this method of avoiding the risk of being disturbed in his relations with others. This may show itself in timidity and shyness or in the tendency to keep apart and enjoy solitary activities.

PHYSICAL SIGNS OF DISTURBED SOCIAL RELATIONS. There are a number of physical manifestations of disturbed social relations. Most of them are signs of sympathetic nervous discharge, such as blushing, going pale, perspiring, and increased urinary and fecal urges. There may also be motor disturbances such as trembling, rigidity, and various accessory movements in the form of useless gestures. Stammering is one physical manifestation of a disturbance in social relations.

The hermit is one who withdraws himself from the society of others. Thoreau's much admired experiment in living by himself at Walden Pond was no doubt related to a need to escape the anxiety aroused in him by his relations with others. His attitude toward paying a poll-tax indicates his extreme rebellion against authority. This interest in avoiding anxiety by withdrawal from the temptations of social contact is given religious recognition by monasteries and convents where a safe retreat from the temptations of the world is provided. This tendency is evident in the incapacity to show oneself to advantage on important occasions, or in dependence on the judgment of others.

On the mental side there are the feelings of inferiority: not being wanted, not finding the right thing to say, and general discomfort in having to perform in the presence of others.

STRIVING FOR INDEPENDENCE. Some achieve independence of others by more positive methods. For instance, a young woman will strive for independence from the family by preparing herself for some kind of work. There are cases where individuals have piled up possessions in wealth as a way of isolating themselves from others thereby achieving freedom from anxiety. Feigning stupidity is still another method of losing anxiety by decreasing social contact. There is no doubt but that individuals on occasion may simulate blindness or deafness as a way of withdrawing their social contacts and protecting themselves from anxiety, like the old woman in the folk ballad who was extremely deaf until something was said that directly concerned her or her interests.

This social withdrawal also has its narcissistic side. As a person withdraws from others he becomes more concerned with himself, and finds satisfaction of his drives and impulses by devoting himself to his own concerns rather than in sharing his experiences with others.

AGGRESSIVE WITHDRAWAL. A child may try to avoid anxiety by more positive methods of aggressive withdrawal or resistance. The negativistic child who refuses to coöperate with the wishes of parents and teachers is using this as a method of avoiding anxiety which would be aroused if he permitted himself free expression along these lines.

Secretiveness. An interesting form of defense against anxiety is secretiveness. The individual who attempts to hide his personal affairs and concerns from others is probably, in part, protecting himself from too open concern and awareness of them. There are many ways of concealing one's impulses from others. Sly and underhanded acts enable a person to give expression to his hostile impulses without letting others know their source or who is involved. A person may attempt to conceal his own thoughts and interests by questioning others.

Taboos and Scruples. Taboos and the observance of scruples form another defense against anxiety. The Methodist, who has been taught that certain forms of recreation are sinful, will set up strong scruples against dancing, card-playing, and theater-going.

Indecision. Another method of defending oneself against anxiety is by postponing decisions and thereby refusing to meet certain issues squarely. Anxieties are frequently shown by indecision in thought and action. Because of aggressive or erotic impulses to which danger is attached, the individual is caught between the desire for expression and the need for inhibition. This may result in a state of indecision in which the individual is perplexed, distraught, and unable to decide upon a clear course of action.

The need to avoid anxiety arouses resistance to seeking advice about one's personal problems because a discussion of them might be involved, although many individuals, especially those with neurotic difficulties, would benefit by talking them over with a competently trained specialist. Akin to this is the denial that one cares, and the adoption of a stolid, stony attitude toward the problems of oneself and of others. These inhibitions may lead to an actual decrease in mental activity and an interest in affairs about one and can even reach a stage of pseudo-feeble-mindedness. When the defense against anxiety goes to this length, the individual has to be taken care of by others, and mental hospitals are filled with patients whose defenses against anxiety have incapacitated them for the active pursuits of life.

Repression of Experiences. We repress not only things we do, but also things which may have been done to us either in act or in thought or in fantasy. Little children who are the recipients of sexual advances from adults usually have no memory of them.[12] They become deeply repressed. However, they may later cause personality disturbances and grievous conflicts which are difficult to manage. Likewise almost any traumatic or

---

[12] Landis (Carney Landis, and others, *Sex in Development* (New York: Paul B. Hoeber, 1940) reports that "only three individuals in the entire group (of 295 women) reported incidents of a sexual nature (before the age of five)."

painful experience of childhood is rapidly forgotten, which means it is repressed. Children seldom remember the extreme dangers encountered in early childhood, the extreme punishments which they received, the accidents which befell them. Where such memories persist, and these are not usually the really dangerous, harmful or painful experiences, it has been found that they represent screen memories which protect one from the memories of really traumatic events. Most persons have repressed their childish wishes to be seen in naked form and in fact have protected themselves against such wishes by modesty which may become excessive in the need to create resistance against the tendency.

Time sequence of repression. Enough has been said to make it evident that the important repressions and a large part of the content of the unconscious arise in earliest infancy. The beginnings of love and hate toward parents and siblings, which later are repressed, occur in the earliest years. Erotic feelings toward one's parents, as well as hatred and aggressive tendencies that are shown to them because they are rivals or competitors or because of restraints and prohibitions which the parents have exerted, receive their maximum repression at around the ages of four and five. Through the age of about five or six to the beginning of adolescence is called the "latency period," another probably cultural phenomenon. Earlier tendencies are strongly repressed during that period, and since no new libidinal tendencies are in the process of volcanic eruption, we think of children during these middle years mainly as learning the process of growing up and taking on civilized ways. Naturally, there are great individual differences in repression in this age, and many infantile tendencies, as every parent knows, are not by any means completely repressed. Adolescence is the time when new forces destroy the balance that has been achieved in the control of inner tendencies. Many adolescents manage these new and powerful forces by meeting them with increased repression. Shyness in adolescence may be interpreted as due to the repression of sexuality. Repression may take place throughout life, and everyone is continually putting aside his memory of unpleasant and unsatisfying experiences. However, repressions made in later years do not have the importance of those made earlier in life. The unconscious forces persisting from infancy are the ones which may have the greatest influence on untoward personality development and in causing pathological disturbances.

Laws relating to degree of repression. *Degree of Strength of Repression in Part a Function of Strength of Impulses Repressed.* Those impulses which are strongest are the ones which the ego must repress the most deeply in order to manage them and keep them in control. One may conclude from this that those characteristics in a person which seem to be absent from his personality are not infrequently the very ones which are strongest in him but which have necessarily had the deepest repression. According to this principle, an individual who is sweet and gentle in manners and bearing is the individual who is harboring the strongest urges toward aggression in his unconscious. The individual who is cold and forbidding in his relations to others is the one who is repressing the strongest urges to love.

The Weaker the Frustration the Greater the Probability of Repression. Putting this in the opposite fashion one may say that the stronger the frustration, other things being equal, the greater the tendency for aggression to occur as a response to it. The boy who reaches the limit of his endurance when being tormented finally turns and attacks his tormentors (unless, of course, his fear of their retaliation continues to mount also). A weak frustration may be hardly sufficient to arouse aggression, and the response to it may be more easily repressed. Actually, the extent of repression is determined by the degree of frustration, but what is repressed depends on the specific motivational factors in the individual.

The Greater the Amount of Anticipated Punishment the Stronger the Inhibition. The stronger the blow or criticism which is anticipated the stronger the tendency to inhibit. The stronger the punishment threatened the more of a deterrent it is, other things being equal, to behavior.

Counter-cathexis. Repressed drives are constantly being restimulated by the experiences of living, and consequently there is a continuous striving for expression in behavior and repetition in consciousness of repressed tendencies. For example, every day there are instances when one feels annoyed at the interference or competition of someone with whom one has to work or plan. One feels like attacking and destroying this interference, but then again there are forces inside to declare that such hostile and retaliatory impulses are bad and dangerous. To resist lunging out in full-fledged aggressive attack, the tendency to repress aggression must be constantly asserted. Likewise, the tendency to express openly erotic tendencies in one's relations with others requires constant check. It also appears true that repressed drives, representing inner needs, possess an urge to expression even when not stimulated by the experiences of living, and one recognizes the presence of these drives by general tension, restlessness, sleep disturbance, general fatigue, or by limitation of interests and a narrowing of the span of attention.

The continuous effort exerted against the normal play of basic drives may be called *counter-cathexis.* Repressed and unconscious material is excluded from expression in behavior and consciousness by living forces which have to do with the maintenance of the good opinion of others, and, in the last resort, keeping one's own good opinion of oneself. This latter, of course, is derived in final analysis from the standards that constitute the good opinion of others, particularly one's parents. Freud, in his earlier work, gave these forces the picturesque name of the "censor." He used this concept in explaining the phenomena of dreams which apparently let certain unconscious material through to expression when these resistances are relaxed during sleep.

Resistance. Counter-cathexis as a function of the ego, is quite unconscious. Counter-cathexis employed by an individual during a process of psychoanalytic treatment has been called *resistance*. Psychoanalysts have made extensive studies of the process and influence of resistance. They find that when a person is threatened with having unconscious material presented to him, he will fight it off with certain well-known methods. Every psychoanalyst knows that lateness to sessions, failure of the flow of free association material, the fertile flow of stereotyped and repetitive material, and a variety of red herrings drawn across the trail, all tend to help an individual escape the necessity of facing in awareness unconscious tendencies which the analyst brings to his attention. Repressed material actually achieves a certain independence of the ego. It cannot be voluntarily recalled. As we saw earlier, when a name is forgotten a person cannot recall it even though he very much wants to. So, although repression and resistance are functions of the ego, the process is an unconscious one, and repressed material seems to be out of reach.

Signs of Resistance. It is important for a counselor to recognize the signs of resistance as they express themselves in the counseling situation, inasmuch as a great deal of personal counseling can proceed only when the resistances which keep repressed material unconscious have been dissipated. Resistances are shown by the employment of various mechanisms such as projection and rationalization, to be described in subsequent chapters. The skilful counselor must acquaint himself with these mechanisms so as to recognize them as they are employed. One method of resistance is to appear late at a counseling session or to be absent altogether. It is not uncommon for a person to come late to his appointment after the first two or three sessions. Generally he presents such a realistic excuse that the counselor feels that it would be entirely improper to even suggest that the person was reluctant to be on time at that particular session. A pursuit of the inquiry will more times than not reveal that the lateness is an expression of resistance. Mothers frequently cancel appointments because their children have developed bad colds or for other essential reasons. Again the counselor has to take these reasons at their realistic face value, although the chances are again good that behind the reason is resistance. A break in the flow of conversation is a very trustworthy sign that repressed material has been touched, and that further discussion along these lines would prove very uncomfortable to the client. Irrelevant talk is another frequent method of showing resistance. A person will talk steadily and fluently about inconsequential affairs, perhaps unconsciously avoiding topics that have greater emotional loading and are more indirectly pertinent to his problems. Persons not infrequently take the bit in their teeth and control a counseling session by steering the topics under discussion away from their real problems. Forgetting some incident or name can readily be recognized as a resistance device. Sometimes resistance is shown by counter-attacking. When a person feels that the conversation is beginning to tread on an area to which he is sensitive, he may manage the situation by turning the conversation to the counselor, perhaps with a veiled note of criticism or depreciation. Still another method of avoiding a realistic facing of unpalatable truth about the self is to adopt a playful, light, frivolous, or jocular attitude. When a person refuses to take things seriously it is a sure sign that he is treading dangerously near something that is of most serious consequence. Suspicion helps to divert self-condemnation by projecting one's own difficulties onto the other person. These represent some of the more obvious methods of resistance which are emotionally encountered in the counseling process, but the skilful counselor must become sensitive to the manifold shades of variation in the expression of resistance.

CHARACTERISTICS OF THE UNCONSCIOUS

Unconscious not identical with what is repressed. It is true that all repressed material either in act or in thought is unconscious. However, the boundaries of the unconscious go beyond that which is repressed. We have seen in the foregoing discussion that the ego is actually unaware of the act of repression and also of the tremendous load of resistance which has to be borne daily in order to keep repressions in their place. So in addition to repressed material which makes up part of the unconscious, there is also a part of the ego that says, "Do" and "Don't" that is also unconscious. Actually, not only is forgotten and unacceptable material unconscious, but also the highest strivings and aspirations of a person, which may show themselves only in the strength of his ambitions or the zeal of his endeavor.

Unconscious is dynamic—not descriptive. As we said earlier, we are using the term *unconscious* in this chapter to mean not what has been forgotten and hence, latent and passive, but to stand for those drives and the ideational representation of them which are potentially active and which may be called out by appropriate stimuli. The unconscious is not a passive or resting state but is active—processes and movements go on in the unconscious. They may be aroused to activity by the experiences of the day but kept in the unconscious by repression. They may express themselves in disguised form, in dreams during the night, or in various disguised kinds of symptomatic behavior.

The unconscious our historical past. W. A. White has called the unconscious "our historical past." [13] Much of the unconscious is derived

[13] W. A. White, *Mechanisms of Character Formation* (New York: The Macmillan Company, 1916).

from experiences, thoughts, and fantasies going back to earliest infancy. One frequently finds that the meaning of a theme in a dream must be traced back to fantasies of early childhood even though it was called up by some experience of the previous day which stimulated it into activity. As we have already seen, these thoughts and fantasies have been pushed down into the unconscious because they are unacceptable in modern civilized life.

When an unconscious idea is brought into consciousness, it is accompanied by a painful affect. This may not be very acute, as in the case of a person to whom a rationalization is pointed out, causing him a temporary discomfort which is soon dispelled if he is well adjusted. However, most unconscious tendencies would constitute a grave threat to the personality were they to be immediately taken into consciousness. It is for this very reason that resistances are strong. They protect the individual from pain. To help a person become aware of his unconscious is to increase anxiety. This arousal of pain is a necessary part of the process of getting into touch with unconscious processes. Many persons find pain so intense that they cannot go through with psychoanalytic treatment, and their resistance may show itself in a ridiculing of the process or other form of resistance.

EVALUATION OF REPRESSION

Positive values in repression. Repression is both good and bad. On the positive side of the ledger, we may find that repression is necessary in our civilization for social progress. Civilization is based on the possibility of repressing infantile tendencies. Children naturally, before they have been trained, tend to soil themselves without restraint. Civilization, however, demands control of the excretory processes and confines them to certain times and places. Civilized homes today have their bathrooms. In like manner, in civilized life aggression must be controlled and regulated. We speak of World War II as a return to the primitive. The best qualities of personality are a result of repression. Qualities in a man that are most highly admired, and that are spoken of in his citation are built on a structure of repression. No man becomes generous, prudent, or reliable without the necessity of repressing certain fundamental infantile impulses which lead to the opposite kinds of behavior and personality. Through repression anti-social tendencies can be transformed into social tendencies. The process of sublimation by which an individual becomes socialized implies the repression of more childish traits.

The most complex mental associations are possible without the coöperation of consciousness. We recognize the value of a consciously intellectual approach to the problem of living. However, it should not be forgotten that in great discoveries and inventions the unconscious plays an important part. Art, too, is in part a product of the unconscious and only as the artist permits his unconscious to speak through his creative medium will his art possess characteristics of genius. Indeed, it is difficult to conceive of a personality whose structure depended entirely on conscious processes. Such an individual would have to find the solution to each problem as it arose and build this solution into the unconscious habit structure of his personality. The unconscious part of personality is rigid and inflexible. The person who depends entirely on unconscious control becomes an automaton, incapable of flexibility in the face of new emergencies. The presence of unconscious tendencies gives personality the uniqueness that makes it the rich and human thing it is, but deprives personality of flexibility and resilience.

Repression is a guardian of mental health. If the dissatisfactions in our experience were always presented to us in conscious awareness, life might become a hideous thing, and we would suffer untold agony. The way in which soldiers in World War I forgot their experiences was a most interesting phenomenon. H. M. Pulham, Esquire,[14] a member of the American Expeditionary Forces, on one occasion performed heroically in the front lines of the trenches under shell-fire. However, back in civilian life, he was not only extremely modest but never alluded to this experience. No one ever heard him tell in an evening's reminiscences of those terrible experiences on the battle-field. It was not that he had them in mind but preferred not to tell his listeners how ghastly his experiences were; he actually put them out of his own mind and, to a large extent, was not able to recall them. Fortunately, the coverlet of the unconscious graciously overspread these terrible memories and protected him against suffering from them. So repression helps to keep us sane. Successful repression provides freedom from anxiety.

Negative values in repression. This does not mean, however, that repression is the best way of handling the painful experiences of life. As a matter of fact, repression not only is the guardian of mental health but has dangerous potentialities for it as well. If impulses are weak and repression is adequate, mental health is safeguarded. But if impulses are strong or are put under intense stimulation, and repressive forces are not adequate to the situation, then there is danger of mental breakdown. When frustrations become severe and arouse strong conflicts, then repression may be inadequate to keep down unconscious tendencies. When there is this failure of repression or even partial failure, the result is neurotic or even psychotic behavior. Those who do not permit their aggressive impulses to find open expression as children may have difficulty in later life in establishing any sort of personal relationship except

[14] J. P. Marquand, H. M. Pulhan, Esquire (Little, Brown & Company, 1941).

on the basis of extreme dependency—a characteristic childhood attitude toward their parents.

THERAPEUTIC AND EDUCATIONAL IMPLICATIONS

Therapy. Therapy, which is the treatment of unsuccessful adjustment, cannot be described completely in terms of any simple or single process. However, there is no doubt that therapy is concerned in part, at least, with the management of unsuccessful repressions. One phase of psychotherapy is that of helping an individual to bring his unconscious tendencies into conscious awareness. This is the first meaning of the therapeutic process envisaged by Freud. He thought, somewhat too naïvely, that a neurosis could be cured merely by bringing unconscious material up into consciousness. This concept is still valid so far as it goes, but is considerably oversimplified and fails to take into account certain of the emotional and relationship phases of the process. Before repression can be uncovered, it is necessary to break through the resistances which hold repressed material in the unconscious. A large part of the work of the psychotherapist is concerned with discovering and revealing the resistances and helping the individual to be less bound by them.

The process of making the unconscious conscious is summed up under the general heading of interpretation. Interpretation which is intellectual and an ego process is the only gateway that can be employed in helping to bring to awareness unconscious feelings and tendencies and ideas. But the process of therapy is considerably more than an intellectual one and consists principally of a modification of feelings and motor tendencies.

One way of looking at the therapeutic process is that of helping the ego to be reconciled to the primitive drives. As has already been pointed out in this chapter, through pressure of parents and others, drives are often considered bad and dangerous and hence are repressed. Later these repressed tendencies may run into head-on conflict with conscious tendencies so as to disrupt the adjustments of the personality. Some reconciliation must be found between these infantile tendencies and the demands of the reality of the present situation. As this reconciliation is affected and the individual becomes aware of and is able to accept these unconscious tendencies, the reconciliation becomes not only a mental process but shows itself clearly in behavior. There is no longer the need that these processes be kept unconscious, to find expression only by devious and circuitous methods in symptomatic behavior. Consequently, one outcome of the therapeutic process is the disappearance of symptoms. The ego does not find it necessary to repress its infantile tendencies, but is able to assimilate them and make use of them in a larger integration that can find expression in adult living. As a matter of fact, when infantile processes are brought into consciousness they suffer deflation, and what may have appeared unconsciously as toweringly dangerous assumes its rightful insignificance.

This might also be thought of under another facet of maturing or growing up, for, as the unconscious impulses are released and the ego accepts them, they may be utilized for more mature adjustment. Once unconscious processes are accepted by the individual they can become assimilated into the ego. It becomes impossible again for them to take flight into the unconscious unless the individual under extreme frustration must resort to regressive methods. There is no longer a need that the personality be split into warring factions but these different tendencies become integrated into a more dynamic whole.

The process of therapy necessarily releases anxiety. Because of this there is a certain amount of danger in the therapeutic process and the psychotherapist must be in a position to handle the difficulties that arise in connection with this release of anxiety. Consequently, the psychotherapist should have the closest of contacts with his patient, at least in the early stages of the treatment, by daily sessions with him although as a general rule treatment sessions should be held as infrequently as is consonant with the management of anxiety.[15] The outcome of successful psychotherapy is an exurbance of feeling and a freedom and spontaneity of behavior which was not experienced before. This is a natural outcome of the release from repression and the consequent integration of tendencies in the personality.

Education. This discussion of the process of repression in handling painful experiences has direct educational implications. In the first place, it may be noted that children need from their parents and teachers a certain degree of firmness in order to help them to form repressions and in this way master their dangerous and unacceptable impulses. A parent who does not exercise firmness and control is not only failing to induct his children into the culture in which they are expected to take their place, but also may be permitting the growth of dangerous conflicts —giving children too much freedom leaves them at the mercy of their own harsh strivings. Children need the help that adults can give them in regulating their behavior, thoughts and feelings.

On the other hand, it is possible for parents to exert too much suppression and thereby create difficulties of another kind for their children. Many parents find it difficult to tolerate any kind of sexual or autoerotic expression or permit aggression in their children.

Mrs. F. is greatly concerned that her daughter will not grow up to be ladylike and gentle. She is much exercised because her little girl is discourteous toward

---

[15] Franz Alexander and T. M. French. *Psychoanalytic Therapy* (New York: The Ronald Press Company, 1946).

her companions, quarrels with them, even slaps them, or throws dirt at them. She thinks of the time when her daughter will no longer be a child and may be ostracized because she has not learned to control her aggressive tendencies. Consequently, she takes great pains in suppressing any inclination in this direction and in teaching her daughter that she must not show aggression in any form.

Parents who inhibit their children's sexual interests and curiosity too severely, or who can tolerate no form of boisterousness or initiative are placing definite handicaps on the development of their children. These children in later years may find that these strong repressions which they have assimilated may be met with equally strong desires, and the impact of them may give rise to serious conflicts and possible neurosis. Mental health requires a balance between control and freedom, and wise parents will be careful to avoid extremes in either of these directions. Children need firmness within reason, and yet parents should not be extreme in the degree to which they suppress their children's spontaneous activity.

Dramatic play in children is a sign that healthful development is being safeguarded. Some parents and teachers consider children's fanciful play as unrealistic and wasteful and that their preoccupation with fairy-tales and other fanciful stories is not helping them to meet the exigencies of real living in the modern world. However, these activities show that dangerous tendencies are working themselves off in harmless expression rather than being wholly repressed in the unconscious where they continue an indefinite number of years, and where they may erupt in time of stress when the resistances prove unequal to the occasion.

UNDERSTANDING THE UNCONSCIOUS MAY HELP IN UNDERSTANDING SOCIAL PROCESSES

It has been said that irrational, foolish, inappropriate behavior is an indication that this behavior is motivated in part by unconscious processes. Today the big problem of the age is that of social control. The secrets of nature have been wrested from her, and man has learned through technology to use the energies of nature to satisfy his needs, but he has not learned to control himself in the process, and the structure of civilization is threatened by the selfish impulses of individuals who may run amuck with the huge amount of power at their disposal. To control these tendencies one needs more thoroughgoing understanding of the unconscious and the process of repression. It is in these areas of mental life that an understanding of these dangerous tendencies in man must be found. It is through control of these unconscious processes that the hope of civilization rests.

QUESTIONS FOR DISCUSSION

1. Psychologists object to the use of the phrase "the unconscious." Why?

2. Give illustrations of conscious processes, preconscious processes, and unconscious processes.

3. Many unconscious processes are processes once conscious but now repressed. May there be other unconscious processes which are not the result of repression?

4. Distinguish between inhibition and repression.

5. It has been said that much that we call forgetting is really repression. What evidence is there for this? What causes repression? What causes the actual weakening of learning connections?

6. Freud once said that repression leads to anxiety, but later stated that anxiety leads to repression. Today it is believed that both of these are true. Explain and provide illustrations.

7. What is the relation between punishment and repression?

8. A number of signs of resistance are given in the text. Can you give others?

9. Why is the return of repressed material to consciousness frequently painful and anxiety arousing?

10. Do you believe it better for a person to go his way and let his repressions stay buried or do you recommend that a person become acquainted with his unconscious drives and processes? Justify your position.

11. Must psychotherapy always result in the release of anxiety? Why?

12. It has been stated that to consider psychotherapy mainly in terms of bringing unconscious trends to consciousness is an oversimplification of the process. In what way is this true? What other factors enter into psychotherapy besides insight into unconscious phases of the personality?

RECOMMENDED READINGS

1. FREUD, SIGMUND, *A General Introduction to Psychoanalysis* (New York: Liveright Publishing Corporation, 1920; 1935; first published in German in 1916).
2. FREUD, SIGMUND, *The Interpretation of Dreams* (New York: The Macmillan Company, 1913; 1933; third edition, 1937; first published in German in 1900).
3. GOULD, ROSALIND, "Repression Experimentally Analyzed," *Character and Personality*, 10 (1942), 259–288.
4. ISAACS, SUSAN, *Social Development in Young Children* (New York: Harcourt, Brace & Company, 1933).
5. LUNDHOLM, HELGE, "Repression and Rationalization," *British Journal of Medical Psychology*, 13 (1933), 23–50.
6. SEARS, R. R., "Functional Abnormalities of Memory with Special Reference to Amnesia," *Psychological Bulletin*, 33 (1936), 229–274.
7. SEARS, R. R., "Experimental Analyses of Psychoanalytical Phenomena," in J.McV. Hunt, editor, *Personality and the Behavior Disorders* (New York: The Ronald Press Company, 1944), Vol. I, Chap. IX, 306–322.

XI

Introjection and the Superego

DEFINITION OF THE SUPEREGO — *right & wrong*

id — drives etc

Although the superego is one of the most important concepts in all of dynamic psychology, the term itself is one of the most awkward and inexpressive. It superseded an earlier term, *ego ideal* and was supplied by Freud,[1] who thought of the superego as developing out of the ego, forming a sort of superstructure to it. In his formulation, the superego was out of the reach of the ego and yet had an intimate relation to it. Freud thought of the superego as establishing itself around the age of five or six. However, later work with children indicates that the superego has its beginnings long before the age of five or six, making its appearance in the first year of life, and actually preceding the ego in its development.

Efforts to find a more descriptive term to take the place of superego have not been fruitful. "Internalized parents" or "internalized objects" may be more descriptive, but they are also more awkward phrases requiring considerable explanation. It seems unfortunate that our language is inadequate to express this important concept which has implications over a wide range of human affairs.

Superego may be defined as those thoughts, feelings, attitudes, and behavioral tendencies of an individual taken over from the parents or other persons occupying a parental rôle and made his own. Superego is to be distinguished from thoughts and feelings and behavior that develop as a result of learning from experience. One illustration of the superego would be the tendency of a child to refrain from looking in the closet where he knows the Christmas presents are kept because his parents have said that this closet must not be opened before Christmas. At first his response is to his parents' suggestion; later, however, he takes this suggestion as his own, and entering into the spirit of the festival, he refrains voluntarily from investigating what is in the closet. Another illustration of the superego is the child who feels that he is bad when he has done something which his parents have told him he should not do.

---

[1] Sigmund Freud, *The Ego and the Id*, International Psychoanalytical Library, No. 12 (London: The Hogarth Press, 1927; first published in German, 1923).

On previous occasions his parents have called him bad when he has taken a toy away from his little sister. Now when he has teased his sister he has been observed to say to himself, "Sammy is a bad boy." A third illustration is the child who may take as his own the ambition to get a perfect paper in arithmetic, which his parents have set for him. At first this is the parents' wish; later perhaps, the child may make this wish his own desire. In all of these illustrations the child has taken on as his own prohibitions, feelings, attitudes, ambitions which were originally those adopted for him by his parents.

MOTIVATION OF SUPEREGO

Ambivalence toward parents. Superego is motivated by the conflict in the feelings of a child toward his parents. A child is frustrated in satisfying some drive and shows aggression. This aggression provokes retaliation and punishment from the parents. The parents' punishment in turn provokes hate and hostility in the child toward the parents, but the child fears the consequences of his hostility if he openly rebels. He is afraid, in the first place that if he annoys the parents too greatly the parents will turn away from him, will desert him and leave him without a way of satisfying his inner needs. He is also afraid that his parents will show counter-hostility and revenge and will probably add punishment. If the child did not feel afraid of the consequences of his own hatred, he might pass by his parents' admonitions and prohibitions without responding to them, but he knows that his parents' will is stronger, and that if he does not fall into line greater dangers may still await him. For instance, the parents might punish him still further, might ridicule him, send him away, or use any of the devices that parents have at hand in order to control and discipline their children. Acceding to the parents' wishes may be the line of least resistance. One may go a step further and say that hostility toward the parent is a necessary condition for the formation of the superego. By conforming to his parents' wishes the child assures himself of their approval.

Many persons may find it difficult to believe that children will adopt as their own their parents' wishes only through fear, but this seems to be the primary motivation. At a somewhat later age, rivalry with the parents comes in as the little child feels strivings toward growing up and becoming a match in prowess for his elders, but because at the same time he fears the overpowering strength of his parents, he satisfies these strivings by acceding to their demands.

The superego would not be formed, however, if hostility to the parents alone were present. It is because the loss of the parents is so greatly feared, the parents who supply food and comfort and security, that the child bends himself to his parents' wishes and desires. The child's love for his parents, in the first place, is a selfish love; he likes them for what they give him, and he fears the loss of these comforts and the security of their love. It is for this reason that he does not dare to oppose them too strongly and finds it necessary to bring himself into harmony with them.

Introjection—an adjustment of the superego conflict. The process by which a child accedes to his parents' wishes, by taking into himself either their prohibitions or their ideals and ambitions, is known as *introjection*. Introjection may be defined as the taking for one's own the feelings, attitudes, standards, restrictions, prohibitions, even physical gestures and characteristics of parents or parental figures. Introjection is a process by which these reactions and tendencies to reaction are incorporated by the individual into his own stock of mental and behavioral tendencies. Psychoanalysts have often dramatized this by speaking of the process as one of incorporating the parents by taking them into oneself. Superego refers primarily to the negative tendencies of denying or restraining oneself. In general, there are two types of tendencies which are to be restrained. The first is the inhibition of sadism or hostility and aggressive tendencies. The person who never says anything depreciatory about another is inhibiting his aggressive tendencies, and this behavior may have originated in childhood by following the wishes of parents. Self-restraint may also include the erotic tendencies. As is well known, sex is subject to deep inhibition in our culture, and much of this repression is due to early parental teaching that gratification along erotic lines is not acceptable.

Introjection also implies the adoption of positive ideals of kindness or helpfulness. The individual who is a Good Samaritan, who gives generously of his time and resources to others has undoubtedly picked up these tendencies by incorporating the characteristics of some person in early life whom he respected and admired, and the loss of whose love he fears.

In a more general sense, introjection may refer to the tendency to incorporate the environment into ourselves, or to put it differently, to widen one's interests and to expand one's personality. For instance, one might feel glad and proud of persons or groups with whom he is related. A parent may feel pride in the success of his children; the youth may be proud of the achievements of his school team or the success in the Olympic meet of his country. One may also feel hurt at the criticisms leveled at some person or institution with which he is related. We may feel offended at the criticism of our work, our school, our team, our business or our family. The process by which we extend our sympathy, our pride, or our humiliation to include persons and objects outside of ourselves may be thought of as similar to incorporation or introjection. It is through these mechanisms that the personality expands. One avoids the dangers of the external world by taking the world inside oneself.

Purposes of introjection. *To Avoid Pain, Discomfort, Belittlement.*
The primary purpose of introjection is avoidance. In the first place, a
child introjects his parents' wishes or prohibitions in order to avoid punishment, that is, the pain that counter-hostility and punishment might
bring upon him if he were to refuse doing his parents' bidding. Psychoanalysts sometimes symbolize this motivation of introjection by reference to castration, which is perhaps the most dreaded and severe of all
possible punishments.

Introjection is also motivated by the desire to avoid the withdrawal
of love, good-will, and approbation. The child fears the loss of the person
he has loved, and who is so necessary for providing the satisfaction of
his basic needs. As personality develops, this fear of separation and loss
of love is shown in fear of belittlement, criticism, censure. Perhaps the
strongest driving force toward conformity is the fear of ostracism and
humiliation and the need for "saving face." A. Kardiner [2] points out
how, in some societies, customs are acquired by children not so much
from a fear of punishment as from a sense of shame if they depart from
established practice. The reader may also note that these are the factors
which are responsible for the rise of anxiety, and so we may assume that
much, if not most, anxiety is accompanied by introjection, and we shall
see later that a considerable part of this anxiety following or accompanying introjection is better known as guilt.

In addition to avoiding punishment and loss of parents' love, introjection may help a child to control his parents. Out there his parents'
demands are inexorable. But if he takes his parents' requirements and
prohibitions as his own, then he has some small measure of control over
them, for he has taken their wishes inside himself. Actually the demands
a person makes of himself may be more severe than the demands of
others: one may be far more strict and rigid with himself than his parents
ever intended to be, so that the danger that he attempts to avoid by
internalizing his parents turns about and becomes a greater danger than
ever. Parents may relent, but a person's internalized objects are relentless. They never relax.

To Control Impulses. Introjection is also motivated, not so much by
fear of outer threats of harm and provocation, as by a need to control
and manage the inner surging impulses which make one liable to dangers
from without, that is, from punishment. A little child soon learns to
recognize that his own angry impulses can get him into trouble, and that
he must learn to control them. He also learns the best way of controlling
them is to fall into step with his parents instead of opposing them and

[2] Abram Kardiner, *The Individual and His Society* (New York: Columbia University Press, 1939), 74.

allowing his angry feelings to get the upper hand. Superego in an adult may show itself as guilt or feelings of inferiority, and these serve as signals of danger from these infantile aggressive or erotic impulses.

To Provide Substitute for Person Who Is Lost. Introjection may also be motivated through a desire to provide a substitute for the person who is lost, in fantasy, as a result of the child's hostile impulses and bad feelings. A child feels hostile toward his parent who wishes to block him in some gratification. Or he may wish something which would be injurious to his health or would be inconvenient to his elders, and momentarily a hot anger arises. The child desires to rid himself of the parent, so that he may have his way in reaching the desired pleasure. Immediately, however, he also feels the possible loss of the parent whom he would like to get rid of, and there is, at the same time, a wish to have back the parent who a moment before was in the way of his desire. So introjection is an attempt to stabilize the outer environment by taking it inside the self, where he may always depend upon it. A child may wish to compensate for the love which he both needs and receives from his parents, but which in his fantasy he gives up as lost. He does this by taking into himself the things that his parents stand for and by concurring with his parents' wishes. So we find that the love of his parents is taken into himself and becomes self-love or narcissism. He feels satisfied with himself for doing the things that his parents wish him to do. A great deal of self-satisfaction in life grows out of this early tendency of fitting oneself into the plans and desires of others and perhaps being called a good boy or girl for so doing.

To Bolster One's Weaknesses. Along this same line, introjection also helps a child to bolster up his own weakness and to maintain his earlier feeling of omnipotence. To the very young infant the whole world belongs to him. At a cry his parents run to his aid, and he is master of them all. As he matures and finds that he is a separate person, and a helpless one, he may attempt to perpetuate this feeling of omnipotence by aligning himself with those who are stronger and more powerful than he. By doing his parents' bidding he partakes of a measure of their strength. As one takes on the strength of others he is helped to hide his own weaknesses. Infantile omnipotence at first is maintained by merely wishing it or crying for it. Then it is maintained by incorporating the parents through introjection. Later, however, this process is further expanded, and one looks for support by acceding to the wishes of society through its laws and customs, so that one feels secure as a member of the group and derives power from the group. A still further development is to align oneself with the universe and to look to God for strength. So the religious person, by obeying the rules of morality, is continuing this process of gaining strength for himself by aligning himself with superior forces. In a somewhat different sense the child, by submitting and acquiescing, may buy himself from obligation externally imposed and secure the right to be left alone. A "good" child thus becomes a free and independent child, having substituted internal aims for those which may be imposed by external authority; and this is the origin of "free will."

Superego a Façade. Horney points out that the superego is not wholly genuine, but that it is a façade to impress the onlooker as well as the self. It is a front to hide underlying weakness and to bolster up one's courage and the sense of one's own importance. However, perhaps one should distinguish between the neurotic superego, which is just such a protective device against the weaknesses of infancy, and the normal superego, which more genuinely helps an individual fit into the culture of his group.

Horney [8] pictures three distinct parental attitudes that may help to create different types of superego: righteous parents who exact obedience because of their standards of right and wrong, self-sacrificing parents who make demands of the child in payment, and ambitious parents who require the child to fulfil his own unfulfilled ambitions.

This mechanism of introjection can be translated into psychological terms. In its simplest form it may be thought of as a process of conditioning. The wrong deed may be thought of as the conditioned stimulus —the signal; the parents' admonition is the unconditioned stimulus. The response to the parents' admonition is refraining from the wrong deed. Later this response is shifted from the parents' admonition directly to the wrong deed, itself, which is immediately responded to by refraining from it. There is a short-circuiting, and the temptation to commit the prohibited act is blocked internally without the necessity of the parents' warning.

In introjection a child gives up part of himself. Introjection may be thought of as an act by which the child gives up a part of himself, that is, his wishes and desires, in order to retain his parents' love by the act of acceding to their demands and prohibitions. In this sense, it is an economic transaction; the desires are given up as payment for the parents' love. It is a common observation that individuals grow more moral in adversity, whereas they give freer rein to their impulses in fair weather. This observation fits in with the general thesis here propounded. At all stages of life, control of impulses is learned through fear of some greater privation and harm. On the other hand, while it is true that a child gives up part of himself in the process of introjection, he also takes into himself his parents' wishes, and it is by this process of accretion that his personality grows.

[8] Karen Horney, *New Ways in Psychoanalysis* (New York: W. W. Norton & Company, Inc., 1939), 216 ff.

PRIMITIVE STATES AND PROCESSES OUT OF WHICH SUPEREGO GROWS

At the beginning of life the self and the world are not differentiated; before birth the child is actually a part of his mother. Although the process of birth rudely interrupts this relationship, separation is far from being complete, and so far as reactions go, the child is still very much a part of his mother for a long time. It is only gradually, after some weeks, that a child vaguely senses his parents as not being part of himself. At first his mother is mainly a breast, and it is at the breast that this close intimacy is felt. The father at the beginning is mainly a voice, and a deep and powerful voice at that. It is interesting that the superego in later life is largely in terms of auditory imagery. We speak of the "still, small voice," and recognize that the prohibitions and restraints imposed in infancy come primarily through the medium of the voice. Early in life the child is sensitive to the watchful eyes of his parents, who observe him in what he does and notice him when he does things which please or displease them. This watchfulness is also an important part of the superego and later is felt as self-criticism or self-observation—one part of the self critically observing another part. This is undoubtedly the origin of introspection—we can observe ourselves as we have been observed and studied by others. Introjected processes, which are of the nature of thoughts, ideals, wishes, restraints, and fears, come more through auditory sources. Introjections which tend to be acted out seem to be derived more deeply from visual sources. A boy patterns his behavior after what he sees primarily, as well as what he hears. It is well known that training is more effective when a good model is set for a child to copy than when he is told what he should do.

This differentiation between the self and the not-self is a slow growth. The younger the child, the more complete the introjection that seems to involve his total self. In later life the superego may be more highly differentiated. One attitude may be derived from a teacher, another from a book, and so our ideals and scruples are built up from varied experiences; but the first superego development tends to be a more all-embracing affair.

A child frequently learns that which the parents hold secret more thoroughly than that which is openly censured or prohibited. The mystery of secrecy adds to its importance in the child's mind and may give rise to greater fantasy production than that which is talked over in the open. It is for this reason, in part, that greater repression arises over sex than over other topics more openly discussed. What the parent refuses to talk about the child represses from his thoughts.

BEHAVIOR, THOUGHTS AND FEELINGS INTROJECTED

Neutral. Some of the parental attitudes introjected seem to be of a fairly neutral character, so they may pertain to both the positive and negative. The parents' tendency to watch the child, which he later takes in as self-scrutiny, may be of either a positive or a negative character. The parents may encourage the child either positively or negatively by suggestion, by persuasion, by example in their own behavior or by promises.

Balint [4] has even suggested that all learning is a form of introjection, and this is reasonable. So many times it is necessary to "digest" a new idea before one is on friendly terms with it, almost as though it originally had a threatening and hostile aspect. Indeed, the unknown often is thought of as threatening and hostile, and many scholars are driven in their pursuit by an attempt to master their surroundings by understanding and hence controlling them, and thus reduce anxiety about them.

Negative. It is a characteristic of introjection that the person introjected may be split into a bad or a good component. In most of the discussions of the superego in psychoanalytical literature, the negative aspects are emphasized, because they are the first ones to appear, inasmuch as they are the closest to the fundamental motivation of anxiety. First one should mention the prohibitions and restraints exercised by the parent which the child takes into himself. Next the child tends to introject the tendency for punishment and the need for punishment after he has committed a wrong act. He feels that his parents will punish him and that he will deserve it, and later he will take into himself this same feeling of the receiving of punishment and his need for it. This refers not only to physical punishment but to all methods of discipline whatever they may be, whether by bribery, cajolery, threats. A threat of punishment may even be more traumatic than punishment itself, and the threat of punishment in anticipation of wrong-doing in fantasy is a very important part of the superego. More derived forms of punishment, as criticism, condemnation and blame, originally given by the parents, may be introjected and become part of the superego.

Positive. On the other hand, a child may introject positive attitudes on the part of the parents (here called ego ideals) although this would seem to be a somewhat later development. The distinction between ego ideal and superego is not always found in psychoanalytical literature. Freud himself in the *Ego and the Id*, uses these two terms interchangeably. They are used here, however, with a clear-cut distinction. Both are

4 Alice Balint, "Identification," *International Journal of Psychoanalysis,* 24 (1943), 97–107.

introjected or assimilated systems. Ego ideal refers to positive standards, ideals, and ambitions. Superego, on the other hand, refers to inhibitory forces, prohibitions, restraints, scruples, and the like. Both of these aspects of the personality have their origins in the instructions, admonitions, encouragements, and restraints exercised on an individual by his parents or those close to him in his early years. A boy's mother can talk to him about the kind of man she wants him to be and form in him ideals and aspirations which he later takes as his own (ego ideal). A boy's father may threaten him with punishment if he damages property and fails to live up to the moral code, and later the boy is found to have accepted these rules and restraints as his own (superego). (This differentiation is not made by Freud.) He may introject his parents' ideals, the positive standards of thought and behavior for which they stand, their attitudes, their religion, politics, and social standards. A child may introject his parents' ambitions, their strivings, the things that they hold most valuable and worthwhile in life, and take these same values and react to them by striving. As a child tends to introject the need for punishment following a wrong-doing, so he may also introject the need for reward in the tendency to seek reward as the result of conforming to his parents' ideals and standards. Little has been written in psychoanalytic literature on this need for reward, but undoubtedly it is as powerful a tendency as its opposite—the need for punishment.

NATURE OF THE SUPEREGO

Negative superego. The negative superego, which grows out of parental restrictions, prohibitions, threats, and punishments, may be simply defined as *conscience.* In psychoanalytic literature when superego is referred to, its usual reference is to the negative superego and should be so understood, unless otherwise specifically stated. This negative aspect of the introjective process evidently has more dynamic significance than the positive. It is most simply manifested by simple inhibitions which we recognize under such headings as scruples, duty, self-restraint, and puritanism in the person who is correct, strict, rigid, ceremonious, or precise. There is a tendency for these inhibitions to spread from the first prohibitions imposed by the parents, to behavior of an analogous character as the individual builds higher defenses in the interests of maintaining his superego. So the child who is admonished by his mother not to be rude to the visiting neighbor, may generalize his response and adopt attitudes of deference and courtesy toward all persons. One mother taught her daughter the importance of self-control, and the child did not dare to express her feelings openly so that they could be observed by others—it was indecent to let oneself go and cry. These inhibitions may actually spread so as to result in loss of interest, apathy, and idleness. The child in school who is described as being lazy or lacking in interest may be suffering from an overdose of superego following on the heels of an overstrict parental supervision. The mother may have her way in directing the child's behavior in accord with her wishes but does not bargain with the possibility that the restrictions which she sets up may spread to cover more territory than she intended to include. As the superego becomes strong, so the ego may become weak, impotent, submissive, and lacking in assertiveness and daring.

Superego also shows itself in loss of self-respect and in feelings of inferiority and inadequacy. This is definitely a phenomenon of introjection. Just as the parents may make the child feel that he is the scum of the earth, a worthless and good-for-nothing wretch, so the individual may take such attitudes into himself and think of himself in similar terms. Parents who use such harsh and negative methods in the name of discipline, fail to realize that sharp words reach their target with greater penetration than they anticipated, and that these expressed attitudes help a child form his own attitudes with regard to himself. Anticipation of these prohibitions, threats, and punishments, and the anxiety accompanying them lead to guilt, another superego phenomenon more completely discussed in a later chapter. Finally, by the very process of introjection the individual turns the aggression originally directed toward others onto himself and feels the need or the inevitability of punishment, a concept that will also be further elaborated.

Positive superego—ego ideals—ideals and ambitions. As we have already seen, parents can express positive and good ideals and wishes to their children as well as the negative and bad. When a child takes these parental attitudes concerning him as his own, they help to build the more positive side of his character. The parents take the place of the narcissistic perfection and power with which the child once viewed himself. Ego ideal, therefore, grows out of desire and love but may also result from envy and rivalry with the parents. Ego ideal comes later than the superego. It is a part of personality that develops on into childhood. As a matter of fact, whereas the superego is never lacking, inasmuch as every child must suffer restrictions of one sort or another, the ego ideal may be only partially developed. As the ego ideal develops, there springs up a secondary self-love or pleasure and satisfaction with the self, to the extent that a child makes as his own his parents' wishes, ideals, and ambitions. He feels pleased or satisfied with himself, and a glow of self-esteem rises.

Arthur is asked by his mother to water the plants carefully without dripping water on the rug. Arthur pays close attention to what he is doing and carries out the task as directed. His mother notices how well he has done it and shows her appreciation. Arthur swells with pride and feels a glow of satisfaction. On later occasions he will exercise similar care in performing tasks, even those which he sets himself, and will feel a similar satisfaction on doing them well.

So an enlarged ego ideal may arise to take the place of his earlier natural feeling of omnipotence which may have been ruthlessly deflated. This inflated ego ideal may drive the person on to perfection of various drives, to desires to control people, and to accomplish great deeds. Sometimes these strivings work themselves out in reality. Only too often, however, they remain only in the fantasy stage, while the actual ego may avoid tasks in everyday life.

Ego ideal is motivated in part by the desire to keep the affection of the parents. The parents' praise and evident pleasure in the child is a source of pleasure to him and, as with a prized possession, he strives to keep it. In some cases the ego ideal is not in conflict with the ego. If parental wish or ambition is actually introjected and taken by the individual as his own, it becomes integrated with his personality, There are times, perhaps, when one feels obligation or call of duty against which there is considerable resistance. It may require strenuous endeavor, overcoming of fatigue, and encounter with danger, but in all of these it would seem that the ego ideal is on the side of the ego itself and opposition comes from some of the more primitive impulses and drives.

In this connection, it is interesting to stop for a moment to consider compassion or sympathy, which are tendencies to treat others as one would like to be treated by one's own ego ideal. Every person likes to feel satisfied and think well of himself, and when another is in distress or is cast down, then one can project his own feeling of wishing to cast out his negative self-regard and to take on feelings of self-assurance and self-esteem.

Discrepancy between superego and real parents. So far in this discussion, the impression has been given that the superego is a faithful representation or image of the attitudes expressed by parents toward the child. As the parents admonish, so the child admonishes himself; as the parents express their wishes toward the child, so the child takes on these same wishes as his own. Actually, however, this description is not accurate. The parents' prohibitions may become grossly distorted and perhaps exaggerated in the child's mind. A mild rebuke on the part of the parent may seem to the child to be an overwhelming threat, and, as he takes the rebuke into himself, his own self-stricture may be much more severe than his parents ever intended their mild censure to be. This is due in part to the fact that the introjected object is a product of internal states and feelings as well as outer prohibitions or restraints. In psychoanalytic literature the term "imago" is used to indicate the representation of another person in one's fantasy. The imago of a mother is the kind of person that the mother appears to be to the child. This imago may correspond closely to the real mother but also may be a gross caricature, with some mild tendencies on the part of the mother exaggerated in fantasy. The child translates his own inner feeling into the picture of the parent whom he introjects so that the introjected parent takes on the same intense emotional tone that characterizes the child's inner emotional states. It is for this reason that the superego is frequently considerably more severe than the real parent. If the correspondence between the parental punishment and the superego were exact, the child's guilt would be in proportion to the severity of the parents' punishment. As is well known, however, a child of even mild parents may have an exceptionally severe superego, that is, a strong conscience, intense feelings of inferiority, strong guilt reactions, and tendencies toward self-punishment. Indeed, not infrequently a child, one of whose parents died when he was young, will have an excessively strong superego, partly because it is based on fantasy entirely and is not subject to correction by reality, since the parent is not present in reality.

Laforgue [5] points out the possibility that in most cases a child introjects his parents' superego, that is, what they stand for, believe, and hold as their own standards and prohibitions rather than the parents' actual personalities. If a boy's father drinks but feels guilty about it afterwards and teaches the folly of drink, the boy too may drink freely, but he too will carry about with him the feeling that drinking is wrong and feel guilty after a spree. It is the father's beliefs, standards, and the things he feels proud or ashamed of rather than his actual behavior that determines the boy's superego. In this illustration there are two introjected systems in conflict with each other. One voice says, "You ought to be like your father"; the other says, "You are not permitted to do what your father does." A child may identify with his father and copy his behavior, but his superego is determined by his father's superego, that is, his standards, beliefs, acceptances and rejections.

Superego may derive from many persons. Superego springs from the relation of a child to his parents or to those who occupy the parental rôle in the first place. However, contributions to the superego may come from many other persons with whom the child is more or less closely related in his life experiences. A brother or sister who has a more or less responsible rôle in connection with the management of a child may help to form the superego. Teachers, by virtue of their rôle, also play an important part in the formation of the superego. An examiner frequently is placed in a superego rôle.

Superego may also come from institutions and even abstract concepts that influence a child's growing sense of right and wrong, his obligations and his ideals. Early in life a child begins to form a vague concept of

[5] René Laforgue, "The Mechanisms of Isolation in Neurosis and Their Relations to Schizophrenia," *International Journal of Psychoanalysis*, 10 (1929), 170–182.

what is known as society and feels the force of rules and regulations as they may be promulgated in the family, in children's play groups, in clubs and teams, in the organizations in the school, and in the laws of civil society. The threat which binds an individual to social standards is the threat of expulsion and ostracism, deriving from the original fear of losing the mother's love. A child's relation to law is distinctly a superego relationship. It is one aim of education to inculcate respect of law, and a good citizen is one who has taken into himself the willingness to abide by the laws of the country of which he is a citizen. In some primitive society this allegiance to law is first of all an allegiance to a ruler, such as a king or chief, and the obedience of the laws is obedience to the king's word. In a democratic society where laws are decided upon by a majority of representatives of the citizens, this allegiance takes on a more abstract quality. It is not so much the allegiance to a person as it is to a system, and the psychology of the citizen of a democracy is of a higher order than that of the citizen who is a subject of a king.

Even more remote and abstract is an individual's sense of loyalty to a deity. This fealty to the moral code and obeisance to God is a direct outgrowth of earlier attitudes toward one's parents and is explained by the tendency to introject the teachings of one who is stronger and wiser. In primitive religions this allegiance is to a very personal god; in more sophisticated individuals this allegiance is to moral law, or to fate, or to a sense of order in the universe. All of these systems of control within the individual, whether from the simplest taking into oneself of parental admonitions or the widest reaches of allegiance to an abstract ideal, represent the same process which we here call superego.

Harsh threats and punishment increase severity of superego. A point has been made above that the severity of the superego does not correspond with the severity of the parental restrictions and punishments. However, although the relationship is not perfect, it is true that harsh threats and punishments increase the severity of the superego. Parents who are cruel and unreasonable in their treament of a child add greatly to the child's anxiety and intensify his need to introject the parents. In such a case, the parental figure that is introjected is so terrifying that the child has difficulty in living peacefully with it and tends to project it out again onto those about him by means of rebellion, resistance, and hostility. It is common for a harsh and severe mother to complain that her son is defiant, disobedient, and incorrigible. She believes that the more she scolds and whips, the less coöperation the child shows. Actually such resistant children are suffering from intense pangs of guilt; their superegos are more powerful than those in which the discipline is of a less severe nature, and their uncoöperative behavior derives from an attempt to deal with their own anxiety. Instead of being less sensitive to their parents' wishes, their sensitivity is increased to such a high level that they have to expel it from themselves through uncoöperative behavior.

RELATION OF SUPEREGO TO EGO DEVELOPMENT

It is through introjection that a child's social personality develops, and so far from being an undesirable process, it is essential to the child's growing up to fit himself as a member of the society in which he must live. As a child accedes to parental demands, he advances from one stage to another in his development.

Later superego may become integrated with ego. In later life the individual who has had wise, sensible, and moderate parents may integrate the superego with the ego. This is the individual who recognizes the obligatory; he wants to do what is expected of him; he is a citizen who willingly obeys the laws; he does not try to extort or accept special favors. The superego plays an important rôle in the process of repression, for although it is the ego which is actually responsible for repression, what is repressed is at the behest of the superego. The superego dictates to the ego. As the superego comes into contact with reality, and hence becomes less harsh, a process of critical rejection can be substituted for the less critical repression. When parents have been reasonable in the early upbringing of a child, the later superego by no means keeps a rigid and resistant character but is open to suggestion and to reason, and in a normal individual a considerable part of early superego development is later reviewed, accepted or rejected and modified according to the dictates of reason.

The ego can delegate stable responses to the superego and thereby free itself from having to give attention to the details of living, and this permits the ego to focus attention on the more important new adjustments as they arise every day. We do not have to determine the pattern of our clothing, the composition of our breakfast food, or the construction of our automobiles. It would be unfortunate indeed if we had to decide afresh every day how we would carry on the routine of living, and it is well that these decisions have been made for us by our culture so that in much of the day's activities we can follow blind habit.

VALUES OF THE SUPEREGO

As may be seen from the foregoing discussion of the superego, it has important positive as well as negative values. In the first place it is the basis of culture, for only as the mores of a culture are passed on from one generation to another through the teachings of the parent does a culture tend to perpetuate itself. This culture is transmitted from parent to child, and usually through a process of training and without too much critical evaluation. Superego is the basis of morality. One sometimes hears laments on the decline of religion, with a fear that if the supernatural sanctions are lost, the foundations of morality will be disturbed. However, the foundations of morality do not reside in the church but rather in the family. If a nation wishes its morals to be maintained, it should look toward cultivating enduring homes. The individual whose morality is based solely on superego has a blind and not too resilient code of ethics. The mature person is one whose ego, that is, his critical faculties, have replaced his superego, that is, the uncritical adoption of the early moral values to which one is subjected.

Superego is also the basis of most individual standards and values. Political beliefs, religious affiliations, taste in art, music, and housing, the use of language, all are in reality superego formations. A man is a Democrat or Republican usually not because he has carefully reasoned out the merits of these two parties, but because his father before him was a Democrat or Republican, and he has grown up to believe that all merit and honor reside in the candidates of one party, and all infamy and dishonor belong to the other party. In the same way, by virtue of childhood experiences, one religion seems to be right, whereas other religions seem to be foolish or meaningless. These values and affiliations have a deep emotional basis, coming out of experiences in early childhood. Mature persons in these areas also criticize and refine these child-given values and standards, and hence put them on a more rational basis. However, to accomplish this degree of maturity is achieved by only a few persons, and the vast majority of individuals are dependent on superego formation for their emotional values throughout life. Superego then, is the basis of a considerable part of personality growth, and the tolerances and intolerances, acceptances and rejections of the adult are established on a superego foundation.

But the superego puts the individual in chains—the chains of his early experiences. Superego choices are not free choices, and they are not natural choices. The individual who is bound by his superego does not possess the capacity for free and elastic adaptation of which his developing reason makes him capable. Superego loyalty to a leader may deaden the critical faculties of a person, as was well evidenced by the blind devotion of the German people to the leadership of Hitler.

Superego is the basis of much mental illness. The superego and the ego may be in conflict, and this conflict gives rise to various pathological conditions. A person may have impulses to go in one direction, but the superego says "No, this is not right; it is bad, evil, dishonorable, unclean, disgusting." As these two forces war within the individual, he may be forced to adopt meaningless behavior as a pseudo-resolution of the conflict. The stricter the superego, the more intolerant it will be of satisfactions of the basic needs of man, and the sharper the conflict.

The problem of civilization, then, is that of harmonizing the controls that individuals must adopt for social living with the fundamental individual needs. As civilization grows more complex, it requires more and more repression, restriction, and restraint. Individuals must exercise greater control over longer periods of time. The machine tends to channel man's activity along repetitive and meaningless lines. There is a limit to which the individual can chain certain basic impulses in favor of the greater satisfaction of others. Must a man submit to regimentation and the attenuation of his erotic and aggressive impulses in order to produce more goods for various sensuous enjoyments?

EDUCATIONAL IMPLICATIONS

The process of superego formation raises many important questions with which education is vitally concerned. One such issue is how parents can combine the setting of restrictions and prohibitions, which is part of their duty as transmitters of the culture, with the acceptance of the individual child, which is needed by him as a basis of emotional security. A parent must tread a narrow, middle course. On the one hand, if a parent is too strict and severe in his training, the child will feel threatened, frustrated, and insecure. On the other hand, if a parent becomes too lax and fails to exercise proper care in training, the child again fails to mature and develops insecurity from another direction. The wise parent, then, must find a way of accepting his child at the same time that restrictions are set in training. This can be done by placing the emphasis on the positive aspects of training rather than on the negative and repressive. If a parent can express his belief in, as well as show his love for a child at the same time that restrictions are set, the child will grow in security as well as in the ways of society.

We have seen that harsh methods of training are destructive: they breed an overaggressive and tyrannical superego with which the child does not feel comfortable. This, as we have seen, results in feelings of inferiority on the one hand, and a tendency to project hostile feelings out onto the world, on the other.

Parents would do well to place their emphasis on the positive rather than the negative in training. Formation of the ego ideal has far greater constructive values than the building up of the negative superego. Indeed, one can safely disregard restraints and prohibitions if one has given a child positive encouragement and stimulation.

Both the aggressive and erotic impulses ought to be directed rather than repressed. Parents should feel less need to prevent their children from being disorderly or destructive or aggressive toward other children, and should place more emphasis on helping their children to channel their aggressive tendencies along constructive lines. Likewise, parents would do well if they felt less concern for children's erotic impulses, and less need to choke them off, and could turn their attention toward help ing children form wholesome social relationships, and finding pleasure in salutary and harmless ways.

Finally, the importance of consistency in training and harmony in family relationships, cannot be overemphasized. We have already stated that inconsistency and disharmony are very disruptive to the developing superego. A child tends to introject what a parent does rather than what a parent says. If a parent does one thing but preaches another, it arouses conflict in the child and tends to separate the child from the parent. If the superego is to become stable and strong—but not too strong—then family relationships should be harmonious and integrated.

QUESTIONS FOR DISCUSSION

1. In what way does the superego grow out of hostility to parents? In what way is love of parents necessary for the formation of the superego?

2. Give examples of positive superego (ego ideal). Give examples of negative superego.

3. What is the relation between superego and "free will"?

4. Explain the statement that the superego is an attempt to provide a substitute for the person who is lost. What person might be lost? Why should he be lost? What does lost mean in this connection?

5. What is conscience in terms of superego theory?

6. How is the ego ideal developed? What factors lead to the establishment of ego ideal as distinguished from the superego?

7. What happens when a person's superego is a very distorted replica of what his parents are and stand for?

8. How do men and women differ in superego development?

9. In what way may a person's mental conflicts be related to an overstrong and harsh superego? Give concrete illustrations.

10. In what way is the superego the basis of morality? What implications does this have regarding the origin of moral standards?

11. What relation is there between the superego and religion?

12. How can parents build a superego which will help a child become a member of society without at the same time undermining his emotional security and stability?

RECOMMENDED READING

1. FREUD, SIGMUND, *Group Psychology and the Analysis of the Ego,* International Psychoanalytical Library, No. 6 (London: Hogarth Press, 1922; first published in German, 1921).

2. FREUD, SIGMUND, *The Ego and the Id,* International Psychoanalytical Library, No. 12 (London: Hogarth Press, 1927; first published in German, 1923).

3. FREUD, SIGMUND, *Civilization and Its Discontents,* International Psychoanalytical Library, No. 17 (London: Hogarth Press, 1929).

4. FREUD, SIGMUND, *New Introductory Lectures in Psychoanalysis,* International

Psychoanalytical Library, No. 24 (London: Hogarth Press, 1933; New York: W. W. Norton & Company, Inc., 1933).

5. FROMM, ERICH, *Escape from Freedom* (New York: Farrar & Rinehart, Inc., 1941).

6. HORNEY, KAREN, *New Ways in Psychoanalysis* (New York: W. W. Norton & Company, Inc., 1939).

7. ISAACS, SUSAN, *Social Development in Young Children* (New York: Harcourt, Brace and Company, 1937).

8. JONES, ERNEST, "The Development of the Concept of the Superego," *Journal of Abnormal and Social Psychology* 23 (1928), 276–285.

9. MURRAY, J. M., "The Conscience During Adolescence," *Mental Hygiene*, 22 (1938), 400–408.

10. PEARSON, G. H. J., "Some Theoretical Considerations on the Formation of the Superego," *Psychoanalytic Review*, 19 (1932), 164–167.

11. STEPHEN, KAREN, "Introjection and Projection: Guilt and Rage," *British Journal of Medical Psychology*, 14 (1934), 316–331.

12. WEISS, E., "Regression and Projection in the Superego," *International Journal of Psychoanalysis*, 13 (1932), 449–478.

XII

Projection

Projection and introjection may be contrasted as mechanisms of defense against anxiety. Whereas introjection is a mode of embracing in the personality elements that are admired in other persons, projection is a mode of throwing off from the personality onto other persons or objects elements that one holds in low regard.

DEFINITION

As most commonly used, projection is the reference of impulses, thoughts, feelings, and wishes originating in the person himself to persons and objects in the outside world. Projection, in short, is taking one's own thoughts and impulses and attributing them to another person. It is the mechanism by which one is able to deny the reality of his own disagreeable thoughts and feelings, by attributing similar thoughts and feelings in fantasy to other persons.

A simple illustration of projection is shown in the person who complains that he is being snubbed by others on the street because they do not like him and will not accept him as a member of the community. The truth of the matter is that he actually is hostile toward other people and is critical of them but finds this difficult to admit to himself and so attributes to others his own coldness. Another example is the stepmother who, feeling that there may be some criticism in regard to her treatment of a stepdaughter, accuses the stepdaughter of being unkind and ungrateful.

FUNDAMENTAL CONSIDERATIONS

Projecting the bad. Almost without exception the thoughts, feelings, impulses, and wishes which are projected are bad, unworthy, dirty, or dangerous. Man is essentially self-seeking. The things that he takes into himself from the outside are the things that he admires. Those things that he despises about himself he has a tendency to put out of mind, and one method of doing this is to project these attributes onto others. It is more difficult to find illustrations in which a person projects onto others attributes of himself of which he is proud. When a member of Phi Beta Kappa congratulates an initiate on his scholastic achievement, he is projecting on him (perhaps with some unconscious envy) his own desires to make a high scholastic record; or when, after a game of tennis, the winner congratulates the loser for his skill—"It was a tough game. You made me fight for it"—he is projecting his admiration of a skill which he would like to believe he possesses in no small measure himself. And if, in addition to praising his opponent's skill, he remarks on his own bad luck, he adds a little aggressive note of disparagement. Another illustration of projection of praiseworthy attributes would be that of the father who projects his own ambitions onto his son, with whom he has identified himself. Ordinarily a person projects his hatreds, his moral delinquencies, his desires that he feels are bad and sinful, his limitations, and inadequacies.

Projecting the good. In the case of projection of worthy attributes, there is also a coincident introjection giving rise to the phenomenon of identification, as will be described in the next chapter. That and other tangible forms of self-expression can be thought of as a kind of projection. Raphael, in painting the Sistine Madonna, put on canvas a conception which at the time represented his own inner longings and which subsequently has been considered through the centuries as an expression of the highest impulses of man. As the artist projects his inner impulses into his art product, he is also identifying himself with what he has painted. As we project ourselves in various constructive activities into the world, we are at the same time making the outside world part of ourselves. In sublimation we have a kind of projection which is socially valued and accepted.

Unconscious nature of projection. The projected attributes of the self may be conscious or unconscious. As Horney suggests, projection may be nothing more than merely attributing to another person the same feelings that one has himself. I may assume that others, too, enjoy the distant view or despise treachery. The person who holds himself in high esteem may believe that others do also, but the person who despises himself may believe that he is despised by others. But projection, if unconscious, helps a person to protect himself against painful or dangerous attitudes which he may unconsciously hold about himself. To admit self-limitation is most difficult for the average person so he tends to repress hostile impulses or ignoble thoughts, refuses to admit them as representing himself and saves himself by believing that these uncomplimentary attitudes about him originate in some other person.

Motivation. Projection, therefore, is another mechanism by which a person (through his ego) protects himself against his own dangerous impulses, first, by repressing them and making them unconscious, and then by attributing them to others. Thus, he not only protects himself from

he couldn't have meant that — he isn't like that etc.

the necessity of admitting and dealing with these painful and dangerous tendencies, but by referring them out onto others, he makes it possible to attack them or run away from them as he cannot do when they
seemed to apply to himself.

For instance, a little child may have an impulse to be untidy, but because he
has already learned to be intolerant of untidiness in himself, he cannot tolerate
the recognition of his own untidy tendencies. If he sees another child tracking
mud into the classroom or putting dirty hands on the wall, or failing to wipe
the candy off his face, he may become very outspoken and critical.

In general, when one sees a person more than ordinarily critical of another it may be suspected that he is having difficulty in managing in
himself these same tendencies.

Not only can a child flee from danger by projective methods, but he
can ward off threatened attacks by this device. For instance, a child
will run to his defense and find excuses for his lapses and faults even
before the threatened scolding descends upon him. Projection, then, is
one method for getting rid of punishment.

Projection increased by fear. Murray,[1] in an interesting experiment,
has demonstrated that in a state of fear there is an enlarged tendency to
project suspicion and evil thoughts and designs onto others. When fear
has been aroused one imagines all sorts of dangers. Fantasy grows by
leaps and bounds. When it was discovered that the Germans were able
to penetrate into Norway and Holland through the treachery of the
fifth column, every other country that feared Germany in any way immediately became suspicious of fifth-column activities on the part of its
German residents.

Projection influenced by outer conditions. Recent experiments by
Rodnick and Klebanoff [2] indicate that frustration increases the tendency
to project aggression, as well as decreases the projection of self-satisfaction. This has been demonstrated in the use of the Thematic Appercep-
tion Test—a projective technique. When stories which subjects tell are
criticized, the subsequent stories contain more themes of aggression and
less superiority in the central characters.

Projection implies error in perception. Projection implies a certain
amount or kind of error in perception of the outside world. Naturally,
one cannot ascribe all illusion to projection, but it can safely be said
that all projections are in a sense a form of illusion. The real world
outside is falsified. The reality of things is distorted and reshaped in
terms of one's own needs. Insofar as one ascribes his own tendencies to
another, he incorporates a subjective element, not evident to an outside

[1] H. A. Murray, Jr., "The Effect of Fear upon Estimates of the Maliciousness of
Other Personalities," *Journal of Social Psychology,* 4 (1933), 310–329.
[2] E. H. Rodnick, and S. G. Klebanoff, "Projective Reactions to Induced Frustration
as a Measure of Social Adjustment," *Psychological Bulletin,* 39 (1942), 57, 489.

observer, into his perceptions of the external world. The frequency of projection as a mechanism testifies to the amount to which our perceptions of the real world are distorted.

Projection of drives. One may project an impulse, emotion, wish, or thought that is felt or experienced at the time. A mother who insists that her son feels very bad because he was not promoted in school probably is projecting her own feelings of frustration by attributing them to the child. Another mother complains of the vanity of her daughter while she was at the very instant applying cosmetics to herself. Grace, on learning that she was going to be promoted to the next grade said, "Now Mother will be happy." So, in general, one projects one's own immediate feelings. However, it is possible for one to project feelings in the present which actually were held long ago, perhaps even in childhood, although in such cases the early impulses will probably have been expressed in repetition on many subsequent occasions. An adult, for instance, who held toward a parent hostile feelings which were successfully repressed as a child may project these hostile feelings onto others on later occasions. The boy may feel that his teacher is his enemy because of his hostile feelings not toward her as a teacher but toward others, his parents perhaps, in his earlier development.

Following projection there is sometimes what has been called "retaliation fear." When a person has enmities or grudges toward another person, these may be really projections of the bad critical feelings which the person holds toward himself. He may go further and imagine that the other person knows that he feels this way toward him and in return will retaliate. Consequently, the person who projects hatred onto other persons is likely to imagine that the other persons feel hostile toward him even when there is no objective basis for this belief. Naturally, since the projection is wholly in the realm of fantasy, the fear of retaliation is also.

Manson is a timid child, who has been very much suppressed by a dominating mother. This has left him with unconscious feelings of hostility inwardly but outwardly with a very timid and retiring character. Manson believes the big boys in his neighborhood are "down on him." He believes that they wish to attack him and torment him. He must find his way home from school through back alleys so as to avoid them. Ascribing these hostile feelings to the other boys is, in the first place, a projection on his part, and his fears of them grow out of the strength of this fantasy. Because he actually does cringe from them, they may respond in kind by becoming overbearing and threatening toward him, so that his fears in part are based on reality as well as on projection of his own dangerous aggressive tendencies.

PROJECTION RELATIONSHIPS

The simplest kind of projection is the one just illustrated, in which a weakness in oneself is directly projected or referred to another person.

In the first place, the individual refuses to recognize the projected impulse as part of himself. This is reflected in the child who turns on his accuser, or even seeks out an accuser under the demands of a harassing conscience with "I didn't do it—you did it," or "You made me do it," or "You want to hurt me or spoil my fun." Other illustrations are: the child who is intolerant of others who cheat on examinations in school, but who has had to resist similar temptations in himself; or the child who, having the task (at school) of keeping himself orderly and in line which he does not want to face directly but prefers to do by managing the behavior of others, becomes the very efficient monitor or proctor in keeping other children orderly. The widespread hatred of Hitler may have indicated that everyone had a little of Hitler inside himself. The victim of the hatred of the mob or the lynching is accused of the very motives which reverberate in the members of the mob themselves, and the fury of the mob may be in direct ratio to their own feelings of guilt for these unconscious tendencies. In the first type of projection, the attribute is projected onto another person who is carrying out in actual behavior the tendencies which the person feels implicitly within himself.

Projection of child onto parent. It is possible for a child to project onto his parents his concept of what his parents are like. For instance, he may think of his mother as being warm, affectionate, and protective, or hostile, punitive, dangerous, and neglectful. These projections naturally arise out of actual real experiences with the parents at an early age. Some of these, having been incorporated by introjection, may then be projected onto the parent at a later age. A little boy who unconsciously hates his father because of real or fancied insults may imagine that his father is hostile to him—much more hostile, in fact, than he really is. At a later time, these projections may correspond very little with the real character of the parent, partly because the original impression or fantasies with regard to the parent have been exaggerated and partly, perhaps, because the parents themselves may have changed. This projected image of the parent, called the "imago" (see p. 215), is the fantasy concept of the parent that the child has built up and acts upon. This fantasy concept of the parents may be displaced onto other persons in later life. It will be seen from this that projections based originally on reality may become so distorted in fantasy that it is difficult to trace them back to their source.

Projection of parent onto child. Contrariwise, the parent may project himself onto his child. The mother, for instance, may project onto the child her own longings, ambitions, fears, and attribute these same feelings and qualities to the child. In interviews with parents it is common to find the parent describing certain fears of the child with regard to school or teacher, certain hatreds that the child has developed toward other persons, certain ambitions that the child possesses: to be a good scholar or a good musician. One must always suspect that these statements made by the parents may not actually represent the child's feelings but are projections of the parents onto the child. It is reasonable to assume, in the first place, that these qualities attributed to the child are really feelings and possibly attributes of the parents. Actually, one finds in many instances that parents do not know what their child is feeling and what his attitudes toward life are.

For instance, Mrs. S., who was unable to satisfy her childhood ambition of going to college, held that as a goal for her daughter, Eileen, who heard from early childhood that she was slated to go to college. Pressure was put upon the girl in elementary school and with increasing force in high school. Unfortunately Eileen did not act as desired, and the more pressure put upon her, the less interesting she found school, and the more interesting she found boys and the possibility of a career as a waitress in a local hotel. Eileen's lack of interest in school was a bitter blow to Mrs. S., who seemed once again to be thwarted in achieving her ambition through projecting herself onto her daughter.[3]

Projection of pupil onto teacher. Projection of feelings by a pupil onto his teacher illustrates another relationship in which projection is commonly used. For instance, instead of accepting blame himself for difficulties and lack of progress in school, a pupil may blame the teacher and ascribe his difficulties to her dislike for him or favoritism for the other children, whereas the teacher is in all probability most fair. Indeed, in proportion to the pupil's own guilt projections his teacher becomes dangerous and unfair. On the other hand, it is possible for the child to ascribe to his teacher wisdom, fairness, and affection, attributes representing his own standards of life, which may not really discribe his teacher at all. Such a child will approach his teacher with trust and dependence. Later he may find that he has misjudged her by depending on her. Every person projects onto another person attributes stemming from his own outlook on life, which perhaps may have to be modified in the light of real dealings with the person.

Projection of teacher onto pupil. Contrariwise, the teacher may project onto children in her class attributes which really are her own, but which she would like to see fulfilled again in her pupils. For instance, having struggled all through her own childhood to be a success in school, she may attribute the same ambition to her pupils, being attracted to those who actually are successful in achievement and irritated by those who fail. A teacher may project to children many other attributes besides success in school. She may expect them to be deceitful, tricky, inaccurate, disorderly, and the like, according to her own repressed tendencies.

[3] There is an interesting relationship in this illustration between identification and projection. One might say that Mrs. S. *identified* herself with her daughter by *projecting* onto her her own ambitions. We shall later see how other emotions, notably guilt and jealousy, can be projected onto a second person with whom one has identified oneself.

Projection of client onto counselor. A particularly important form of projection of relationship is that of the client onto a counselor or therapist. As a matter of fact, in modern therapeutic procedure the counselor expects the client to project onto him his or her main unconscious trends, thereby making it possible to bring them into the open so that the client can become aware of them and hence accept them and learn to manage them. In the counseling situation the counselor then exerts as little of his own real personality as possible, repressing his usual feelings and responses in order to meet the client's projections as objectively as possible. He behaves neither aggressively nor masochistically.

The client projects onto the counselor whatever rôle he needs to assume at the particular time. It may be love or hate, disgust, fear, distrust, need for support, shame, repentance, pride, or condemnation. For instance, a college student may ask for a loan of money, projecting onto the counselor an attribute of indulgence which for years past has been characteristic of the student's general irresponsibility. This may be one of the problems with which the student is struggling. The counselor must expect to be the recipient of these projections and try to understand them for what they are so that he can communicate his understanding at the proper time to his client. One aim of the therapeutic process is to encourage and to permit the expression of feelings that cannot be expressed to individuals in the normal course of life.

Projection of counselor onto client. The counselor is most effective when he is aware of his own tendencies toward fear, anxiety, shame and so forth, and when he does not have the need to project these tendencies onto his client. Insofar as he does find projection necessary, he forces the client to react to him as a real person rather than as a projected person, and makes it necessary for the client to respond in kind. To the extent to which the counselor is able to recognize, accept, and manage his own tendencies, he makes it possible for the client to use him in whatever way the client needs during the therapeutic hour.

Projection onto some inanimate object. An irate golf player may blame his poor drive on the bit of mud sticking to his golf club, or the basketball player may attribute his poor passing to the fact that he is playing in a pair of borrowed shoes. Watch a little child and see how he will animate objects about him by speaking of the "naughty" basin that has spilled the water or the "bad" wall that has been dirtied by his fingerprints.

Projection onto part of the body. When a child breaks some object, he may find some such excuses: "My finger slipped," "I didn't hear you coming," "I couldn't see very clearly," "My ankle turned just at that moment," any of which is calculated unconsciously to put the other person off the trail of possible intent in the damage done.

Projection onto groups, institutions and the social order. The club, team, business firm, or nation which uses dirty tactics or is unscrupulous, unfair, or grasping may indicate inhibited tendencies within the in-group. When a member of the opposing team is accused of slugging, he has taken an advantage which the accusing team would like to have taken, but which its own code of ethics inhibited. Fenichel [4] shows in detail how hatred of the Jews is a projection of disliked tendencies within the self. Some persons project their defects onto the social order and attribute to institutions, government, labor unions, the same ill-will, mistakes, lack of charity, and inefficiency which in reality represent their own outlook on life.

PHASE OF SELF PROJECTED

Bad wish-self. The most common kind of projection is that of the bad wish-self. It is possible to speak of this as the projection of the fundamental drives. In this kind of projection one's own bad and dangerous impulses are thrown off and referred to as belonging to another person. The *tu quoque* (thou also) arguments of little children may be seen as a simple variety of this projection. The little child, for instance, is criticized for having a bad temper. She immediately retaliates and says: "You have a bad temper, yourself." The person, who, after being criticized, watches the other person closely in order to find some error or slip which can be the occasion for counter-criticism is probably utilizing this mechanism of projection.

Hostility. The first type of projection of the drives would be the projection of hostility, in which a person's own impulses are thrown off and ascribed to another person. We see this in a primitive form in hating and in a less extreme form in simply not liking the other person. A boy of eight, for instance, with strong sibling rivalry may say of a brother or sister, "Isn't he greedy?" "Doesn't he leave his clothes thrown around in an untidy pile?" The person who commonly asserts that he is not liked by others, that they shun him, fail to speak to him on the street, go out of their way to avoid him, act cold and distant when they meet, is really in many cases projecting his own strong feelings of hatred. Horney [5] speaks of the "feeling of being victimized," which really results from one's unconscious tendencies to take advantage of others. Complaints that others are not helpful and do not come to one's aid, are actually disguises of an unconscious wish to defeat or surpass another person. In general, it may be stated that the more aggression one finds in others, the more he has repressed it in himself. The boy who is picked

[4] Otto Fenichel, "Psychoanalysis of Antisemitism," *American Imago*, 1 (March, 1940), 24–39.
[5] Karen Horney, *The Neurotic Personality of Our Time* (New York: W. W. Norton & Company, Inc., 1937), 245.

on by others is the one with the most repressed aggression. Attributing anger or rage to another person by, for example, pointing out the occasions on which he loses his temper, may be a form of projection. With small children these fantasies may be extreme. An adult does not readily think in terms of killing. The little child, however, does not know the full significance of this term and readily releases hostile feelings to the extent of saying, "I will kill you." However, if this has been suppressed he may project his feelings out and in fantasy believe that other persons want to kill him. The adult who believes that people about him are murderously inclined, who must carry a revolver in order to protect himself from dangerous gangsters, is in all probability, harboring similar unconscious hostile feelings himself.

Little children not only ascribe these deeply hostile feelings to others, but many simpler, unlovable or disagreeable characteristics as well. Jimmy is rude. Margaret is a tease. The tendency of children at a certain age to be tattle-tales is an illustration of this common mechanism of projection. Older persons will assert that others are attempting to humiliate them, to place them in awkward situations, to destroy their reputations, to criticize them unjustly—all projections of similar unconscious tendencies within the individual.

A common form of projection ascribes envy to another person.

Mr. B. believes that he is not getting along in his profession because his previous success had given him so much prestige that his colleagues became envious of him and have banded together to prevent him from securing the recognition and consequent advancement really due him. Actually, however, this may be a pure projection on his part of the envy which he unconsciously feels toward those about him. When he believes he is being neglected, he may really be trying to hide his own envy and possessiveness of others.

Immorality. A second type of projection of the bad wish-self has to do with ascribing to another person various kinds of dishonesty, dishonor, or immorality. A principal, who, in attempting to locate the child who has stolen a fountain pen from his desk, finds a boy who is much interested in the episode and is extremely coöperative in attempting to locate the culprit, may suspect that he has had a part to play in the stealing. Whether or not he is actually the culprit, one may suspect that this boy, who takes great interest in putting the blame on someone else, has himself had similar impulses and has projected them. The same will apply to those who are eager to criticize or help to levy harsh punishment on those who have broken the rules.

In other instances, projection of guilt onto the culprit is absent, and there is projection of guilt onto the attacker. It is as though one felt guilty at one's own aggressive tendencies and projects this guilt out onto a third person who is doing the same thing (attacking another) unconsciously recognized in oneself.

For instance, Thomas, age seven, is extremely jealous of his younger brother, Bobby, age three. On many occasions Bobby has teased and tormented him. Now we find that the mother is about to punish Bobby, who has been playing with some of his father's working materials that he is not supposed to touch. In this case Thomas becomes violently angry at his mother and goes to the defense of his brother. Actually, Thomas becomes so angry at his mother because he recognizes in her the same hostile feelings and the same wish to hurt Bobby that he has himself felt on various occasions. Now when he sees another person, his mother, about to punish Bobby, he can easily become angry at her because he is projecting onto her his guilt and need for punishment for the very feelings which he unconsciously harbors in himself.

Similarly, it is possible to accuse another person of exploiting others, of lying, of being greedy, of being unclean, and the like. Bernard Shaw has said that the chief punishment of a liar is not that he is not believed but that he cannot believe others.

Superego projection. It was mentioned earlier that the first kind of projection was that of the bad wish-self. A second kind is the superego, with one's incorporated injunctions derived from parents and others. It is possible to project onto others the very feelings and restrictions which, at an earlier time, one has introjected from others. For instance, the child who feels the necessity within himself to be strict may project strictness as a characteristic onto others. He feels a need for others to be strict because they will support his own introjected strictness. Such a child will look upon another person as being strict even when he has no intention of being so. This child will be docile, polite, very eager to follow the rules and please another person. Approaching the teacher as a person who is expected to be strict is more likely than not a projection of the child's inner need to be strict himself. Such a child has great difficulty in accepting an older person who permits a good deal of freedom. To the little child such a person represents his own bad wish-self instead of his strict super-ego, which he would like to be able to find in other people outside of himself. Insofar as other people are found to be critical, condemnatory, cynical, this may be a projection of similar tendencies within the self. The child who expects his teacher to be critical, who expects his parents to be strict and dominating, who is looking for cynicism in others, is probably projecting self-castigatory tendencies within himself onto others. Insofar as a child is expecting others to punish him, we may suspect that he is projecting onto others self-punishing tendencies within.

Robert looks upon his teachers as his enemies. He suspects that they have evil intentions directed against him. Actually, these attributes which Robert finds in his teachers are projections of his own need to be checked up and punished for his faults and misdemeanors. It is important to understand Robert. He is not the tough, hardened boy who has no sense of responsibility. Actually, he has a more severe superego than others, and his own sense of guilt drives him to see similar condemnatory attitudes in others. His own need for punishment causes him to look on others as possible tormentors and punishers.

Likewise, the person who finds others intolerant may be projecting onto others intolerant tendencies within himself. Parents sometimes project onto their children their own harsh superego and become exceedingly strict and severe with them. Mothers sometimes distort their children's outlook on sex by their own inhibitions and prudishness.

It is possible for a self-pitying person to project this pity out onto others and wish to give them the help which he feels he did not receive himself. Two quotations taken from autobiographies illustrate this point:

My mother and father did not show any signs of affection for each other or toward the children. I always wanted to be loved the way other children were. I hardly remember my mother ever kissing any of us. . . . I want help in trying to meet the urges and needs of my boys and girl in school so that they can get, before they are grown, satisfactions that I was not able to get.

I take special interest in helping children to read and still do. I am getting some of the satisfactions that I wanted when a child.

Note in this last statement that by projecting help and affection out onto her children she is thereby gaining for herself some of the satisfactions that she felt were denied her when young.

Finally, it is possible to project feelings of inferiority and worthlessness onto others. Insofar as others seem to be poor scholars, poor teachers, poor teammates; insofar as society seems to be all bad, and the institutions of society going from bad to worse, there is a possibility that the person is projecting out similar feelings of unworthiness and inferiority and inadequacy from himself onto others.

This projection of the superego is not necessarily all on the negative side. It is possible to project onto adults the image of the good and accepted self. Insofar as the child has had good and accepting parents he looks upon himself as a good person and accepts himself. Then he has the tendency to project this view of himself out onto others and tends to find others about him as good and accepting persons. Such a child expects to see a kind world about him and looks for kindness and fair treatment in others. Unfortunately, in reality he is doomed to be disappointed. There may be, therefore, some value in having a child experience both the good and the bad in his parents, so that when he comes to meet people in reality in later life, he will be able to project onto others attributes which will match the reality of the situation.

Projection of self-love. A third phase of self that may be projected is self-love. It is one of the few varieties of positive aspects of the self which may be projected. As examples one may mention the parents' projection of their self-love onto their children, so that they tend to love their children for the qualities in them which they have previously admired in themselves. The child who is loved selfishly is loved only when he is successful and adopts the qualities which his parents have admired, perhaps unconsciously, in themselves. Such a child is not loved for himself but is only loved for what he can produce. He is loved because he is beautiful and people admire him; because he is making a good school record and people speak well of him. A child who is loved selfishly is fundamentally insecure, and, because of this, often develops neurotic symptoms. Selfish love may also have a homosexual quality. A man finding it necessary to love someone who resembles himself will find these qualities most completely expressed in another man, or he may admire in his wife the feminine qualities that he sees in himself. Or a woman who previously has identified herself with her father may find the masculine qualities in herself attractive in another man whom she meets. In selfish love one is loving the other person not for his own realistic qualities but for the qualities which one finds in the other one that are projected from the self.

Projection of difficulty or failure. A person may blame another for being the cause of his failure, whereas the real cause lies within himself— his inadequate ability or skill or his inattention. A child may blame the teacher or outside activities for his inability to get along in school; failure in work may be ascribed by a person to the fact that his abilities are not appreciated by his employer or that a rival is using unfair means in order to forge ahead of him. The poor workman quarrels with his tools or the weather or just bad luck.

Self-regard a projection process. Our self-regard is in fact a kind of projection. We like to think of ourselves in terms of what we believe others think of us. But this is a projection of our attitude toward ourselves. If we believe that others think highly of us, this is in part a projection of our own high self-evaluation. But if we believe others despise us, we again are in part projecting our own self-belittlement. Of course, beliefs concerning evaluations by others are constantly subject to realistic corrections.

HOW PROJECTION IS EXPRESSED

Thoughts and fantasies. Projection is expressed most commonly in thoughts, feelings, and fantasies. A person looks about him and finds fault with people and institutions. In projecting off onto others the ignoble and dangerous characteristics which are really his, a person's thoughts and attitudes and dislike of the world are thereby concealed. Naturally, since projection is of the less desirable characteristics, these thoughts tend to be aggressive in character, concerned with hating, criticizing, and finding fault with other people. Suspicion is a very frequent expression of projection. A man may suspect that another person has hostile designs and is plotting his downfall, or a woman may imagine that a man has been attracted to her and is about to make amorous approaches.

Parker sees things through dark-colored glasses. He is certain that he has been given the poorest teacher in his building. He continually finds fault with her, insists that she assigns too much homework and that she does not make things clear, that she picks on him. Parker also finds fault with the Boy Scouts. They do not meet on time. They do not take enough camping trips. They are not strict enough about passing the tests for the various classes in Scouting. Parker also finds things to criticize about his Sunday school. He is sure that they have more fun in the Presbyterian church across the tracks. There they have plays and parties and, in the summer time, picnics. Parker is always looking at what the other fellow is doing and bemoaning his own lot in life. One may suspect that Parker is projecting onto the people with whom he works and plays his own feelings of inadequacy.

Open aggression. Projection can be expressed, however, in open aggression. Isaacs,[6] following Freud, speaks of projected guilt. "When children call other people 'dirty' or 'horrid' or when, for example, Harold says sententiously, 'I don't like big boys to tease little ones,' or Paul tells Mrs. I. he is very ashamed of her because she has been cross with him when he teased Dan, he was himself really very guilty about having teased Dan." This open aggression by which children try to project their bad wish-selves off onto others may be in the form of bodily attacks or in the less obvious but equally telling habit of calling names. Sometimes projection is accomplished by urging another person to do what the person wishes to do himself. A child, for instance, may entice another child to destroy school property, to write a derogatory note to the teacher, or to play the Hallowe'en prank, something he may not dare to do himself. Placing blame on another person is a telling method of projecting one's own guilt. Then there are a number of more subtle methods, for example, pouring scorn or contempt or ridicule on another person either directly or by innuendoes. Persecution and intolerance may be thought of as forms of projection. When a group has failed in carrying out its ambitions, it may place the blame on some minority group. It is said, for instance, that the persecution of Jews in Germany was the method by which the Nazis projected Germany's downfall onto a special group which was to bear the brunt of responsibility. Intolerance of various kinds, whether religious, racial, or political, may be the projection of blame for one's own defeat or inability to completely dominate the situation. Criticism has been spoken of many times as a common form of projection. An especially telling form of projection is "righteous

6 Susan Isaacs, *Social Development in Young Children* (New York: Harcourt, Brace and Company, 1937), 366.

indignation," for the very righteousness of the indignation protects it with respectability.

Going to one's own defense. The man who flies to his own self-defense with a multitude of excuses is really projecting outward his own inner self-reproach. There is a French expression, "Qui s'excuse, s'accuse," meaning he who excuses himself, accuses himself and with a freer translation, "A guilty conscience needs no accuser," or as the saying goes in the South, "Hit dog always hollers."

Little Arthur, who has dropped the box of strawberries which he was bringing home from the garden, is quick to find an excuse. There was a hidden stick lying across the path, and he could not help but stumble over it.

Naturally a child who feels it necessary to run to his own defense is the child who is likely to have poured upon him a torrent of abuse.

Law and authority. In a sense, the whole system of laws and penal procedure is a projection on society of the individual's feeling of guilt. Take for example, the child in school who wants rules made that will keep pupils orderly and will eliminate competition and unfairness. In such a case, a pupil may be afraid of his own tendencies to be disorderly or to be unfair and wants to be buttressed against these tendencies by rules made and enforced by the group. In school courts pupils will impose penalties far more severe than the school authorities would for the same offense, in part, perhaps, because each is projecting his own guilt and need for punishment onto the offender for his own unconscious wishes which are similar to the offense. So in the larger realm of public affairs, society, being afraid of its own tendencies to aggression and disorder, buttresses itself against these tendencies by the institution of civil law, the basis of our present civilization. Laws were not necessarily formed originally as projections but are accepted as binding today by most citizens because they institutionalize projecting tendencies. Many features of group control are in essence projections of controlling tendencies within the individual of which he is not quite aware. The leader is the incarnation of the group's conscience. In other words, projection is a mechanism by which man helps to keep himself in better order and control.

Exclusiveness. Projection can also be expressed by exclusiveness and turning away. It can be seen in the simple act of cutting another person on the street, or, in another case, lifting one's skirts so as not to be dirtied by those whom one thinks inferior. Members of a society who have had difficulty in gaining admittance themselves are the very ones who wish to protect their feeling of superiority by enforcing rigidly the entrance requirements of others, thereby projecting their feeling of inferiority. Perhaps the same would hold with respect to the application of immigration laws in a country.

Projection in fantasy. *In Play.* A very significant mode of projection is play. This may be seen so clearly in children's play with dolls and other figures. A little girl will project all of her wishes and feelings onto her dolls as she plays with them. Sometimes the doll will be a little baby to be put to bed, to be taken out to ride, to be washed and clothed and fed. Sometimes a doll will be the stern and strict mother who has the care of a family of dolls which she talks to in commanding and forbidding fashion. Some of the time a doll will feel happy, and at other times a doll will feel neglected or sad. The use of play is proving to be very helpful in understanding children who present problems. In their play they project their own feelings, wishes, and conflicts out into the play situation. The careful observer in watching a child at play will be able to discover many of the child's personal problems. The boy with his toy trains can think of himself as the powerful engineer, or his model airplane permits him to feel himself in the rôle of the pilot.

In Art. In a more sophisticated sense, much art is a form of projection. Projection as a mechanism may be recognized as a particular form of the general tendency to give outer and concrete expression to inner thoughts, feelings, and attitudes. Projections, therefore, may be thought of as special cases of the general tendency to express oneself by word or deed or creative act in the world of reality. The artist projects into his art his own feelings, his hopes and fears, his loves and hates, his joys and disgusts. This projection is probably most obvious in the graphic and plastic arts. The sculptor expresses his feelings of strength or of weakness, of fear or of hate, in the models which he creates. The artist paints into his pictures his moods of gaiety or depression, his compulsive need for detail or his more primitive need for bold execution, as expressed in large patches of color and bold strokes. The musician projects his mood into his music. The mood in Wagner's *Die Meistersinger* is in marked contrast to that in Tschaikowsky's *Sixth Symphony*. Women project their prevailing mood into their clothing and their houses. Even one's handwriting, so we are told [7] is a projection of one's impulses to be bold, precise, erratic, sharp, peculiar, and so forth, although here, as in other forms of art expression, it may be the deeply unconscious which is being expressed and which may not coincide with the more open modes of expression of the personality. Art, then, serves as a welcome form of release through the mechanisms of projection and thereby serves as a safety-valve for repressed tendencies, a reputable and even socially valuable safety-valve which might have other much less desirable modes of expression.

In Literature. A particularly significant form of projection is found in literature. The novelist projects his feelings, his conflicts, and his wishes into the tales that he creates. When a novelist creates a character, that

[7] Werner Wolff, *The Expression of Personality: Experimental Depth Psychology* (New York: Harper & Brothers, 1943).

character must correspond to something inside the person who finds expression in this particular mode. Most persons have only limited capacity for projection, perhaps because they have had limited identifications. A man like Dickens, who created innumerable characters running the whole gamut of human types and emotions, must have identified himself easily with all sorts and conditions of people and been able, in addition, to project these out onto the characters that he created in his fiction. One can only speculate how two such sheltered persons as the Brontë sisters could write such melodramatic stories as *Jane Eyre* and *Wuthering Heights*. It seems fair to assume that they were projecting, in this manner, impulses and fantasies which had no other more direct means of expression. The playwright visualizes even more vividly the scenes and characters created by him, and in producing them on the stage creates actual scenes with which hundreds of people can later identify themselves and thereby live through experiences similar to those which are called for by their own needs. The poet also projects his feelings, not in quite such a direct manner as the novelist, but in more subtle and delicate shadings and nuances. Wagner, in his operas of the Ring, was working out on a gigantic scale the tremendous conflicts with which his tempestuous life was involved.

VALUES OF PROJECTION

On the whole, projection as a mechanism is considered a rather poor kind of adjustment. It may be thought of as an attempt at cure of the conflict within the self, but it is an ineffectual cure. As has been seen by the many illustrations given, projecting certain characteristics in oneself out onto persons or objects represents a failure to permit awareness of these characteristics in oneself and a failure to manage them. Insofar as the internal tendencies are repressed, they may cause needless anxiety and guilt, needless conflicts and suffering. The person who can learn to recognize and hence to tolerate and possibly accept his own impulses is on the road toward managing them.

On the other hand, where these impulses seem too dangerous, and where there is no one on whom one can lean in order to gain sufficient security, a way is found for managing them alone, even though somewhat lamely, by projecting them onto others. It has even been said that we *need* other persons in part so that we may hate them. Projection of our impulses onto others helps us to regulate and order our own lives. This is seen most clearly when laws are considered as projections of one's own tendencies toward self-regulation, where the self feels hardly adequate to manage its own dangerous erotic and aggressive tendencies. These can be projected out onto other people who will serve as regulators and arbiters of these tendencies, thus effecting a certain degree of security. This is the method that society has worked out in order to control the dangerous impulses and bring them into some semblance of order.

· QUESTIONS FOR DISCUSSION

1. What might be the motivation for projecting good attributes of the self?

2. What is retaliation fear and how does it grow out of projection? What form of mental illness develops out of retaliation fear?

3. Explain how a teacher's dislike of subnormal children could be a form of projection.

4. It has been suggested that whenever a person talks about another person he is projecting. What could such a general statement mean? Explain how a mother describing her child's problems could be a form of projection?

5. Give an example of superego projection.

6. How can law and government be thought of as projections so far as the individual reacts to them?

RECOMMENDED READING

1. BELLAK, LEOPOLD, "The Concept of Projection, an Experimental Investigation and Study of the Concept," *Psychiatry*, 7:1944, 353-370.

2. FLÜGEL, J. C., *Man, Morals and Society* (New York: International Universities Press, 1945).

3. HORNEY, KAREN, *New Ways in Psychoanalysis* (New York: W. W. Norton & Co., 1939).

4. ISAACS, SUSAN, *Social Development in Young Children* (New York: Harcourt, Brace and Company, 1937).

5. STRECKER, E. A., and APPEL, K. E., *Discovering Ourselves* (New York: The Macmillan Company, 1931; second edition, 1943).

6. WEISS, EDOARDO, "Regression and Projection in the Superego," *International Journal of Psychoanalysis*, 13 (1932), 449-478.

XIII

Identification

First meaning. Identification is a very common phenomenon observ-able in all human relations. Identification has two distinct meanings that should be clearly differentiated. Modeling of oneself in thought, feel-ing or action after another person is the most common use of the term. This may be accomplished in two ways. Most typically, identification takes place when a person copies another person. In this sense identifica-tion is practically synonymous with imitation. In common language, a child may be said to imitate someone else whom he admires. Mary ob-serves that girls who are personally attractive receive the most attention, and she copies the dress and mannerisms of one of the smartest girls in her class. Kardiner [1] calls this an "enriching" type of identification be-cause by means of it the personality is enlarged.

Second meaning. A related, yet much more subtle, meaning is found in those cases in which a person, instead of copying another person directly, attempts to live out his wishes in the life of another person. One example of this would be a woman who hopes to achieve some of her unfulfilled social and scholarly ambitions by seeing them fulfilled in her sister. Another example is the case of the citizen who insists on having a severe penalty imposed on some other citizen found guilty of a misdemeanor. He himself has not been guilty of this act, to be sure, but he has dreamed of committing it, and it would make him feel a great deal of guilt were he actually to be the culprit. In these cases there is an interesting connection between identification and projection. One might say that the first woman identifies herself with her sister and then projects onto her some of her own unfulfilled ambitions. Kardiner calls this an "impoverishing" type of identification because the person projects himself in fantasy onto another person.

Identification is present in all persons. It can be observed very early in life even in the first days and weeks. It has been said to be primary basis of character formation. One may look to identification as an ex-planation for many of the traits and characteristics of a person. One

---

[1] Abram Kardiner, *The Individual and His Society* (New York: Columbia Univer-sity Press, 1939), 64.

hears it commonly said that Mary takes after her mother, or that Tom is a chip off the old block. Children are frequently heard to say, "My mother said," or "My father said."

FUNDAMENTAL CONSIDERATIONS

Unconscious nature of identification. Probably we should not use the word identification to describe what takes place when a person systematically looks over his acquaintances and decides which one he prefers to be most like. Identification, as it typically operates, is unconscious, and the person is not aware of the fact that he is modifying his own behavior to pattern it after that of another person.

Distinction between having and being like. Freud [2] has made the distinction between *having* another person and *being like* another person. Having another person as a friend, as an enemy, as an intimate, as a confidant, as an object of love, is what Freud terms "object relationship." Being like another person has been given the name "identification." One can identify oneself with another without having any relationship with him. On the other hand, it is possible, indeed it is a very frequent occurrence, that one has both a relationship with another person and also an identification with him. For instance, it has frequently been noted that married persons tend to grow like each other. Not only have they entered into a relationship with each other, but they have adopted the same tastes, standards, and points of view. It is possible for one to identify oneself even with an intimate, if for no other reason than that the intimate possesses characteristics that the person himself would like to emulate.

Fenichel [3] points out that identification is a more primitive process (that is, occurs at an earlier age) than love, and that love in a sense grows out of or is a derivative of identification. That is why (as we shall see) when a love relationship is prevented, identification sometimes takes place by regression.

Identification a modification of the self. Identification is in reality a modification of the self. It is a method by which the self becomes enlarged and takes on new interests, new patterns of behavior, new attitudes, and new feelings toward persons and objects in the environment. The larger the number of identifications, the wider a person's interests. The very process of growth may be thought of, in part, as the taking on of additional identifications: first, simple kinds of behavior and feelings with

[2] Sigmund Freud, *New Introductory Lectures in Psychoanalysis*, International Psychoanalytical Library, No. 24 (London: Hogarth Press, 1933; New York: W. W. Norton & Company, Inc., 1933).

[3] Otto Fenichel, *An Outline of Clinical Psychoanalysis* (New York: W. W. Norton & Company, 1934).

respect to persons in the immediate environment, later extending these identifications as maturity increases to people, institutions, and movements in the larger society. A person is as broad as his identifications. So the unique character of the personality is determined by a person's identifications.

Motivation. Identification may be thought of as one of the methods that a person can adopt in order to satisfy his needs. As needs develop, there is a search for methods of satisfying them. It is only natural that a child should look about him and find how others are satisfying these same needs and then adopt these methods as his own. Typically, the person with whom one identifies himself is both loved and hated. He is loved because he is a person who is admired and who can, through the identification, be of service. He is hated, on the other hand, because his very power, strength, ability, or beauty is envied.

Identification has also been described as a means of compensation. By identification with a person whom one admires, one may bolster up one's own weakness or gloss over deficiencies. It may be truthfully said the greater the need for a person to identify himself with another, the greater the personal insecurity. A person gains strongly by identifying himself with someone else whose prowess he wishes to emulate and whose virtue or achievement he can take for himself. This use of identification as a means for compensation is wholesome when it leads actually to taking over the other person's behavior, attitudes, or feelings; it can be actually destructive if the identification is made in fantasy only, without feeling the necessity of taking on the characteristics of the other person in reality.

Identification is a method of adjusting to rivalry and hostility. Identification absorbs and substitutes for the rivalry. A boy may manage the rivalry he has felt for an older brother by striving to emulate him. This permits him to praise and admire his brother instead of to criticize and disparage him.

Identifications once made may be abandoned as increasing maturity shows other and better ways of meeting these same needs. However, old identifications may be readopted at a later time, if necessary, by regression in case the older identifications still seem to serve in the new situations as the best form of adjustment that can be made.

Identification and regression have interesting relationships. "Backward identification," that is, identification with a person younger than the self, is sometimes called regression. Identifications which are extreme also have been referred to as being like regression. For instance, the identifications of the very little child are frequently fantastic. He magnifies in his mind the characteristics of other persons, and these exaggerations come out in play through the characters that he adopts. It is easy for him to play the part of a bandit, a gunman, or a giant. The older person who makes fantastic identifications is said to have regressed because his identifications are similar to those made by a little child.

IDENTIFICATION RELATIONSHIPS

Boy with father. Of the first type of identification the most typical example is the identification of a boy with his father. The boy looks forward to the time when he can be stronger, more powerful, and have greater control. His father is one whom he admires and perhaps envies because he is stronger and can do so many interesting and difficult things, all of which have prestige in the boy's eyes.

Arthur, aged five, likes to play automobile. He will sit in the driver's seat as his father does, blow the horn, shift the gears, and talk back to policemen.

Jennings is called Junior and seems to follow in his father's footsteps. In high school he played on the ice-hockey team as his father had done years before. He chose to go to Dartmouth, his father's college, later deciding that his career would be in the law, and hoping that he would be able to become a member of his father's firm. The father was proud that Junior was interested in carrying on the family tradition.

Imagine the responses of three fathers to the bill collector who knocks at the door. One parent will be stormy and blustering, will shout that the charge was unjustly made, and will threaten violence to the collector. The second will be unctuous and canny. He will make glib promises of paying at some indefinite future date. The third will be humble and apologetic, candidly explaining his difficulties. Many years later we may find their sons, who were silent witnesses of these episodes, using similar methods of dealing with similar situations. In identifying themselves with their fathers they unconsciously have assimilated patterns of social behavior.

Girl with mother. Equally common is the identification of a girl with her mother. Betty, who is eight years old, likes to dress up in her mother's clothes, put on her high-heeled slippers, apply rouge, lipstick, mascara, and red nail polish, and then set about acting the part of her mother by entertaining guests, pouring tea, and dealing out cards. Thus in her play she identifies herself with her mother in her social activities and anticipates the time when she herself can play a similar rôle in real life.

Agnes, who is sixteen, would like more freedom to have dates with boys and resents her parents' insistence that she be at home before eleven o'clock in the evening. One would think that Agnes would like to break away entirely from her home and family. However, there are many signs that Agnes has identified herself closely with her mother. She adopts the same style of hairdress that her mother does and has the same taste in jewelry. She seems to agree with her mother when there is an issue as to how flowers should be arranged or what draperies should be chosen. She also resembles her mother in the way in which she pouts when she cannot have her own way, her fear of being alone, her quickness in making decisions, and the gracious way she has of meeting people.

It has been said that there is a stronger and more persistent tendency toward identification among girls than among boys. Boys turn their energies outward and work out their needs in the world of reality. Many girls, however, remain bound by their identifications—they work out their needs through their identification with another person rather than by their own efforts and activities.

It should be mentioned that identification may, and usually does to a degree, take place between the child, whether boy or girl, and the parent of the opposite sex. A boy may take on the beliefs and philosophy of life of his mother; a girl may take on the aggressiveness of her father. When this becomes prominent we speak of homosexual tendencies, and we call the boy a "sissy" or a "fairy" and the girl a "tomboy." If a boy identifies himself with the feminine rôle, he does not have to seek a woman to love—he has the woman in himself; and inversely with the girl.

With parent substitute. Identification may be made with a parent substitute as well as with the parent.

Tim likes to play policeman, will strut around, ordering people to stand back, and will bawl out imaginary traffic-law offenders. Martha likes to play school but always wants to be the teacher. She arranges other children as they should sit in her school, is patient with them in their lessons, but is firm with them when they act silly or start to wriggle. Henry has never found anyone whom he admires so much as his mathematics teacher. He positively idolizes him. He follows him closely in class and adopts some of these same manners while president of the debating team.

Identification in the form of hero-worship is a common phenomenon in adolescence. In the need for recognition and establishing status, an adolescent through identification will appreciate to himself the success of his hero. As one girl stated: "I recall that I could play the piano better with my hat on because one of my heroines was a fine pianist and was usually seen playing at afternoon affairs wearing a hat."

Zim in a study of *Science Interests and Activities of Adolescents* states: [4]

Younger adolescents may develop interests in science in emulation of some adult whom they admire, who is their hero. This association is frequently expressed and even if not conscious is easily observed. It may be an envisioning of himself in the rôle of his father, or the hero may be some relative, teacher, friend, or even a person known only through stories or books. The author has known a number of adolescents who felt that a particular scientist was their hero and wished to read his original papers, duplicate his experiments, etc. The

[4] Herbert Zim, *Science Interests and Activities of Adolescents* (New York: Ethical Culture Schools, published privately, 1940), 127.

family doctor is a frequent hero of boys interested in science. Famous men, such as Einstein, Pasteur, and Marconi, are important as heroes.

These substitute identifications should be recognized as a natural and necessary part of the act of growing up and breaking away from the dependence of family ties. The adolescent girl who successfully identifies with teachers, movie idols or classmates is attempting to free herself of infantile dependence on her mother. However, by imitating sexual behavior of less admirable characters in early adolescence there is danger of a weakened rather than strengthened self-control. It has been frequently observed that the oldest son in a family may resemble the maternal grandfather. The boy is unconsciously identifying himself with the man whom the mother has loved and admired the greater part of her life—her own father. The oldest son wants to stand in the same relation as his grandfather in his mother's regard and identifies himself with him.

With siblings. It is very common for brothers and sisters to identify themselves with each other provided they are spaced somewhat in years. In my observations, brothers or sisters who are close together in age or who are the first two in the family are quite likely to have dissimilar characteristics. The older one may be cautious, reserved, and orderly, while a younger brother may be carefree, sociable, and disorderly. However, if brothers or sisters are separated by a few years, the younger brother may look up to the older one as a hero and his highest ambition may be to emulate his brother. He will look forward to working his way through college as his brother is doing, will want to take the same studies and maintain an equally high standing, and in many ways will look to his brother as a pattern and model.

Quite the reverse, the child may identify himself with a younger brother or sister if the younger child seems to be favored in the family in some way. It has been commonly noted that when a baby is born in the family an older child may take on babyish ways such as using baby-talk, wetting himself, spilling his food, and the like.

Identification with sibling substitute. Another common form of identification is with a sibling substitute. A boy, for instance, instead of identifying himself with a member of his own family will identify himself with one of his school or college group whom he admires very much.

George seems to have a crush on the football captain in his school. He insists on having his hair cut as the older boy does, wants to wear the same kind of square toed shoes, plaid woollen socks, and sport shirts. He also adopts some of the older boy's characteristic racy vocabulary.

Identification of parent with child. Not infrequently a mother, finding herself thwarted in her love life or in her ambitions will identify herself with her children and attempt to live out her frustrated plans through them. This identification relationship has received more extended analysis and discussion in the chapter, "Projection."

Identification of husband with wife and vice versa. Not infrequently marriage partners may identify with each other. This may be seen not only in those instances in which husband and wife develop similar tastes and interests as they grow older, but also in those cases of selfish love of a homosexual type in which one partner secretly and unconsciously admires traits and characteristics in the other that he would like to possess himself.

Identification of counselor with client. The identification of a counselor with his client is a common therapeutic procedure. Identification may be used loosely in this connection, since certainly if the counselor intends it, it cannot be wholly unconscious, but the process is meant to simulate identification.

Henry was sent to Mr. A., the school psychologist, because he had been caught cheating on an examination. He found out that Henry had a very severe stepfather who would whip him if he did not bring a good report from school. Henry was faced with a terrific conflict. He had either to fail and receive a severe whipping at home, or find some way of passing the final examination. He chose the latter as the easier way. Mr. A. put himself in the boy's place in imagination and sympathized with him. This completely disarmed Henry who found it possible to relate his own feelings and tell Mr. A. in his own words some of the difficulties he was facing. By thus encouraging and permitting Henry to talk openly about his problems, Mr. A. helped him to face them with less anxiety.

Identification of one person with third person. A typical example of the second type of identification is the successive identification of mother, sister, and wife.

Mr. F. lost his mother when he was only seven years old. However, an older sister became the housekeeper and took charge of the family of seven children. Mr. F., as a boy identified this sister with his mother and transferred his attitudes of compliance and resistance to this sister, who took the place of his mother. Later on, he picked a girl for his wife whom he again identified with his mother and also with his sister. His wife combined in her person the same dominating characteristics with motherly care. Mr. F., therefore, went through life under the domination of this series of women who took the place of a mother for him, praised his successes, condoned his failures, and helped him with his decisions.

A similar identification may be seen of father, brother, and son.

Mrs. T. vents her bad temper on her young son. She nags him constantly and upbraids him for any small deviation from her strict standards. In general, she is identifying him with her own father and later with her brother for whom she had similar hostility as a girl but which she has now entirely repressed. As a matter of fact, Mrs. T. now has to contribute to the support of her elderly father and feels strong devotion toward him.

EXTENSION OF IDENTIFICATION

Behavior and attitudes. In the illustrations which have just been given, the identifications are of a simple, obvious kind in which the imitation is of behavior or of general attitude. Identification, however, can take a number of different courses. For instance, unconsciously one may identify oneself with another by mannerisms and tastes. Social attitudes are largely a result of early identification. One finds himself when grown up holding allegiance to the Republican or Democratic party and often is called upon to justify this allegiance. The actual truth of the matter is that this allegiance was an identification in early childhood with the attitudes and beliefs expressed by father or mother in the home circle. In like manner, one finds himself adhering to a religious sect for no other reason than that it is the religious sect of one's childhood family, and belief in it has been taken over by the process of identification.

One not only identifies with people but also with social movements, with one's family as a cultural entity, with its prestige and honorable history, with one's school or college or fraternity. The feeling of "we-ness," that one is a member of a group, may be extended as a product of the process of identification.

Sidney speaks of his school with the greatest loyalty. He boasts of its football team, takes pride in the newspaper of which he is an editor, and is proud to display his school emblem and his class numerals on his sweater and the class pin on his lapel.

Philosophy of life. One's philosophy of life and attitudes with regard to class and caste, one's idealism, one's repressions, the acceptance of a culture, one's moral standards, one's ambitions, all stand out as an outcome of this same mechanism of identification. The habits of thought of the earliest family associations are adopted without critical review, and then in later life there is an attempt to justify them.

In identifying himself with those whom he loves, hates, and emulates, a boy thereby is adopting the rudiments of his own philosophy of life. His moral standards, tendencies toward selfishness, self-sacrifice, idealism, ambition, and repression all grow out of these early identifications with members of the immediate family circle through a process of identification. The taboos with respect to murder, cruelty, theft, incest, and sex are formed on the basis of these early identifications. Later in life the persons who were the original models for these identifications may be forgotten and all that is left are impersonal or even personified ideals. It is for such ideals that men take their stand and often fight.

IDENTIFICATION IN FANTASY

Identification with imago of parent. Many of the identifications which have been described are identifications in fantasy rather than in reality. For instance, the child's identification with his parents is likely to be with the imago of the parent rather than with the actual parent. Children build up fantasies of bigger, stronger, more important, and more powerful persons than the parents actually are, and the child identifies himself with this imagined parent rather than with the parent who actually exists. We are all magnified in the minds of our children, and it is with this magnified self that our children identify themselves.

Identification with imaginary companions. When a child does not have a suitable model with whom to identify himself, he may manufacture one. Many children have imaginary companions who serve in fantasy as the person with whom the child would like to identify himself. These imaginary companions live in far-away glamorous places, have unusual toys or pets, are permitted to do interesting and forbidden things, all of which have allurement for the child himself. We might say, then, that the child identifies himself with the imaginary companion. The question still remains as to where the child finds the characteristics of the "ideal" that he manufactures. We know very well that these "ideals" are not fabrications of his imagination—the elements, at least, are derived from his familiar experience. Commonly, they find their origin in characteristics of father or mother, brother or sister, grandmother or grandfather, aunt or uncle, however much these persons have characters which do not permit him to identify *in toto*.

Identification with toys, animals, objects. The child may identify himself with his toys. A girl, for instance, dresses her doll, puts her to bed, feeds her, takes her out to ride, as she herself would like to be treated. Children in their play may take the position of father or mother, teacher, cops or robbers, kings or queens, each one of these characters being a person whose position they would like to occupy and with whom in fantasy they can identify themselves. A boy may identify himself with an animal. He may wish to run like a dog or be strong and fierce like a lion or a bear. It is an interesting pastime, when one is with a group of people, to identify persons with animals, in a spirit of ridicule. Here is a man who reminds one of a bulldog; another of an ox; another of a race horse; another of a baboon; another of a pig. One may also identify himself with an object. Boys, for instance, will identify themselves with their toy automobiles or airplanes and wish for the power or speed which they attribute to these objects. A girl may identify herself with her bedroom and take the same interest in furnishing it with frothy curtains and bed coverings as she has in adorning her person.

Identification with person absent or dead. A very different kind of identification in fantasy is with a person who is dead or is absent. When a parent dies, the child's identification with the parent still persists; in fact, it may be even stronger with the parent dead or absent than it was when the parent was alive. This is one method that a person adopts for keeping still intact that part of his personality that was contained in the relationships with the late person. And it is by this method that a person defends himself against unconscious aggressive impulses which he may have held toward the person when he was alive. Many times these identifications with absent persons are heightened to the extent that they are controlled only by the memory and hence are likely to be more permanent in character than if they depended on a living relationship. In such cases, the person may try to restitute the lost person in his own life. A widow may, for instance, try to carry on her husband's business, finish her husband's book, or adopt some ideals that her husband stood for. Or, the child will in fantasy adopt the vocation of the missing parent or take on his habits of thought, his activities, and his standards.

Although Harry, age ten, does not speak of his father who died four years ago and apparently thinks of him very seldom, the fact is that he is actually much influenced by the memory, mostly unconscious, of his father. If he thinks of his father at all, it is of a very good and wise man, a man who was outstanding in achievement. Harry bases these memories on childish incidents which are very much magnified in his imagination. These thoughts of his dead father serve as a stimulus to Harry's effort in school and as an incentive to his bearing and conduct. His mother and aunts and uncles do not know of this and they merely think of Harry as growing to be a splendid, manly boy, who in many ways reminds them of his father.

Identification with characters in fiction. One may mention as an identification in fantasy that which is made so frequently with actors on the screen or in the play, or characters in a book. It is well known that as one sees a play he tends to identify himself with one of the characters in the plot, to take his part in all conflicts and struggles, to want very much for the outcome to be in his favor. In short, he "roots" for his favorite characters, just as he roots for his favorite team in a game. These identifications with characters in fiction may play an important part in character development, as is well known by teachers of literature. These identifications do not have to hold to sex lines. A man can identify himself with the actress, a girl with her favorite hero. In their play children may take the part of gasoline-station attendants, judges, doctors, Spanish senoritas, cowboys, teachers, Pilgrim Fathers, and especially movie stars. Identification frequently takes place with radio, movie, and comic-book heroes.

VALUES IN IDENTIFICATION

Positive. Identification is universal and common to all men, a potent mechanism in character formation. It has positive value when it helps an individual to find a way of satisfying any of his needs. Identification is recognized as good when it gives a person ambitions, ideals, and goals; and when it spurs him on to greater activity. It is also valuable insofar as it gives a person security. When a child can ally himself with his father or his older brother and gain strength from this alliance against his own weakness; when a man gains strength by allying himself with his state or nation or his school or club, then we find such identification good.

Identification is also a basis of sympathy. When we sympathize with a person we have in part identified with him. Even when we sympathize with a person in distress we identify with him in the sense that we would like to have had the secret satisfaction for which the misfortune is a punishment and to share the punishment. Freud [5] illustrates this by the spread of hysteria in a girl's boarding-school when one girl is provoked to jealousy by the contents of a love-letter. The other girls would secretly like to have had the same experience.

Negative. Identification, on the other hand, may be considered less desirable when it tends to become exaggerated and fantastic. Men and women who permit themselves to become so strongly identified with some character in history or fiction and, at the same time, dissociate themselves from the affairs of real life become psychotic. Delusions of grandeur, a characteristic of paranoids, is an illustration of identification gone haywire. The individual believing himself to be Jesus Christ or Napoleon or Einstein or some other religious or scientific hero may so immerse himself in this rôle of fantasy that he loses his capacity to adjust to the real world in which he must live. Identification is bad when it is without discrimination. A small boy may identify himself with his favorite airplane pilot, spend his time tinkering about on engines, and dream of the time when he can span the continent. On the other hand, if this leads to being careless in dress, or going about with soiled hands, or lateness at meals or at school, this identification can give parents and teachers considerable concern. Identifications can become fixated and hence prevent growth. It is possible for a child to hold a childish goal or ambition to such an extent that he fails to grow more mature in his outlook and to adopt a more adult point of view. If there is a lag between goal and achievement, as when identification takes place only in fantasy,

[5] Sigmund Freud, *Group Psychology and the Analysis of the Ego,* International Psychoanalytical Library, No. 6 (London: Hogarth Press, 1922; first published in German, 1921), 64.

there may come a feeling of worthlessness or discouragement, even of guilt, which can be destructive or which can negate any of the benefits which come from the spur given by the identification.

EDUCATIONAL IMPLICATIONS

Identification, therefore, because it is a common mechanism in the formation of behavior, feeling, and thought, may be used as a powerful educational tool. In general, children respond readily to appeals to identification. Whatever a teacher wishes to inculcate in her children can be most easily accomplished not by directly urging them but by pointing tactfully to some other person who may be admired and who possesses these traits and characteristics. Parents and teachers should also remember that there is a natural trend for a child to identify himself with them; and that, insofar as they themselves carry in their persons the traits and characteristics which they would like to see in their children, they can be sure that their children are on the road to adopting them by the process of identification.

SOCIAL IMPLICATIONS

In the chapter on projection leadership was mentioned as a projection of inner authority. Leadership is also an identification as the leader becomes a substitute for the goals and successes which we are unable to attain by our unaided efforts. The tendency to identify with a leader blindly can be prevented by (1) an amelioration of the situation so that the individual feels more confident and secure, and (2) strengthening of the group and its defense resources so that there is less to fear from the aggressiveness of other groups. As a group grows inherently strong there is less need to project authority on and to identify with a strong leader.

QUESTIONS FOR DISCUSSION

1. It has been said that a person's basic character is a result of his identifications in infancy and childhood. Explain the possible meaning of such a statement. Name some traits of character that could have developed from identification.

2. It is also said that some identifications serve as disguises to hide the basic underlying character structure. Give illustrations.

3. How is identification a method of adjusting to rivalry and hostility?

4. In what way is the person with whom one identifies loved? In what way hated?

5. The statement is made on page 242 that a person is as broad as his identification. What does this statement mean? Give illustrations.

6. If identification is a way of mastering rivalry, why is it that frequently two

brothers near of an age have different characteristics? Why is identification sometimes used and sometimes not used as a method of mastering rivalry?

7. What is meant by saying that a counselor ought to identify with his client?

8. Why does a child frequently identify with a dead or missing parent?

9. Discuss the principle of identification in connection with the novelist, the dramatist, the actor, the reader, radio listener, or theatergoer.

10. Discuss leadership as a phenomenon of identification. As a phenomenon of projection.

Recommended Reading

1. BERGLER, EDMUND, "The 'Leading' and Misleading Identifications," *Psychoanalytic Review*, 32 (1945), 263–295.

2. ENGLISH, O. S., and PEARSON, G. H. J., *Emotional Factors in Living* (New York: W. W. Norton & Company, Inc., 1945).

3. FREUD, ANNA, *The Ego and the Mechanisms of Defense*, International Psychoanalytical Library, No 30 (London: Hogarth Press, 1937; also, New York: International Universities Press, 1946; first published in German, 1936).

4. FREUD, SIGMUND, *Group Psychology and the Analysis of the Ego*, International Psychoanalytical Library, No. 6 (London: Hogarth Press, 1922).

5. HENDRICK, IVES, *Facts and Theories of Psychoanalysis* (New York: Alfred A. Knopf, 1934 revised edition, 1939).

6. ISAACS, SUSAN, *Social Development in Young Children* (New York: Harcourt, Brace and Company, 1933).

7. KNIGHT, R. P., "Introjection, Projection, and Identification," *Psychoanalytic Quarterly* 9 (1940), 334–341.

8. SCHILDER, PAUL, *The Image and Appearance of the Human Body*, Psyche Monograph No. 6 (London: Kegan, Paul, Trench, Trubner and Company, 1935).

9. SPERLING, O., "On Appersonation," *International Journal of Psychoanalysis*, 29 (1944), 128–132.

10. STRECKER, E. A., and APPEL, K. E., *Discovering Ourselves* (New York: The Macmillan Company, 1931; second edition, 1943).

XIV

Conflict

In Chapter III frustration was discussed in connection with the satisfaction of wants. But frustration, by and large, presents problems to an individual in relation to his adaptation with the outer world, and does not immediately concern problems of the integration of the individual himself. Most of the serious problems of adjustment in children and in adults are based on conflicts. An understanding of the nature of conflicts and how they are resolved is necessary for an adequate understanding of how persons can achieve satisfactory adjustments and integration of personality. While not a mechanism, conflict is introduced and discussed at this point because the ground work has been laid for a recognition of the structure of personality by the discussion of introjection, projection and identification.

DEFINITION

Conflict differs from frustration in that it is the simultaneous operation of two incompatible action systems—drives, needs, wishes, purposes, tendencies, impulses, and so forth. Normally, when there are two incompatible action systems stimulated, one is inhibited giving the other freedom of action. We see this most clearly in the action of antagonistic muscle groups. For instance, it is obviously impossible for the biceps and triceps muscles of the upper arm to contract at the same time. One flexes the elbow and the other straightens the elbow. The nervous system is so organized that there is complete coöperation between these two groups of antagonistic impulses. When the biceps is stimulated, the triceps muscle is relaxed and vice versa. This coördination is the way in which the body manages its muscle groups which have opposite functions. In mental conflict, two antagonistic behavior tendencies are aroused, and there is a failure in the inhibition of one of them. Somehow they both are operative and cause confusion and tension. As an example, conflicts may be recognized in difficulties in making a choice or a decision. The small child finds that it is not possible to enjoy eating his cake and also to have it to save as a prized possession. The older boy finds it difficult to choose between an opportunity of attending the ice carnival and going to the basketball game, both of which are scheduled on the same evening. The young lady has difficulty in deciding whether to wear her white or green dress. She feels that she looks better in green but that most of the other girls are going to wear white.

Conflicts arise and continue because two antagonistic drives are aroused. Both of these drives are important and necessary in the individual's economy. They may, however, apparently belong to quite different departments of life, and ordinarily, perhaps, a person can satisfy both of them at different times and on different occasions without any difficulty. However, the time may come when it is not possible to satisfy both. They may come at the same time or require different uses of the same materials or lead in opposite directions. Both wants, however, are real and not easily restrained, and consequently conflict results.

In conflict opposing forces approximately equal. Conflict implies that these opposing forces are of approximately the same strength and importance to an individual. If one action system is stronger either because it serves a more basic purpose, or points to a more direct and easy way of achieving a desired end, or because learning has been more adequate, this behavior will have the preference and the conflict will not be so acute.

The stronger the drives or avoidance tendencies the more intense the conflict. In general, the stronger the cravings, or the stronger the avoidance tendencies, the more intense the conflict. One does not feel a very strong conflict about things for which he cares very little. Conflicts over minor wants are not likely to be very intense. If there are signs of intense conflict over apparently trivial decisions, one may feel assured that the desires involved go deeper than they appear to on the surface and probably unconsciously are connected with broad and underlying trends in the personality. For instance, one may apparently have great difficulty in selecting some simple gift and the conflict seemingly causes great mental distress. One does not know, however, to what extent the difficulty in selecting the gift is related to conflict of friendly and hostile attitudes toward the person for whom the gift is meant.

In describing the various kinds of psychological conflicts, the classification to be used will follow, roughly, that given by Lewin,[1] whose topological and vector psychology has been most fruitful in the derivation of dynamic laws of behavior. Lewin's analysis and classification of types of conflict is based on the distinction between wants and avoidances. He recognizes three types of conflict: (1) that in which the individual is confronted with two opposing or contradictory wants, (2) that in which the individual is faced simultaneously with a want and with a desire to

[1] Kurt Lewin, *A Dynamic Theory of Personality* (New York: McGraw-Hill Book Company, Inc., 1935), 88–94.

avoid the same situation or activity, and ③ that in which the individual is faced with need to avoid two situations, from both of which he wishes to escape. The meaning of these three types will become clearer as they are illustrated by examples.

Conflict between two competing or interfering drives. The first of these types is a conflict between two competing contradictory action systems within the individual. Lewin gives the simple example of a child who has to choose between going on a picnic and playing with his comrades.

Conflict Between Basic Drives. There is a reference in the Freudian literature to "instinctual conflict," meaning conflict between the basic drives. However, there is good reason to believe that basic drives such as love and hate are not fundamentally in conflict with one another, but that if such a conflict arises, it in some way involves the structure of the personality. It is perhaps too simple to think of love and hate as being two opposite forces which naturally run into conflict with each other. Where such a conflict arises, and one drive has the ascendancy and the other is repressed, probably what takes place is that some critical faculty intervenes to make the one attitude acceptable and the other unacceptable. It is as though an individual finds hate too dangerous and puts the tendency to hate aside, leaving the tendency to love with a free field. Or perhaps, because love has been rebuffed so many times, to express love becomes too great a threat to the person, and this tendency is repressed, leaving hate the undisputed master of the situation.

Conflict Between Immediate Wishes. Besides conflicts between the basic drives, there are a myriad of *more immediate* and *minor* antagonistic action systems, which come into conflict at every hour of the day. For example, one must make a choice between staying in bed in the morning where it is warm and comfortable, and getting up and going about one's daily pursuits; or, in the evening, there is a choice between going to bed in obedience to the demands for rest and sleep, and staying up to finish an interesting novel or to listen to the radio. There is the choice between talking to one's friend or preparing one's assignment for the next day's class. While it is true that in these simple conflicts involving a choice, the wishes are antagonistic in the sense that they will take an individual along two different lines of activity, there is not the fundamental antagonism and wrench to the personality that results from the conflicts involving the more fundamental drives. Consequently, it is possible for both of these simple drives to be tolerated in consciousness, and since the person is aware of the conflict he retains it clearly in consciousness to be handled in problem-saving fashion.

Conflict Between Immediate and Remote Drives. There may also be conflict between *immediate* and more *remote* wishes, ideals, duties, or ambitions. Tom Sawyer, for instance, was caught between the necessity of painting the fence and the desire to go with the gang up Cardiff Hill. An adolescent finds that the drives toward sexual pleasure and expression are in conflict with his wishes to achieve. He finds that he may have to choose between having a good time in the present and putting his emphasis on his studies in order to win a high scholastic record and hence gain admission to college. The conflict here is between a goal which is consciously, even though perhaps uncritically, accepted, and the more pleasure-seeking driving forces within. Washburne, in his *Social Adjustment Inventory* [2] has used conflicts between immediate and more remote wishes as diagnostic of social adjustment. He will ask "If you had to choose between having a very fine automobile right now (with expenses paid, a driver's license, and knowledge of how to drive), or a million dollars next year, which would you take?" Washburne found that the adolescent who chose to have the automobile, to have his immediate wish satisfied, was, on the average, less well adjusted than the adolescent who could postpone his gratification to secure a larger reward in the future.

Conflict Between Two Ideals or Ambitions. Two *ideals* or *ambitions* are frequently in conflict. In our complex modern life, many goals beckon, and yet time and energy are insufficient to permit their realization.

I once knew a young man in college who was a good student and had ambitions to make Phi Beta Kappa. He also had an excellent physique, and could easily make the college football team. During the football season, however, the schedule was so arduous that it interfered with his scholastic ambitions. He accomplished both goals only by a high degree of tenacity and careful planning.

Women today are torn between raising a family and having a career. These are goals, both of which may be ardently wished for, and yet both are so consuming of time and energy that they run into sharp conflict.

A child whose parents are mismated, quarreling and disagreeing in their family relationships, is almost forced to adopt standards and ideals which are in conflict. Perhaps the parents separate, and the child goes to live with each for part of the year. From each parent he learns a different set of ideals. His mother wants him to go to college and enter upon some professional career. She has standards of honesty and a restricted point of view with regard to relations with girls. His father, however, wishes him to go into business and is not too scrupulous in his own business methods. His son well knows that his father is somewhat free and loose with women. The boy is fond of and loyal to each parent and assimilates the ideals and ambitions of each. However, they conflict, and it is impossible for him to reconcile these conflicting standards that are held up to him. Consequently, he is frequently in grave conflict in making choices and decisions.

[2] J. N. Washburne, *Social Adjustment Inventory* (Yonkers-on-Hudson, N.Y.: World Book Company, 1940).

Conflict Between Two Duties. Sometimes *two duties* conflict. Andrew Jackson, for instance, had to make a choice between remaining with his invalid wife at the Hermitage and serving his country in the Battle of New Orleans. Parents are frequently torn between the demands of their children. Wishing to do their duty by each of their children and give them the very best preparation for life in most cases inevitably involves choice and conflict over which children can be sent to college or given other similar advantages.

Conflict Between Duty and Ambition. Sometimes *duties* and *ambitions* conflict. A teacher, for instance, is ambitious to advance herself professionally and would like to attend the summer session or take part in teacher institutes. However, her invalid mother also makes demands on her time and energies, which means that her professional ambitions must be indefinitely postponed. Many a person has to make the choice between sending a younger brother or sister to college or spending the money on his own professional advancement.

Conflict Between Two Antagonistic Beliefs. In this same group will be included conflicts over competing *attitudes* or *beliefs*. The conflicts already described have been between competing tendencies to action. However, these conflicts may arise even in the planning stage when one is merely thinking about the stand to be taken on various issues. Sometimes when these concern the fields of politics or religion, they are distinct enough to be described under a separate heading. Culture conflicts, which we have earlier stated to be essentially sociological, may be psychological to the degree that the individual has assimilated within himself points of view of two or more cultures. He may find that certain forms of behavior are both accepted and condemned, and he is perhaps sympathetic to both points of view. The adolescent today frequently finds severe conflicts between earlier religious views learned as a child at home and in church, and views with regard to the universe learned in science classes. These conflicts may be very intense. The science teacher not infrequently has a boy or girl come to him and ask if he believes in God, if science sees no plan or purpose in the universe, and similar philosophical questions. We frequently find conflicts of this type between sex standards and religious teachings or between points of view expressed by church and state with regard to military service. In 1940, for instance, this country was committed to conscription of men between twenty-one and thirty-five, and discussions in the newspapers and in forums preached and upheld this action. On the other hand, certain idealistic church groups discussed the issues as to the individual's responsibility toward war, and one group of Christian gentlemen expressed opposition to conscription. John Haynes Holmes, for instance, said, "So my resolve is fixed, as it has been fixed for many years. If America enters this war, I will not. As far as the law may allow, and my spirit dictate, I will oppose the war." [3] These divergent points of view meant severe conflicts to some young men who were struggling to adopt a definite position and who were influenced both by their allegiance to country and to religious teachings.

Wishes concerning one's own adequacy and abilities may conflict with a belief that one's abilities may not be up to standard. A mother may become terror-stricken over the suggestion that her son may be feeble-minded or may have delinquent tendencies. This belief is in conflict with her belief and hopes that he has high potentialities and will grow up to become a great success in life.

The conflict of loyalties also comes in under this heading. In the case of the boy whose parents are separated, underlying all issues of his standards and conduct is the conflict of divided loyalties. Shall he hold himself loyal and deferent to his mother and equally so to his father? This becomes more difficult to the degree that their ideals and standards diverge, and he has a desire to adopt standards of both. Or if a boy with separated parents lives in a foster home, there is the additional conflict between loyalty to his mother whom he adores and to his stepmother for whom he has the greater respect. Then there is the conflict between loyalty to one's mate and to one's parents, particularly where both make conflicting demands. This conflict is especially harsh in cases where there is fixation on a parent, with emotional ties which are unduly strong. Then there is the conflict of loyalty to a friend. Shall one be true or false to a friend? Shall one be loyal to a friend when the friend has done something of which one does not approve and which goes against one's conscience? In such cases, shall one be true to the person or shall one be true to one's ideals? These and similar issues of choice and decision form the basis of many difficult conflicts.

Conflict between an action system and a frustration. Lewin's second group of conflicts is that in which an individual is faced simultaneously with a want and also with a desire to avoid the same situation or activity. He gives as an illustration the boy who wants to climb a tree, but is afraid; or the child who is offered a reward for some activity, such as a school task, which he does not really want to execute. In these illustrations there is an external stimulus beckoning the child on, but at the same time there is a barrier, either external or internal, that makes the activity difficult.

Conflict Between a Drive and External Frustration. This conflict between a drive and its control may be seen in early infancy, when a parent finds it necessary to restrain a child. Here the conflict is between a drive and an external frustration. The child reaches out its hand to touch some attractive object, and the mother slaps its hand or places

[3] J. H. Holmes, "If America Enters the War What Shall I Do?" *The Christian Century,* 57 (Dec. 11, 1940), 1546–1549.

the object out of reach. Slapping the hand is a punishment. The infant soon learns to recognize these occasions, in which an adult forcibly restrains him and uses pain to enforce the restriction, as punishment. He may even go beyond and interpret any pain or injury which he experiences, whether or not given intentionally by another person, as a means of restraining him. Many of the subtle and distressing conflicts of adult life, those which bring anxiety and guilt and which drive a person into neurotic behavior, originate in these simple conflicts between a child's primitive impulses and the restraints in the form of punishments placed upon him by his parents in the earliest days and weeks of his life. Here is an illustration of the importance for later personality adjustment of the apparently insignificant experiences of a baby in its earliest years.

Conflict Between a Drive and Inner Restraint. Growing out of this conflict between a drive and external frustration is the large class of conflicts between drives or wishes for immediate and pleasurable activity and inner restraints. A good example of this type may be found in the conflict between the desire to grow up and the need to be dependent. If a child has been intimidated and represses his outgoing adventuresomeness, competition, and assertiveness, he may develop retiring and dependency trends. But the natural forces of growth will supply urges toward independence, authority, and aggressiveness. Resulting from this conflict one commonly finds criminal tendencies that are a protest and compensation against the dependency needs.

CONFLICT BETWEEN A DRIVE AND EGO RESTRAINT. The first of these is the conflict between the aroused drives and the demands of the ego, known in psychoanalytic literature as the ego conflict. For instance, consider the conflict between the alcoholic who wants a drink and his tendencies to hold himself in check. He recognizes that if he does drink he will be late to work the next morning, he will lower his efficiency, and there is a chance that he will lose his job. He is afraid of deterioration and loss of efficiency. Such a conflict between caution, on the one hand, and impulse on the other is well recognized in discussions of morals.

CONFLICT BETWEEN A DRIVE AND SUPEREGO RESTRAINT. *Basic drive— superego conflict.* A second variation in this group may be the conflict between basic drives and the assimilated *unconscious* inhibitions. This is known in the psychoanalytic literature as the basic drive-superego conflict. It is this conflict that is the basis of much neurotic behavior and suffering. Just as the child may recognize his parents' prohibitions as representing danger to him if he does not submit, so he may recognize his own standards and internal restraints as dangerous if he does not accede to them, and when he does act contrary to his own self-imposed standards, he is filled with guilt and remorse. The little child, for instance, may be observed to feel annoyed when his hands are dirty, to feel ill at ease when he has left the cover off a box, or has left his toys scattered around, or has a spot on his clothes. He may be timid in the presence of other children as though he were afraid that his own tendencies toward them will be aggressive.

These prohibitions and restraints, arising originally in the culture but taken into the self and accepted by the individual as his own, meet the impulsive side of a person's nature in a head-on collision. This is probably one of the most striking and distressing forms of conflict that exists. Usually the individual is well aware of his repressing attitudes. He knows that he believes it wrong or sinful or improper or lacking in sportsmanship if he were to steal, commit adultery, tell a lewd story, or cheat in a game. The tendencies to do each of these things he probably fails to recognize in himself and if questioned would deny their presence with some vehemence. One can recognize this *conflict* between urges and internal restraints in situations in which one feels guilty, embarrassed, or ashamed. A child feels guilty when he has stolen something, told a lie, broken a window-pane, torn his clothes. He feels ashamed when he has made a mistake in his lesson, when he has forgotten to comb his hair, when he has not done as well as a brother or sister.

Conflicts of this type occur most frequently in connection with tendencies toward sexuality,[4] partly because sexual expression is so strongly condemned in our culture where every individual grows up with strong superego attitudes toward it, and partly because the sexual urges carry such a large amount of feeling with them. The excitement of romantic love is undoubtedly due to the conflict between these sexual urges and prohibitions against them. On the one hand, there is the arousal of the impulses toward love, and, on the other hand, the belief that in yielding to these impulses one is doing something that is considered wrong. One finds this conflict in a little child who, when he is first reproached for playing with his genital parts, has to face the fact that this is prohibited as well as his strong urge to gain gratification in doing it. Later he finds that sexual love for his mother is treated in the same manner, and the incest fear develops. In adult years this same conflict persists. As an illustration, consider the woman who falls in love with a married man and has to contend, on the one hand, with the emotions that are aroused, and, on the other hand, with the scruples assimilated from her early teaching that it is wrong to yield to this love. Charlotte Brontë's story, *Jane Eyre,* presents the exquisite torture that this conflict can engender.

---

[4] When the sexual is mentioned, it should be recognized that the word "sexual" is not being used in its limited and customary sense but refers to many activities in infancy and childhood which have a sexual significance. There are many components of the sexual impulse in childhood, each one of which is pleasure-giving in its natural form of expression, and many or most of them are prohibited by parents in our culture in their natural and undisguised expression by children.

Tendencies toward aggression may likewise be subject to this same type of conflict. Children are taught at an early age that aggression is not acceptable in present-day society, and that it is wrong to strike, bite, or harm any person. Yet his impulses to hate and tendencies to harm another person are aroused at every turn, and these tendencies are constantly met by the opposing, assimilated inhibiting tendencies which tell him that they are wrong. This conflict is recognized by the individual himself as guilt. Every basic desire that is repressed in early years may serve as a basis for later conflict. For instance, the desire to exhibit oneself, which is well recognized in infancy, later comes in conflict with the acquired tendency to feel that to do so is wrong and shameful. This type of conflict becomes especially strong with children who have grown up in strict homes where there has been much moral teaching or where there has been overprotection.

CONFLICT BETWEEN DRIVES AND ANTICIPATED SELF-PUNISHMENT. One may go a step beyond this conflict between basic drives and tendency to hold them in check by recognizing that the expression of these basic drives in young children has often been followed by punishment, and that the need for this punishment has been introjected or assimilated into the self, just as the prohibitions themselves have been. Consequently, when an impulse arises and there is also aroused a feeling that this impulse is bad and hence is subject to punishment, the person has a tendency to inflict on himself, if not actual physical injury, at least all sorts of hardships and deprivations. Naturally, a person wishes to avoid self-inflicted punishment, as one avoids punishment that is to be imposed by another person. Just as there is inhibition of an impulse, on the one hand, arising from fear of punishment which may be imposed by parents or teachers, so on the other, there may be conflict between one's impulses and one's fears of one's own inner tendencies toward self-punishment or self-deprivation. Since both the impulse itself may be repressed and unconscious, as well as the introjected tendencies toward self-punishment, this conflict itself is wholly unconscious, and is known only to the person as guilt or feelings of inferiority.

CONFLICT BETWEEN DRIVES AND THOUGHTS OF ONE'S OWN LIMITATIONS. A fourth variety of conflict between drives and inner restraining systems is that in which the restraining force is thoughts of or beliefs in one's own limitations. These conflicts arise very often. A little girl wishes to receive and show affection in her family, but she has often been told how much of a beauty her sister is and how ugly she is with her straight, stringy hair and freckles. Consequently, she believes herself to be an unworthy child, and fearing that her affectionate advances will not be accepted or reciprocated she represses them and is known as an odd, unapproachable child. The adolescent youth may feel his sexual powers arising, but he may be troubled with thoughts that because of some unfortunate early sexual episode or masturbation he has made himself impotent. Consequently, a grave conflict arises, and he becomes timid and retiring in his relations with the opposite sex, unconsciously believing that he lacks certain essential qualities which would make him altogether acceptable to them.

This discussion has been concerned with drives toward immediate and pleasurable activity. However, there may also be poignant conflicts between the remote drives in the form of ideals or ambitions and inner restraints. In the first place, there may be a conflict between an ideal or an ambition and restraint imposed by the ego. For example, one may have an ambition to learn the touch system in typing, but finds that it is difficult to afford the time necessary for the acquisition of this skill; or one might wish to perfect himself in some sport, but, again, realizes that while there might be genuine satisfactions in being able to display one's prowess, such a skill must take a secondary place as compared with skills necessary in one's business or profession. Sometimes common sense comes to the rescue in preventing a person from following the will-o'-the-wisp in the form of some chimerical goal or aspiration.

Conflict Between Introjected Systems. A third large group of conflicts between action and restraining systems are those in which both forces are of introjected systems. By an introjected system we mean some action tendency which has been assimilated uncritically from the culture, usually by teachings of parents and others in early childhood or merely from accepting the current modes of behavior and attitude in the surrounding culture.

CONFLICT BETWEEN EGO IDEAL AND SUPEREGO. A first type in this group is the conflict between an *ego ideal* and the *superego*. These two sets of introjected forces may come into conflict. For instance, in the illustration of the youth whose parents have separated, we may find that the father, on the one hand, sets the example of promiscuous sexual activities (ego ideal). The mother, on the other hand, has from early childhood attempted to teach her son the value of chastity. She has scolded or threatened, shamed or ridiculed all his expressions of interest in girls and through these prohibitions has created in him, at least in one side of his character, strong ascetic tendencies. His father's ideals and his mother's restraints, both of which he assimilated, are in strong conflict.

CONFLICT BETWEEN EGO IDEAL AND ANTICIPATED SELF-PUNISHMENT. A second type is conflict between the ego ideal and anticipated self-punishment. This type does not differ so much from the conflict between basic drives and anticipated self-punishment except that in this case instead of a basic drive, the drive is an introjected one in the form of an ideal or ambition or goal. A boy, for instance, has a strong drive to pass with a high grade on an examination. He knows that if he were to fail he would blame himself for failing to study or for going out with the crowd and staying up late at night. He is dimly aware that were he to make a low grade on the test he would feel the necessity of denying himself all sorts of pleasures. That self-denial is a punishment for his failure to take the test seriously and properly prepare for it would be unconscious on his part. Consequently, he anticipates the test with considerable apprehension and "examination fear." In this case the drive is conscious, but the anticipated self-derogation and punishment is mainly unconscious, showing merely itself in vague apprehension.

CONFLICT BETWEEN EGO IDEAL AND THOUGHTS OF ONE'S OWN LIMITATIONS. The third type of conflict is between the ego ideal and thoughts or beliefs in one's own limitation. We may divide these beliefs into two groups: first, beliefs about one's past deeds or accomplishments; and second, beliefs about one's own potentialities. The conflict between one's ambitions and attitudes toward one's deeds and accomplishments may be severe. On the one hand are high ideals set for oneself and, on the other hand, are the more or less tangible evidences of failure to live up to these ideals. This conflict shows itself in feelings of unworthiness and inferiority, which can become most painful in their intensity. The second group under this type are those conflicts between belief concerning one's aptitudes and potentialities and the ideals that one holds. A boy, for instance, wishes to make a success in his career. His father, however, has committed a crime and has been in the state penitentiary for years. This boy believes that he has within himself similar criminal tendencies, which he fears will prevent him from making the success in life which he would like to win. Fantasies with regard to one's own limitations are widespread and the cause of many severe conflicts. The person may fear that he is going insane because of insanity in the family, that he lacks intelligence or special ability to carry through the goal that he has set for himself, that he lacks certain character qualities which will give him the needed persistence and endurance to carry through to the end, or that he lacks normal sexual potency. These beliefs coming into conflict with ideals produce grave disturbances in personality.

Conflicts Between Inner Restraining Systems and Outer Encouragement. It is also possible to find conflicts between restraining systems, that is, inhibitions, and various forms of stimulation or encouragment from the outside. These conflicts reverse those which we have just been considering. First of all, the original drive must have been suppressed so that the inhibition becomes assimilated within the personality. Then as this inhibition becomes strong, there may be heartbreaking conflicts between it and outer encouragement or stimulation. On the other hand, there may be conflict between a repulsion, that is, a feeling that something is wrong or bad or ignoble, and outer encouragement or sanction of this act. For instance, a young man coming from a strict and puritanical home may find himself with a bid to become a member of a fraternity in college.

Upon getting acquainted with his fraternity brothers, he finds that they sanction many things that are in conflict with the standards of his home, church, and community. He finds that he is expected to drink, to experiment with relations with women, to place bets on athletic events. These newer sanctions coming into conflict with his childhood standards may give rise to extremely severe conflicts. The conflict may not be merely one of feeling. He may have rationalized his position and have built up elaborate structures of ethics based on religious beliefs whose sanctions become even stronger bulwarks against the new mores into which he finds himself plunged.

These conflicts grip the individual with special force when outer sanctions and encouragements have become introjected and assimilated into the individual's set of values. He then finds one part of himself which says that it is all right to go in for petting, to play a little poker, to join the fellows in a drink, and his newly acquired sanctions which still must contend against deeper inhibitions, repulsions, vague feelings that what he is doing is not wholly right.

Conflict between two restraining systems. In his third group of conflicts, Lewin includes conflict between two restraining systems in an individual. As an illustration, take a boy in school who wishes to escape from a certain assignment but also wishes to escape from a penalty which will be imposed upon him if the assignment is not completed. Here he has a necessity of avoiding two disagreeable situations that impinge upon the same act and either force him to accept one or the other of the disagreeable consequences or to escape from the situation altogether.

In this group, the conflict is not between an inhibition and a sanction, but between an inhibition and some external force in the form of a punishment. Here we have those situations in which a boy is forced to do something which is distasteful or against which he has inhibitions. A boy may be forced to cheat, something that he recognizes as bad, by the fear of punishment which he will receive if he brings home a poor report card.

Here again, the conflict becomes the more acute when the outer force becomes assimilated as an inner duty. The child, for instance, may engage in petty thieving, which he knows is wrong, in order to avoid the beating awaiting him at home if he returns empty-handed. In these conflicts, there is a desire to escape, on the one hand, from the immediate situation which has become untenable, and on the other hand, from a duty which has been inhibited from past experiences.

Hovland and Sears [5] believe that there is a fourth type in this group, which is a combination of the first and the third. They find, for instance,

[5] C. I. Hovland, and R. R. Sears, "Experiments on Motor Conflicts. I. Types of Conflict and Their Modes of Resolution," *Journal of Experimental Psychology*, 23 (1938), 477–493.

that there are frequently two wants with positive valences, the neglect of either of which will produce some kind of disappointment or punishment. As an illustration, take the situation in which a person has two appointments at the same hour. It is impossible for him to be in two places at the same time, and yet failure to attend either of the meetings results in disappointment, which is the equivalent of punishment.

HOW CONFLICTS ARE REACTED TO

Significant recent experimentation has placed on an objective basis our knowledge of the ways to which conflicts are reacted.[6] This modern experimental analysis follows the classification of conflicts into approach-approach situations, avoidance-avoidance situations, and approach-avoidance situations first given by Lewin.[7]

Approach-approach situations. Miller points out that in true approach-approach situations, that is, situations in which an individual is attracted to two different goals without any negative factors being present, there is no real conflict. Two pure choices could not balance for long in perfect equilibrium on a knife edge. One would soon demonstrate its superior strength and would gain ascendancy. As Miller[8] points out, Buridan's ass standing starving between two bundles of hay is pure fiction. In such a situation a person or an animal will go in the direction of the strongest impulse, or to the nearest stimulus. Such a situation seeks to be governed purely by the strength of the various forces operating, and when one path is chosen the other path loses its pulling power. Where there seems to be conflict and indecision in the face of two alternate choices, Miller believes that there are avoidance factors present as well as the pull of the attractive goal.

However, in human affairs the solution to this simple double-approach situation may have another outcome. It is possible to satisfy each of the alternatives in turn, granted that a person goes in the direction of the strongest impulse or the nearest stimulus. After this impulse has been satisfied, then he may turn in the direction of the other goals and satisfy them in turn. One can sometimes postpone one satisfaction until another has been achieved. One can plan a trip so as to see several points of interest by driving a little further around. When the visitor drops in at lunch

---

[6] J. S. Brown, "Factors Determining Conflict Reactions in Difficult Discriminations," *Journal of Emperimental Psychology*, 31 (1942), 272–292; N. E. Miller, "Experimental Studies of Conflict," in J. McV. Hunt, editor, *Personality and the Behavior Disorders* (The Ronald Press Company. 1944), Vol. 1, Ch. XIV, 431–465; R. R. Sears and C. I. Hovland, "Experiments in Motor Conflict. II. Determination of Mode of Resolution by Comparative Strength of Conflicting Responses," *Journal of Experimental Psychology*, 28 (1941), 280–286.

[7] Kurt Lewin, op. cit.

[8] N. E. Miller, op. cit.

time, he may be invited to lunch, and thus make it possible to continue the conversation.

Avoidance-avoidance situations. The typical response to a situation in which a person or animal wishes to escape from two opposite undesirable stimuli is by withdrawal. The boy who has been assigned a difficult task attempts to escape from it by finding some excuse for not doing it or by leaving the room. When withdrawal is impossible, and an individual is confined on all sides, he tends to respond by blocking or by vacillation. (By vacillation is meant a turning from one alternative to the other.) When the situations to be avoided become more intense, the individual may break down emotionally and develop any one of a number of expressions of strong emotion and disorganized behavior.

Approach-avoidance situations. In those situations in which the stimulus has both a pulling and a repelling power, the typical response is blocking, that is, a cessation of all activity. Lewin [9] has described a form of response, which he calls "encysting behavior," in which an individual seemingly becomes impervious to outside stimulation and becomes concerned with his own immediate affairs and interests. Autoerotic behavior would perhaps come under this term. Sears and Hovland [10] found that blocking is five times as great in avoidance as in approach responses. This block increases in strength as the two tendencies approach equality. In approach-avoidance situations one also finds a tendency to oscillate both toward and away from the stimulus. First, if the animal is some distance away the avoidance drive loses its force and the animal tends to approach. However, as the stimulus object comes nearer, the avoidance drive becomes greater, and the approach is turned into a retreat.

Shift in conflict with shift of drive and avoidance tendencies. J. S. Brown [11] has shown that as drives and avoidance tendencies are strengthened or weakened there is a shift in the point of conflict. If the drive increases with the amount of avoidance tendency remaining constant, a person will move closer to his goal. That is, as a prize becomes more enticing and desirable a child will put forth more effort and will overcome, to a greater extent, his fear of failure. And if the avoidance tendency increases it will drive a person still further from his goal. If a child becomes embarrassed in speaking before a public because he is ridiculed, he will stay even further from the group that is preparing for

[9] Kurt Lewin, "Environmental Forces in Child Behavior and Development," in Carl Murchison, editor, *Handbook of Child Psychology* (Worcester, Mass.: Clark University Press, 1931), Ch. XIV, 590–625.

[10] R. R. Sears and C. I. Hovland, "Experiments in Motor Conflict. II. Determination of Mode of Resolution by Comparative Strength of Conflicting Responses," *Journal of Experimental Psychology*, 28 (1941), 280–286.

[11] J. S. Brown, "Factors Determining Conflict Reactions in Difficult Discriminations," *Journal of Experimental Psychology*, 31 (1942), 272–292.

the play or debate. Increasing the strength of the drive is the equivalent of decreasing the strength of the avoidance tendency.

Miller [12] points out that the gradient of avoidance, that is, the change in the strength of the avoidance tendency, is steeper than the gradient of approach. The reason for this is that impulses toward approach are relatively stable inasmuch as they reside within the economy of the organism, whereas tendencies to avoid are directly proportional to the nearness of the stimulus, and as the distance from the stimulus changes, these avoidance tendencies will change in like ratio.

Double approach-avoidance situations. Several investigators have pointed out that one rarely gets a simple approach-approach situation. Almost always there are negative factors operating along with the positive factors. For instance, if one approach becomes invested with the fear of loss, especially when a goal must be given up in order to achieve another, this fear operates as a negative or avoidance factor. When an individual is between two attractive goals and he starts toward the stronger of the two, a negative factor with regard to the other goal sets in, namely, his regret at having to give it up or the fear of losing it. Consequently, in a pure choice situation, there are also usually negative factors which lead to vacillation and ultimately to blocking. The difference, however, between this and the avoidance-avoidance situation is that there are inherent pulling factors toward each goal, so that no barriers are needed to hold the subject in the situation. Most choice situations probably include the double approach-avoidance factors.

Choice in conflict situations. Barker [13] has added some significant facts with regard to choice in a conflict situation. He experimented by having children choose between two beverages. Some of the beverages were those which children ordinarily like, such as lemonade or cocoa, and others were those which are bitter and distasteful, such as salt water or castor-oil. In preliminary experimental work, Barker was able to place these drinks on a liking-disliking scale. He found that the greater the distinction between items in choice on the scale, the shorter the time for making a decision and the less hesitation and vacillation there is in making the decision. In other words, children have less difficulty in deciding between lemonade and castor-oil than they do between lemonade and cocoa. In actual trials, it was found that it is more difficult for children to make a choice when they had to actually relinquish one of their choices than when they were promised that they could have both of them. Choosing between disliked items required a longer time, and more hesitation

[12] N. E. Miller, op. cit.
[13] R. G. Barker, "An Experimental Study of the Resolution of Conflicts in Children," in Quinn McNemar and M. A. Merrill, editors, *Studies in Personality* (New York: McGraw-Hill Book Company, Inc., 1942), Ch. II, 13–34.

and vacillation than choosing between liked items. On the other hand, choices between neutral items, that is, those neither strongly liked nor disliked, took the longest and led to the most hesitation and vacillation. There was greater conflict in a real choice than when the choice was hypothetic, and the answers were to be given on paper.

Meeting conflict through fantasy. The results of these experimental studies of conflict, however, do not take care of all of the contingencies in the resolution of conflicts in actual life. One method of running away from the conflict in actuality or fearing to come to grips with it in real life is the attempt to achieve the ends desired through fantasy. The boy whose desires to succeed in school conflict with his belief that he cannot succeed, may meet the situation by indulging in day-dreams of becoming a successful aviator.

Meeting conflict through repression. Another reason why the experimental studies do not take care of all of the varieties of conflict in actual life is that they do not take into account the possibility that one or both conflicting tendencies may be repressed. A common method of managing conflicts is to repress into the unconscious one vector of the conflict and allow the other to have free expression and this is what is usually done with the conflicts in basic drives as described on p. 255. Usually this method of handling conflict is satisfactory if the outer frustrations are not too great. If, however, the outer frustrations become too intense, an individual may not be able to manage his tendencies in this way. Both may press for some form of outward expression, and the conflict itself then becomes intense and hard to manage.

Meeting conflict through compromise. Compromise is the typical neurotic method of handling a conflict. An attempt is made to satisfy both demands without actually satisfying either.

For instance, a teacher feels an obligation to stay with her mother during the summer but also wishes to be away from her where she can be free and independent. She will then try to satisfy the claims of her conscience and also her wishes by planning to take an extended trip or to attend a summer-school (the latter preferably because she can justify it by rationalization of her need to make professional progress), while she plans that her mother shall stay at a pleasant hotel and will receive a daily letter from her. In this case, neither wish is completely satisfied for, on the one hand, she is actually not with her mother, and on the other, would continue to feel guilty for having left her.

Neurotic behavior is, to a degree, meaningless behavior in the sense that it does not seem to be wholly appropriate to the situation. The reason that it seems to be meaningless is that it is attempting to provide expression of the unconscious trend as well as the conscious. In that sense, much neurotic behavior has a symbolic significance. For instance, ceremonious hand-washing, which has been mentioned as a way in which conflict may be expressed through compulsive behavior, may indicate both that the individual has gratified himself through masturbation, and feels that this is wrong and must somehow be expiated and cleansed. Consequently, the hand-washing illustrates both the gratification through fantasy of the forbidden tendency and the effort to satisfy the superego demands that the tendency be expiated. Hand-washing repeated many times throughout the day is meaningless in the real world. Its true meaning comes only in terms of its symbolic significance in the light of the conflict.

Integrated solution to conflict. Finally, there is the integrated solution. If such a solution is to be carried out, both sides of the conflict must be fully in view in consciousness, so that the individual is aware of both tendencies. He must be in a position to weigh their relative values, to see to what extent, through modification of them or through substitute gratification, values in each may be realized. By some sort of adjustment of his want, the maximum satisfaction, in view of the circumstances, can be achieved. Naturally, the integrated solution is, theoretically, the one most open to commendation, but it cannot be achieved until the unconscious side of the conflict is clearly brought into awareness so that is can be dealt with on the basis of reality.

As an illustration, consider the mother who loves her son and yet hates him because he reminds her of her dead husband whose name he holds, a husband who failed to support her and debauched himself with drink. Because she unconsciously feels guilty because of these hostile feelings, she tends to give the boy more expensive toys and clothing than she can afford as an atonement. If she could be helped to realize the reality of her feelings toward her son and their origin and the fact that in a way she is not to be blamed for having them, then two things would happen—she would be better able to tolerate her feelings, and the hostile feelings themselves would diminish in intensity.

Sometimes the integrated solution can be achieved by a new gestalt or perspective on the problem.

The Methodist minister is unable to condone attendance at the movies because his church has placed a ban on theater-going. But if he sees the movies as an agency in character education, then he may be able to incorporate them into his accepted values.

A person does not naturally outgrow his conflicts. Conflicts are resolved by adaptation and not through the natural process of development. Parents or teachers cannot assume that the maladjusted child will outgrow his problems by the mere process of growth. He has to manage his problems by finding a better solution to them. One should not hesitate to remove a child from situations which are causing marked frustration, because in so doing one removes the cause of serious conflicts. There is no harm in helping a little child master his fear of the dark by going with him and tucking him in bed.

Resolution of conflicts through psychotherapy. Psychotherapy is the art of helping a person to tolerate and to resolve his conflicts. The maladjusted person is one in whom drives have been jammed and are forced to seek expression in circuitous and meaningless ways. In psychotherapy the individual must be helped to discover and break down these barriers so that the driving forces within may receive more immediate and uninhibited expression. The chief aim in psychotherapy is to help an individual accept the reality of his drives, that is, to bring the unconscious tendencies into consciousness where they can be seen and evaluated, and where plans for meeting them or managing them can be worked out. This is done through the aid of a second person, the counselor, who encourages the person to express himself freely by giving him every kind of security so that repressed tendencies may find expression safely. Education, on the other hand, is mainly concerned with helping an individual to become adequate to meet life's situations, both for maximum satisfaction to himself and for the protection and advancement of society. Psychotherapy and education, therefore, have different goals, but both are concerned with the furtherance and more adequate expression of drives within the individual.

VALUES AND EDUCATIONAL IMPLICATIONS OF CONFLICT

Conflicts are inevitable and normal. Conflicts are inevitable and hence normal. It is no disgrace to be faced by a conflict. As a matter of fact, it is only through conflicts that one is able to grow and to reach functional maturity in the world about him. The individual who is protected from conflict is missing an opportunity of reaching a higher, more stable integration of his desires. Sherman,[14] who has devoted much thought to the meaning of conflicts in human life, would judge them on three scores: first, directly in terms of the issues involved and how deep-seated and fundamental they are in the individual's hierarchy of drives. Secondly, he would judge them in terms of their frequency, and thirdly, in terms of their intensity. One might say that the individual is better adjusted whose conflicts are more immediate and superficial rather than those which involve deeper and more fundamental aspects of the personality, are fewer in number, and are less intense in quality.

Conflicts may interfere with good adjustment. Conflicts may become a detriment if they usurp too much of a person's time and energy. The well-adjusted child in school is the child who has relatively few personal conflicts to contend with and hence can give his attention to the immediate tasks and activities at hand with full zest in attempting to adjust to them. The child who is upset by a severe emotional conflict will have difficulty in adjusting in school. He will be the child who either becomes maladjusted and anti-social or inhibited. The child who is subject to

[14] Mandel Sherman, *Mental Conflicts and Personality* (New York: Longmans, Green and Co., 1938).

severe frustrations and beset by doubts in regard to the security which he can expect from other people is faced with severe conflicts. Many times they are conflicts with regard to aggression: tendencies to wish to express aggression toward others and fear of doing so. When these conflicts are intense they, of necessity, drain off energy and attention from more worthwhile pursuits. No one can fully give his mind to his task until it is free from disturbing conflicts.

The happy man is one in whom conflicts are at a minimum of depth, frequency, and intensity. His life is one that has a straightforward pattern. He can face outward and meet, with zeal and adequacy, the situations that each day presents. The successful resolution of the conflicts, both minor and major, which beset one in daily living is the road to maturity. Integration depends on the successful resolution of the conflicts inevitably met at all stages of development. A person's emotional stability is closely related to his conflicts. The stable person, that is, the one who is unperturbed in the face of severe frustrations and can find a solution for them, is the person who has at an earlier age found a way through his conflicts. On the other hand, the person whose conflicts are intense gives way early to emotion, and we recognize him as an emotionally unstable individual. Conflicts are at a minimum in the individual who has grown up in a secure relationship in the family situation and hence dares to face the reality of the opposing arms of conflict which beset him.

How severe conflicts may be avoided. Severe conflicts may be avoided by avoiding frustrations that are too severe, that is, those which cause regression. A child is fortunately brought up who is protected to the extent that he does not have to face frustrations which overwhelm him and which he finds unsurmountable although, as was stated in a previous chapter, a certain amount of mild frustration is necessary for growth. Many parents feel that they tend to mollycoddle their children. They believe that character is developed by thrusting a child into situations through which he must find a way by himself. There is widespread belief in the values of discipline. However, to thrust the child into emotional situations for which he is unprepared is to present him with frustration for which he is not likely to find satisfactory solution, and this is sure to arouse conflict. Conflicts have less power over the emotionally secure person, that is the individual who was brought up in a home where through personal relationships emotional security was fostered.

QUESTIONS FOR DISCUSSION

1. Give illustrations of the conflicts between a basic drive and superego restraint.
2. Why is a compromise solution to a conflict called neurotic?
3. Why is an integrated solution to a conflict impossible as long as the

individual is unaware of or unconscious of either (or both) of the forces operating? Does this suggest a method of eliminating internal conflicts?

4. What are the implications of the statement that a person does not naturally outgrow his conflicts? (P. 269.)

5. Discuss the issue of removing a child from frustrations so that his conflicts will be less severe. What are some of the arguments opposed to this practice? In favor of it?

6. Discuss the respective goals and methods of education in helping a person resolve his inner conflicts.

RECOMMENDED READING

1. ALEXANDER, FRANZ, "The Relation of Structural and Instinctual Conflicts," *Psychoanalytic Quarterly*, 2 (1933), 181–207.
2. ANDERSON, H. H., "Conflicts in Personality Development," *Mental Hygiene* 20 (1936), 605–613.
3. BARKER, R. G., "An Experimental Study of the Resolution of Conflicts in Children" in Quinn McNemar and M. A. Merrill, editors, *Studies in Personality* (New York: McGraw-Hill Book Company, Inc., 1942), Ch. II, 13–34.
4. DEUTSCH, HELENE, *Psychoanalysis of the Neuroses*, International Psychoanalytical Library, No. 23 (London: Hogarth Press, 1932).
5. GUTHRIE, E. R., *The Psychology of Human Conflict* (New York: Harper and Brothers, 1938).
6. HORNEY, KAREN, *Our Inner Conflicts* (New York: W. W. Norton & Company, Inc. 1945).
7. LEWIN, KURT, *A Dynamic Theory of Personality* (New York: McGraw-Hill Book Company, Inc., 1935).
8. MASLOW, A. H., and MITTELMANN, BELA, *Principles of Abnormal Psychology* (New York: Harper and Brothers, 1941).
9. MILLER, N. E. "Experimental Studies of Conflict," in J. McV. Hunt, editor, *Personality and the Behavior Disorders* (New York: The Ronald Press Company, 1944) Vol. I, Ch. XIV, 431–465.
10. MUNN, N. L. *Psychology* (Boston: Houghton Mifflin Company, 1946).
11. RIVIERE, JOAN, "On the Genesis of Psychical Conflict in Earliest Infancy," *International Journal of Psychoanalysis*, 17 (1936), 395–422.
12. SHERMAN, MANDEL, *Mental Conflicts and Personality* (New York: Longmans, Green and Co., 1938).

XV

Guilt and Self-Punishment

The topic of guilt comes as a climax to the series of dynamic concepts beginning with drive and continuing through frustration, aggression, punishment, anxiety, and introjection. In guilt these forces come to a focus and result in the strongest motivation for growth and adjustment. Just as in the literary plot the climax must be followed by some sort of conclusion, satisfactory or not, so guilt must be followed by some sort of resolution whether it be love and reparation on the one hand, or self-punishment on the other.

NATURE OF GUILT

Guilt a variety of anxiety. Guilt is a variety of anxiety, and so far as can be determined, the nature of the feelings and emotions and their physiological concomitants are precisely the same in guilt as they are in anxiety. Guilt is sometimes called conscience anxiety or social anxiety as distinguished from objective anxiety toward some outside stimulus or event. Guilt, then, is a form of fear, although, because of its derived nature, the feared object is not immediately discernible. Guilt is anxiety arising from the superego, that is, from the demands and prohibitions of parents and other parental figures which have been introjected. Anxiety, as we have seen, is the fear of anticipated danger. Guilt, then, becomes the fear of those tendencies within the self which disapprove and threaten punishment. The boy feels guilty when he has thrown a baseball that has broken a window. To be sure, he may also be anxious because he firmly believes that when his father comes home in the evening he will be punished, but even though his father may not discover the broken window for a long time, the boy may still feel uncomfortable about it, that is, guilty. Something within him tells him that he has committed a fault, has been careless, has broken something for which he deserves to be punished. It is this uncomfortable feeling, stirred up by his own inner standards of what is right and wrong, standards which are, of course, the result of the teachings of his parents and society in general, which we call guilt. Sometimes guilt arises from things that are left undone, as when a man discovers that he has forgotten some important business engagement, or the housewife that she has forgotten to set the table for supper.

Guilt is based on previous introjections. Guilt comes only after the process of introjection. It is not found in the very young child before he has assimilated into his own behavioral patterns the teachings of his elders. It is not found in the psychopath for whom no superego has been formed because of absence of standards, conflicting standards, or the failure of standards to develop due to hostility. When the superego is being formed in the very young child, and the child's behavior is still largely dominated by the wishes and restraints of his parents, the tendencies toward guilt are weak. It can easily be resolved in the child by the adult's forgiveness. In later life, however, when the superego has become established and is to a large extent independent of outside influence, guilt also is independent of the attitudes which others may take. The adolescent or adult, even though forgiven by the person toward whom an offense is committed, still feels guilty about his misconduct. In the adult guilt is determined almost completely by the standards that an individual holds for himself, and it makes comparatively little difference what attitudes others hold toward them. It is for this reason that adults resist change in standards of thought and behavior and take on new ways slowly.

Guilt not possible when objective anxiety is too great. Guilt is not possible when objective anxiety is too great. This is another reason why guilt is not found in the very young child whose anxiety, due to exaggerated fantasies of the attitudes of his parents, becomes overwhelming. The young child has difficulty in accepting his superego and the feelings accompanying it, and he tends to project it in hostility and destructiveness toward those about him. The superego anxiety becomes reduced in degree only as maturity brings a sense of reality in a family that does not arouse too much hostility. So it is only at about the age of four or five that we find true guilt developing, indicating that the individual has formulated his own standards of right and wrong and has developed feelings of discomfort and unworthiness when he does not live up to them. Often in later years when guilt becomes strong, it assumes the peculiar qualities of conscience and is felt as a form of anxiety against which defenses must be raised.

Origin of guilt. Guilt arises from fear or loss of self-regard and also from the dread of punishment. With regard to the first, guilt arises from the fear of being at odds with oneself, that is, the parents within, and from fear and loss of self-love. This form of guilt usually goes under a different name and is called variously, feeling insufficient, feeling inferior or inadequate, feeling isolated or lonely. All of these states result from the fear of what is called loss of self-esteem, self-respect, self-regard or self-love. Just as anxiety has its primary cause in fear of being left alone and deserted by one's parents, so guilt originates from a similar dread of losing oneself, that is, the part of oneself that one respects and admires.

Probably guilt is more commonly recognized as originating from the dread of punishment. However, it is not the actual punishment that is dreaded, but rather the sense of deserving punishment following defection from the standards which the individual has assimilated and taken into himself. Guilt then follows from that part of the self that judges, condemns, reproaches and criticizes. For instance, a man may feel guilty because of the aggressive or sexual impulses released when he is drunk, not because he is criticized by others but because of standards within himself which are the residue of punishment received long ago. The person most critical of others is the one who will feel the most severe guilt himself. This shows itself in such divers ways as the fear of making a mistake when embarking on some new enterprise, anticipating failure, or being acutely aware of one's own shortcomings. Guilt also shows itself in the fear of annoying people and arousing their hostility even before there is anyone to be annoyed. Guilt is a product of one's own fantasy, but always in the background is a reference to the attitudes of other persons —a fear of retaliation or censure or punishment from parents, and in a more remote sense, from society and its laws, or even from Divine anger. So the citizen who fails to get his income tax in before the deadline, may have that uncomfortable feeling of having transgressed the laws; or the religious man may dread the vengeance of the all-seeing Eye.

Part of the motivation in guilt is the desire for union and harmony with the object toward which the aggression is directed and from which the punishment and retaliation is feared. The guilty person wants, first of all, to be at peace with himself, but in the background is his desire to establish good relations with others. He wants to restore his self-regard by clearing himself of his faults and misdemeanors, but, at the same time, he wants to be able to look others in the eye without flinching, and to feel that he is an acceptable member of their society.

Guilt a conflict phenomenon—discrepancy and tension between ego and superego. It must be evident from the foregoing that the forces making for guilt are all within the individual. This means that within the individual there are two sets of conflicting forces. One of these, the superego, represents those tendencies that hold standards, criticize and recognize the need of punishment. The other part of the individual that is held responsible for guilt is the ego. So in guilt the superego representing the introjected parents becomes critical of the ego; the ego perhaps has failed to live up to the behests of the ego ideal, and feelings of inferiority develop. As a child he may fail to make the marks in school that his parents would like; in later years he becomes dissatisfied with his own achievements in school and at work, and develops feelings of unworthiness and inadequacy. Or perhaps the ego has transgressed the prohibitions of the superego, and there is guilt and conscience. Here too, one feels that one is unworthy and a sinner. The little boy is told by his parents that it is wrong to play marbles for keeps. When he grows up he may find that he becomes most uncomfortable when he is asked by a group of friends to place a bet on the outcome of a race.

It is interesting that feelings of guilt and of inferiority spring particularly from the fear of being detected. This undoubtedly goes back to the stage in early years when the child knows that he will be punished only if he is caught doing a misdemeanor. So anxiety is conditioned by the watchful eye of the parent, and the fear of being caught is as much a part of anxiety as the fear of the punishment for the misdemeanor itself. Being seen by the parent (visual response by the parent) becomes the cue to later admonishment (vocal response by the parent). Fear of being observed by the critical parents is the first cue or signal of coming danger and hence is a stimulus for anxiety. So Horney [1] sees guilt as the disparity between the impulse and the defense against it. Guilt is a fear of being unmasked, of having one's real weaknesses revealed both to oneself and to others.

When one feels guilt he dreads letting others know about it. There is a certain comfort in keeping one's weaknesses, failures and shortcomings to oneself. Guilt is intensified when secrecy is abandoned. The detection of one's faults and failings by another person breaks the barrier between the façade and its background. The true self lies revealed in all its nakedness, and the fact that it is revealed, not only to others but to the self, increases the guilt feelings.

Secrecy, then, helps to maintain the discrepancy between the ego and the superego; if one can prevent the world from knowing one's faults, one can also hide them from himself to a degree. Letting the world know makes it necessary to face the reality in oneself, and guilt breaks out with full force. It is for these reasons that persons find it necessary to maintain a poker face and to hide their real feelings, and, as Horney [2] points out so clearly, it is just this failure to admit one's weaknesses and shortcomings that is the basis of neurotic tendencies.

On the other hand, when one is at harmony with one's conscience a deep feeling of peace arises; the tension and strain and feeling of unworthiness and inadequacy melt away. Accordingly, one sees that it is not the weakness or the inadequacy, however severe these may be, that is the cause of guilt and feelings of inferiority, but the discrepancy between the standards one holds and the feeling of shortcomings with regard to them.

[1] Karen Horney, *New Ways in Psychoanalysis* (New York: W. W. Norton & Company, Inc., 1939), 238 ff.
[2] *Ibid*, p. 244.

FUNDAMENTAL CONSIDERATIONS

Guilt highly intolerable. Guilt, like anxiety, is an intolerable state of affairs, one which the individual goes to any extreme to avoid or to disguise. Guilt is probably more intolerable than hate, for it carries with it not only the emotion itself but also the conflict of forces within the individual. The intensity of guilt varies with the degree of aggression that is repressed. The more violent the hostile impulses causing guilt, the more severe the guilt tendencies. Guilt is felt to the degree that aggression is repressed and not expressed openly. Somehow, the open expression of aggression serves as a release of feeling, whereas impulses toward aggression not actually expressed may carry more than the average load of guilt. MacKinnon,[3] for instance, found in an experiment that non-violators of certain prohibitions set up during an experiment expressed more guilt than those who violated the prohibitions.

Guilt a composite of criticism from many sources. One should not assume that guilt always arises from specific wishes or prohibitions of parents or others. Actually, the standards which occasion guilt result from a variety of sources, so that it would be difficult to pin responsibility on any one person. An act may be criticized by one person and condoned by another; hence guilt arises from the total set of values which an individual has absorbed from all portions of his environment.

Guilt over infantile faults may last through life. One becomes impressed with the continuity of dynamic tendencies in an individual. The standards and values which a person absorbs when very young are retained by him throughout his life, and even in adult years he can become sensitive over faults which were criticized in his childhood. To be sure, there is a constant modification of our standards and values as experience accumulates. However, the more immediate experiences are relatively weak in deciding the basic values of a person as compared with those influences which were operating on him and directing him when he was very young.

Guilt involves consideration of the ethical. Guilt is always concerned with and closely related to our sense of moral values. One may say that guilt arises as a warning of departure from accepted standards, but it should be recognized that these standards are not fixed, immutable laws as some religious and philosophical systems have considered them, but are those standards which were inculcated in the individual by the culture in which he grew up, especially as it was interpreted by his own parents.

[3] D. W. MacKinnon, "Violation of Prohibitions," in H. A. Murray, Jr., *Explorations in Personality* (New York: Oxford University Press, 1938), Sec. 14, Ch. VI, 491–501.

OCCASIONS FOR GUILT

Guilt because of aggressive impulses. One feels guilty concerning two things: sadistic tendencies and tendencies to gain erotic satisfaction. In the first place, to the extent that sadism has been punished, tendencies toward its expression are an occasion for guilt. An individual in our culture feels guilty when he expresses hostility, hatred or revenge, whether in deed or in fantasy. Indeed, as has been stated, the most poignant guilt is frequently felt for fantasied hostile impulses rather than those actually expressed in deeds. These hostile impulses in fantasy imply that the aggression has been repressed, and guilt is always stronger when aggression is repressed than when it is given active expression.

Guilt is not felt when hostility is believed justified, but only when the hostility is condemned or criticized. A child will feel guilty because of his hostile tendencies only as a parent tends to put him in his place by appropriate restrictions and punishment. There are occasions in our society when aggression is not only overlooked but actually approved. For instance, one expects a boy to be aggressive in sports, in achievements, and enterprises. Righteous indignation at social evils is generally applauded. In war men are not only given permission but are expected to kill and are rewarded for killing. Juries will acquit an assailant who can prove that he has acted in self-defense. Not only does society condone these kinds of aggression, but the individual is, to a degree, freed from the sense of guilt concerning them. The heroes who are decorated with awards of merit for valor on the battle-field are relieved of guilt over their exploits, for their actions have been justified in honor.

High standards which an individual has adopted for himself can easily become the occasion for guilt. One can explain this as due basically to guilt for the aggression which one feels against the person requiring these high standards. For instance, an individual feels that he must make Phi Beta Kappa in college. When he comes to the end of his senior year and has failed to make his goal, he feels most humiliated, which of course is directly related to the fact that there is a discrepancy between his accomplishment and the goal set for himself. This humiliation, however, stems originally from the fact that his goal grew, at one time, from similar goals set for him by someone else, as for example, a doting parent, and the feeling of inadequacy arose out of the attitude expressed toward him when he failed to meet his parent's expectations.

In general, one may say that the greater the degree of hostility, the greater the degree of guilt which will be felt. A person who has had reasonable parents and who has been only mildly frustrated and given security when young will have little occasion for strong feelings of hostility in later years, and, consequently, will be relatively free from guilt. On the other hand, the individual who has been severely frustrated and punished, particularly for his aggressive behavior, will be the one who feels the most inadequate, and in him guilt will be most strongly aroused in later life.

Guilt for erotic impulses. It is well known that guilt is aroused not only from hostile feelings but also for enjoying forbidden pleasures. Some writers seem to believe that guilt following erotic pleasure comes almost instinctively, but the probabilities are that this guilt is aroused only to the extent that erotic pleasures have at some previous time been punished. As these autoerotic pleasures have been frowned upon by parents, so in later years a man or woman may himself feel guilty and uncomfortable when he has enjoyed too much pleasure. One would have to explain why any individual should feel uncomfortable or guilty at receiving benefits from pleasures, as there seems to be no obvious connection. For instance, if one receives more money than he deserves, or if he is undercharged there may be a slight tinge of guilt. Many persons feel uncomfortable if they do not pay their bills promptly. This is undoubtedly related to guilt and a fear of punishment which accompanies undeserved pleasure, as though one had to pay in pain for the pleasures one enjoys.

Guilt because of criticized characteristics. Apart from these two main occasions for guilt, there are other lesser and perhaps derived occasions. Aside from behavioral tendencies to action, a child may feel guilty or inferior in connection with characteristics possessed by him. A lamed, deformed, mutilated or scarred child is liable to taunts and ridicule, and as Adler [4] has pointed out so clearly, possession of physical defects is a prime cause for feelings of inferiority. More important, perhaps, is guilt that comes from having sexual characteristics not approved by the father or mother. A father, for instance, who unconsciously has difficulty in accepting feminine characteristics in his own personality may find it difficult to accept his daughter in her own feminine rôle. Such a girl may strive to play the boy's rôle when young and take on the characteristics of a tomboy. In similar manner, a boy whose mother finds masculinity dangerous and difficult to tolerate, may have difficulty in accepting his own masculinity. He may veer away from rough and tumble boys' games in sports, and his interests will turn to those activities of a more refined and less competitive nature. In thus denying the rôle of their own sex, these individuals are responding to the guilt which their parents' attitude has forced on them.

In all of these illustrations guilt has been fostered by the attitude

[4] Alfred Adler, *Study of Organ Inferiority and Its Psychical Compensation*, Nervous and Mental Disease Monograph Series, No. 24 (New York: Nervous and Mental Disease Publishing Company, 1917).

which the parents have taken toward the aggressive or erotic tendencies in the very young child. Parents make known their attitude by word and deed in the form of punishment, verbal prohibition, ridicule, and obvious signs of revulsion. Guilt, fundamentally, has its origin in punishment and overstrict treatment by the parent.

EXPRESSION OF GUILT

It is important for the counselor to be able to recognize guilt in its many forms of expression. Guilt shows itself directly in behavior and speech; it shows itself in fantasy productions and in the play activities of children. It also becomes expressed in various projections whereby the individual attempts to deny his guilt and pin it on others.

Anxiety also indicates pressure guilt. Almost any expression of anxiety may also be an expression of guilt in so far as the occasion for the anxiety has been introjected and made part of the individual himself. So there are certain infantile methods of expressing guilt. Crying, which we have seen to be a method by which the very young child shows his anxiety, may also be an expression of guilt. A little boy who cannot do the sums assigned to him may burst into tears. If we knew him better we would recognize that these tears were in anticipation of the scolding that he believes he will receive when his failure is discovered. This, of course, is definitely anxiety because the punishment to be feared is a real external punishment. Later, however, this same child may show signs of despair at his own failure and ineffectiveness, even though no one else is around to show their disappointment. This would be a true expression of guilt. A child who when visiting breaks some object may plead for mercy, although the aunt with whom he is staying may have no thought of scolding him.

Conflict and disorganization indicate guilt. Since guilt represents a conflict within the person, any signs of conflict or disorganization are prima facie evidence of guilt. Various kinds of confusion in thought and speech are telltale signs. The child who stammers or becomes confused in making an explanation is probably struggling with guilt tendencies. Proneness to error, mistakes in copying, errors in arithmetic or reading, in carrying out errands, point to confusion in thought and conflict within the self, which are signs of guilt. Likewise, the inability to concentrate, so common in children in school, may also be taken as a sign of feelings of guilt and inferiority. Mind-wandering and day-dreaming in school are almost certain to indicate emotional conflict and a fear of censure either from teacher or parent. Even simple hesitation may be a token of guilt. In a more general sense, the loss of interest, listlessness, lack of ambition, point to the presence of guilt and feelings of inadequacy. Failing to remember tasks, appointments, errands or responsibilities and procrastination point to the same kind of confusion in thought and arouse a suspicion of guilt tendencies. A person may show his guilt on the intellectual side by doubt.

Fears a possible sign of guilt. Guilt shows itself most clearly in a variety of fears more or less openly expressed. Perhaps the most basic expression of guilt is the fear of loneliness, of isolation, and the loss of love, because this fear is basic to guilt itself. Guilt arises, in the first place, from the threat of rejection and withdrawal of love, and it is this fear that ever hovers about the individual lest he antagonize others and isolate himself from them. So the person who has a need to be one of a group, to join the club or the gang shows his feelings of inadequacy if he is forced to shift for himself, alone and without the support of others. This will show itself in the fear of annoying people and arousing their opposition. The person who cannot bring himself to contradict another and who has adopted ingratiating manners and politic tactics is struggling with underlying feelings of guilt.

The person in whom guilt is easily aroused is the one who fears the retaliation of others; he is the person who is sensitive to criticism and uses various devices to cushion himself against the critical attacks of others. Such a person is always sensitive to the possibility of criticism; he even interprets harmless remarks as slurs although they were not so intended. He is much concerned about public opinion and wants to feel assured that others think well of him. He wonders if others are disapproving of his behavior or point of view, and finds it necessary to ingratiate himself with others so that he may feel secure with them. Sometimes guilt is shown by sharp resentment at criticism, and the tendency is to run to one's own defense. Others show their guilt by ignoring insults for fear that they might further alienate the person who attacks them. He who fears retaliation from others is the prophet of disaster; he is always expecting the worst and has suspicions of evil intentions jumping out at him from dark corners. In this connection, much irrational and unexplained behavior is determined by guilt, since we tend to react to our imagos of another person rather than to the real person. So when there is some uncalled-for outburst against another person, it is more than likely due to the guilt from otherwise unexpressed hostile impulses than to some real occasion for the outburst aroused by the other person.

Guilt shown by feelings of inferiority. Guilt is also shown by expressions of feelings of inferiority, smallness and weakness. The individual who protests his unworthiness, his inadequacy, is giving expression to his tendencies toward guilt and feelings of inferiority. On the other hand, the individual who boasts of his exploits, his travels, his accomplishments in an extravagant fashion may be recognized as one who is trying to hide from himself as well as from others his underlying feelings of unworthiness. Sometimes these feelings of inferiority are expressed by doubt, uncertainty, lack of resoluteness.

Secrecy as an indication of guilt. Another fear experienced by the guilty person is that of being found out, hence the individual shows his guilt by secretive tendencies: the hushed word, the comment passed behind the hand or in the cloak-room, the muffled step, the furtive look. Secrecy is motivated as a means of avoiding the loss of love and of punishment and actually of guilt itself. It shows itself in many ways. A child may hesitate to tell his parents about his comings and goings. Many parents complain that whereas in earlier years they felt very close to their son or daughter, at adolescence a barrier of reserve has sprung up, and they no longer are the confidants of the inmost thoughts and feelings of their children. A young girl will want to have secret boxes and diaries with locks on them. The locket which carries the secret picture is both an expression of wishes and also guilt concerning them. There is a tendency toward the obliteration of clues, and even in flight itself from one's wishes and thoughts. The person who runs away from pleasures, tasks, difficulties, and obligations is one who feels inadequate concerning them and guilty for his inadequacy. Perhaps the desire to conceal guilt may be attempted by such devices as casualness, levity, or coldness of feeling.

Fighting back—warding off punishment as a sign of guilt. There are many ways in which an individual may protect himself against the fear of his own hostility. Most prominent of these is the tendency to fight back. Aggression, which has shown so many meanings in these pages, takes on another one here as a telltale sign of guilt. Unprovoked hostility, criticism, and the reproaches of others are almost certainly signs of guilt. The tendency to argue one's point out indefinitely shows a struggle with one's own tendencies toward feeling hostile; and the belief that this hostility will arouse the antagonism of the other person causes one to go to his own defense against this imagined hostility. The person who bristles when criticized, coming to his own defense, and the person who is unwilling, resistant, uncoöperative and rebellious, give evidence of their fear of the retaliatory measures which others may take toward their own hostility, and give clear evidence of their own feelings of guilt concerning them. Sometimes one jumps the gun in stalling off the feared hostility or criticism by blaming or unjustly criticizing another, or by being rude or defiant. In cases where the attack on the other person seems to lack sufficient provocation, or to be unnecessarily harsh, one may suspect guilt tendencies.

Self-justification and defense as signs of guilt. To protect oneself against the imagined attack of others, one's aggressive tendencies may take the form of defense rather than attack. The guilty person is ready with excuses and explanations for his failure or forgetfulness. Many times these excuses will be given even before the other person is aware that there is any fault. The boy who apologizes to his teacher for the delay in handing in his paper or for his untidiness, is forestalling expected criticism, thereby showing his own guilt over his omissions. Likewise, the person who avoids humiliation by a preparatory build-up is equally protecting himself against his guilt and inferiority. So some persons adopt gracious manners, dress with exquisite taste, or select decorative ornaments for their houses, their automobiles or their writing paper to ward off criticism and possible challenge to adequacy. Others may fear the challenge to their thoughts and points of view and may build up elaborate defenses to their arguments lest they topple over and crash into discard.

Avoiding expression of aggressive tendencies as indication of guilt. A third method of meeting or forestalling the attacks and criticisms of others is to avoid giving offense and to adopt a character of submissiveness and docility. This goes a step beyond the first method and the aggression whose purpose is to ward off punishment is now repressed. The individual who withdraws from competition, who refuses to play games or to lay himself open to any sort of challenge or attack apparently is, first of all, afraid of being defeated and having to suffer the ignominy accompanying it. He may not be afraid of the jeers and taunts of others, but he may feel uncomfortable at the pride and assurance which accompanies their victory and his own humiliation at his defeat. Withdrawal from competition is stimulated primarily because the individual wants so much to prove himself the victor. In a more general sense, this person avoids any act which might give offense to others. He is careful not to antagonize them by any assertions on his own part or by any claims to eminence. He ignores his accusers and takes no steps to justify himself or to retaliate. In thus refusing to compete, he is tacitly claiming his superiority.

Guilt and feelings of inferiority are also shown by obedience, subservience, and humility. A boy may show his guilt by submitting without protest to the wishes of his parents by becoming very good. The person who leads a moral and righteous life, who does not cheat or lie or steal, who is polite, courteous, and proper is one that has put aside all tendencies to resist, to rebel, or to defend himself against the attacks of others. He shows his guilt primarily by avoiding the occasion of it. The purer the life, one may be sure the more poignant the feeling of guilt associated with back-slidings from the high moral standards set. The perfectionist is the person who must hold himself to his high standards in order to avoid feelings of discomfort were he to relax or fail in any principle.

Showing guilt by defending a person or cause. Guilt may show itself not only in those tendencies that an individual adopts with regard to himself, but in the attitudes that he takes toward another person. Many a man will defend a friend or a cause where he would not lift a finger to protect himself in a similar extremity. However, to defend a friend or a cause is tantamount to admitting that whatever is defended is somewhere within the person himself, and by going to the defense of another person, he admits that he is sensitive to just such an attack. Far from criticizing the person who is guilty, we find here an illustration of how guilt serves as the basis for one of the most highly admired of human characteristics.

REDUCTION OF GUILT

Since guilt is such an intolerable emotion in man, he goes to any extreme to avoid or to reduce it, and the present section will review some of the methods by which this is accomplished. In the first place, it should be noted that a man is unable to rid himself of guilt unaided from the outside. Guilt, as we have seen, is an anxiety response to tendencies within the self; consequently, self-forgiveness is impossible and an individual needs some sort of assurance from outside sources in order to rid himself of these distressing feelings.

Self-punishment. The principal method by which guilt is reduced is that of self-punishment. As has already been indicated, guilt implies a sense of deserved punishment, and as guilt is aroused, this sense of deserved punishment is followed by steps taken to see that punishment, or its equivalent, is actually suffered.

Motivation of Self-Punishment. HOSTILITY TOWARD OTHERS DANGEROUS. The motivation for inflicting pain on the self, however, is not immediately evident, in fact would seem to represent an impossibility and hence requires careful explanation. In the first place, there is sadism, or the infliction of pain on others—dangerous because it arouses hostility and punishment from others and threatens loss of their love. So this sadism is repressed. First it is suppressed directly by the restraining influence of others who do not particularly enjoy being the objects toward which sadism is directed and take steps to protect themselves from it. Later, however, sadism is repressed by the individual himself, that is, by his superego, which accepts for himself as wrong that which has been taught him to be wrong by others. So far this reviews what has already been previously stated.

FRUSTRATION OF HOSTILITY TOWARD OTHERS INSTIGATES HOSTILITY TOWARD SELF—THE SOURCE OF FRUSTRATION. As an individual represses his hostility *he becomes the frustrating agent,* and the hostility then becomes turned against the self, which is recognized as a new source of the frustration. Here, then, we see the motivation for aggression turned inward. The aggression toward others is repressed, but the impulse remains unexpressed, and it becomes directed inward against the self (the repressing agent) as a substitute. Since hostility, for example, toward the actual parents is barred, the hostility is now directed toward the parents within who have taken their place. One may see this in the supporting motor control that accompanies the repression of aggression. One may, for instance, bite his lips when he represses saying an unkind word. But biting the lips is biting oneself rather than another person. Likewise, one may dig one's nails into the palms of one's hands when he refrains from hitting another person. Here, again, the tension becomes turned inward as a direct outcome of the restraint from turning it outward. It may be mentioned in passing that sadism directed toward the self hurts others too, inasmuch as the person toward whom the sadism is originally directed is one who loves and consequently is hurt when the loved object, namely the person who is aggressive, finds it necessary to injure himself.

This fear that punishment will follow an offense sets up a tension within the individual, and this tension is the expectation of punishment, originally an expectation in reality. However, if the parent is not present, or if the individual keeps his act secret from the parent, punishment is not forthcoming, and there is no way for the tension set up to be relieved. Suspense is often worse than reality, for the punishment in reality does serve as a relief from the anxiety aroused. Indeed, this tension becomes more vivid and distressing with the continued default of punishment. The need of punishment is in reality the tension and expectation of punishment set up by ordinary processes of conditioning. Indeed, this need for punishment, being the distressing state of affairs that it is, leads the person to seek punishment to bring it on himself in fantasy and in reality. It is this dynamic sequence that led Freud [5] to substitute the term "need for punishment" for "unconscious guilt."

TENSION OF EXPECTED PUNISHMENT CAN BE RELIEVED BY SELF-PUNISHMENT. The tension of the expectation of punishment is assuaged by self-punishment and with this release and reduction of tension, guilt is thus resolved and disappears. It is for this reason that suffering sometimes reduces guilt, and in a sense it is only through suffering—that is, aggression turned inward—that the pangs of guilt can be relieved. It would almost seem that the tension created by the need for punishment is self-stimulating, constantly building up pressure, so that punishment in some form is required as a way of realizing and draining off this increasing tension.

SELF-PUNISHMENT BETTER CONTROLLED THAN PUNISHMENT BY OTHERS. There are other ways of looking at self-punishment which may help to explain its motivation. For instance, it is thought that punishment may be better controlled by the self than by others. One never knows how severe or disastrous punishment by a parent may be, but if given by the

5 Sigmund Freud, *New Introductory Lectures in Psychoanalysis*, International Psychoanalytical Library, No. 24 (London: Hogarth Press, 1933; New York: W. W. Norton & Company, Inc., 1933).

person himself, it should be under his control and hence made no more painful than the individual can bear.

SELF-PUNISHMENT AS FACE-SAVING. In this sense self-punishment may be thought of as a form of "face-saving." Attached to punishment delivered by another is a certain humiliation and degradation. On the other hand, if one punishes himself, and particularly if this is done so that it seems to be a blow of chance or fate, then the challenge to self-esteem and self-respect is mitigated.

SELF-PUNISHMENT BRINGS SYMPATHY. Self-punishment may also bring the person sympathy, care, affection, and reassuring statements from others.

75% of accidents caused by 25% of people

Jackie is always getting hurt; queerly enough, this usually results in injuries to his head. At one time he fell off a fence and landed on his head; another time he fell downstairs, and on a third occasion he was struck behind the ear by another boy. On a fourth occasion he was injured on the scalp in the gymnasium by the swinging rings. All these appeared to be accidental occurrences, but the nature of the accidents were too similar to make them wholly a matter of chance. One would only have to see the concern and solicitude of his parents to recognize the gratification that these painful accidents carried with them. That there was some motivation to them was all the more evident, because in other respects the boy was never quite sure how he stood with either parent.

To bring oneself to task by failure or bad luck following some misdeed, poor judgment, or moral delinquency may be a cause for self-approval and self-gratification by indicating that the person has good moral judgment after all, and is reaping the whirlwind that was sown.

SELF-AGGRESSION PROTECTS AGAINST RETALIATION FROM OTHERS. Finally, to turn aggression on the self protects the person from having to accuse others, with all of the danger of possible retaliation that might ensue. It is not uncommon to observe a person turn on himself a depreciatory remark intended for a friend whom he wants to criticize. The result is that instead of criticizing the other person, he is actually absolved from his fault. A mother who is angry because her son does not make a good record in school, will say, "I know that I am partly to blame for not giving him the proper encouragement and for devoting so much of my time to afternoon parties, bridge, and teas." One can easily observe cases in which self-blame is in reality a backfire from blasting criticism really intended for others.

THE HARSHER EARLY DISCIPLINE, THE MORE SEVERE THE SELF-PUNISHMENT. In general, the harsher the early discipline and punishment by the parents, the more severe the self-punishment. Frequently a parent will complain that although she whips her child many times a day, the more he is punished the less he seems to care and the more obstinate and wilful he becomes. This latter may be true, but the parent is not noticing that at the same time the child's guilt is also greatly increased, causing him to inflict self-punishment: failure to learn to read, failure in school, or the development of other undesirable characteristics. Self-punishment is also punishment of the parent, inasmuch as when the child prejudices his interests, and fails in one activity after another, he also humiliates her before her friends and neighbors. What is taken for pure naughtiness or laziness is actually his own tendencies toward inflicting on himself punishment as severe as that which his mother administers physically.

Form of Expression of Self-Punishment. SELF-PUNISHMENT DIRECTED TOWARD THE PERSON. Under this heading ways in which an individual harms himself and prejudices his interests will be commented upon. The best reference is Menninger's book, *Man Against Himself,*[6] which describes methods found to come under the heading of self-punishment. First of all, however, let us mention some of these methods primarily in the realm of feeling. One response to guilt is remorse or compunction. The guilty person feels sorry for his misdeed. Even before he tries to make amends for it and to pay the penalty, he himself feels sorry, and this remorse or sting of conscience may become so sharp and painful as to be a sufficient punishment in and of itself.

Self-Depreciation. Similarly, persons who have the need for self-punishment may castigate themselves by self-blame or self-depreciation, self-renunciation, or self-reproach. All of these methods of scolding or criticizing the self are direct outgrowths of similar forms of criticism that a person may have received from others. It is an interesting observation that of the various forms of self-punishment presently to be described, an individual usually finds satisfactory explanation for them in terms of accident or illness or chance or fate. Seldom does one want to admit to himself that he has had a direct hand in bringing on himself the restrictions, the failures, the accidents, of which he is apparently the innocent sufferer. He will not admit his error and blame himself for his part of the self-punishment, and will not want it to appear that he was a partner in the responsibility.

Of the many ways in which a person may hurt himself, perhaps the most general is that of refusing to take advantage of opportunities presented. How many times does a person turn away from invitations and opportunities because he feels unworthy or guilty and cannot avail himself of them? The feeling that pleasures are too good for one, that they may be for others but that one is too clumsy or unpopular or hideous or old to participate, may really stem out of the deep-seated feelings of one's inadequacy and guilt.

Martyrdom. One of the most widespread ways of invoking punishment on the self is through the various forms of *martyrdom*. There are, for instances, tendencies toward self-sacrifice, of turning oneself away, or of

---

[6] K. A. Menninger, *Man Against Himself* (New York: Harcourt, Brace and Company, 1938).

leaving victory to others. We are encouraged to show good sportsman-ship, which means to accept defeat gracefully, and even perhaps to give one's opponent every advantage so that he may win fairly, if not even with advantage. All forms of asceticism and self-denial represent an-other form of this same martyr tendency. One sees this characteristically in adolescents who may turn, in one of their moods, to extreme denial of pleasures, glutting themselves with restrictions and hard work, passing by opportunities to feast the senses. The young girl who denies herself ice-cream and chocolates in the interests of reducing, or the boy who, in a similar manner, abstains from smoking and late hours because he is in training during the football season, are voluntarily enduring self-punishment, although for obvious reward. Then there are the tendencies toward self-discipline, also a common phenomenon in adolescents. Here we see the serious-minded youth who rises before dawn, immerses him-self in a bath of cold water, undertakes an arduous schedule of study or work, skimps at meals, denies himself the pleasure of the bull session or midnight feast. We see it again in the individual with an overdeveloped sense of duty whose conscience pricks when in some way he falls short of his obligations and the expectations of others. He labors long and late to get the magazine copy in on time or to complete arrangements for the spring trip of the baseball team. Many of the men whom we admire as successful and who point back to the hard road on which they have toiled, have reached their eminence in part because of the self-castigation from earlier guilt. There is a touch of this form of self-punishment in all of us, because these tendencies toward self-denial, asceticism, disci-pline, responsibility, and hard work are generally admired and win the approval and plaudits of most serious-minded persons. When one looks at the matter from this perspective, one has to conclude that the moti-vations must be strong to cause a person to leave a life of ease and pleasure and whip himself so mercilessly, and to adopt all kinds of hardships and abnegations in order to achieve a doubtful goal. One can endure all sorts of hardships when he feels guilty and unworthy.

While on the topic of martyrdom, perhaps religious penance should be mentioned. It is not so fashionable today but it played an important rôle in certain eras of human history. Under the sting of religious guilt a person may pay exacting penalties decreed by his particular religion. Perhaps today in our nationalistic culture people are taking on equally severe personal penalties and deprivations as the religious zealot of gen-erations ago.

Prejudicing One's Interests. Another way in which one can punish himself is by prejudicing his interests with others. For example, one may let his appearance deteriorate and hence become offensive to others. By procrastinating or by putting off one's duties and obligations, one may disappoint others and thereby fall from their high regard. One may even take more active measures of increasing the aversion or contempt of acquaintances by vague insults or criticisms, by failure to show proper appreciation, by forgetting other persons' names, or uttering vague insinuations or deprecations. One may even hurt the person who wishes to help by failing to appreciate the help given or by finding unnecessary fault with it. One usually excuses the untactful and uncouth person by saying that he knows no better, or that he has had a poor upbringing. The truth of the matter is that many times one incurs the hostility of or prejudices his interests in others' eyes with unconscious purposefulness, as a way of hurting himself and thereby of paying the penalty for actual or fantasied misdeeds.

Many persons become failures not entirely because of the blows of fortune or ill-luck but because they manage to pervert circumstances to their own disadvantage. The reader may be inclined to believe that ordinary events of life are being strangely twisted and given unnecessarily distorted meanings and interpretations. Why would one ever wish to fail, one may well ask? However, cases have been studied in which the failure of a child in school indicates that the failure was intended. In part, the child failed because his parents considered him a failure, and he was almost compelled to live up to the reputation which had been attributed to him. Sometimes children fail in school not only to punish themselves, but also to hurt their parents and to force them to reveal that the extent of their affection for their children depends upon progress in school. The child with a good level of intelligence whose parents show that they have high regard for him, and who thereby insure his high regard for himself, is more likely to succeed in school than the child whose parents do not show high regard for him and who consequently lacks confidence in his own abilities. Indeed, it is possible for ignorance, stupidity, or even low intelligence to have a functional origin. It is well known that persons sometimes feign stupidity. Perhaps, in a wider sense, they may compromise their success in the world by mental confusion and incapacity. But this statement should not lead anyone to hope that mental deficiency usually has such a functional origin; on the other hand, one is safest in taking expressed intelligence as the best indication of real intelligence.

Another method by which individuals prejudice their interests is by the development of personality traits of shyness and withdrawal. However much one may enjoy companionship and association with others, something within him cuts him off from them and makes for him a lonely and isolated existence.

SELF-PUNISHMENT THROUGH THE BODY. Here we come to this large field, which in recent years has been publicized under the heading of "psychosomatic medicine." It has become increasingly clear that many forms of illness and organic suffering have a psychogenic origin; these are in part psychologically motivated. This is not to deny in the least that the disease or the infirmity is real. The pain, the lesion, the inflammation, or the fever is real, but at the same time it may have been induced, in part, through mental instigation. The exact mechanism by which the mind in this way has influence over the body is only beginning to be dimly recognized, but the existence of such control can no longer be doubted. Suffice it to say here that illness and suffering serve admirably as forms of self-punishment, both by their incapacities and the pain which accompanies them. One investigator, Fromm-Reichmann,[7] is convinced that migraine headaches are always one specific expression of deeply repressed unconscious hostility against beloved persons. They also serve, at the same time, to bring punishment on others who grieve at the suffering and are forced to expend time, money and care in treatment. They serve the needs of self-punishment admirably, since they seem so convincingly to be the result of physical causation and consequently are entirely out of the control of the individual who succumbs to the illness. They absolve the person completely from responsibility. He sees no necessity for finding fault in himself for his own aggressive and erotic impulses. One has only to observe how readily persons look to a physical handicap for an explanation of their psychological difficulties to discover how widespread is this form of self-punishment.

Accidents and injuries come under this same category of self-punishment through the body. In these cases too, the responsibility seems to lie outside of the individual and points to chance or fate for the explanation of the suffering. It is indeed difficult to picture the motivation which would cause a person to swerve in his automobile-driving at just the right moment to have a collision, but the unconscious forces at work are nevertheless certain.

Punishment Relieves Guilt. Guilt is reduced in intensity by punishment. In this sense, punishment then is a satisfaction, even though it can hardly be admitted that it is a pleasure. The tension aroused by the guilt may be even more unpleasant than the punishment which releases it and permits it to flow through and drain off. Punishment also, besides relieving guilt, seems to reduce the repression which was kept effective by means of the guilt. After punishment, behavior is no longer restrained and inhibited, and since there is no longer the same need for maintaining secrecy, the personality relaxes and the behavior may become more natural and spontaneous.

On the other hand, punishment, as we have already seen, does stimulate the superego, so that punishment cannot be thought of as a cure for guilt but merely as a temporary relief. As impulses and behavior that are unacceptable to the superego, and consequently arouse guilt, are

---

[7] Frieda Fromm-Reichmann, "Psychoanalytical Remarks on the Clinical Significance of Hostility," *Medical Annals of the District of Columbia*, 5 (1936), 260–263.

repeated on some subsequent occasion, the need for punishment with its accompanying tension returns and this time it is stronger than before. Like a habit-forming drug, punishment, while affording temporary relief, actually requires a larger dose following each administration.

Efforts of Self to Provoke External Punishment. A person may find that his own self-punishing tendencies may be far more severe than those which he can expect from kindly parents and teachers. In order to avoid his own severe superego, he may reach out again and attempt to instigate punishment from others. Every child knows how to provoke punishment by annoying or hurting others or their interests, so that the hate which was introjected in order to avoid the hostile reactions of others is again projected outward for the very purpose of arousing anger in others. Here, then, we find the not uncommon phenomenon of the child's being naughty in an increasing tempo for the precise unconscious purpose of bringing punishment on himself. The sequence of behavior operates somewhat in this way. The child has to be increasingly naughty and disturbing in order to get the reaction which he requires from his parents. Sometimes one can see this in the child in the growing intensity of his passion or temper tantrum. Parents who are slow to wrath and who have their own tempers well under control are the very ones against whom the child with the severe superego must go to extreme limits in order to gain punishment. It may be that the parent himself is afraid of aggression and represses it until—as mothers frequently say—"they lose their patience and fly off the handle." When the punishment is meted the child's naughtiness and guilt subside, and for hours or days he is an uncommonly "good" child. However, as temptations arise and hostile fantasies once more put in their appearance, the child's guilt once again demands relief and the cycle is repeated. Many teachers readily recognize that this cycle of bad behavior is followed by a period of relative calm.

Function of Self-Punishment in Testing Reality. Susan Isaacs [8] points out in telling fashion the function of punishment in testing reality. In her observations she has seen that children often invite punishment to see how severe it will be, in order to determine whether it is something which can be endured. In fantasy, a child may even go much further than this and seek punishment in order to discover whether his parents really wish to injure him or destroy him. In other words, it is a test of the extent to which the child can count on the parents' fundamental acceptance or rejection. Because the child has such an overwhelming need to be loved, he must test the reality of the parents' hate.

Here too, we see the phenomenon of prohibition increasing a child's desire to experience the very thing which is prohibited. A boy who is told that he must not say the forbidden word seems possessed to utter it.

---

[8] Susan Isaacs, *Social Development in Young Children* (New York: Harcourt, Brace and Company, 1937).

This even looks as though it were a challenge to the parents' authority, but in reality is more an attempt to test the danger of the punishment which is threatened. In a more general sense, this process of testing the reality of danger situations is a wish to test and demonstrate one's ability to master a situation. Boys will take dares from each other in order to prove their own mastery and to dispel the reality of their fear.

Efforts to redeem and purify the self. We are speaking here still of methods of reducing guilt. Going beyond self-punishment, the individual takes steps to clear away the stain of guilt aroused by his misdeeds. We see this in tendencies toward repentance, penitence, and contrition. Repentance, while a form of self-punishment, is a weakened form. We spoke earlier of remorse and compunction, and the suffering which they produce, as being forms of self-punishment. In repentance, however, this suffering is mitigated, and there is an attempt to restore the self-respect. Repentance also protects the individual from punishment from without. The penitent individual is already on the road to paying the penalty and, consequently, has absolved himself from the need for punishment by others.

Then there are attempts at purification through reform and resolution to lead a new life. These promises to refrain from prohibited thoughts and acts in the future are all efforts of the self to seek redemption and purification. Religion has formally recognized such activities and has given them symbolic representation through various rituals.

Efforts to bring about reconciliation with the outside world. One may not only seek to propitiate himself, but may also take steps to reconcile himself with others. For instance, one may take definite steps to secure love and affection. There are many ways of going about this. Perhaps the most obvious is that of giving gifts, a device commonly used to win favor. The gifts may be actual physical objects, such as food, clothing, jewels, or they may be in the nature of kind deeds, "good turns," assistance with tasks, and the like. An interesting behavior constellation not infrequently seen in children who carry heavy burdens of guilt, is that of stealing money in order to buy candy or other favors for which to exchange friendship and affection. In this single series of acts, one may see combined the desire to bring punishment on the self at the same time that one is attempting to conciliate others. Conciliatory acts for the reduction of guilt can usually be recognized through their exaggeration, for any form of generosity or helpfulness—however sincere—may carry with it an unconscious effort to eliminate guilt.

The Excuse or Apology. Another form of conciliation is the excuse or apology. This humbling of the self has a masochistic quality about it and partakes of the nature of self-punishment, as well as the desire to reinstate oneself in the good graces of others.

Confession. Perhaps the most important act of a conciliatory nature is confession. In confession the tendency to secrecy is abandoned; the nature of the forbidden act is revealed; and the person throws himself on the mercy of those whom he has offended. One can see in the act of confession most clearly the extent to which guilt is really a fear of punishment, for as a person confesses, he throws himself open without defense to whatever retaliatory measure the other person wishes to exact. The hope is, of course, that by abandoning hostility and making himself defenseless he pulls the teeth of anger from the other person and thereby saves himself from his vengeance.

VALUES OF GUILT

Guilt has both its positive and negative values. It may seem strange to ascribe any positive values to such a distressing emotion. However, it is through the fiery furnace of guilt that some of the finest human values are derived.

Negative values of guilt. The most obvious negative value of guilt is the intolerable distress that it causes, driving people to unfortunate extremes to rid themselves of it. Insofar as guilt leads to some form of self-punishment, it restricts and harms the self. To this extent, then, it prevents the self from deriving full enjoyment of life. The man who brings on himself misfortune, poor health, failure, self-denial, or martyrdom is failing to find the maximum enjoyment of life.

Positive values of guilt. In the first place, guilt should be recognized as an important motivating force for morality and civilized culture. One frequently hears religious persons bemoaning the fact that religion has lost its grip in modern times, thereby threatening the moral foundations of society. Religion, however, is only an expression of guilt and a method of resolving it. Guilt is as strong today as it has ever been. One must depend on the family and the standards and moral ideals of parents as the fundamental bulwark of our culture. So guilt serves an essential function which cannot be dispensed with in present-day life.

Civilization with its restraints implies a certain degree of self-aggression. All inhibition of natural impulses, in a sense, means that a certain amount of aggression, normally directed outward toward others, has been turned inward on the self. Inhibition, to the extent that pleasure has been choked off, is a form of self-punishment. While we may decry the fact that self-punishment restrains and restricts the full enjoyment of life, we believe that this is necessary in order to live together in civilized peace and harmony. Those who have given consideration to what can be done to reduce the destructive forms of aggression now running rampant in the world, believe that part of them must be absorbed through the controls of self-aggression.

It should also be recognized that guilt can never be wholly avoided.

Parents can go to whatever extreme they wish to avoid censure, blame, criticism or punishment; they can give a child free rein to self-expression and place on him a minimum of restriction. Even so this child will have guilt; in fact, more guilt than the normal child.

Most important of all is the fact that on the foundation of guilt are built some of the most valuable of human characteristics. The mechanism of sublimation develops on this foundation. In Chapter XIX we shall see that love in its most fully developed form is based on dissatisfaction with the self and the desire to find another person who will supplement the self which feels so inadequate. Reparation and all other constructive activities apparently depend on a primary guilt for which amends must be made. So the highest achievements of man find as their fundamental motivating force the desire to make amends for early inadequacies. It is the striving to overcome infancy, weakness, and failure that gives man the driving power to mount to successful achievement.

EDUCATIONAL IMPLICATIONS OF GUILT

In the last section it was pointed out that there are certain positive values to guilt; nevertheless the development of guilt should not be an educational aim. Guilt is altogether too easily stimulated, and it can too easily rise to uncomfortable and uncontrollable heights. However, in mild amounts, it undoubtedly serves as a stimulus for learning and for the taking on of constructive activities. Education has a great deal to learn about the methods of stimulating that exact amount.

Damaging guilt arises from extremes of parental control and discipline, and, as we have seen, from weak, submissive control as well. So the reduction of guilt depends in large measure on the nature of the parent-child relationship.

It was pointed out above that a certain modicum of guilt was necessary to uphold moral standards of the community. However, periodically these standards take extreme directions and put too much stress on the controlling mechanisms of human beings. While a certain amount of regulation is necessary to civilized life, the tendency to regulate must be kept in constant check. By and large, the individual who has been made to build a strong superego and guilt tendencies when young, is a candidate for neuroticism in later life.

QUESTIONS FOR DISCUSSION

1. Discuss the distinction between anxiety and guilt in terms of the relation of the ego and superego.
2. How is guilt an outcome of punishment?
3. Discuss feelings of inferiority. How are they related to guilt? How do feel-

ings of inferiority express themselves? What are some of the factors in development which give rise to feelings of inferiority?

4. Why should guilt be related to the sense of moral value?

5. By what signs can guilt be recognized in another person?

6. Discuss the statement that "a man is unable to rid himself of guilt unaided from the outside." (P. 284.)

7. Cite examples of ways in which a person prejudices his own interests by making himself offensive to others as a self-punishment in order to reduce guilt. Of what might a person feel guilty in such circumstances?

8. Cite examples of efforts to provoke external punishment to mitigate guilt by (1) children in school (2) workers in industry (3) criminals. In each instance speculate what the person may feel guilty about.

9. Discuss confession as a method of handling guilt. How is confession related to self-punishment? How does confession help to resolve inner conflicts?

10. A person without normal guilt is frequently called psychopathic. Discuss the possible causes of lack of guilt in terms of developmental experiences.

11. What are some of the positive social values of guilt? Although guilt is one of the most distressing human experiences, it is said that out of guilt grow some of the most commendable human characteristics—how is this possible?

Recommended Reading

1. ALEXANDER, FRANZ, *Psychoanalysis of the Total Personality*, Nervous and Mental Disease Monograph Series, No. 52 (New York: Nervous and Mental Disease Publishing Company, 1929).

2. ALEXANDER, FRANZ, "Remarks About the Relation of Inferiority Feeling to Guilt Feeling," *International Journal of Psychoanalysis*, 19 (1938), 41–49.

3. DUNBAR, H. F., *Emotions and Bodily Change, A Survey of Literature in Psychosomatic Inter-Relationships* (1910–1933) (New York: Columbia University Press, 1935; revised edition, 1938).

4. FENICHEL, OTTO, "The Clinical Aspect of the Need for Punishment," *International Journal of Psychoanalysis*, 9 (1928), 47–70.

5. FREUD, ANNA, *The Ego and the Mechanisms of Defense*, International Psychoanalytical Library, No. 30 (London: Hogarth Press, 1937; also New York: International Universities Press, Inc., 1946; first published in German, 1936).

6. FREUD, SIGMUND, *New Introductory Lectures in Psychoanalysis*, International Psychoanalytical Library, No. 24 (London: Hogarth Press, 1933; New York: W. W. Norton & Company, Inc., 1933).

7. HORNEY, KAREN, *New Ways in Psychoanalysis* (New York: W. W. Norton & Company, Inc., 1939).

8. ISAACS, SUSAN, *Social Development in Young Children* (New York: Harcourt, Brace and Company, 1937).

9. LEWINSKY, H., "On Some Aspects of Masochism," *International Journal of Psychoanalysis*, 25 (1944), 150–155.

10. MENNINGER, K. A., *Man Against Himself* (New York: Harcourt, Brace and Company, 1938).

11. NUNBERG, HERMAN, "The Source of Guilt and the Need for Punishment," *International Journal of Psychoanalysis*, 7 (1926), 430–433.

12. REIK, THEODOR, *Masochism and Modern Man* (New York: Farrar & Rinehart, Inc., 1941).

XVI

Sublimation

Sublimation is the one mechanism which comes closest to the affairs of everyday life. Consequently it is the mechanism which has been subject to the most vigorous and persistent attacks from academic psychologists. However, it occupies a place along with the other mechanisms, describing one way in which a person manages his primitive tendencies and impulses. Whatever one may think of sublimation as a theoretical concept, there is no doubt that a better understanding of the possible underlying motivation of much of daily activity in the workaday world, whether in terms of sublimation or not, will prove of help in interpreting behavior.

DEFINITION

Sublimation is the adoption of behavior or feelings which are a substitute for the original or natural expression of an impulse or wish, and which are at the same time harmonious with the native impulse or wish and socially acceptable. Since it is thus acceptable in the world of reality, sublimation has been spoken of as a highly valuable mechanism, a kind of adjustment extolled as altogether laudable and commendable.

Many games, such as football, would represent a sublimation of the tendency to strike and kill. Putting oneself forward, in occupying a prominent place in a group, speaking loud and forcibly, or wearing sporty and ostentatious clothes, may be a sublimation of a more primitive tendency to display the naked body.

FUNDAMENTAL CONSIDERATIONS

Comparison with repression. Sublimation has been contrasted with repression as a method of managing forbidden or unacceptable impulses. Repression crushes these impulses and forbids their actual or direct expression. Part of the energy released is piled up and escapes in roundabout substitute ways through symptoms or fantasy. Sublimation is the way of giving these impulses, whose primitive and natural expression is unacceptable in civilized life, an alternate yet socially acceptable outlet and mode of expression.

Since the natural or primitive form of expression is unconscious, the person who has adopted a sublimated outlet is unaware that a more natural form of expression is repressed; in fact, he would probably resent as ridiculous any such suggestion. For this reason sublimation as a mechanism has been severely criticized.

Motivation. Motivation to sublimation is similar to that of a number of other symptomatic forms of behavior. Sublimation is set into action when there are obstacles to the direct gratification of impulses which prevent the primitive forms of expression. Typically there are interferences by another person, presumably, in infancy, the mother or father. This is accomplished by threats or ridicule and even punishment. For instance, parents will usually make the processes of defecation and urination seem repulsive and dirty and will attempt to establish habits of cleanliness and order to bend the growing child to their ways. Later the child finds that the domination and restraints by the parents are seconded and reinforced by general social taboos. He finds that society in the shape of schoolmates, police, in fact all our social institutions, expects certain standards of behavior and does not tolerate certain forms of expression. The little child, for instance, soon learns that certain things he can talk about freely with his mother when he is going to bed are not acceptable at the dining table when company is present. Later he may sublimate this desire to refer to some of these prohibited taboos by telling obscene stories or jokes which have a racy implication.

Sublimation may also be an expression of selfish tendencies. Insofar as one's impulses are turned inward whatever he does is for himself and is a form of self-love. Self-love, however, undergoes modification as one grows older, becoming concerned less with sexual and bodily satisfactions and more with one's place in the social group. Self-love goes through a process of idealization which is at the same time a process of sublimation. Ideals for the self can also become ideals for better social service, scientific discovery, or executive leadership. It is possible for self-love to become idealized and socialized and to lose its more primitive sensual and emotional qualities.

Sublimation may also be motivated by superego or introjected interference with the direct and natural expression of impulses. Not only does one have to contend with prohibitions from without, but the time comes when one has built up his own standards of what is right or wrong, clean or unclean, acceptable or unacceptable, and must shape his behavior to these standards. From this it may be seen that a child growing up toward puberty does not need the constant domination of his parents but has already taken into himself, sometimes with terrifying force, his own set of prohibitions. These prohibitions may be maintained by adopting substitute forms of expression, which may also be recognized as sublimations.

Develops in an atmosphere of security. Sublimation develops best in an atmosphere of security. The child who readily adopts sublimation is a child who is accepted by his parents and is given the warmth and affection that leads to personal and emotional security. The child who is accepted, therefore, dares to experiment with people and things in the real world, and thereby finds substitutes for the kinds of expression which are suppressed. Severe rejection or intimidation or punishment in suppressing activities is not likely to be a fertile condition for the development of acceptable sublimations. If tendencies that are thwarted, either from without or from within, are to be sublimated, they must not be too intense. It is probably true that sublimations will not follow readily when the suppression is traumatic, for in such cases the inhibition is too intense and tends to spread to any form of related or cognate activity. It has also been suggested that excessive indulgence in infantile sexuality probably hinders sublimation. Where the infant has been overstimulated sexually or there has been seduction, the impulses aroused are probably too intense, and the need for direct gratification too severe, to permit the release by substitute sublimated activities.

Sublimation requires a certain freedom on the part of the individual—freedom from external pressure or requirement and also from the compulsiveness of his own demanding superego. The child who studies because he is afraid he will be punished or will lose his mother's love if he does not, is not sublimating; neither is the child who is driven to study to placate his own demanding superego. Sublimation implies spontaneity and freedom to enlarge and unfold the ego.

A function of the ego. Sublimation is essentially a function of the ego or personality and is not merely concerned with the satisfaction of an isolated drive. It represents the child's contact with reality. It enables him to use his higher mental processes to the limit of their capacity. It favors the application of intelligence to the problems which the person meets. Insofar as it requires intelligence it is a conscious process, but the individual may not be aware of its use as a defense against more primitive expressions of the impulse. Sublimation, therefore, serves as a partial explanation for the normal activities in which a person engages.

A mechanism of early childhood. Sublimation is a mechanism of early childhood. It appears in most pronounced fashion between the ages of five and twelve, the so-called latent period. It is in this period that the original impulses, particularly those of a sexual nature, have been finally successfully suppressed, and the child for whom the repression is successful is launched out into his exploration and management of the world about him. It is probable that the major sublimations which a person adopts begin in childhood. Later sublimations are to a large extent only repetitions of the patterns which were laid down in the first sublimations following the period of infancy. One commonly sees sublimations taking on form in adolescence. It is at that time that the growing boy or girl finds meaning in art and science, in sports, in religion and social service, but it is probable that these are only the blossoming of trends which were laid down several years before.

Made possible by identification. The kind of sublimation adopted is undoubtedly preceded and made possible by identification. This again is a common observation. Children slowly adopt patterns of behavior which others around them whom they admire provide as models. The kinds of sublimations adopted are determined by the patterns of behavior found in the home and in the school. Parents and teachers should recognize that their own sublimations are going to be adopted by their children and pupils without their having to make these the object of direct instruction.

Related to choice of occupation. Sublimations play an important part in determining the choice of one's profession or employment. One's occupation ought to provide him with experience which not only helps him earn a living and gives him the necessities of food and shelter, but ought also to permit him the exercise of some creative faculty, which in itself would have the manner of a sublimation. The teacher, for instance, is a person who may have sublimated her desire for children of her own in her work with children for whom she is responsible as a teacher. The butcher may have selected an occupation which gives him an opportunity of expressing his unreleased aggressive or sadistic tendencies. One could go through each occupation and list the pleasures it provides which represent the satisfaction of basic needs whose original expression has been diverted.

FORMS OF SUBLIMATION

It may be of help to list categorically some of the more important forms of sublimation. Friendship as contrasted with erotic and sexual love is recognized as an important sublimation. In this sense social experiences such as play, picnics, church gatherings, work or visits may be thought of as sublimations of earlier childhood erotic tendencies. These all stem from the sublimation of sexual feelings toward the mother or father which turn into tender and comradely feelings. Social service in its various forms as well as civic activities may be considered as sublimations, even extending the more immediate and direct friendly interests. Art in its various forms, both expressive and receptive, is an important form of sublimation. Science in the form of experimentation or in its applications to constructive work belongs to the list and is prominent particularly in boys during adolescence. As previously noted, an important kind of sublimation is found in one's occupation or work, perhaps even more strikingly in one's hobby or avocation. Religion occupies a prominent place in the sublimations of adolescence. The thrill over, and communion with, nature, as exemplified in such geniuses as Thoreau and Burroughs, represent a sublimation of erotic desire. Finally, some of the aggressive impulses are sublimated through sports and games.

A considerable part of sublimation is expressed through symbolism. Religion uses symbolism to represent some of the deeper impulses to which it gives expression. Symbols are a common feature of art products. The symbol gives token recognition of the need and a token representation of its satisfaction. Even the memento can elicit a mild replica of the more intense experience for which it stands.

TENDENCIES WHICH ARE SUBLIMATED

Practically every original impulse may be found in later life in sublimated form. The nature and direction of some of these sublimations will be mentioned in the following discussion.

Aggression. Aggressive impulses also have their sublimations. This concept of sublimation of aggression is one loaded with great social importance. The world at this time is in great need of a sublimation of aggressive impulses to serve as a substitute for war and brutality. Many years ago William James [1] wrote an essay on the moral equivalent of war, a concept which attracted immediate attention and has been a vague goal of social planners ever since. As a matter of fact, it would seem as though it is relatively difficult to sublimate the aims of aggression, at least much more difficult than the aims of the various components of sexual behavior. Aggression apparently sets up tensions which demand more immediate release than the tensions connected with sex.[2] Consequently the sublimations of aggression are more difficult to incorporate into a social plan. Sublimation of aggression is relative. Terms of aggression are taken over by the photograph devotee to indicate his feelings— a picture is called a "shot." Instead of killing the wild animal one may take photographs of it. One may sublimate his hostile tendencies in the direction of social reform and war against the social evils. Many years

---

[1] William James, "The Moral Equivalent of War," in *Memoirs and Studies* (New York: Longmans, Green and Co., 1911. Originally this was a publication of the American Association for International Conciliation, Feb., 1910, No. 27).

[2] At this point it may be noted that sex impulses are not wholly separated from the aggressive impulses. Indeed Riviere, in M. Klien and J. Riviere, *Love, Hate and Reparation*, Psychoanalytical Epitomes, No. 2 (London: Hogarth Press, 1937), make the point that sex is feared so strongly because in infancy its first expression is linked with aggression.

ago Southard [3] wrote a book called *The Kingdom of Evils,* and spoke of man's organized attempts to combat ignorance, crime, vice, disease, and poverty. Many persons have devoted their lives in an aggressive way toward combating these evils. Menninger [4] in a discussion of Southard's list would add to these evils, ugliness and aggression, itself. With so much of the world turning to war as a way of gaining other satisfactions, it would seem as though there is no more important kind of fight to be waged today than that against aggression itself.

Games and sports form a very wholesome socially acceptable sublimation for aggression. We see this in spectacular form in college football games in which eleven men will pit themselves against eleven other men for an afternoon and a huge crowd looks on with empathic enjoyment. One can gain equal aggressive satisfaction not only in active games and sports such as boxing or wrestling but in bridge or chess, or even slapjacks or old maid. Those working with maladjusted children who have need for releasing their repressed aggressions find that games provide this opportunity very successfully. [5] Some can meet their aggressive needs through mountain-climbing. Politics and competitive business are sublimative outlets for aggressive tendencies for many men.

A large number of occupations contain an element of aggressiveness which enable a man to sublimate his conflicts in socially approved ways. Salesmanship in its various forms has a distinctly aggressive element. The business executive is a man who enters with zest into competition. More sadistic trends can be sublimated in a number of occupations, by the butcher in a very obvious but social way, by the surgeon and the barber in a more refined but equally obvious manner. The variety of ways in which aggression is sublimated is legion; laughter, even when it is directed toward another person's mistakes and misfortunes, is a socially acceptable expression of aggression. In this connection it might be worth mentioning that certain occupations quite obviously are restitutive in nature, possibly to make amends for aggressive fantasies over which guilt is felt. The nurse, for instance, is concerned with healing. The masseuse combines vigorous bodily manipulation, punching, kneading, and knocking with the intent of correcting strains, displacements, and tensions. Even the teacher, a person with a protective aim, in many cases obviously finds in her work a restitutive significance. This is particularly obvious

---

[3] E. E. Southard and M. C. Jarrett, *The Kingdom of Evils* (New York: The Macmillan Company, 1922).

[4] K. A. Menninger, *Man Against Himself* (New York: Harcourt, Brace and Company, 1938). p. 424.

[5] One teacher contributed the following: "A pupil of mine was so exasperatingly full of mischief that, at the end of the day, I was worn out. In seeking some means of sublimating this impulse, I hit upon dramatics. My classes were constantly engaged in dramatizing, and there were many 'chores' to be done in connection with preparing for the performances. Marjorie, the mischief-maker, put the same energy into helping make the dramatic presentations a success as she did into her trying escapades."

in those persons who have positions in guidance in education and who have as their function helping young persons either avoid trouble or escape it. The social worker attempts to patch up some of the evils of the present social order and the psychological conflicts resulting therefrom. One even sees this tendency toward restitution in those statesmen who lend their services to weak and helpless nations and who propose giving them assistance in times of crisis.

Sublimation of erotic tendencies. Erotic tendencies supply the most obvious and at the same time most spectacular illustrations of sublimation. Around the ages of four and five there are marked erotic feelings toward the mother. Later, however, these are suppressed, and in their place one finds tender feelings later recognized as sentiment. These tender or sentimental feelings remain strong throughout life. In place of physical expressions of sex there will be sublimated forms of handshaking, slapping on the back, embracing, kissing the hand. These all are forms of personal contact which are permitted in ordinary friendly relationships representing the husk of a more intense sexual response. The fires of sexual ardor may burn out, but friendships and marriages based on a community of interests have enduring qualities because they encompass larger segments of life so that they can resist the ravages of time.

Many occupations represent sublimation of these erotic tendencies. Practically every occupation that brings people into friendly relationships may serve this purpose. Social service, teaching, the ministry, and medicine, in fact practically all the professions are those in which strong social relationships are expected but on a strictly impersonal or friendship basis. There is a barrier over which one is not expected to step in a professional relationship which marks it off from one with a definitely erotic or sexual significance. Much of religion is a sublimation of the erotic tendencies. Religious worship represents a satisfying yet sublimated expression of love and reverence.

VALUES

Positive values. By definition sublimation has social value, which may be divided into utility value, play value, and esthetic value, each of which has been amply illustrated in the foregoing discussion. Sublimations are legitimate activities as contrasted with the forms of expression they replace. Sublimation directs the individual's attention and energies to the environment and helps him produce changes in it. When a sublimation fails in its social acceptability, as happens occasionally, we give it the term *eccentric*. Even then it is possible to distinguish between unacceptable forms of experience, which are bad, dirty, dishonorable, repulsive, and the sublimations that take their places, which, even if they are not wholly socially acceptable, are recognized as amusing or just plain queer. This frequently happens with sublimations which lose their social significance or are carried to extremes. Collections, for instance, as when a child collects stamps or shells or pictures, are recognized as a form of sublimation of obsessional tendencies. If, however, the collection has no social value and is carried to an extreme, it is still recognized as a sublimation, although it has lost its capacity to excite admiration.

That social acceptability is not an invariable characteristic of sublimation, however, is indicated by the difficulty in reconciling the two in many recognized instances of sublimation. Could delinquency be considered a sublimation? Certainly delinquency is not socially acceptable, yet it represents a deviation from, and partial substitution for, more primitive forms of aggression. And what shall be said of war, which is both a socially approved and condemned form of aggression, a sophisticated substitution for primitive aggression and yet a return to its most barbaric form?

Money-Kyrle [6] once suggested that the essence of a sublimation is that it is overdetermined, that is, that it is an act that serves (or partially serves) two or more needs and therefore forms a reinforcement which is absent in the partial satisfaction of either need alone. One might redefine sublimation as that act which satisfies both some primitive need and ego prestige. The second requirement (ego prestige) would always be met by social acceptability, but it could also be met by the approval of a small sub-group of society (as in a group of criminals) or temporary approval in cases of emergency (as in a nation at war). The definition of sublimation in terms of overdetermination, one element of which shall be the enhancement of ego prestige, eliminates one criticism of the usual definition of sublimation which implies a value judgment and gives it a moral significance.

Mental Health Values. Sublimation has been spoken of by psychoanalysts as a highly commendable method of dealing with difficult, dangerous, and forbidden impulses and with the dangerous disorganized fantasies. Sublimation, by moving in harmony with original impulses, fulfils and enriches life. By its social acceptability it acts as a stabilizer; by its objectification of internal impulses and tendencies it serves as a contact with the world of reality and hence helps to make more adequate adjustments in the world of people and events. At the same time it has been pointed out that the average man has severe limitations to his capacity for sublimation.

Because sublimations are generally socially acceptable, they are substitute reactions which help to lessen the amount of anxiety. It is perhaps

[6] R. E. Money-Kyrle, *The Development of the Sexual Impulses*, International Library of Psychology, Philosophy and Scientific Method (London: Kegan Paul, Trench, Trubner and Company; New York: Harcourt, Brace and Company, 1932).

this feature as much as any other that gives sublimations their mental hygiene value.

Relief of Tension. W. S. Taylor,[7] who has written at length on sublimation, compares it with other forms of behavior which act as tension reducers. When impulses are released but prevented from complete expression, there results a piling up of residual tension in the muscular system. For instance, when one who is angry inhibits striking another person with his fist, the impulse started may be dammed up temporarily and expressed later and perhaps partially in some substitute way, as cursing the other person or even taking it out later on the ticket agent or the secretary in the office. Sublimation, however, does not refer to the method of handling the frustrations of everyday living but rather to the modes of socially acceptable expression of the continuing drives and impulses which are prevented from immediate and natural expression in the long course of development from infancy through childhood and into adult life.

It will be readily seen that sublimation in most of the illustrations which have appeared in psychoanalytic literature is concerned with the reconstruction of various aspects of the sexual impulse. This is reasonable because sex is the one impulse which has had the most drastic control exercised over it by society. Many of the immediate and obvious expressions of sex as they would occur in infancy and childhood are roughly suppressed by parents and teachers, and it is little wonder that this drive seeks expression in acceptable and substitute fashion. The fact that sublimations usually are found in the sexual area has led to much of the criticism and ridicule of this mechanism. When one looks at the need for some such substitute activity, though, it would seem not only reasonable but necessary.

Difficulty in Attaining Complete Sublimation. It is extremely doubtful, however, whether it is possible ever to achieve complete sublimation, that is, without the necessity of some direct expression of the original impulse. Taylor, who had studied the sublimation of the sex instinct in men, believes that no form of substitute activity, whether art or science, sport or work, ever quite drains off, and takes the place of, the needs for direct sexual expression. Tension may be partially reduced, but the physical and glandular basis for sex still remains, calling for some sort of direct expression. It is for this reason that sublimation does not succeed as a substitute for the more direct forms of expression with everyone. In fact, probably only a small proportion of persons are successful in making sublimation a satisfactory substitute for some of the more direct and natural forms of expression. Even when it apparently is a success, it may be punctuated by periods of lapse. Some of the primitive orgies

[7] W. S. Taylor, "A Critique of Sublimation in Males: A Study of Forty Superior Single Men," *Genetic Psychology Monographs*, 13 (1933), 1–115.

and ceremonials apparently were institutionalized and regulated occasions when sublimations were tossed away and more direct forms of expression were accepted. We can see similar reversals in our present civilization, for instance, in war, in the fanaticism of certain religious groups, in the loosening of ordinary restraints in connection with riots, lynchings, and the excesses in hazing by college men and women. In particular, sex expression can never be completely satisfied by sublimation. This very fact makes one pause to consider again the problem of the youth who is forced by present economic conditions to interpolate a period of abstinence between the time of his maturing and the time when society is willing to recognize sexual expression in the formalized institution of marriage. Many writers have suggested the possibility and desirability of taking up the slack of this period when sexual powers are at their maximum by various sublimations, but it is doubtful whether this is a complete solution of the problem.

That sublimation requires a constant expenditure of effort is not readily recognized. It sometimes happens that the sublimatory value of an activity wears away and there is a tendency to regress to the need for a more direct and primitive expression of an impulse. What happens sometimes to *work* is an illustration of the fate of an activity which serves as a sublimation. While work serves as a sublimation, it is entered into with zeal and enthusiasm; but if it loses its value as a sublimation, the zeal for the work may fall away. Then, when the work no longer has its interest, it becomes onerous and there may be a breakdown from overwork. This undoubtedly is the basis for some cases of "nervous breakdown."

Sublimation as Therapy. Sublimation is useful as therapy for persons who have reached impasses in their conflicts and must seek some sort of relief. Where direct aid is not available in the form of psychoanalysis, it is possible to offer considerable relief through various sublimated activities. A considerable amount of sublimation is required for healthful living. Indeed, even where adequate and fundamental therapy is available it is possible that healing, constructive efforts can be put into motion through helping a person adopt sublimations which fit his needs. In this sense, therefore, art, science, social service, sport, and work all may be thought of as factors in healthful, constructive living.

A very wealthy woman had no interests in life, no duties or encumbrances, and to all intents and purposes was very ill, but her doctor could find no physical basis for her illness. Someone interested her in a children's home that needed supervision and money. She became the "fairy godmother" to that home, and her illness miraculously disappeared.

Relation of Sublimation to Education. A description of the processes by which sublimations are acquired would be a description of the process of education itself, for sublimation is practically the equivalent of education. Sublimations, as a result of educational processes, develop slowly and gradually. There is a long process of conditioning growing out of early primitive impulses. This is the learning process which is so completely described in studies of child development and learning. Sublimation, therefore, in its long process becomes further and further removed from the original native forms of expression. As a child learns to read and write, to become interested in history and geography, in plays and games, he may develop and elaborate his sublimated processes to such a high degree that to all intent and purposes the motivating impulse from which they originally grew and which continued to nourish them is lost. Sublimations receive their start in infancy. As E. Jones [8] says, "The weaning of the child to external and social interests is the essence of sublimation and the most important single process in the whole of education." Every traumatic situation successfully mastered is a sublimation. However, sublimations, proceeding as they must outward from within, cannot be forced. The task of education is that of providing an opportunity for the development of sublimations which are appropriate to the individual rather than of forcing a uniform set of sublimations on every child.

Dangers of sublimation. Sublimation also has its dangers, which have been pointed out in convincing fashion by Chassell.[9] He speaks of the danger of carrying all one's eggs in one basket. By that he means that insofar as one depends upon a single kind of sublimation to take care of the adequate expression and release of a set of impulses, one may be courting danger. It is possible that this particular sublimation, whether it be work or play, art or science, may in time prove to lose its effectiveness, and then the individual will be stranded with no acceptable outlet for his impulses. Many persons, for instance, who have put all of their energies into their work may find that in middle life their work fails them and they are left without resource. A more popular way of saying the same thing is that one should take up a number of hobbies or avocations as well as devote one's energies to work.

A second danger that Chassell mentions is that sublimation may become sacred and be set up as a barrier against underlying guilt feelings and anxieties. As long as the moral standards or the artistic or scientific ideals are not threatened, all is well, but if there is danger that they may become undermined by new discoveries or by new ideas which may percolate into one's system, there is also danger that the whole fabric of sublimation will collapse and expose one to the full force of the anxieties

---

[8] Ernest Jones, *Papers on Psychoanalysis* (London: Bailliere, Tindall and Cox; Baltimore: William Wood and Company, 1913; second edition 1918; third edition 1923; fourth edition 1938).

[9] J. O. Chassell, "Vicissitudes of Sublimation," *Psychiatry,* 2 (1938), 221–232.

and guilts he is for the time being successfully managing through his sublimations.

In the third place, there is a danger that sublimations may fail when they are based largely on repression. The young woman who sublimates her hostility toward her mother by managing a business with a firm hand, may find that in periods of fatigue or strain her calmness and self-assurance are punctuated by resentment and open hostility and aggression toward her mother.

In the fourth place, there is a danger that the sublimation may take on a compulsive character when the person finds it so necessary that he does not dare to drop it. When the sublimation is something to which one clings, there is evidence that the conflicts banished are welling up through the unconscious barrier and the structure which apparently gives equilibrium is actually tottering.

Finally, one wonders to what extent civilization will go on adding to restrictions of native expressions of impulses. It is possible that civilization has already gone so far that the culture of our cities is too far removed from nature and too much dependent on machines, printing, and all the artificial fabric of living. This is a point of view expressed years ago by Wordsworth and Rousseau. One honestly queries whether the time will not come when there will be a reaction and a demand for a return to simpler and more immediate expression of the urges and impulses which are natural to man as an animal and from which he cannot depart too far without making the strain unbearable. Indeed, one can see trends in this direction in the "back to the farm" movement, and the popularity of such outdoor recreation as skiing and swimming.

QUESTIONS FOR DISCUSSION

1. What are some of the conditions for forming sublimations instead of other methods of mastering anxiety?

2. Discuss the process by which selfish tendencies become changed into ideals of social service.

3. Discuss the sublimation of sexual drives. To what extent is it possible for other activities to take the place of the need for physical sexual expression?

4. What is the relation of sublimation to repression? When one sublimates his aggressive or erotic tendencies, are the more direct physical expression of these drives inhibited, or is there a draining off of energy into related activities?

5. One criticism of a sublimation is that it shall be an act having "social value," but it is evident that this is not a necessary condition. For instance, illustrations are given in the text of collective delinquency and even war that might conceivably be called sublimations, but in such instances social value is certainly doubtful. Discuss ego prestige as a criterion of what should be called a sublimation.

RECOMMENDED READING

1. ALEXANDER, FRANZ, *Psychoanalysis of the Total Personality*, Nervous and Mental Disease Monograph Series, No. 52 (New York: Nervous and Mental Disease Publishing Company, 1929).
2. CHASSELL, J. O., "Vicissitudes of Sublimation," *Psychiatry*, 2 (1938), 221–232.
3. HORNEY, KAREN, *New Ways in Psychoanalysis* (New York: W. W. Norton and Company, Inc., 1939).
4. JAMES, WILLIAM, "The Moral Equivalent of War," in *Memoirs and Studies* (New York: Longmans Green & Co., 1911).
5. LEVEY, H. B., "A Critique of the Theory of Sublimation," *Psychiatry*, 2:239–270, 1939.
6. MURSELL, J. L., "The Logic of Sublimation: A Criticism," *Journal of Abnormal and Social Psychology*, 21 (1926), 75–84.
7. STRECKER, E. A., and APPEL, K. E., *Discovering Ourselves* (New York: The Macmillan Company, 1931; revised edition, 1943).
8. TAYLOR, W. S., "A Critique of Sublimation in Males: A Study of Forty Superior Single Men," *Genetic Psychology Monographs*, 13 (1933), 1–115.

XVII

Compensation

Compensation one of the principal methods of adjustment. Compensation has sometimes been listed as one of the mechanisms, but strictly speaking, it is hardly to be thought of as a mechanism inasmuch as it covers a wide variety of behavior. Actually compensation as a method of adjustment uses many mechanisms. Compensation as method will be described in this chapter very generally; while the specific mechanisms used in compensation are discussed each in its own chapter.

Compensation is a form of adjustment to a real or imagined personal defect. It is, in short, an attempt to overcome, or substitute for, the defect in some way. In this sense, compensation is found as a biological phenomenon at all levels of organic development.

For instance, if one lung is incapacitated, the other lung will take up the burden and actually over a period of time become enlarged so as to perform the function of two lungs. Likewise one kidney will attempt to perform the functions of both if the other becomes impaired. The process of homeostasis described by Cannon [1] is compensatory in character. The body contains mechanisms whereby the chemical equilibrium in the blood is maintained, and when it becomes too acid or too basic, compensatory processes are automatically instituted.

The defect for which compensation is made may be a real defect, as for instance, poor eyesight, or it may be an imagined defect which exists only in fantasy, as, for instance, when a person whose intelligence is at least average believes himself to be mentally inferior.

Compensation a defense. Compensation may be thought of as a kind of defense which the organism sets up against a defect or limitation in its structure or functioning. Sometimes the term *defense mechanism* has been used to indicate one of the more important modes of compensation that a person has available against his weaknesses and limitations. In fact, when broadly used, compensation is a term which may be used to

[1] W. B. Cannon, *The Wisdom of the Body* (New York: W. W. Norton & Company, Inc., 1932; revised edition, 1939).

cover all types of defense against anxiety. In particular, a person finds it necessary to set up defenses or to compensate for feelings of inferiority. It is true that an organism sets up compensations somewhat automatically against defects in structure or functioning. However, in human beings compensation for personal defects hardly takes place unless the defect is recognized and the person feels his inferiority, real or imagined. Compensation, therefore, concerns itself not only with overcoming or managing a weakness or defect, but also with establishing oneself in the favorable regard of others. We are so constituted that we care as much what others think about our achievements as we do about the actual achievements themselves. So compensation is concerned not only with freeing ourselves from our feelings of inferiority but also with securing favorable attention from others as an indication that they do not recognize any inferiority in us. In this sense, then, compensation is like drawing a red herring across the trail. It is an attention-getting device. It helps to divert attention from unfavorable characteristics and direct it toward strong or favorable characteristics. A person who has many weaknesses or defects to compensate for and who must continually strive for the favorable attention of others comes eventually to adopt a mendicant or "gimme" complex or attitude. He finds it necessary at every turn to demand favorable attention from others. This tendency to exaggerate some trait in order to draw attention away from a weakness or deficiency in another direction has been called "overcompensation" by Adler.

Compensation a method for maintaining self-respect. In addition to defending oneself against one's weaknesses and securing the favorable attention of others, compensation is also concerned with maintaining one's own self-respect and self-regard. Self-respect may be thought of as an incorporation through introjection of respect shown us by others. However, it becomes eventually an intrinsic part of one's personality, and most of us find it necessary to satisfy our own needs for self-respect as well as to secure the favorable attitude of others. We have our own ideals to live up to and satisfy as well as the standards set by the society in which we live.

Compensation stimulated by competition. The necessity for compensation is greatly stimulated by our competitive society. One can imagine a society where it makes little difference whether a person has certain possessions or talents. However, in our society we are measured by our achievements and possessions to such an extent that there is a strong and relentless drive toward at least normal or average and, if possible, superior attainment in these directions.

Origin of compensation in childhood. One might say that compensation has its origins in childish inadequacy. Everyone has been little at one time as compared with father and mother and others who have nurtured him in his formative years. The little tot feels his inadequacy, and all his striving is toward growing up and being able to meet competition. Compensation is an attempt to manage this feeling of littleness. Compensation also has its origin in rejection of children by their parents, nurses, and others to the extent that a child who is not wholly accepted, cared for, and protected is bound to feel inferior and inadequate.

Consequently compensation, in part, is an attempt to overcome this feeling of not being wanted or loved or accepted, not having one's due place in the family, school, and community groups.

FACTORS COMPENSATED FOR

Physical defects. One can feel inadequate or inferior in practically any way, whether physical, mental, social, or personal. Adler,[2] who has developed the theory of compensation for inferiority most extensively, placed his original emphasis on compensation for physical defects. Almost any bodily anomaly becomes a weakness and limitation for which a person feels it necessary to compensate. Being tall, or short, fat or thin, having poor eyesight, poor hearing, scars and blemishes on the skin, particularly on the face, excessively large or small features, may make one feel inferior and require compensation. Lameness, a poorly functioning heart, weakness caused by some exhausting disease, or malnutrition are functional bodily weaknesses. Then one finds that even such attributes as acne on the face, freckles, red hair, straight, stringy hair, prominent teeth, pop-eyes, sloping shoulders, and many other deviations from the normal in physical development are characteristics which, if they cause one to feel inferior, require compensation.

Low mentality. One of the most depressing factors causing feelings of inferiority is low or inadequate mentality. Of course, if a person has a very low mentality, he does not recognize its significance and goes on his way quite oblivious of the pity that he engenders in others. A person who feels most inferior would seem to be the person who is of average or even above average intelligence but who has had to live in a family or community where there are others much brighter who have been given respectful recognition for their intellectual gifts. So high a premium has been placed on intellect that the feeling that one is intellectually inferior would seem to be the most poignant of all feelings of inferiority. When one child in a family is praised for being bright, another child will frequently compensate for his lack of distinction along these lines by developing social charms or striking beauty.

Economic or social status. Inferior social or economic status when comprehended is painful and must be compensated for. Feelings of in-

[2] Alfred Adler, *Study of Organ Inferiority and Its Psychical Compensation*, Nervous and Mental Disease Monograph Series, No. 24 (New York: Nervous and Mental Disease Publishing Company, 1917).

feriority in social and economic status are wholly a matter of comparison. One can feel superior to those in the class below, inferior to those in the class above. If one lives in the midst of his own class and has no contact with others in the class above or below, he has little feeling with regard to class position. If, however, he lives on the border of his class or even in the midst of the class above or below, his feelings become more intense. In particular, if a person is thrown into a class above his, he is made to feel inferior and must find some way of compensating for this feeling. The college student, for instance, who finds it necessary to earn his way in the summer by waiting on table at a hotel or tutoring in a private family is often made to feel uncomfortably inferior because of the indignity of his position in comparison with those whom he serves, especially in view of the fact that during the year he may be on a par with those whom he serves during the summer. The man who suffers a loss in the stock market may attempt to overcome his loss by keeping elaborate charts.

One man of my acquaintance who was destined by his mother to become a gentleman but has never been able to hold a position which equals the goals which he set for himself, compensates for this by extremely neat and elegant dress. He lives the part of the gentleman in his dress even if he is not able to attain the position that would permit him to live the life of the gentleman in actuality.

Moral status. One can also feel inferior and be forced to make compensation for evil or ignoble impulses in the self. One's moral standards of right or wrong and his ambitions may not always be lived up to, and he is driven to find some way of compensating for them.

TYPES OF COMPENSATION

Overcoming a handicap. The first and most important kind of compensation is that which attempts directly to overcome a handicap or limitation or defect. The boy who has had a long lingering ailment and comes out of it somewhat weak and emaciated may attempt to build up his muscular tone by systematic exercises and recreation. Theodore Roosevelt, by cultivating an active outdoor life, developed into a hardy and robust man from a sickly boy. Glenn Cunningham became one of the world's greatest runners as a result of exercise which he took to restore use of his legs after severe burns. The boy who is a poor scholar in mathematics may give all of his energies to the study of mathematics in an attempt to overcome this deficiency. I once talked to a school headmaster whose theory of education was that every person should specialize in those subjects in which he had the most difficulty so that he could overcome these weaknesses and hence develop himself into an all-round scholar. This particular individual found languages gave him the greatest difficulty in high school. He specialized in language in college in an attempt to bring his competence in languages up to his competence in science and mathematics.

The child who has grown up on the wrong side of the railroad tracks may have set for himself the goal of accumulating a fortune, and he persistently follows this goal so that eventually he can build himself a fine house on a large estate and take his place in the society from which at one time he felt himself an outcast. The boy in adolescence who has come up from childhood with an overwhelming sense of guilt, and perhaps unconscious feelings that he has transgressed the moral code, may attempt to compensate for this imaginary moral defect by straight-laced asceticism and rigid observance of the moral code.

When compensations are adequate, that is, when a person can be recognized for his talents along some line, he can afford to repress aggression and to accept dependency. The artist or scientist who devotes his life to his pursuits and thereby sublimates many of his desires can afford to transfer the management of his affairs to another person.

Turning the handicap into an asset. Some defects cannot be corrected. A second method of directly overcoming a handicap is by turning the handicap into an asset. This is called overcompensation, but that is not the customary meaning of the term. (See the meaning by Adler cited on page 310.) It is only the unusual person who can do this, however. Many persons suffering defects have devoted their lives to a study of the ways in which persons with these defects can be made to live useful and happy lives. Helen Keller, who is both blind and deaf, has been a source of great inspiration to others who are afflicted with the lack of these senses of sight or hearing by what she has been able to accomplish in spite of her handicaps. The person who is blind or deaf naturally is not able to regain the use of his senses except in the most exceptional cases. The boy who is lame or who has a cleft palate must find some way of compensating for such handicaps by developing a situation in which the defective function is useful. The slender boy will find himself wanted as the coxswain of the crew or the jockey in the horse-race. The tall boy will find that his height is an asset when he applies for a job as doorman at a motion-picture house or hotel. Actually it has been found that in some occupations too high an intelligence is a handicap rather than an asset. The bus driver or delivery man whose mind is so active that it flies away from the monotony of the task is less effective in such positions than the man for whom the job offers a greater challenge. There would seem, therefore, to be a place for the person who deviates from the normal in many directions, and one way of compensating for these abnormalities is by finding the place in which he will be most useful.

Substitution of one function for another. A third and common method of compensation for personal limitations is by the substitution of another function for the function which is weak. Sometimes this is done by developing the opposite of the function. The tall girl, for instance, will slouch in order to compensate for her height, while the short man will strut about and bluster. A whole science of dress has been developed which helps a woman to conceal any exaggerated feature by the skilful use of line, color, or contrast. A manufacturer may pay his labor inadequate wages and then compensate to ease his conscience by establishing hospitals, parks, social services, each with his name inscribed in a prominent place as the gracious donor. A poor man may be satisfied if he can convince others (and himself) of his uprightness.

Most frequent, however, is the development of allied functions, and this probably will constitute the most obvious and frequent kind of compensation.

Marvin has always been a sickly boy and has not been able to participate in games like the other children in his block. He has compensated for this by much indoor play and by becoming interested in the books in his father's library. He has developed a studious interest in history and will spend much of his spare time reading in the public library. He is known to the boys as a bookworm and as a grind. On the other hand, they are forced to respect him, particularly since at graduation time he was called up to make the valedictory address, which was very mature for a boy of his age.

Jack, on the other hand, has an I.Q. of between 90 and 100. School work is difficult for him, and he has never cared much for it. This is due in part to the fact that his older brother has always done well in school. Jack compensates for his low marks by his interest in athletics. He is extremely fond of sports, goes out for football in the fall, basketball in the winter, and baseball in the spring, and in the summer loves tennis and swimming. During the summer months he had no difficulty getting a job in a summer camp, while his older brother was forced to stay home. Jack will undoubtedly be successful, as he makes friends so readily, in spite of the fact that he has not been able to do well in school.

Zim [8] describes how interest in science can serve as a compensation for deficiencies in other directions:

In a sense attempting to gain security through a science interest is one form of compensation. Compensation is a strong drive in interest development. An adolescent may increase his interest and activities in science because of academic difficulties, physical defects, or social maladjustment. Lack of affection at home, birth of a new brother or sister, splitting of the family or other internal family problems may lead to compensatory efforts in a field of science interests. In many cases the adolescent attempts to compensate for some personal deficiency through activity in science. Such compensations may hinder normal growth for the student. They may be attempts to intellectualize some personal or emotional problem and to solve it by intellectual means. Personal sex problems may be intellectualized into a study of reproduction or genetics but success with these problems does not mean that the student will find a way through his own difficulties. More frequently success in the science will not touch the areas compensated for, unless there is careful guidance at the same time. Frequently the personal nature of problems involved precludes any help in the school situation, but the teacher who is aware of the function of a science interest for the boy who is trying to find such compensation may be able to broaden the boy's activities in a way that will ease his personal problems.

[8] Herbert Zim, *Science Interests and Activities of Adolescents* (New York: Ethical Culture Schools, published privately, 1940), 126, 127.

One may suspect that almost any trait or characteristic which is exaggerated in an adolescent or a child is a compensation. Loud tastes in dress, wisecracking and tomfoolery in the classroom, taking up such hobbies as playing the saxophone, making woodcuts, collecting cacti or birds'-nests, when such activities are overdone, may be suspected of representing a compensation.

Anti-social behavior as compensation. In many cases anti-social behavior can be thought of as a compensation. Sometimes anti-social behavior is a compensation for some defect or limitation. The child who is failing in school attempts to secure recognition by creating trouble. It seems strange that recognition is so strongly desired that the child will attempt to gain it by undesirable as well as by desirable conduct, but such seems to be the case. Very obviously and directly a boy who comes from a poor family and is denied the privileges of a child in a better-situated home or who lacks toys or even food may compensate by stealing. In many cases delinquency can be attributed part to the desire of an adolescent to achieve for himself notoriety, glory, or even crude compensation in reality for his social status. It must be recognized, however, that the motivation for delinquency involves many more factors than can be included under the heading of compensation.

Compensation through play. When a child is not able to succeed through achievement in the classroom or through developing skills, he may compensate for this by play. In play the competitive element provides an opportunity of asserting oneself in an endeavor to win. Many persons engage in games of chance with the hope that if they cannot succeed through their skill, chance will give them the success which they crave.

Compensation through symptomatic acts. There are a large number of meaningless acts and gestures recognized as expressions of neurotic tendencies which can be thought of as representing compensations or substitutes for other forms of adjustment which have failed to yield satisfactory results. A child may resort to temper tantrums as a last resort in having his way and exerting influence over his parents. If the temper tantrum is a substitute for more direct persuasive methods, it can be thought of as a form of compensation.

Speech offers the most convenient vehicle for the expression of compensatory tendencies. By boasting or bragging one may cover up his real feelings of inferiority. A boy may boast of having ridden in the cab of a locomotive or flown in a four-motored bomber to strike awe and respect in the hearts of his listeners, but he is also hereby bolstering himself against his feelings of his own essential unworthiness. By belittling others one can assume a more lofty position in one's own regard.

Fantasy as a compensation. Fantasy may be a type of compensation. Rather than attempt to make up for one's limitations by some sort of substituted behavior, it is possible to compensate in fantasy. The boy that is handicapped physically may day-dream of his exploits on the athletic field. The girl who is plain and homely or whose mother has old-fashioned ideas of dress may compensate by imagining herself a modern Cinderella. In fact, much of the day-dreaming that goes on in childhood and adolescence is of a compensatory nature, acting out in fantasy the successes and exploits denied in the actual world. Fantasy has one advantage over open verbal boasting, in that is can be done in secret out of sight of public gaze or hearing, and consequently can become wild and exaggerated.

Compensation through a second person. Finally, compensation may be accomplished through a second person.

Mrs. K., growing up in a minister's family where one had to watch one's step, missed the normal experiences of adolescence, apparently because a minister's child is held up as a model in the community. Mrs. K.'s mother herself was a very narrow-minded person and believed that a great many harmless enjoyments were sinful. Mrs. K.'s father was likewise a stern and uncompromising man. Consequently when Mrs. K.'s young daughter was entering adolescence, Mrs. K. wished for her pleasures and experiences which she herself was denied as she was growing up. She encouraged her daughter to go to dances and week-end parties. Mrs. K. stinted herself in order that her daughter could have a number of sport and party dresses. She encouraged boys to come to the house and pushed her daughter forward into social life.

This process has already been amply illustrated in the chapters, "Identification" and "Projection."

RESOURCES FOR COMPENSATION

Vocation. Among the resources for compensation may be mentioned first one's vocation. Many a person has selected his vocation as a way of compensating for some limitation. When one has been a failure in his vocation, how does he compensate for it? One way is to teach the skill of which he has not quite made himself a master. It is a fact that some of those who go into teacher-training institutions as instructors have actually not been wholly successful themselves as teachers in elementary or secondary schools. There is a well-known saying that "those who can, do; those who can't, teach." One may suspect that many famous teachers of voice or piano or of golf or tennis have been almost champions, but not quite having championship caliber, they have compensated for this by taking on the task of instructing others.

Avocation. One's avocation in many cases becomes a very effective form of compensation. Many a person's hobby actually becomes his most important contribution, and often a person has won through his hobby the fame and esteem he has been unable to gain in his vocation. The same trait has already been mentioned with regard to pupils in school. When a pupil has not made a success of his school work, he may gain compensation by taking up some fad or hobby and devoting much of his time to it and may make himself a success to compensate for his lack of success in school work. I have in mind a young man who was not altogether a failure in school but compensated for his low marks in some subjects by establishing for himself a successful stamp business which nets him a small amount of money each year.

Personal characteristics. Personal characteristics can be used as compensations. One may compensate by fine manners, by courtesy, by good conversational ability, by striking or chic appearance, or by ability to manage large undertakings successfully.

Possessions. Some persons compensate through their possessions. By owning a fine automobile, a fine house, a kennel of championship dogs, a man may compensate for his lack of ability in his work or for his lack of social graces.

Play. Children in their play often compensate for real or imagined personal limitations. Lehman and Witty [4] in studying play in school among children, came to the conclusion that children gain a good deal of compensation by this make-believe play. These authors point out that playing school is a favorite game among Negro children, and they believe that by playing school Negroes compensate for their actual inferiority with regard to school work or perhaps more often for the treatment that they receive at the hands of others.

Philosophy. The philosophy or point of view has already been spoken of as one of the resources for compensation. Sense of humor may be mentioned in this connection. A man with a sense of humor who can turn aside a slight or slander by seeing the funny side of it has equipped himself with the most valuable compensatory aid for meeting rebuffs. Of quite a different sort but still of the nature of fantasy are those readjustments that a person makes in his attitudes by which he is able to accept or tolerate his limitations in his situation and hence adapt himself to them. One's philosophy of life, whatever it may be, whether that of denying his wishes or taking the blame for his limitations on himself or finding some other rationalization for them, is a form of compensation.

VALUES OF COMPENSATION

Positive values. Compensation has both its good and its bad implications. On the one hand, it is one of the important and necessary methods of adjustment to be adopted where there seems to be a real or imagined personal defect or deficiency. When it leads to satisfying and useful fields of endeavor, compensation is a good method of adjustment. Its results

---

[4] H. C. Lehman and P. A. Witty, "Playing School: A Compensatory Mechanism," *Psychological Review*, 33 (1926), 480–485.

can be considered good when they yield superior accomplishment. Compensation represents an active outgoing method of adjustment. Insofar as it stimulates ambition and leads to increased effort, it may be thought to be an acceptable and beneficial kind of adjustment. Compensation, to be wholly acceptable, ought to make a person attractive to others, and in many cases it does accomplish just this. Insofar as the compensation results in a changed attitude by making the person less sensitive to his inferiorities, it makes it possible for him to accept his status, which should result in a relief of tension leading to satisfaction and calm. Compensation, therefore, may help a person to be happy himself and also more acceptable to others.

Negative values. On the other hand, compensation is bad when it does not lead to the results just mentioned. For instance, if it tends to alienate and isolate a person from others, making him less socially acceptable, it cannot be said to be a good form of adjustment. If the form of compensation adopted is one of attention-getting which annoys and interferes with others, leading eventually to asocial behavior and delinquency, it again can be thought of only as harmful and injurious. Compensation is not the best form of adjustment available when it results in some sort of exaggeration of behavior. Most of the substitute forms of compensation are effective only when they are exaggerated, and in this sense they do not represent a satisfactory solution to a problem. The person with the perfection complex or the need for surpassing others finds that his problems are not solved and that he has chased himself from one state of unhappiness to another.

When important areas of life are neglected, as may be the case when one activity is substituted for another, compensation is harmful. For instance, if a child who has average intelligence and is made to feel inferior because of his unsatisfactory work in school is encouraged thereby to give up all interest in school and turn his interests to athletics or social affairs, his education may thereby suffer, and in the long run this form of compensation will be a detriment.

Compensation is bad when it takes place only in fantasy and leads to cessation of effort instead of increased effort to overcome the deficiency. However, indulgence in the movies may be a valuable safety-valve insofar as the fantasy is somewhat removed from our daily lives and we are not likely to remain immersed in it. It is interesting that the attitude toward withdrawing through fantasy is not valued the same way in adults as in children. The denial of reality is regarded as normal in children, and they are expected, even encouraged, to live in a fantasy world. It is all right for a child to enjoy reading fairy-tales, but one would think an adult who spent his time reading Grimm and Andersen had something wrong with him. Living in the world of reality and of fantasy can coexist in a child, provided he shifts readily from one to the other at the appropriate time. The child is expected to drop his fantasy play at the appropriate time and to wash and clean himself for dinner. In the adult, however, these opposites are much more completely segregated. He is expected to live in the world of reality in his daily life and to indulge in fantasy only at appropriate times in the theater or with his detective story. Indeed we suspect the person who introduces fantasy into his living, for this is the beginning of the development of schizoid trends and is liable to the danger of more extensive personality disorganization.

Compensation is bad when emphasis is placed on only temporary activities or possessions. The man who compensates for feelings of inferiority by flashy, loud clothes or a sporty automobile is making only an ineffective attempt to meet his problem. When the clothes and automobile become out of style, his problem of meeting his inferiority will still be present with him. Compensation that represents a temporary solution to problems can at best be only a palliative.

Finally, compensation is not an acceptable method of adjustment when the substitute achievement does not wholly take the place of felt inferiority. For instance, if the child compensates for his failure to excel in school work by undertaking some collection or becoming a social lion, he will find that so much emphasis is placed on success in school that none of his substituted activities will completely free him from his feeling of inadequacy with regard to school progress. In this sense, then, many substituted compensations only temporarily or momentarily relieve the basic feeling of personal limitation and inadequacy. In such cases the problem of adjustment still remains to be worked out in a satisfactory manner. Finally compensation may lead to eccentricities, exaggerations, and oddities in personality, and if these become pronounced, they may alienate an individual from others as the group makes him the butt of ridicule, causing him distress and unhappiness.

QUESTIONS FOR DISCUSSION

1. Give illustrations of (1) the method of turning a handicap into an asset (2) of substituting one function for another.

2. Freud has stated that in compensating against inferiority a person wants to be loved and accepted, as well as to believe himself to be adequate. Discuss the relative importance and relationships of these two factors.

3. In what ways may coöperation be thought of as desirable form of adjustment?

4. Psychoanalysts do not include compensation as one of the defense mechanisms. What other mechanisms described in this book could explain in part the phenomena commonly referred to under the term compensation?

5. Adler originally developed his theory of compensation with reference to physical defects. What other limitations or handicaps may a person attempt to overcome by compensation?

6. What methods have you observed that people adopt to compensate for

(1) shortness (2) tallness (3) lameness (4) poverty (5) lack of education (6) poor school achievement (7) low mentality?

RECOMMENDED READING

1. ADLER, ALFRED, *Study of Organ Inferiority and its Psychical Compensation*, Nervous and Mental Disease Monograph Series, No. 24 (New York: Nervous and Mental Disease Publishing Company, 1917).
2. MORGAN, J. J. B., *Psychology of Abnormal People* (New York: Longmans, Green and Co., 1928).
3. MORGAN, J. J. B., *Psychology of the Unadjusted School Child* (New York: The Macmillan Company, 1926; revised edition, 1936).
4. SHERMAN, MANDEL, *Mental Hygiene in Education* (New York: Longmans, Green and Company, 1934).
5. STRECKER, E. A., and APPEL, K. E., *Discovering Ourselves* (New York: The Macmillan Company, 1931; second edition, 1943).
6. VAUGHAN, W. F., *The Lure of Superiority* (New York: Henry Holt and Company, 1928).
7. WOLFE, W. B., *How to be Happy Though Human* (New York: Farrar and Rinehart, Inc., 1931).

XVIII

Rationalization

Rationalization should be a well-known mechanism because it is so common and widespread in human affairs. It is the one mechanism which has been most generally recognized by psychologists, perhaps because it has to do with thought processes and comes the closest to dealing consciously with unconscious material.

DEFINITION

Rationalization may be defined as faulty thinking which serves to disguise or hide the unconscious motives of behavior and feeling. Rationalization, therefore, takes its place as another one of the defense mechanisms—a defense against having to recognize unconscious motivation in everyday life. It is a device frequently resorted to by many a person in attempting to reassure himself of his own prestige. It is a way of fooling oneself, of making oneself seem more able, more successful, more moral, and more honorable than one really is. Rationalization is the blanket which we throw over our own infirmities and weaknesses so that it will not be necessary for us to have to face them directly. A boy excuses himself for failing an examination by saying he did not study for it, whereas the examination was actually too difficult for him to be successful in.

FUNDAMENTAL CONSIDERATIONS

Rationalization as fallacious thinking. Rationalization is fundamentally fallacious thinking. In terms of the syllogism, rationalization is a selection of facts that can be used as minor premises in order to justify certain conclusions already reached. One notes three things in this analysis of the process of rationalization: first, that the conclusion is given. Usually this is an act performed, since rationalizations are very frequently explanations justifying behavior which has already taken place. Second, in a rationalization the major premise is also given, and with this no particular fault is found, except that it may not always be a sound generalization. The essential feature of rationalization is the search for a particular circumstance to be used for the minor premise which, taken with the major premise, will lead decisively to the conclusion. Rationalization, therefore, represents a selection of possible circumstances or reasons which will justify the course of action already pursued.

For example, Max comes late to school and on being sent to the office of the principal finds it necessary to have a reason for his lateness. Lateness is the action which must be justified. Among the real reasons are the boy's dislike of school, the pressure that he is under at home to make a good record, and the convenient way of showing his hostility toward his parents provided by the demerits he receives. Max, however, is only vaguely aware of the former reason and is entirely unaware of the latter. When faced with the necessity of finding an excuse to satisfy the principal, he begins to search for a reputable one. First it is necessary to persuade himself that it was not possible for him to get to school any earlier: "Yes, as I was coming down the walk I noticed a trolley car just leaving, and it was five minutes before the next one came. I am sure that there must have been a delay in the street-car service." This seems reasonably convincing to him, and so he plans to use it as his excuse. The syllogism in this instance would run something like this: Major premise—if there is a delay in the street-car service, I shall be late to school. Minor premise—there was a delay. Conclusion—therefore, I was late to school.

The distinction between a rationalization and correct thinking is the distinction commonly made between the good and the real reason. The real reason is the state of affairs essentially and necessarily connected with the conclusion which is to be justified. A good reason is a circumstance selected out of many that could have been chosen which contains a superficial or concomitant explanation.

In this analysis, the implication is that certain facts are overlooked, and necessarily so, since they are repressed and therefore are facts of which the individual is unaware. In rationalization there is a disproportion of emphasis. Uncomfortable facts are disregarded in favor of ones which will not serve as deep-seated threats to the essential integrity of the person concerned.

Motivation. Rationalization is an effort to guard one's pride by escaping the necessity of recognizing the real basis for behavior for which one feels ashamed and guilty. In rationalization, behavior is not repressed as is the case of other mechanisms, but is an attempt to distort its meaning or significance so as to make it acceptable in the pattern of living. One rationalizes to avoid wounding one's self-pride by acknowledging the underlying and fundamental motives for the behavior which one finds it necessary to justify.

Rationalization is primarily an effort to effect a compromise between an impulse or compulsion and the demands of social propriety. In this sense, it is an effort to resolve the conflict between the basic drive and the superego or cultural standards to which an individual is sensitive. Rationalizations always appear to be attempts to justify oneself to others, but more basically they are attempts to reconcile conflicting tendencies within.

A subsidiary motive for rationalization is the attempt to minimize the successes and virtues of another person toward whom we feel hostile or with whom we are in competition. As in the primary form of rationalization, one tends to find arguments and reasons for depreciating and degrading the behavior and motives of another person.

Characterized by inflexibility. Rationalization as a method of thought is characterized in general by inflexibility, fixity, and stubbornness. Since in rationalizing the person is not entirely free to cast around for possible explanations from which to select one that seems, by all the canons of logic, most fundamental, he must protect his reasoning artificially, and this is frequently accomplished by the force of the assertion and the stubbornness with which the reason is held. One reason why rationalization is inflexible is that it usually is accompanied by or follows the arousal of emotion, and emotion notoriously leads to an exaggeration of response and inflexibility.

Logic-tight compartments of the mind. The person who rationalizes also tends to show dissociation in his mental processes. The term, "logic-tight compartments" of the mind, has been used as a picturesque description of the mental processes of selecting reasons in rationalization. The person who rationalizes, for instance, is usually inconsistent. He may stand for liberalism in philosophy but he is quite reactionary in his political or economic views. He may stand for social security and be an active worker in various charitable enterprises, but when it comes to passage of laws which would limit the income of a corporation in which he has invested or which would increase his taxes, he takes a very reactionary stand. It is almost as though barriers were erected in his mind preventing him from seeing the essential relation between his point of view with regard to social security, on the one hand, and the necessity for the redistribution of wealth on the other. The same person will claim that cigarettes steady his nerves and stimulate him. People whose minds are divided into logic-tight compartments tend to accept things on authority rather than investigate all of the implications of their beliefs.

Signs of rationalization. In the following illustrations of rationalization, one may feel as though all reasoning tended to be a form of rationalization and may even begin to distrust any of his own reasoning. Of course this is not true; all reasoning is not necessarily a rationalization. Rationalization can be recognized by a number of clearly defined signs. One signal is the person's attempt to hunt for reasons. If the principal in asking Max, for instance, finds that Max stumbles and halts in his effort to produce a good reason for being late, he may suspect that Max will never give the real reason even if he knew it, but is searching for an approved one that will be a rationalization. Secondly, the extent to which a person avoids rationalization in his thinking can be determined by the consistency of his thought. If in discussion one uncovers certain inconsistencies that the other person fails to recognize, or, recognizing them, attempts to justify further, one may suspect that rationalization is at work.

For instance, Mr. M., who is at a bridge party where it is proposed that they play for small stakes, refuses on the grounds that it is against his principles. On other occasions, however, it has been noticed that Mr. M. does not have the same scruples in regard to living up to some of his other standards with rigid consistency. If Mr. M. is willing to compromise in one situation, one may suspect that there is some unexpressed reason behind the refusal to do so when playing bridge. Perhaps at the bottom of his expressed conviction is some deep-seated feeling with regard to playing for money which outweighs any possible gain in wealth or prestige.

Another sure method of detecting rationalization is by noting the amount of emotion shown during a discussion. A person who rationalizes is almost sure to lose his temper if the adequacy of the reasons which he gives is questioned. The man who is not rationalizing meets challenges on their merits and pits one argument against another with a flexibility and a willingness to change his position, giving reputable explanations for doing so.

Rationalization as a disguise. Rationalization may be thought of primarily as a disguise of the self for the self. First and foremost, we wish to protect ourselves against recognizing our own motives which a part of our personality would consider ignoble, mean, and discrediting. In order to maintain a certain integration of the personality and to find ways of making all kinds of behavior and circumstances acceptable, one resorts to rationalization. However, the integration is not complete; hence, the logic-tight compartments. It is after one has persuaded himself of his rightness and integrity that he then attempts to justify himself to the world and persuade others also that his reputation is still unsullied. One naturally thinks of rationalization as an attempt to prove to others that one's motives are noble, but it should not be forgotten that preceding this attempt is the necessity of persuading oneself.

Rationalization used to justify fundamental values. Rationalization may be used to *justify fundamental values*, which are acquired through the process of identification in early childhood. Every person grows up a citizen of a country, a member of a church, and a member of a political party with certain basic personal values and philosophy. Later he finds it necessary to justify his membership in his political party, his adherence to a certain church, his loyalty to a club or state, and searches for reasons and arguments which will justify his choice. It is because of this that one must suspect much of the campaign oratory, for the arguments used in political speeches are more for the purpose of justifying choices made long ago rather than the attempt to help people form their opinions anew.

Use of rationalization to justify behavior of another person. One can use rationalization not only to justify one's own behavior, but also that of another person with whom one has identified oneself or for whom one feels responsible. A mother, for example, may explain away the behavior of her naughty child by saying that he is tired. However, in this example, it may well be that she is protecting herself, as well as the child, by trying to hide her inadequacies as a mother. But as a parent identifies himself with his children, he will run to their defense and offer excuses for their delinquencies. Generalizing, we find a tendency to rationalize for the failure or shortcomings of our school, political party, golf club, or even state or nation. Whatever we feel a part of, that we must uphold and justify.

Relation of rationalization to projection. Rationalization is not unlike projection. In projection, however, an individual clears himself by projecting his faults onto external circumstances or another person. To the extent that in rationalization one is transferring the real reason for behavior from one's own motives to some external circumstances or to blame of another person, one is rationalizing by projection. In short, rationalization is a method for protecting the ego's narcissism or wish to be loved and admired.

TYPES AND EXAMPLES OF RATIONALIZATION

To attempt to classify all the varieties of rationalization and to give illustrations of them would be an impossible task, since rationalization enters into every phase of human affairs. The best that can be done is to point out a number of these varieties in the hope that with them in mind the reader will become sensitive to the presence of rationalization in any form. In this analysis the rationalization will be broken up into two components. On the one hand, there will be a discussion of the personality limitations and motives, wishes and impulses which can be justified by recourse to rationalization and, on the other hand, the excuses commonly given as protective devices of rationalization will be illustrated.

Personality limitation. Practically any personality limitation, either real or imagined, is subject to justification by one who feels the need to be protective. The carpenter finds excuses in the grain of the wood; the tennis player in the uneven surface of the court; the billiard player in the fact that the table is not exactly level. Most persons in our culture find it necessary to rationalize their status and excuse their failures, whereas the real reasons may lie in their own deficiencies. The person who is in debt to another can usually find many excuses for postponing payment. One also finds it necessary to rationalize his social status. Persons in minority groups are especially given to rationalizing about their conditions and failures in life. This is possibly one of their greatest handicaps in that it keeps them from evaluating their circumstances in true perspective. The Negro business man rationalizes that he cannot succeed because Negroes prefer buying from white dealers when, as a matter of fact, he may not have used business tactics that insure success.

Incapacity. It would make an interesting study to ascertain what kind of incapacity makes people feel sensitive and inferior. Most persons do not feel it necessary to give excuses for not being good athletes, good musicians, good artists, or good scientists. On the other hand, most persons find it very necessary to justify their mental abilities. Probably there is no area in which people are more sensitive or in which it is more difficult to admit incapacity. This may be due to the pressure put on children to succeed in school. The school boy or girl must find a reputable excuse for failure if failure comes his way. In a study undertaken sometime ago the question was asked of pupils who had left school at the end of eighth grade, "Why did you find it necessary to leave school?" All sorts of reasons were given, but excuses on the ground of poor health and necessity of going to work were among the most frequent. Undoubtedly, there was some truth in these reasons, but the explanation of lack of ability to do the work in the succeeding grades or lack of interest in school was given much less frequently than should be expected.

A person who has an incapacity for being aggressive will feel particularly virtuous for the kind consideration which he has for the feelings of others. The person who is unable to defend himself against the attacks of others will satisfy himself on the basis of his capacity to understand other people. The man who is unable to go after what he wants will feel a glow of self-justification at his unselfish aims. There are many persons who because of infantile experiences find it difficult to have adequate sex experiences in later life. Most of these persons find it necessary to adopt certain rationalizations. Many unmarried women, for instance, have love-affairs but are blocked from consummating them in marriage because of fixations on earlier persons, perhaps on the father. They will rationalize each of these experiences, however, finding that the man in whom they were interested did not really measure up to their ideals of what a husband should be. One man, for instance, spends too much time following the racing news. Another is slack and untidy in his person, and still another, in the final analysis, lacks the push and drive to be the success which his sweetheart feels he must be. In each of these cases the affair is broken off and some such superficial excuse is given, whereas the real reason lies in the unresolved fixations coming from early life experiences.

Eccentricity. Most persons with eccentricities, for instance, obsessions, which are their bulwark against disturbing duties and anxieties, find it necessary to rationalize them, usually on the grounds of their social value. Indeed, most neurotic persons will find rational excuses for pampering their neurotic tendencies. The man who must have his whole household quiet from two to three every afternoon so that he may have a nap justifies his behavior on the grounds of his health. The mother who has an obsessive need to nag at her son day in and day out about his work in school justifies the action on the ground that in no other way will Arthur be able to get through school.

Anxiety and fear. Many people carry around a burden of anxieties and fears which they find it necessary to rationalize either verbally or in behavior in order to protect themselves. Many women, for instance, are afraid of approaching old age, and they do everything in their power to retard its advance. The cosmetology industry has been developed largely to help women ward off the encroachments of age. Most persons adopt a variety of rationalizations against disease and pain. They will try to persuade themselves that the pain does not exist, or that its treatment can be postponed. Other commonly held anxieties against which most persons find it necessary to bolster themselves are the fears of being neglected, of being poor, and of being ugly. Fear of social disapproval and losing caste with others is a basic cause for rationalization both in word and in behavior.

Character weaknesses. Then there are any number of character weaknesses which must be justified by rationalization. One person may attempt to justify his selfishness on the grounds that he must look after his own interests first, because only when he himself is healthy and satisfied can he be of service to others. Then there is the need for justifying the taking of personal advantage of others and being domineering. For instance, a man takes an active interest in politics, justifies this interest on the grounds of national and state welfare, and makes generous contributions to the campaign funds of the Republican party. He maintains that the economic well-being of the nation is possible only when the Republican party is in control. Actually, however, this may be a façade to cover up his interest in possible greater profits in connection with his own business.

Jealousy is frequently covered up by rationalization. Members of a society will institute rigid tests for membership and will carry on elaborate initiation rituals, all designed by the unconscious as a way of proving their own superiority and humiliating the newcomers who threaten their position.

A group of high-school seniors were discussing the personnel of an important committee. Theirs was the job of nominating the members. Betty, a prominent girl in the group, objected, unjustly, to Lorraine; Lorraine would be a competitor of hers later on for citizenship honors, and she did not want her to be given this additional honor.

Mrs. Y. protested against the appointment of Mrs. X. on a committee in the women's club. Mrs. Y. maintained that Mrs. X. lived too far out in the country and attempted to mollify her protests by saying that Mrs. X. was already carrying so many responsibilities that she would not have time to take on this additional one. Actually, however, underneath this reasonable protest was jealousy of Mrs. X. as a rival.

A man may attempt to justify his penuriousness by saying that he must save up for his old age or that he is looking forward to a vacation trip or to buying a new home. The reason this is called a rationalization is that the man cannot help being "tight"—it is a character trait ingrained by early infantile experiences.

The tendency to hate, which many persons seem to hold irrationally, is often justified by finding superficial reasons for disliking or hating the other person. The man who frequently finds it necessary to escape from responsibilities must also accompany his refusals with reasons almost certain to be rationalizations.

Idealization. The process called *idealization,* in which a person in love tends to overvalue his loved object, rests in part on rationalization.

James rhapsodizes over his sweetheart and in his fantasy attributes to her the most extravagant excellences. He gives expression to these spiritual merits by poems addressed to her. He fails to recognize the sensual basis of his attraction and worship, but rationalizes the sensual by reference to spiritual charms.

Sex. Finally, in our society where sex expression is taboo except in the institution of marriage, it becomes necessary to rationalize all premarital experiences.

Kathryn, an emotional girl of seventeen, had sex relations with one of the boys in her high-school class. She justified her actions by saying that she was getting the experience which every woman should have before she marries. "No man wants to marry a woman who is a novice in such matters."

It is also common for adolescent girls who regret early sexual experiences to blame their parents for not informing them of the dangers involved or exercising firmer control, although this very control was bitterly contested at the time.

EXCUSES GIVEN IN RATIONALIZATION

To list all the varieties of possible excuses that might be given as rationalizations would be quite out of the question. All that can be attempted here is to give a few examples of certain recurring types. We hear daily such simple rationalizations as, "I can't," as an explanation why one does not do a certain task, or, "I had to do it," "I couldn't help it," "It's nothing at all," for explaining away some aggressive act.

Liking or disliking as an excuse. A common excuse is simply that of *liking* or *disliking*. The girl who was not invited to the dance said she did not go because she did not like the crowd. The man who buys himself expensive cigars insists that he does not like any of the inferior brands and finds particular enjoyment in the more expensive ones. Of course this latter explanation may well be a real reason, but underneath it may have been some other equally important unconscious explanation, such as the necessity to punish his wife by spending more for cigars than he could afford. Many teachers profess a special interest in counseling. Were the truth known, they wish to transfer to counseling sometimes because they are not wholly successful as teachers, and also because they hope in that way to work through to a solution of some of their own problems.

Placing blame on extenuating circumstances and other persons. It is very common to place the blame on *extenuating circumstances*. "My watch stopped," "The car was late," "My tools were dull," "The light wasn't good," and so forth, are excuses which we hear every day. Of almost equal frequency will be the excuses given of physical incapacity: "I did not hear," "My eyesight is not good," "I have a lame back," "I am just getting over a cold." The mountain climber feels that he is justified in not reaching the peak because of mountain sickness, when actually he has lost his enthusiasm for the hardship and physical effort necessary to accomplish his goal.

It is also very easy to place the *blame on other persons*. One rationalizes by projecting. Complaints are made that other persons were not prompt, that one had to stay home to look after the baby, that one's teacher did not give the expected help, that one's father did not arrive with the car, and so forth.

Rationalization in reference to authority. Acts are commonly justified by pointing to others in positions of authority or respect. A boy who did not wish to comb his hair might refer to Lindbergh, following his elevation to a hero, or a married woman who continues to use her maiden name in business may refer to former Secretary of Labor, Madame Perkins. In these rationalizations there is also an identification which brings one close to the unconscious significance of the rationalized act.

Blaming oneself. Next to blaming other persons, a frequent form of rationalization is *blaming oneself*. The need for self-depreciation is never simple, and the mechanism involved is never solely that of rationalization. There is always some way in which aggression has been turned in upon the self to take the form of self-depreciation. Some examples of this have already been given. The man who justifies his lack of aggressiveness on the ground of humility, which he terms a virtue, is an example of this. The Beatitudes have been used by persons for centuries as ways of justifying their low estate and lack of worldly success. It is common to find excuses for accidents where the accident may have been unconsciously brought about to shield or blind the observer from noting some other less acceptable personality limitation. For example, a child may have blotted his paper and berated himself for his carelessness, when the accident, which was unconsciously permitted or even intended, only covered up his inability to do the task called for. Some individuals frankly admit their faults, thereby unconsciously excusing themselves from having to correct them in reality.

Various excuses. One may use *relative importance* as an excuse. For instance, one young boy reads the newspaper on Sunday morning with remarkable thoroughness. When he is reminded of certain chores that are his responsibility, he snaps back, "There is nothing more important than current events. One just has to know what is going on in the world." Similar excuses have been heard from boys and girls who insist on listening to the news on the radio instead of doing their homework, and then continue to listen to the next skit. Another excuse which is frequently heard is the necessity of *making an exception.* "Just this one time" is commonly used as a rational excuse, as though the oneness in carrying its own weight against the general rule made the excuse valid.

Mrs. K.'s four-year-old daughter uses the expression, "Just this one time" to gain an opening wedge in her mother's objection. Later she expresses her argument with, "Well, you let me do it before."

Those who have anxieties whose cause is buried in the unconscious may find it necessary to rationalize them by *adopting a real object to fear.* This is the basis of most phobias where fear of a specific object is only an excuse for the real fear buried deep in the unconscious.

Sour grapes. In psychological literature two excuses have been given specific names, although these forms of rationalization are not more important or more frequent than many of the other varieties illustrated here. One of these is called "sour grapes," and refers to the excuse so often given that what was wanted is not worth having after all.

Mary T., who was not invited to the party, explains that it is a low-brow party anyway, that they never have a good time at parties given by Catherine, and that she has other things more interesting and important to do.

Allen, who failed his entrance examinations for the college of his choice, later explains that it is just as well since the standards of work at this college are not very high and hence it would be a waste of time to go there.

The boy who could not marry a rich girl later is heard to say that rich girls in general have bad characters. The truth of the matter is that this boy had particular financial needs which could have been filled had he married a wealthy girl, and had to find some excuse to justify his failure.

Sweet lemon mechanism. Opposing this, the other type of rationalization has been named by Gates,[1] "the sweet lemon" mechanism; it is also sometimes called, "the Pollyanna" mechanism. Here an undesirable state of affairs is rationalized as having its merits. One takes a new apartment which necessitates walking up three flights, but one rationalizes that the benefits of better light and cleanliness outweigh the hardship. A boy who has to walk to school four miles each day finds recompense in the fact that he is toughening his muscles and getting an education despite many difficulties. This form of rationalization is more highly regarded than others because it relieves anxiety and, at the same time, makes use of other constructive forces in the situation.

Doctrine of balances as rationalization. There is a pernicious *doctrine of balances* which many persons fall into as a way of justifying their circumstances. A rather ugly girl may convince herself that good looks are not so important as success in school. It is argued that brightness and beauty are not natural companions. Slow learning is justified in the saying, "Easy come, easy go." And those who have reason to be jealous of bright children will argue that bright children tend to be unsocial and to have poor health.

Rationalizing by reinterpreting motives. In some cases, where one starts off on a course of action which later proves difficult to maintain, there is the necessity for a *reinterpretation of motives*.

Mary H., for instance, gives up smoking but later finds that it is more difficult to abstain than she thought it was going to be. Finally, she returns to the old habit and justifies what she has done by saying she wanted to prove that she could give up smoking if she wanted to and, having satisfied herself that she could, sees no reason for further abstention.

In reinterpreting motives, another familiar excuse is the appeal to duty.

Essential right of the status quo. Richard C. Cabot in his book, *The Meaning of Right and Wrong*,[2] supplies a number of illustrations of wrong thinking, which he makes the basis of his discussion of negative moral values. According to Cabot, the essence of badness may be found in rationalization, that is bad thinking. Several of the illustrations which follow are taken from Cabot's discussion. Many of these habits of thought that Cabot refers to are deeply ingrained in thought and action and are more common as rationalizations than verbal excuses. For in-

[1] A. I. Gates, *Psychology for Students of Education* (New York: The Macmillan Company, 1923; revised edition, 1930).

[2] R. C. Cabot, *The Meaning of Right and Wrong* (New York: The Macmillan Company, 1933).

stance, there is the argument of the *essential right of the status quo,* particularly of privileged persons. Wherever a person gains a certain advantage either through rank, wealth, or position, he comes to feel that these advantages are his by right. It is as though he said, "I have power and privilege. Therefore, I ought to have them. They are my rights." If the advantages or privileges are denied him, he will act like a spoiled child. Differences in rank and prestige soon settle into crystallized and permanent forms which are difficult to imagine as changing.

Ignoring the other person. Another subtle form of rationalization mentioned by Cabot is the *tendency to ignore another person's needs as though one did not know of their existence.* This is a subtle form of selfishness all too common in our great cities where down-and-out persons can be ignored on the street by thousands.

Procrastination. In *procrastination,* another form of self-deception, there is a disagreeable task to be performed which can be postponed, thereby postponing the discomfort of it also. This is an insidious form of self-deception and may be classed as one of the forms of rationalization carried out not by verbal excuse but by a form of behavior.

Argument of necessity. The argument of *necessity* is a common form of rationalization. A man wishes to purchase a new automobile even though he cannot afford to do so. In order to justify his purchase he persuades himself that it is necessary to the health of his ailing wife who needs to get out into the country. At the present time, advertising plays on this form of rationalization. It creates a necessity for the many mechanical and electrical gadgets of our era. A person is cruel to himself, to his family and friends if he does not provide the latest labor-saving device to make life easy and comfortable. One can argue for almost any course of action by the appeal to necessity.

Appeal to morality. Another form of rationalization may be called *pseudo-morality.* This is illustrated by the employer who, wishing to run his business on the principle of the open shop, argues that he has treated his employees for years in a most magnanimous way. His wages are above the level of many of his competitors whose employees are unionized. He maintains that for his own employees to unionize would be detrimental to their cause. These arguments, however, serve merely as excuses to permit his continued autocratic direction of the factory. By arguing that he is a benevolent autocrat and stressing the word, *benevolent,* he believes that he has presented a fair and telling argument against turning his factory into a closed shop.

Appeal to fundamental principles. There are many varieties of appeal to *fundamental principles,* all of which are varieties of rationalization. For instance, much sloppy thinking has been disguised as liberalism. The appeal to be mature in all things, the challenge to be tolerant and broad-minded, and its opposite, the calling of names such as "old-fashioned" and "conservative" cover up tendencies to protest against conditions which work hardship on the individual. One finds that the individual who has not been able to achieve a position or salary or social status according to his ambitions will use these arguments.

Appeal to magic. It is queer how universal the tendency is to get *something for nothing.* Even in the mental sphere, we delude ourselves into thinking that facts can be brought about by a form of magic. We go about ordering or forbidding ourselves by auto-suggestion without realizing that change of habit requires a certain expenditure of energy as well and usually depends upon some sort of change in conditions or at least a change of stimulus or cue. A subtle and deep-seated form of rationalization is an *appeal to self-preservation* as a fundamental right superseding all other motives and reasons. "I had to cheat, otherwise I would have failed the test."

Arguments based on comparison with others. Another subtle argument representing a curious twist of mind is one that attempts to make *two wrongs equivalent to a right.* A pupil who has committed some misdemeanor lets another pupil take the blame, arguing as follows: even though it was I who slipped up, my fellow-pupil had previously created disturbances, so that he too was culpable and hence punishment meted out to him is justifiable. Another similar excuse commonly heard in schools is that *someone else did something worse.* By pointing to the faults of another person, a boy hopes to justify his own blameworthy course of action. Or one justifies an act of aggression toward another by saying, "He deserved it." Parents and teachers frequently justify punishment by this flimsy rationalization.

VALUES OF RATIONALIZATION

Positive. Rationalization cannot be thought of as a commendable mechanism. Its values are mainly negative. The only positive values that one can see are those which make it possible for a person to avoid facing disagreeable and distressing motives. This device may for the time being alleviate the anxiety, but it is an unstable form of adjustment and is always in danger of being toppled over by force of circumstance. In general, one may say that good adjustment involves facing of all kinds of reality, which is the very thing that rationalization attempts to prevent. As has already been noted, if rationalization at the same time, as in the "sweet lemon" variety, seems to hold other constructive values, it can be considered as a worthy method of meeting and accepting difficult conditions.

Negative. Rationalization has more dangers than advantages. It tends to blind the man to the rational solution of his problems in the real world. It encourages postponing of the solution of real problems and helps a person to excuse himself from facing his problems. In rationalization there is also the danger of actually harming others. For instance, the mother who rationalizes concerning her child is putting off a realistic meeting of the child's problems. The mother of a dull-normal child may refuse to recognize the reality of his dullness. Her anxiety over school progress increases as the child continues to show increasing retardation. This anxiety leading to increased pressure may create neurotic disturbances in the child.

EDUCATIONAL IMPLICATIONS OF RATIONALIZATION

Rationalization is encouraged in a child by putting too much pressure on him and forcing him to justify his every act. Parents and teachers should recognize that children are continually acting from unconscious motives and for this reason should not be forced to justify their behavior on rational grounds. Often a teacher asks a child, "Why did you do that?" and the child is forced to answer, "I don't know." The teacher, then, persists in trying to get the reason from the child, a reason of which he is unconscious. It would be much more important if parents and teachers could understand the unconscious motives back of the child's behavior rather than attempt to force him to produce reasons which have only a rational basis. If parents were to accept children's behavior with all of its irrational qualities, it would be easier for the child to approach his problems more realistically.

Arguing with a person encourages rationalization since it forces a person to defend his position. He is encouraged to discover more and more rationalizations rather than to admit the uncomfortable unconscious motives back of his beliefs and attitudes. Accepting and acting on the rationalizations of another person helps also to establish them. A child should neither be forced to find rationalizations to justify his behavior, nor should his rationalizations be accepted once they are given. When a child offers an excuse for some lapse or delinquency, parents should recognize the nature of this excuse. This does not mean that the child who gives an excuse should be punished or forced necessarily to change his behavior in accordance with the parents' standards. On the contrary, when rationalizations have been given, less pressure than ever should be placed on the child so that he will find it easier to recognize and accept his underlying motivations. It must be remembered that rationalization occurs, in the first place, because certain motives appear wrong, bad, sinful, and dangerous. Parents and teachers must compromise between holding their children up to the standards expected in contemporary society and in not making basic motives seem unpleasant and dangerous.

Finally, controversies cannot be settled by labeling arguments as rationalizations. This will only add to the confusion and force a person to discover still more subtle forms of deception. The best way of helping children to face reality is through the identification with parents and teachers who themselves are able to face reality and are under no immediate necessity to justify their behavior by resorting to rationalization.

QUESTIONS FOR DISCUSSION

1. It has been said that every attempt to excuse the self or to explain failure or inadequacy contains a rationalization. Cite some example which seems to disprove this statement.

2. Give illustrations of rationalization other than those given in the text.

3. Rationalizations can be used not only to justify the self, but some other person, organization, or principle with whom a person is allied. Give illustrations of rationalizations in which a person justified (1) some member of his family (2) his school (3) his town, state, or country (4) his political party (5) his religion.

4. What other dynamic factors enter into self-blame besides rationalization?

5. Give other illustrations of the "sour grapes" mechanism.

6. What are some of the dangers of rationalization? To the self? To the child in school? To the state or nation?

7. How would you go about helping a person to discontinue his practice of rationalization?

RECOMMENDED READING

1. BAGBY, ENGLISH, *The Psychology of Personality* (New York: Henry Holt and Company, 1928).

2. CABOT, R. C., *The Meaning of Right and Wrong* (New York: The Macmillan Company, 1933).

3. JONES, ERNEST, "Rationalization in Everyday Life," *Journal of Abnormal and Social Psychology*, 3 (1908), 161–169. Also in *Papers in Psychoanalysis,* third edition (London: Bailliere, Tindall and Cox; Baltimore: William Wood and Company, 1913, 1918, 1923).

4. MORGAN, J. J. B., *The Psychology of the Unadjusted School Child* (New York: The Macmillan Company, 1926; revised edition, 1936).

5. MORGAN, J. J. B., *Keeping a Sound Mind*, revised edition under title *How to Keep a Sound Mind* (New York: The Macmillan Company, 1937, 1945).

6. SHERMAN, MANDEL, *Mental Conflicts and Personality* (New York: Longmans, Green and Company, 1938).

7. STRECKER, E. A., and APPEL, K. E., *Discovering Ourselves* (New York: The Macmillan Company, 1931; a second edition, 1943).

8. TAYLOR, W. S., "Rationalization and Its Social Significance," *Journal of Abnormal and Social Psychology*, 17 (1923), 410–418.

XIX
Love and Self-Love

One may search through most of the popular texts of psychology without finding love even remotely considered, and yet the very fact that the word *love* produces so pronounced an emotional reaction on most persons indicates its psychological significance in human affairs. Psychology has dealt adequately with the strong emotions but on the whole has ignored love. Its importance cannot be overvalued, and no topic in psychology has more profound implications.

DEFINITION

Love will first be defined in terms of feeling. As used in this chapter it will refer to the positive feelings of liking, satisfaction, and enjoyment. Even as the first pleasures are experienced, so the person who is associated with this pleasure is enjoyed; and this is the beginning of love. When one loves, one cherishes. The object of love is approached with admiration and reverence. When one loves another person, one even tolerates his waywardness and foibles and overlooks minor limitations and irritations. In love some feel gratitude and a sense of appreciation and obligation toward the other person, even when direct gratification from the other person has ceased. Love is linked to gratification in such a way that through love it is possible to tolerate the suffering (frustration) that is necessarily bound up with it. Sometimes the distinction is made between *liking* and *loving*. One likes when he feels mildly toward another person, but he loves when the feeling becomes intense and passionate. In this chapter love will be used for all degrees of positive feeling, whether mild or intensely passionate.

The second meaning of love grows out of the first. As one feels fond of another, one is attracted toward him and wants to come closer. There is pleasure in proximity, and love ripens into a deep "attachment" which indicates the element of closeness. There is a striving for contact. There is a desire for physical contact which may show itself in caresses and tenderness; but there is also a desire for social contact—being in the same circle of friends—and for communion of thoughts, attitudes, and ideals.

Love may be thought of in a more general sense as the *affirmation of value*. It is the recognition of whatever we consider to be good, valuable, and worthy, and toward these persons or objects we show our positive emotions. This affirmation is not limited to the mere nod of a head but expresses itself passionately and with energy. In love there is a striving for the happiness, the development, and the freedom of an object or person. In this sense love is the opposite of hate. What one hates he wants to destroy and to put away from himself, but what one loves he wants to nourish and foster. A mother who loves her child should want the child to grow and become a person in his own right. It is impossible for a person to love evil, or that which is negative or which is based on compulsion. Love is not an intellectual evaluation but is expressed by the attitude and activity of the whole personality. Love as the affirmation of value is indicated by those objects which have been found to symbolize love in the dreams of some persons: money, or a coat, or a job—all objects of value—or fire or flood, which represent its passionate and engulfing element.

Love not only represents an *attitude* toward what is valued, but indicates further a *search* for these objects of value. Love represents a search for the person on whom one can lavish his affection. One searches for understanding, for fame, and for possessions, each one of which shows the direction that his love is taking. "For where your treasure is there will your heart be also." [1]

Finally love represents a drive of the individual for wholeness, completeness, reconciliation, and personal adequacy. As we shall see later, love grows out of a sense of personal incompleteness, smallness, and inadequacy. Reik has said that the person wholly satisfied with himself can never love another. As an individual finds value in others, he enlarges himself and finds a completeness which is lacking when he stands alone. So personality fusion and integration can be accomplished only by giving oneself to persons and interests and enterprises outside oneself.

Love is a spontaneous response. Love is not something that can be forced or coerced. It presupposes freedom and spontaneity on the part of an individual to act in accordance with his own values and not at the behest of another person. It is difficult for the compulsive person to love freely. Love and compulsion do not readily coexist.

Love is not permanent. Love is in a sense a momentary thing and represents the values existing at the moment. What is valuable today may lose its value tomorrow, and new loyalties and interests may arise to take its place. Life is made up of movement, development, and change,

[1] Matthew VI, 21.

and one must expect love to follow the tide of development. Love has value because it contributes to the growth and unfolding of personality rather than something that must be clung to permanently. Love may fade as experience reveals inadequacies in the loved object. The reality of the object and the overestimated fantasies concerning the object do not coincide.

Reik [2] also points out that the ego ideal is not always single but may be a mixture of contradictory features. Whereas one person may satisfy certain of these ego-ideal requirements, he may not satisfy others, and shifting needs in the individual may mean that the loved object contributes less to the individual's needs. Reik believes that the withering of love is due not entirely to the fact that a change takes place in the loved object, but also and in large part to a change in the ego needs of the person himself. It is customary to project blame on the other person and believe that he is an impossible person to live with, but much of the difficulty may be within the individual himself.

INFANTILE LOVE—PRIMARY SELF-LOVE

Bodily satisfaction. Love finds its origin at the start of life in the infant's experiences of pleasure. An infant's first expressions of love are erotic, as he finds pleasure in the stimulation of certain sensitive bodily zones. In early infancy the erotic (pleasurable) and personality needs coincide. As a matter of fact personality has not yet emerged, but finds its first expression in these pleasurable reactions to the stimulation of stroking and rubbing. A baby's first love is in nursing, for it is in this act and in the stimulation of the lips, gums, and tongue, that the little baby finds pleasure. At first this pleasure is entirely receptive, but later on the infant becomes more energetic and this pleasure enters a more active stage. There is a wish to swallow, to control, to dominate others, and an attempt to win satisfaction by active effort. This active sadistic self-love is to be contrasted with passive self-love, which is represented by the tendency to surrender oneself to another person in order to be given things and to gain satisfaction passively. The passive person expresses love by his need for receiving gifts and attention rather than demanding or striving for them.

Ego satisfaction. The previous section has dealt with the infant's concern with his body. At the same time that this is going on there is a growing sense of value for the self as an individual, separate from the distinct concern for the body. Self-esteem must wait for the development of the perception of the self as different from other persons. The infant is originally at one with his mother. It is only gradually that she takes

[2] Theodor Reik, *A Psychologist Looks at Love* (New York: Farrar & Rinehart, 1944), 138.

shape as another person, sometimes present and sometimes absent, with the power to give or to withhold. This growth of the perception of self as distinct from the world without is accelerated by the process of weaning. Gradually the self acquires value and becomes important apart from the pleasures centering around eating and excreting. As the self is recognized as separate from other persons, it becomes libidinized, that is, feelings of value and pleasure become attached to it. Self-love as used in this sense is the complement of egoism and means that the self not only is *acting* in self-interest but has *feeling* and *value* attached to it. This feeling helps to mold and strengthen the self. Gradually distinct emotions are built up around the self as contrasted with these which pertain to others. One can see this clearly in childhood as a child shows signs of jealousy and hurt feelings when attention is given to another child who is a rival. As the self acquires value, the individual is helped to develop prudence and foresight, and self-evaluation provides a check on the unrestricted expression of the basic drives. One stops eating because one has feelings of satiety, but one may also stop eating in order not to become ill or in order not to offend one's elders who would call one a pig or glutton. This development of love of the self as a person—primary self-love—not only gives the self value, but places the self in a vulnerable position, for when one loves, he not only cherishes the loved object but feels hurt if in some way it is damaged or slighted. The very growth which gives the self value may also make it possible for the individual to feel slighted, offended, insulted if in some way he is not given the privileged position or the attention which he craves.

Primary self-love is concerned only with the self and the advantages it can gain. It is not concerned with others, hence primary self-love is not concerned with, or related to, good or evil. Moral issues do not arise in connection with primary self-love, and the individual who regresses to this primitive stage is beyond reach of ethical considerations.

Self-love is a term which has been loosely and inexactly used throughout literature, so that several serious inconsistencies have arisen in connection with its use. Probably there are many kinds of self-love, and at least two kinds can be clearly distinguished. One kind is based on parental acceptance. The child who is accepted by his parents tends to feel secure and confident in himself. He has genuine self-esteem, rooted in emotional security and based on a realistic appraisal of the self. This kind of self-love is not dependent on anxiety and, as we shall later see, is the basis of object love; for only as a person genuinely respects himself can he love another person.

The child rejected by his parents possesses self-love, but in quite a different way. The child who is denied love by his parents is thrown back on himself for love. He is forced to find pleasure in himself rather than in persons and experiences outside and frequently is driven to autoerotic practices in an attempt to derive the pleasure denied him in his contacts with others. Such a person builds a fantasy, instead of a reality, appraisal of himself. He magnifies himself through day-dreams as he becomes his own hero in fantasy exploits. He becomes aggressive, forced by the necessity of wresting a good opinion of himself from the outside world by forcible means. His attempt at gaining power is his insurance against the underlying belief in his own unworthiness. Self-love based on rejection is rooted in emotional insecurity and is tinged with anxiety. The person who is fundamentally unsure of himself but builds himself up in fantasy and self-stimulation is unfit for social relations with others.

SECONDARY SELF-LOVE

Secondary self-love still refers to self-love but represents a step toward object love,[3] or love of another person. Secondary self-love has two meanings. It refers to the recognition of the other person, but only for what the other person can contribute to the self, and this in two senses: (1) to use the other person for the self, and (2) to make the other person part of the self. Both of these require exposition.

Secondary, like primary, self-love grows out of situations in early infancy. It is only natural for a little child to become fond of persons, particularly his parents, who cater to his comfort. This fondness, however genuine it appears, is rooted in the fact that the other person supplies the infant's needs and that through the mother his distresses are relieved and his pleasures are received. Self-love experiences a recrudescence in adolescence as the growing boy or girl is deluged by fresh needs for emotional relationships. The adolescent wants very much to be admired and respected and becomes extremely sensitive to criticism. He (or she) welcomes each evidence of physical development as a sign of growing up, and a cult of body worship may develop. The adolescent girl, in particular, may give more time and attention to the cultivation of charm and beauty. But this self-love is unstable because it is constantly threatened by shame of, and disgust with, bodily functions, an attitude inherited from infancy; and the adolescent girl may try to hide and efface evidences of approaching feminine maturity.

In secondary self-love the ego has not developed beyond the need for being supported and protected. One finds adults who have never grown beyond this kind of relationship with other persons, using them only for

---

[3] The terms *object relationship* and *object love* are used throughout this chapter in a special or technical sense to refer to love of something (or someone) outside the self as opposed to love of the self. Probably in nine times out of ten object relationship or object love refers to relationship with, or love of, another person rather than some material object.

what they can bring. The individual whose only need for others is their catering to his pleasure is essentially insecure. This form of relationship with others originates in anxiety. A person who depends on others for what they can contribute to him is really afraid of losing the love and support of others and has nothing within himself that he can rely on independently. Many times fear of the loss of others' love is due to underlying and unconscious hostility. It is as though the individual fears his hostile impulses will antagonize and alienate others, and it is this fear which is the basis of his clinging to them for support.

Selfish object choice then, is the love of another person only for those advantages for the self which can be derived from the relationship. A person who is capable of forming only this kind of relationship with others finds that his own self-regard is dependent on the attitude others take toward him. If he is loved, then his self-regard is raised; but if he feels that others do not love him or actually despise him, his self-regard sinks. He is in constant need of praise to prove to himself that he is lov-able and worthy of love. The only basis of his love for others is the fact that this attitude contributes to his esteem for himself. In this kind of self-love relationship another person may be loved for providing safety. Just as the drowning person attempts to raise himself from the water, disregarding how much he is submerging the other person, so in self-love one cares little about the burdens placed on the person from whom the "love" is received. One also loves another person for pleasure, but a person who seeks relationships with another *only* for the gratification it affords to himself is not offering the most mature form of love. One may also love another for the sake of prestige. A child may be exploited in order to bring prestige to his parents. A man may marry a woman because her beauty testifies to his good taste. A woman may marry a man because he can provide her with riches and comforts or social position.

There is an urgency or compulsiveness about self-love. One feels pan-icky about the strength of the love tie, and any small sign of defection arouses anxiety. Self-love also has an insatiable quality. There can never be enough of it. Tokens of love must be repeated at every succeeding moment. Doubts arise on a brief separation or when the loved one shows any sign of directing his affections toward another person.

Object love is impossible as long as a person serves only as a dispenser of affection and admiration. One cannot be directly fond of another person as long as that person serves only to build up one's ego. In self-love there is a failure really to enjoy the other person. As a matter of fact, there is so much doubt and insecurity with regard to the devotion of the other person that anxiety replaces true enjoyment. Concern with oneself prevents a person from giving himself freely to others and over-shadows any feeling of affection.

To make the other person part of the self. The foregoing discussion has considered the use of the other person for selfish purposes. When, however, the selfish person (a child) has demands made on him by another person—the parent, for example—whose love he wishes to retain, he has to find ways of winning and keeping his approval at the same time in order to avoid threats or harm to his self-esteem. As the parents criticize, belittle, or punish him, he must take steps to avoid developing feelings of inferiority and guilt. And so he tends to take into himself the wishes and ideals his parents express for him. He develops an ego ideal, a picture of himself as the kind of boy his parents show they want him to be. In this way he can win from his parents expressions of approval, and they will say, "What a fine boy George is growing to be." As he takes for his own his parents' ideals, he gains in strength by identifying himself with his parents. If he can find satisfaction in himself by becoming the kind of boy his parents would like him to be, then he also retains his self-esteem to the extent that he—that is, his ego—lives up to the demands of his superego. It is here that conscience comes in, for this serves as a watch-dog to see that the self lives up to the ideals the parents hold for the child.

Achievement Substituting for Pleasure. As a child builds an ego ideal and attempts to live up to this ideal, achievement gradually begins to take the place of pleasure. Parents can create a glow of satisfaction in the child by saying, "What a big boy you are growing to be," and the child can think to himself, "What a big boy I am getting to be." Admiration and recognition become substitutes for love. In later years a child cares more for his parents' opinion of what he can do than for the physical expressions of love they gave him at an earlier age. So self-love becomes the basis for later achievement. Some who achieve, for instance athletes and thinkers, are those who have developed secondary self-love. They find that in order to retain the love of their parents they must build ideal pictures of themselves and strive to live up to, and accomplish, these ideals. It is true, however, that when the drive for self-esteem is too strong, this achievement may be a superficial striving for show rather than an honest performance.

MATURE LOVE—OBJECT LOVE

Fondness that results from familiarity. The genuine fondness of another person, apart from any advantage to be gained for the self, arises originally from a very simple and common phenomenon; namely, that fondness always results from continued contact and familiarity which has been pleasurable. We grow to love the things that we experience.

As I was traveling across the flat prairies with a friend, I commented on what seemed to me an ugly group of buildings, surrounded by one or two trees, set in the midst of the boundless, unbroken plain. I discovered that this little group of buildings was a beautiful and hallowed spot to my friend. To him it meant home and all the associations of childhood. Any surroundings, no matter how commonplace or ugly, can seem beautiful through pleasant associations.

In spite of this obvious explanation of object love, the fact that a person can become fond of another person presents certain dynamic difficulties. Individuals are so completely self-centered that attachment to, and finding value in, another person is not the obvious thing psychologically that it might appear to be from its frequency and our familiarity with it. The present analysis makes love grow out of the less lovely aspects of personality. Love is made to seem like a corrective process and a way of avoiding a greater evil. Such an explanation strikes a person at first thought as ridiculous and far-fetched. However, observation of children and individual analyses point strongly toward the dynamics presently to be outlined.

Object love grows out of dissatisfaction with the self. Fondness for another person grows out of the fact of infancy, the fact that everyone has been at one time small, insignificant, helpless, and dependent. If we were totally satisfied with ourselves, there would never be need for finding value in another person. As one enters childhood, he finds that he cannot always have his way with others and that in many respects he fails to come up to the ideals which others have for him and which he has developed for himself. Love grows out of this dissatisfaction with the self. It is based on the loving criticism and reproaches administered by parents and teachers. It grows out of the comparison of himself with others of his own age, playmates or other children in the family. It grows out of the doubts of his erotic capacity and the need to demonstrate to himself that he is capable of loving another. Thus love grows out of feelings of inferiority and inadequacy; but if it is to be mature love, these feelings must be healthful and normal, not based on anxiety, rejection, or emotional insecurity.

Dynamics of object love. *Love Grows out of Envy.* Love, then, grows out of envy of another person who is older, stronger, more beautiful, or more competent than he. There are two methods for maintaining self-respect: one by the road of achievement, the other through love of another person. The child who is envious of another may overcome his envy by turning it into admiration. The other person then is admired and praised. Because one finds value in him, he is cherished and becomes precious. The well-being of the loved person becomes as important as the well-being of the lover. A parent, for instance, by identifying with his children renews his own childhood.

The loved person represents a better person—the ego ideal. In the discussion of secondary self-love, we spoke of a person's taking into himself the wishes and ideals of another person whose love he does not wish to lose and making them his own, his ego ideal. But if the individual is disappointed in the extent to which he can live up to his own ideals and accomplish them, he may find a satisfactory substitute for them in another person. The loved object then becomes in some respects the kind of person he himself would like to be, a substitute ego ideal. This process of idealization finds its first expression typically in early childhood when a child realizes his parents and gains strength by identifying himself with them.

Little Tommy can hold his own with the other boys when he points with pride to the skill of his father who caught the biggest fish or has taken the longest airplane trip. "Wait until my older brother catches you," is a method by which a little child can dare to stand up against the bigger bully.

This displacement of power which finds its first expression in connection with the parents extends itself to more remote authorities until eventually a person finds his greatest source of strength and comfort in the worship of God, to whom he attributes everything that is good, all-knowing, and all-wise.

Love—a recovery process from dissatisfaction with the self. So we find that love is a healing process to sooth the wounds of broken self-love. Being discontented with the self, one finds solace in the admiration and love of another person. Object love, then, represents a shift from direct attempts to bolster self-esteem to finding self-esteem through the love of other persons whom we may possess as our own. As I find value in the other person, that person becomes mine and to that extent part of myself or my extended self. We feel pride in the person whom we love, and that pride adds to our own pride. So one becomes generous to the other person and is willing to sacrifice himself because value has shifted and is focused in the other.

Self-love Retained in Object Love. Even when object love is highly developed, however, a certain degree of self-love is retained. Genuine object love is based on a security in the self which makes one seek the other person, not for what he can get, but for what he can give and can afford to give because his self-love is of the stable and secure kind based on acceptance rather than rejection. A person who is genuinely fond of others has no doubts that others can be fond of him. He does not have to cling to others for fear of losing them, because he is secure within himself. Self-love can be diluted but can never be destroyed. The secure person can extend himself to many others and give of himself generously and without stint because he feels sure that others will respond generously to him. Friendship has been spoken of as an extended self-love. A friend becomes the alter ego or the substitute for the ego ideal.

Indeed, to reinforce the point that even in the most mature object love self-love is never lost, we may go on to say that one *always* loves another person in order to be loved or appreciated in return. But the difference between selfish love and mature object love is that in the former one loves because of doubt and anxiety as to his relations with the other person, whereas in mature object love one gives himself freely because he feels secure in his relationships with others. As a matter of fact, in true object love self-love is actually increased because a person feels more at ease, more comfortable, and more secure as he gives his love and has it in turn reciprocated. Unrequited love, on the other hand, produces a threat to self-esteem which may be serious and shattering in its consequences.

Love Implies Acknowledging Others as Independent Personalities. Love and admiration of others can be enjoyed only to the extent that the other person is acknowledged and respected as an independent personality. One does not love another genuinely when one wishes to use the other person, control him, or direct his growth and activities. The parent who most truly loves his child is the one who respects him as an independent person, immature to be sure, but one who has a right to be respected as a separate individual. The good parent wants his child to grow up and mature rather than to stay dependent and childish.

Love Enriches a Person. The loved person then, with his admired characteristics, becomes valuable to the lover, and as a person loves he grows in his self-esteem. It is interesting to note a man's pride in his family or possessions. Let a number of families get together, and one can see with what pride a man introduces his wife and children. As the children are growing straight and strong, making out well in school or college, as his wife continues to be a worthy helpmate and possesses charm, the man feels proud of them and permits himself to expand in his own estimation of himself. The man who owns the winning race-horse, acclaimed by many, gathers pride for himself by virtue of this fact. Love helps a person see himself in a more favorable light. A parent lives on through love of his children. As they grow in stature and bring honor to him, he finds that he can translate his satisfactions from his own achievement to those of his offspring.

Self-love is basic in mother love. Children, who were once part of the mother, continue to occupy her hopes and fears. She becomes devoted to them because it is through their development that she is able to realize her own goals and aspirations.

Love reduces the feelings of unworthiness, isolation, and depression. The man who lives for himself and shuts himself off from contact with others is bound to have moments in which he feels that he has failed and that life has robbed him of his just rewards. A lover, however, gathers strength to the extent that he can give himself generously to the cultivation and help of the person whom he loves. A lover feels strong in his recovery from his earlier feelings of unworthiness and inadequacy.

HOW SELF-LOVE MANIFESTS ITSELF

Autoerotism. Self-love is expressed originally through pleasure in the stimulation of one's own body. As has already been pointed out, certain portions of the body are more sensitive, and stimulation of these parts is more pleasurable than others. It is through the stimulation of these parts that the infant first finds value in himself. The outsider can recognize these pleasurable states as the baby shows them by laughter, smiles, coos, gurgles, the cessation of crying, and the reciprocation of affection.

Egocentricity. After the self becomes recognized as a separate entity, self-love shows itself through egocentricity; that is, seeing the world from a personal or subjective standpoint. The little child particularly refers everything to himself. His speech is filled with the personal pronouns, "I," "me," and "mine," and everything thought, said, or done is in terms of what it will bring to him.

Self-absorption. The selfish person is self-absorbed. The child tends to withdraw into an exclusive concern with himself and his own interests, attitudes, feelings, and pleasures. He becomes his own hero; and the child whose self-love is based on rejection builds a fantasy hero-self to take the place of the self crushed in reality.

Self-admiration. The selfish person is proud and vain. These feelings become the symbols of his strength, but they are only the shell to cover the emptiness within, an insurance against the hollowness of the self. They serve as protection and security against the devaluation of the original self-love. Self-admiration may be directed toward the body, and the selfish person may spend hours before the mirror; or toward the mind and its accomplishments; or toward attainments and achievements and the things that he is able to construct and contrive. A person may admire his moral virtues and feel proud that he is law-abiding, continent, temperate, and clean. A man may admire his sexual potency and virility. He may find pride in his wealth and possessions. All these, either personal characteristics or objects that he owns, may contribute to his pride and vanity. A woman, on the other hand, may conceive of herself as a jewel, an object of great value which she will someday present to some man—her lover—as a precious gift. Women tend to feel self-respect for their own inner mental or fantasy life instead of expecting praise for their outward achievements, and it is this quality of superiority in the inner self that adds to woman's charm.

Domineering. Another form of selfish expression may be in the tendency to domineer, to demonstrate power, or in the wish to aggrandize oneself by controlling others and bending them to one's will. In this way one demonstrates that he is a strong man and thereby adds to his own self-feeling.

Demands on another person. The selfish person may place demands on others for attention, praise, honor, compassion, or gratitude. He needs praise as an incentive for his work; he requires praise and admiration from others whether he deserves it or not and frequently hopes to be admired for qualities which do not exist or to be praised for achievements which are not worthy of commendation. He may make demands on others without being willing to grant any payment in return. He may require others to be loyal to him in spite of his provocative behavior, or to be generous without payment or gratitude. He may demand advantages which cost others in time and effort but which pay them niggardly returns. He may even require sacrifices on the part of others for his own benefit.

Fromm, in his paper on "Selfishness and Self-Love," [4] points out how the insecure person is greedy in his demands on others. This greediness may be for the obvious necessities of food, clothing, money, or possessions. One may also impose on another for his time. He may be importunate in his demands for advice or for help in difficulties. The insecure child may ask for gifts. The timid person may ask for information.

In the third place, one may place intolerable demands on another for perfection in living up to high ideals. When a person really loves another, he is willing to accept him as he is with his faults and limitations. The selfish person, feeling insecure in himself, wishes to build the other person up to meet his demands of perfection which he is not able to accomplish within himself.

Being on guard against another person. The selfish person is on guard against another lest he be imposed upon or lest the other let him down. He becomes suspicious and makes unwarranted interpretations of harmless attitudes that the other adopts. Demands made by others are regarded as impositions. Criticisms coming from others are interpreted as humiliations and attempts at discrediting. The interest of another in a third person is interpreted as rejection neglect and sometimes even as hostility.

Disregard of another person. Still another way in which self-love is shown is through disregard of another person and treatment of him as though he were one's property. One may disregard his personality, or his limitations and peculiarities, his deeds and wishes. A wife, for instance, may overlook her husband's need for a quiet evening at home and insist that they go to the night-club; or if a husband has a need for a round of golf or a visit to the races, she may want to have him exclusively for herself on that afternoon. Parents may disregard the needs of a child's development. They may interfere with a child's efforts to grow up and do things for himself. One may disregard another's independence and place restrictions and hindrances on his free movements. In all these cases, the

4 Erich Fromm, "Selfishness and Self-Love," *Psychiatry*, 2 (1939) , 507–523.

selfish person ignores the independence of other persons and uses them for his own needs rather than recognizing that they too may have needs and interests of their own.

Jealousy. One of the most important manifestations of self-love is through the attitude of exclusive possession; that is, *jealousy*. This is commonly taken to indicate the strength of love. The jealous person is thought to be the one who loves more than average; he is hurt because of the depth of his fondness; he becomes angry because the threat of loss of love is so great. Jealousy is popularly considered to be rivalry in love. All this, however, is in reality a perversion of the truth. Actually a jealous person is weak and inadequate in love, or rather his love is selfish. The jealous person projects unfaithfulness onto the other person and puts the blame for the waning of the love impulse upon him. Actually, the truth of the matter is that the jealous person is the one in whom the love has failed, frequently because of the magnitude of his guilt and hate. The jealous person believes that he is not loved because he is not lovable; that is, because he is hateful. Indeed there are some persons in whom passion can be aroused only when hate is thrown off in jealousy. They can find interest in another person only when a rival appears on the scene to threaten the relationship.

When jealousy is shown, there is an undue dependence on the love object. The relationship is not one in which a person freely and willingly gives of himself, but one in which his own needs make imperative its continuance. In the family situation, for instance, the little child is jealous not only because a brother or sister is preferred but because there is, in addition, the threat that he may be ignored as the mother gives her love to the brother or sister.

It need not be repeated, perhaps, that jealousy is an important component of the family situation. The little boy, for instance, wishes the exclusive attention of his mother and finds his father the hated rival standing in the way of his wishes. The success with which he works through this complexity of feelings determines the quality of many of his later social relationships. Jealousy frequently dissolves following the displacement of love. For instance, if a child in the family finds some playmate outside the family with whom he can have interests and secrets in common, the intense rivalry with other children in the family may decrease. Indeed, it is common to find that when children within a family are young they may give their parents considerable concern because of their constant bickerings and wranglings. When they go away to school, however, and form other associations their earlier hostilities may apparently completely disappear, and they will show great loyalty and fondness for each other. Jealousy will sometimes disappear when the person can rise above the petty feelings aroused by the relationships of a narrow circle and take on wider interests and acquire a broader perspective.

Using another person. The selfish person may want, not only to possess another person exclusively, but to use the other person for some selfish purpose. He may wish the other person to provide him with sexual gratification, and this may be his only excuse for interest in the other person. This is the typical attitude toward the prostitute or gigolo. Or one may use another person for the prestige he may bring. In the days gone by American heiresses would seek out members of the titled European nobility as husbands because of the prestige which they would bring, and today many Hollywood marriages have no higher motive.

Making other persons dependent on self. Still another form of selfish relationship is that in which one person is made dependent on another. Women sometimes are only too eager to attach themselves to incompetent or incapacitated men because they find that the responsibility which is theirs in guiding and leading these persons to some kind of effectiveness gives them a sense of importance and accomplishment. Many men, more particularly perhaps in the Victorian Age, felt a sort of power if they could marry a woman whom they could make dependent on them as in a master-slave relationship, as Galsworthy depicted in *The Forsythe Saga*.[5]

Becoming dependent on others. Self-love is also shown in quite the opposite way by becoming compliant and accepting a position of emotional dependence on another person. In adopting this "clinging-vine" attitude, one person gains strength at the expense of another. However, humbling oneself in this way by relying for strength on another person humiliates to a degree, and insofar as it does, is accompanied by unconscious resentment.

Sensitivity to neglect or criticism. The selfish person is sensitive to neglect, to belittlement, and to criticism. A selfish person is concerned over himself. A hypochondriac is one who is obsessed with infirmities and illnesses. He dwells on the state of his health and takes steps to preserve himself from illness or decay. He is concerned with the soundness and functioning of his lungs, heart, and stomach. He worries over his mouth and teeth and becomes sensitive to the least sign of defects in his sight or hearing. The selfish person is more than ordinarily concerned with his appearance and takes pride in adorning himself tastefully and wearing the most modish and appropriate clothing. He becomes concerned over the functioning of his intellect. He worries lest his personal qualities fail to meet his standards of excellence. He becomes concerned over his status and is highly sensitive to the possibility of being ignored or snubbed or not appreciated for his true merits. Where he fails to come up to his own ideals, he indulges in self-pity.

[5] John Galsworthy, *The Forsythe Saga* (New York: Charles Scribner's Sons, 1906, 1922).

Depreciation of others. The selfish person, on the other hand, shows his own self-concern by his tendency to depreciate others. He develops strong antipathies to men in certain occupations—butchers or barbers—or to certain peoples—Jews or Negroes. He easily indulges in fault-finding and criticism. He quite openly shows his antipathies and aversions and belittles their characteristics and disparages their accomplishments.

EXPRESSION OF OBJECT LOVE

Sex. *Sex and Love Not Identical.* The infrequent mention of sex in the foregoing discussion may seem to a number of persons to be strange inasmuch as love and sex are so commonly bracketed in most persons' minds. Love is almost universally used as a term to denote sex. When one picks up a book entitled *The Art of Love,* he expects to find a treatise on sex. Psychoanalysis in its early formulations was severely criticized because it was thought to overemphasize sex and to interpret all neurotic states as due to aberrations of the sexual impulse. It is true that psychoanalytic theory, being based mainly on extensive studies of neurotic persons, has failed to provide a wholly adequate analysis of love, which is in the main a characteristic of normal and stable individuals.

It is an interesting fact, however, that only recently in the history of the human race has love been considered an aspect of sexual activity. One does not speak of love in connection with sexual activity of lower animals, and primitive man by no means linked love and sex together as one and the same thing. Anthropological studies of primitive cultures will show that every conceivable emotional relationship can accompany sexual relations. For instance, Margaret Mead [6] in studying a New Guinea tribe found that a man gives all of his affection to his sister and that his relations with his wife are to a high degree impersonal and even antagonistic.

Even in civilized countries where marriage is arranged between two children by their parents, the marriage is not based on love but becomes an economic and social transaction between families. Love may develop in the marriage relationship, but sex is not accompanied by love at the start. Indeed, romantic love as we know it in our own society has had a

---

[6] "A man gives the allegiance of dependence to his father, occasionally to his mother, mutual affection and feeling of reciprocity and co-operativeness to his sister, playfulness and easy give and take to his female cross cousin, anxious, solicitous, sedulous care to his children. For his wife he reserves—what? Unrelieved by romantic fictions or conventions of wooing, untouched by tenderness, unbulwarked by co-operativeness and good feeling as between partners, unhelped by playfulness, preliminary play or intimacy, sex is conceived as something bad, inherently shameful, something to be relegated to the darkness of night. . . . Married women are said to derive only pain from intercourse until after they have borne a child." Margaret Mead, *Growing Up in New Guinea* (New York: William Morrow and Company, Inc., 1930).

late historical development. What seems so important and inevitable is simply a product of our own culture. It is our way of conceiving sex.

But Sex and Love Have Much in Common. Physiologically, love and sex have much in common. They both represent the operation of the parasympathetic nervous system. The preparatory stages of sexual excitement, including tumescence and a turgid condition of the genital organs, represent a discharge of the parasympathetic nervous system. In a more general sense the discharge of the parasympathetic represents an essential condition for the expression of love. Both love and sex represent muscular relaxation, and freedom from inhibition and fear. They both represent pleasurable excitement. Both represent an outgoingness. Indeed, sex as a basic drive which demands the response of another person for its relief and satisfaction becomes a prime setting for the development of love.

However, love must not be confused with sexual expression. There may be love of food and adventure in just as real and passionate a sense as the love which accompanies sex. On the other hand, sex must not be thought of too narrowly as the relief of physical tension. Indeed, most writers on sex would insist that the forepleasure and the personal relationship are important factors in the consummation of sexual pleasure. In this sense sexual love involves a confluence of two separate streams of expression and feeling, one purely physical, the other, emotional, based on human relationships. As these two come together, they result in a more profound and exalted experience than any other expression of love. Indeed, sexual expression depends for its highest satisfaction not only on the adequacy of the physical act but also on many other factors, just as the pleasures of eating are enhanced by refined appointments and entertaining company. The expectations of the culture determine in a large measure the quality of sexual expression. What custom permits and expects sets the stage for the quality of sexual pleasure. The vitality of the two partners also plays its part. The sexual temperaments of the man and woman as determined by their erotic experiences in infancy also determine the quality of sexual experience. Current discussions of sex put major emphasis on the adequacy of the sex act itself, but this is only one of a number of factors and not necessarily the most important one which contribute to the total satisfaction in sexual relations.

Sex in its narrow aspects is physical. Love implies, on the other hand, the esteem and recognition of another individual as a separate personality. For the most complete sexual relationships other persons must be acknowledged in a double way, first as persons and second as carriers of sex activities.

Sex is one form of joint sharing and activity through which love may be expressed. Indeed, it is the most complete union and sharing of which men and women are capable. It represents the highest degree of intimacy; but it has been emphasized time and again that sex must not be thought of in its narrow physical aspects but in the whole circle of relationships, experiences, and responsibilities which accompany it.

Christian civilization, strangely enough, is opposed to sexuality while at the same time it endorses love. This inconsistent attitude makes all persons in our culture to a degree impotent and frigid. Love could receive a more widespread and deeper expression if society could take a less restrictive attitude toward sex.

Friendship. This long passage on the relation between love and sex would make it seem that sex is the only form of expression of object love. While it does occupy an important place, it is by no means the only form of expression. Indeed, friendship in which the sexual element is minimized or missing can serve as the expression of love quite as effectively as though sex expression were present. Friends can have many bases for common interests, common pursuits, for sharing and helping one another, all of which foster love and serve as its expression. Reik points out that in friendship there is less overestimation of the object, less idealization, and a less intense possessiveness. Friendship usually involves certain qualities of the person and not the whole person himself. Reik sees the relationship in friendship as one of equality, but Fromm makes this equality a requisite of love. In friendship each of the two individuals keeps a stronger separate identity.

Coöperation. Love finds its social expression through various forms of coöperation. One of these is in the various modes of sharing. Husband and wife will find that love is enhanced to the degree in which they can share together in family life either their work or their play. A person feels that he is loved by another when he is invited to do intimate things. Sitting down to eat together is one form of intimacy and a valuable expression of love. The give and take of conversation is another form of sharing. One may give to another person his thoughts and feelings. To amuse him, to inspire him, to encourage him by the capacity to listen and to receive from the other person expresses fondness fully as much as the capacity to give. One must be ready to share grief as well as pleasure; and until one has shared hardships and trials, perhaps the bonds of love are not welded in their closest form. It is possible to establish love on a basis of interests as well as sex.

Helping another person and giving freely of one's time, energy, and wealth is another way of expressing love. The neglect of another person and the refusal to assist him is universally accepted as a refusal of love.

Exchanging gifts becomes an important token of love. A gift is a sign that the recipient is love-worthy. One gives freely objects such as food, toys, or clothing; his service or time; or erotic satisfaction only to a person whom he likes or admires.

Love also expresses itself through gentleness. The lover is considerate, is not brusque or importunate, and shows a quiet consideration of the other person.

Hart [7] has prepared the following tests of romantic love. (1) There is greater happiness in the presence of the loved partner than of any other person (this assumes a love that is exclusive and reciprocal). (2) There is a sense of unrest and dissatisfaction when they are separated. (3) The lovers find a wealth of things to say to each other. (4) There is an eagerness to share experiences. (5) Each is eager to give full consideration to his partner's opinions, judgments, and interest. (6) Plans and interests keep organizing themselves around the partner. (7) The lover takes pride in his partner. (8) He is eager for the success of his partner.

Probably the best description of how love is expressed was given by Paul in the passage from Corinthians. [8]

Love suffereth long, and is kind; love envieth not; love vaunteth not itself, is not puffed up, doth not behave itself unseemly, seeketh not her own, is not provoked; taketh not account of evil; rejoiceth not in unrighteousness, but rejoiceth with the truth; beareth all things, believeth all things, hopeth all things, endureth all things.

CONDITIONS FOR THE DEVELOPMENT OF LOVE

The capacity to be loved. Some persons find it difficult to permit themselves to accept love from others. These individuals are remote, offish, inaccessible. If one lacks a capacity to be loved, he finds it difficult to love in turn. Experience in the clinical study of children indicate that the capacity to be loved depends primarily on being loved by one's parents. If one has been given love in childhood, he finds it easy to accept love in later life. But this love from the parents must not be excessive in amount. Where the parents overindulge a child, they make it difficult for him to be satisfied with smaller amounts of attention. He becomes greedy, ravenous, and highly narcissistic. He finds it difficult to renounce love, even temporarily, when it is not forthcoming. Such an individual becomes panicky when forced to be alone or when he finds himself with strangers. Excessive love from parents encourages overindulgence.

A second condition for the capacity to be loved is the recognition that one is lovable. This depends on being told that, and being so treated and accepted by others. A child who is called a bad child will find difficulty in later years accepting love and praise from others. The child who

[7] Hornell Hart, *Personality and the Family* (Boston: D. C. Heath and Company, 1941), 170 ff.
[8] Corinthians, I, 13:4–7.

has been disappointed in his expectations of what others will give learns to expect little and is afraid to recognize love lest once again he be deceived.

A third requirement of the capacity to accept love is a certain pliability and suggestibility. To be able to accept love, one must be susceptible to the desires of others. One will hardly be the recipient of love if he is stiff, resistant, or stubborn. Such a person will tend to antagonize rather than encourage love from others. Also, to be loved one must be willing to admit superiority, merit, or ability in others. One must not aggrandize the self too greatly but must have a certain amount of humility and reverence. A person has a capacity to be loved only when he recognizes merit in the person from whom it is to be received.

Capacity for self-love. The capacity for self-love, as we have already seen, also grows out of the attitude that the mother takes toward the child. Self-love flourishes in its most healthy state when a child is loved and cherished by his parents. If the child is over- or undervalued, there is distortion to his own self-evaluation. The child who is overvalued by doting parents develops an overweening self-love. His interest in his body develops in the first place because his parents go into ecstasies over him. Parents who sacrifice themselves by too close waiting on a child encourage him to overvalue his self-importance.

On the other hand, the child who is underestimated by critical and punitive parents is thrown back on himself for pleasure. He tries to build up in fantasy the self he does not find mirrored in the attitude others show toward him. Such a child attempts to gain by force and aggression the satisfaction in himself that his parents do not willingly give him.

Self-love, however, may also be dependent on skill, accomplishment, and achievement. The child who can do things with his body, with his hands, or with his mind, or who can control others by his speech thereby gains a confidence in himself and greater capacity for self-esteem and self-love. Any child is aided in making a good adjustment who is helped to gain the basic skills of reading and writing, of graceful bodily co-ordination, and pleasing social accomplishments. Oddly enough, the capacity for self-love of a somewhat different sort may also be strengthened by illness. The child who has had a long confining illness is thrown back on himself for pleasure and amusement and is made overconcerned with self-care. However, as can be readily seen, this kind of self-love lacks the healthful tone of that which has a more positive origin.

Finally, the capacity for self-love depends on sexual potency. A man or woman who is sexually adequate is helped to feel a higher self-respect.

Capacity to give love. A capacity to love is also dependent in the first place on being loved by one's parents in infancy. Here again this parental love should be a mean between two extremes. Children whose parents help them to make good and to grow up give their parents love in return, which is the first of the many forms of object love that find expression throughout life. On the other hand, as has already been mentioned, the child of rejecting parents is thrown back on himself, and the capacity to give himself to others is reduced. The unloved child finds it difficult in later life to take part in effective human relationships; having been rejected once, after approaching his parents expecting to be accepted, he hardly dares to risk offering himself again. On the other hand, excessive parental love tends to encourage fixation. When the parent becomes too important a person, it is difficult for the child in later years to find any other relationship quite as important or satisfying; in this way overindulgence may actually impair the capacity for love relationships with others in later life.

As we have already seen, another factor in the capacity to give love is the individual's good relationships with himself. These things must of necessity go together because they grow out of a single stem; namely, being loved by the parents. As Fromm [9] states, "If a person can love only others, he cannot love at all," meaning by this fact that if he is so unsure of himself that he has to love others (selfishly) in order to regain his self-assurance, then he cannot have genuine love for others. A person who does not have respect for himself has difficulty in offering sympathy and understanding to others.

Object love depends upon finding a good love object. If those who are accessible have unlovely qualities or throw up barriers of repulsion, love is impeded. The other person must not only be physically acceptable but also must meet the requirements of social class, race, and religion. To love another, a person usually must be free from illness, accident, or other forms of incapacitation. He who is ill is of necessity so concerned with himself that he finds it difficult, if not impossible, to give himself freely to others. There are notable exceptions to this, of course, and some bedridden persons have drawn praise by their unselfishness and devotion to various causes; but this attitude is the expression of some special mechanism.

In order to love, there must also be freedom from excessive competition. Intense rivalry makes generous love impossible.

Freud points out that love that is too easily attained may not be deeply appreciated. It would seem that love develops most soundly when the love object is to a degree inaccessible and its attainment represents a challenge. That which can be easily grasped may appear to have less value than that which requires effort to reach. While this feature of love

[9] Erich Fromm, op. cit.

may be commonly observed, it is probably the exception rather than the rule. The studies of Wright [10] on frustration would seem to indicate that the highest value is placed on those objects (and persons) closest at hand and most easily accessible.

The capacity for love depends on the capacity to sacrifice or expend the self without stint or counting of the cost. The person whose self-love will prevent him from any form of exertion which might be harmful can hardly achieve the highest form of unselfish object love. Likewise, there must be the capacity for forgiving or overlooking the slights, the rudeness, and incivility of others.

Love depends on the possession of common interests and the pursuit of common enterprise. Where two individuals diverge in their tastes, their attitudes, and their loyalties, it is difficult for them to maintain the bond of love.

Love varies in the reliability and steadiness of feeling. The shallow arousal of sexual desire which can be easily satisfied by sexual relationships may be accompanied by one kind of love. On the other hand, love may be bound up with the whole personality rather than with the desires and satisfactions of the moment.

Finally, a man loves as he has loved others before. The character of one's love retains a continuity. As the early infantile experiences set the pattern for the nature of love relationships, later love experiences repeat these early characteristics time after time through life. A person's new love relationship can be counted on to bear a resemblance to the loves he has had in the past.

VALUES OF OBJECT LOVE

Love has become the foundation of the Christian religion and is extolled and glorified by everyone old and young. Love is the basis for the most profound happiness human beings are capable of achieving. One's love relations are cherished as experiences of paramount value. If one looks back over the years, his comings and goings, his achievements and successes pale in significance beside the memories of companionships and intimate associations with others.

The richest life is that which is filled with associations with others. Anyone who writes an autobiography entitled, *Across the Busy Years,* records not only his achievements but also his associations and intimate relations with others. A life filled with personal worthwhile contacts is one based on love. Love provides the surest guarantee of security from fear. One can best protect himself from disturbing anxieties when he is

10 H. F. Wright, *The Influence of Barriers Upon Strength of Motivation,* Contributions to Psychological Theory, 1, No. 3 (Durham, N.C.: Duke University Press, 1937).

secure in the gift of his love to another person. The person who loves becomes relaxed and at ease and is able to throw off the burden of tension. Love helps a person to achieve peace of mind and freedom from guilt. The person in love is assured of his potency. The capacity to achieve and the capacity to love and to understand are the two principal weapons or tools for the conquest of, and adjustment to, the external world. Love frees one from crippling dependency on others and from sensitivity to criticism, scorn, and contempt. Love is a successful solution to the threat of loneliness and isolation. Many persons are afraid really to accept pleasure and enjoyment for themselves because of crippling experiences in early years. The highest form of pleasure comes to the person who is able to give himself in love.

Love is the essence of desirable group life. The world today is struggling to recover from a global conflict which has brought misery and terror to most peoples. Efforts are being made to create a world in which this misery will never have to be repeated. In a previous chapter the cause of war was found to lie in aggressive tendencies in man; the basis for peace, on the other hand, must be found in the love tendencies in man. Somehow love tendencies must be provided with an opportunity for expression, and a world organization must be established which can foster the love impulse. Love in the last analysis is the only antidote for hate.

Love is the strongest civilizing factor. There is no doubt that love occupies a more important place in world affairs today than in any time in previous history. It is certain that men are more sensitive to cruelty, to slavery, and to torture and that they hate these things more today than ever before. We have a clearer notion of what kind of world we would like to live in and we have a dim insight as to how this kind of world can be accomplished. The force which has helped men grow out of barbarism is love. Love brings a change from egoism to altruism. It is love that enables men to live collectively, to care for one another, and to establish arrangements for social security.

Love is the basis for emotional security and stability in the individual. It is love from the parents that helps to establish the secure personality in infancy, and the emotionally stable adult is one who has been loved by fond parents in early life. Parents can never love a child too much or too well.

Love is the basis for effective personality development. The finest individuals are those who have been nourished in an atmosphere of love.

EDUCATIONAL IMPLICATIONS

Use of love in learning. Theories of learning have stressed the importance of satisfaction as a factor in the learning process. Children learn better by praise than by blame or indifference. Praise even in mild degree is an expression of love. Children learn most readily in response to love. Anna Freud,[11] for instance, has noted the fact, many times verified, that the most important motive for the learning in school is love of the teacher. Children are motivated less by prizes, competition, and other extraneous incentives than they are by wishing to please the teacher and secure some token of affection from her. Teachers and parents recognize that the threat of the withdrawal of love is the most potent form of punishment. In fact, it is so devastating that it may have disastrous and traumatic effects if used too severely. Parents or nurses who threaten the child with the bogeyman or the policeman or say that they will go away and never come back are creating deep wounds in the child's security and erecting barriers to the child's possibilities of growing toward emotional maturity.

Love as a growth process and product of maturity. Love is a growth process and is not something that reaches full maturity at once. Two persons who marry should recognize that the first flush of physical attraction is far from being the full fruition of love impulses. Love is something that matures as a result of years of mutual coöperation, mutual enjoyment, and mutual suffering. As individuals share experiences with one another they are providing a broader and sounder basis for love.

QUESTIONS FOR DISCUSSION

1. Reik has said that the person wholly satisfied with himself can never love another. On the other hand it is asserted by Fromm that "if a person can love only others, he cannot love at all." Reconcile these two points of view.

2. Distinguish between primary self-love and secondary self-love.

3. A selfish love choice has two phases: in one a person selects another person who will give him love in return; in the other a person selects another person who resembles himself. Reconcile these two phases.

4. How is it possible for mature love to develop out of guilt and feelings of inadequacy?

5. How is introjection a factor in mature love? How is ego ideal a factor in mature love?

6. Both love and identification are said to enrich the personality. What contribution does each make?

7. How does a person exhibit his tendencies toward self-love?

8. Dostoevski in *The Brothers Karamazov* states (p. 462, Modern Library edition) "The jealous are the readiest of all to forgive, and all women know it. The jealous man can forgive extraordinarily quickly and he is able to forgive infidelity almost conclusively proved, if only he can be convinced that it has all been 'for the last time.'" How do you explain this in the light of the discussion in the text?

[11] Anna Freud, *Introduction to the Technic of Child Analysis*, Nervous and Mental Disease Monograph Series, No. 48 (New York: Nervous and Mental Disease Publishing Company, 1928).

9. Love and sex are one and the same in the popular mind. What do they have in common? What values does sex have apart from love? What values does love have apart from sex?

10. What are the essential factors of friendship?

11. It has been said that love shows itself best through service. How is that possible?

12. Explain the statement "love is the basis for effective personality develop ment" (p. 357).

13. What is the relation of love to learning? What place does love have in education? In schools? What attitude should the teacher take toward love? How can a teacher express love?

RECOMMENDED READING

1. ACKERMAN, N. W., "Psychotherapy and 'Giving Love'," *Psychiatry,* 7 (1944), 129–137.

2. BRIDGES, J. W., *The Meaning and Varieties of Love* (Cambridge, Mass., Sci-art, 1935).

3. FLÜGEL, J. C., *Psychoanalytical Study of the Family,* International Psychoanalytical Library, No. 3 (London: Hogarth Press, 1921).

4. FROMM, ERICH, "Selfishness and Self-Love," *Psychiatry,* 2 (1939), 507–523.

5. HART, HORNELL, *Personality and the Family* (Boston: D. C. Heath and Company, 1941).

6. HORNEY, KAREN, *The Neurotic Personality of our Time* (New York: W. W. Norton and Company, Inc., 1937).

7. ISAACS, SUSAN, *Social Development in Young Children* (New York: Harcourt, Brace and Company, 1937).

8. KLEIN, MELANIE, and RIVIERE, JOAN, *Love, Hate, and Reparation,* Psychoanalytical Epitomes, No. 2 (London: Hogarth Press, 1937).

9. MENNINGER, K. A., *Love Against Hate* (New York: Harcourt, Brace and Company, 1942).

10. MURPHY, L. B., *Social Behavior and Child Personality* (New York: Columbia University Press, 1937).

11. REIK, THEODOR, *A Psychologist Looks at Love* (New York: Farrar and Rinehart, Inc., 1944).

12. REIK, THEODOR, *Psychology of Sex Relations* (New York: Farrar and Rinehart, Inc., 1945).

XX

The Ego and the Self

The self is a topic in psychology which has been practically neglected in recent years and only now is beginning to find a reputable place in psychological discussion. Speculations with regard to the self have always been of interest to philosophers and to religious leaders. In our own generation George H. Mead [1] of Chicago has made the self a cornerstone for his philosophy of society. Among the psychologists William James [2] devoted a significant chapter to the self in his treatise on psychology. In general, however, social psychologists have been the only group of psychologists who have recognized the self and have devoted attention to it. At the beginning of the century Baldwin [3][4] and Cooley [5] developed theories concerning the origin of the self. McDougall [6] found self-regarding tendencies to be among the most important of the sentiments. More recently, Gardner Murphy [7] and Kimball Young [8] have developed the concept of the self in their social psychologies. The main body of psychology, however, recognized the self as a reputable topic for psychological research and inquiry only very recently in response to the significant paper by Gordon Allport, "The Ego in Contemporary Psychology." [9] As psychology freed itself from the shackles of its philosophic origins and attempted to meet the demands of scientific methods, it first gave attention to some of the elements of behavior such as sensory perception, reaction time and the like. The time seems ripe, however, for

[1] G. H. Mead, *Mind, Self and Society.* (Chicago: University of Chicago Press, 1934).

[2] William James, *Psychology.* (New York: Henry Holt and Company, 1890), vols. 1, 2.

[3] J. M. Baldwin, *Mental Development in the Child and in the Race.* 3rd edition. (New York: The Macmillan Company, 1895, 1906).

[4] ———, *Social and Ethical Interpretations in Mental Development.* 4th edition. (New York: The Macmillan Company, 1897, 1902, 1906).

[5] C. H. Cooley, *Human Nature and the Social Order.* (New York: Charles Scribner's Sons, 1902, 1922).

[6] William McDougall, *An Introduction to Social Psychology.* (Boston: John W. Luce and Company, 1908).

[7] Gardner Murphy, *Personality.* (New York: Harper and Brothers, 1947).

[8] Kimball Young, *Personality and Problems of Adjustment.* (New York: F. S. Crofts and Company, 1940).

[9] G. W. Allport, "The Ego in Contemporary Psychology," *Psychological Review,* 50 (1943), 451–478.

psychologists to devote attention to larger wholes. The recent work by Sherif and Cantril [10] on *The Psychology of Ego Involvements* indicates the growing strength of interest in the self.

Another line of thought concerning the self comes from Freud and the psychoanalysts. At the beginning of his work, Freud was interested more in the details and elements of the mind and it was only relatively late that he recognized the part the self plays in adjustment. Freud's term, *Das Ich,* has been translated into English as *ego,* and, stemming from the psycho-analytical influence, the term, *ego,* is now widely used in current discussions of the self. Freud's little treatise on *The Ego and the Id* [11] stimulated some discussion on the ego two decades ago, but within the last ten years another wave of papers from the psychoanalytic point of view integrates the ego psychology more thoroughly into the psychoanalytic system of thought.

DEFINITION

James [12] recognized two distinct concepts with regard to the self, which he called the "I" and the "Me." The "I" is the self as observer or knower, the self that perceives the world about it and reacts to this world. The "Me," on the other hand, is the self observed. It is this phase of the self of which an individual is aware and which he holds important. Mead [13] maintained the same distinction between the "I" and the "Me" and elaborated on these two concepts, stressing the social origin of the "Me." Murphy,[14] in his recent book on *Personality,* uses the two terms, ego and self, to stand for two phases of the self which do not, however, coincide exactly with those originally posited by James and Mead. Murphy refers to the self as the object of perception, whereas the ego is a system of activities organized around the self to include both self-enhancement and self-defense.

In the present chapter the two terms *ego* and *self* will also be used because it is believed that there are two concepts with regard to the self which need to be kept distinct and would therefore seem to require two different terms. In this chapter the ego will be used to refer to that phase of personality which determines adjustments to the outside world in the interest of satisfying inner needs. Or to define the *ego* differently, it is an active process for developing and executing a plan of action for attaining satisfaction in response to inner drives. The *self,* on the other

10 Muzafer Sherif, and Hadley Cantril, *The Psychology of Ego Involvements.* (New York: John Wiley and Sons, 1947).

11 Sigmund Freud, *The Ego and the Id.* The International Psychoanalytical Library No. 12 (London: Hogarth Press, 1927).

12 William James, op. cit.

13 G. H. Mead, op. cit.

14 Gardner Murphy, op. cit.

hand, refers to the ego as it is observed and reacted to by the individual. The ego as actor and observer comes earlier in development than the self as observed. The self may have four different aspects. It may be the self as *perceived,* as, for instance, when one sees his physical self in the mirror or listens to his voice in a sound reproduction. The self may also be a *concept.* The little child thinks of himself as good or bad according to whether his father and mother call him good or bad. Thirdly, the self becomes of *value* and an *interest.* One may be curious about the self and the self may be cherished or despised. Fourthly, the self may be a *system of activities* organized around the ego in response to these values. The self is something to be enhanced or to be defended against attacks from without or even on occasions to be punished. Koffka,[15] the Gestalt psychologist, was interested in the self as a figure on the ground or background of the total field of experience. Self from his point of view became one of the principal figures or configurations of perception to which the individual responds.

The ego and the self are by no means totally independent concepts. As the ego develops an adjusting apparatus, and enlarges its powers of perceiving, thinking and acting, so the self, which is the awareness of this growing capacity for control and adjustment, develops concurrently. The concept of the self is determined in large measure by the success or failure of the ego, while, on the other hand, success and failure of the ego are to a degree determined by the adequacy of the self, that is, the individual's concept and valuation of himself. When the self depreciates its own abilities and accomplishments, or when in fantasy it magnifies its potentialities and believes that it can accomplish more than it has the capacity for, then disparity between the ego and self becomes a neurotic or even psychotic adjustment.

THE STRUCTURE OF THE EGO

The ego has three distinct elements: one, perceiving (ego as the *knower*); two, thinking (ego as the *thinker*); and three, acting (ego as the *doer* or the *executive* or the *will*). In short, the ego first of all receives impressions from the outside world, then organizes these impressions so as to form a plan of action, and finally executes this plan of action in order to bring about desired satisfactions.

DEVELOPMENT OF THE EGO

Man is not born with an ego but the ego is the product of learning and development. Ego development begins at birth and is a process which

[15] K. Koffka, *Principles of Gestalt Psychology.* (New York: Harcourt, Brace and Company, 1935).

is never completed. Ego development passes through four stages. At first there is the non-I, the primitive stage where the self is not differentiated from the environment which surrounds it. In the second stage, the I becomes differentiated from its environment. It perceives the environment and responds to it and develops a self which perceives this differentiation. In the third stage, which may be called the "My" stage, differentiation has proceeded still further and discrimination is made between what pertains to the self and what pertains to others. In the fourth stage, which may be called the "We" stage, the ego becomes to a degree subordinate to the larger group and out of the earlier differentiation comes sensitivity to the relationships with others.

Ego development, a process of differentiation. In the beginning, the infant is not separated from its mother. The act of birth then may be considered the beginning of ego development, for in this traumatic act of separation the infant is forced to begin to perceive, think and act for itself. At the beginning of life, before the ego has developed, reactions to stimuli are undifferentiated. At first the ego includes too much. It does not differentiate between the self and the rest of the world. In times of stress or extreme fatigue there are always traces in every adult individual of this undifferentiated state.

The ego grows out of separation and frustration. As the mother is sometimes absent, the infant is forced to look around for her presence and to reach out for her. The baby missing and feeling after the breast is the prototype of all later thought processes. The infant has to learn that the non-ego is that which brings pain and frustration while the ego is that which brings pleasure. Benedek,[16] as a result of her observations, believes that the infant's first perception is the recognition of the face of the mother, coming even before the recognition of objects such as the breast or bottle.

The self develops as we feel ourselves separate and distinct from others. It is probably true that one learns to recognize and distinguish others before one learns to recognize and distinguish the self. Normally at about eight months an infant begins to differentiate faces and at this time shyness may develop which probably is a sign that the infant differentiates between a familiar and an unfamiliar face. As the recognition of the familiar face takes shape, vague notions of the self simultaneously develop. As the mother begins to take shape as a separate person the baby forms vague notions of himself as a separate individual.

Perception is an important factor in this process of differentiation. When the source of satisfaction is temporarily withdrawn the infant is forced to perceive in order to find the source of satisfaction. A vague realization develops that something has to be done by the outside world

16 Therese Benedek, "Adaptation to Reality in Early Infancy," *Psychoanalytic Quarterly,* 7 (1938) , 200–215.

to alleviate distress and to bring satisfaction and this leads to the first longing and directing of attention toward outer objects. The infant's realization that the mother (hitherto undifferentiated from self) cannot always be controlled helps to produce this differentiation. This sorting and interpreting of stimuli helps to make the infant respond to himself as being apart and different from the world around him. The outer world is recognized in its independence of the self by the process of search and comparison. First the baby makes signs of his anticipation and of his expectation of the coming of his mother and this is followed by his recognition of her footsteps, of her singing, of the sounds that she makes in preparing his food, and then finally of her presence itself. There is not only a need to perceive this but to recognize a distinction between one's own action and the action of others. There is a growing realization of his dependence on persons and things outside of himself and of his efforts to adjust himself to them. Growing awareness of this distinction between himself and others may be marked by his fierce opposition to the wishes of others in the second year. But recognition of the differences between self and others must be paralleled by a recognition of the similarities between the self and others.

This process of differentiation is extremely gradual and it is not possible to locate it in any single episode. However, the process of weaning undoubtedly hastens differentiation and the development of the ego. Walking, too, as it makes possible locomotion toward and from objects, increases independence and accelerates the differentiation process. By retarding weaning or the development of walking the infant is forced to remain dependent and his ego development may be retarded.

It should not be thought that differentiation is solely a function of perception. The ego develops primarily in reaction and many writers have emphasized the importance of motor release for ego growth. The child develops his ego to the extent that he is given opportunity to try things out for himself, to explore and gradually to learn methods of adaptation. The ego develops in the self-assertive responses of an active infant to other assertive individuals.

Benedek [17] has proposed the concept of *confidence* as an important factor in the development of the ego. She refers to the feeling that develops in the infant when the mother temporarily leaves and he is assured she will soon return. The infant who has not experienced disappointment in this regard and feels assured that indulgence will follow a brief period of deprivation is the infant who will develop the capacity to tolerate deprivation. This building of confidence, which apparently is a real response on the part of the infant, protects the infant from

[17] Therese Benedek, op. cit.

fear of object loss. Normal babies show confidence when separated from the mother and achieve a certain stability of response. Infants who have been hurt through deprivation will fail to develop this attitude of confidence and consequently fail to develop a toleration of deprivation. Confidence is believed to be a factor in developing capacity to respond to reality and the ego develops more surely in those infants who have developed this capacity for confidence. As experience in child guidance accumulates it becomes more and more clear that the presence or absence of the mother becomes increasingly important and significant in the development of personality.

Ego development a process of integration. Early development must be thought of as a series of loosely related experiences. The infant learns separate reactions to such different situations as nursing, dressing, bathing and fondling. He also learns reactions to different persons who make different demands on him and respond to his needs in different ways. In the very young child, consciousness is intermittent and discontinuous. Waking periods are broken by frequent naps and the change from one activity to another lacks the continuity that it has at later ages. Some writers have referred to ego nuclei, that is, the variety of reactions that characterize early development. These different ego subsystems make it possible for the ego to be a member of many different "Weness" groups. These different ego nuclei are to an extent autonomous and function independently of one another. The child responds in one way to mother, in another way to father, and in still another way to brothers and sisters. Later he responds to playmates, to nursery school teachers, to classmates in school. Each of these groups has different expectations and requires different responses. Not infrequently the child who is unruly and difficult at home becomes coöperative in the kindergarten.

One must recognize that modern society is becoming more and more split up into different culture groups, each with its different set of standards and expectations. In particular, there is conflict between the expectations of an older and stabler society and the newer and more fluid society. Within our own society there are different goals, such as the coöperative versus the competitive, migratory versus sedentary trends, tendencies toward standardization as contrasted with individualization, tendencies toward uniformity in thinking versus independence and individuality in thinking. These various ego nuclei which may be more pronounced in some individuals than in others are fateful for the later strength and weakness of the ego. Where the individual is pulled in different directions he may find it difficult to adjust to new situations in which his previous acquired tendencies are less appropriate.

It is a characteristic of personality to attempt to achieve an integration of these reaction systems. Some present-day psychologists have referred to this process of integration as a natural and inevitable tendency of personality. Rogers [18] has made this tendency to seek consistency a cornerstone of his theory of psychotherapy and Lecky [19] has written on self-consistency. This integration apparently takes form around some dominant goal or core of activity. However, there is no reason to believe that there is some innate or constitutional process which inevitably tends toward integration. On the contrary there is reason to believe that integration is a function of growing intelligence and ability to conceptualize. As intelligence takes on stature, of necessity it tends to comprise more and more within its scope and it is only natural that as intelligence matures the child should begin to see relationships between the different elements of experience. It is always a feature of the higher mental processes to attempt to simplify its material. This tendency toward integration is also a function of the availability of different experiences to consciousness. Where large sectors of experience are repressed it is impossible for integration to achieve completeness. One of the tasks of psychotherapy is to bring inaccessible parts of experience into consciousness where intelligence can assimilate them into the rest of the personality.

Social psychologists stress integration as being a function of the structure of society. They insist that it is more difficult for individuals to be well integrated in a society which itself lacks integration and comprises within itself various forces and trends. Certainly the social aspect of integration must be fitted into the more individual aspects depending on intelligence and the ability to conceptualize.

Rôle of the body image in the development of the self. Some writers, particularly Schilder,[20] have emphasized the importance of the body image in the development of the self and have asserted that the child's perception of its own body becomes the nucleus of awareness of the self. It is important in this regard to differentiate between the inner and outer body. The external body, that is, the body that can be seen and felt to the touch is easier to learn about and is actually discovered earlier than the inner body. As a matter of fact, the interior of the human body remains a mystery for most individuals. A little child can only imagine what the interior of the body is like and he pictures it in terms of models of machines or containers with which he is familiar in the everyday world. Knowledge of the interior of the body remains a mystery for most persons throughout life for actually a true understanding of what

[18] C. R. Rogers, "Some Observations on the Organization of Personality," *The American Psychologist,* 2 (1947) , 358–368.

[19] Prescott Lecky, *Self-consistency: a Theory of Personality* (New York: Island Press, 1945) .

[20] Paul Schilder, *The Image and Appearance of the Human Body* (London: Kegan Paul, Trench, Trubner and Company, 1935) .

lies beneath the skin becomes the property only of trained physicians or students of anatomy and physiology.

The external body becomes differentiated from the rest of the world by the simultaneous occurrence of both outer tactile sensation and inner sensory data. We learn about ourselves when by pressing a finger on a spot on the skin we receive sensations from the skin. The body then becomes learned by the coördination of what can be seen and what can be felt. Actually when the finger touches the skin there are two simultaneous sensory impressions. One is the impression of the touching finger and the other is the impression of the part of the body which is touched. The self becomes differentiated from other selves largely because of the difference in tactile sensation. Pinching another person results in no feeling of pain whereas pinching oneself results in pain. The recognition of the body grows out of these pleasurable and painful experiences. In point of fact we learn to know our bodies better from pain than from pleasure because pain sensory endings are spread over the total surface of the body whereas sensations of pleasure are concentrated in a few erotic zones.

It should be recognized that the body image does not coincide with the objective body but is distorted. A good illustration of this may be found in listening to one's own voice in an automatic recording. Experience is fairly widespread that an individual does not recognize his own voice when he hears it being played back to him from the recording. This only means that the impression which he has built up concerning his voice does not correspond to the impression that he gets when he hears his voice coming to him from a distance. The bodily self that we feel does not necessarily correspond to the bodily self which others may observe.

The body occupies a middle position between the external world and the self as the agent of our perceiving, thinking and acting. Our hair can be cut off or a tooth may fall out and become detached from our body. The body can be viewed more externally and objectively than our inner tensions, thoughts and feelings. The sense of the self proceeds largely from increasing differentiation and localization of body experiences. As the little child learns to identify and point to his nose, mouth, eyes and ears, he is beginning to form a more detailed picture of himself. Later there is a further differentiation of the self as a body and the self as a mind which can experience sensations and feelings, solve problems and make decisions. Throughout this development, however, the body remains as a very solid and substantial core to which the less tangible experiences of the self can be referred.

With regard to concepts of the inside of the body and their coördination with inner feelings, psychoanalysts have pointed out that the little child tends to associate his inner states with outer objects and persons.

In particular, the inner states of tension and need are associated with the withholding and bad parent. On the other hand, inner states of satisfaction and contentment are associated with the providing, attentive and good parent. Consequently we conceive of inner states of tension and need as bad and think of ourselves as bad when distressing inner states are present because we associate them with the bad withholding parent. We also think of ourselves as good when in a state of contentment and satisfaction, because then we associate ourselves with the good and providing parent.

Of special importance is the discovery of differences between the sexes, facts which every boy and girl must eventually learn. These differences come inevitably as a shock when first discovered, perhaps more so to a girl than to a boy. Later in adolescence there is the need to adjust to still further signs of sex difference and the ability to accept these signs and to fit easily into the rôle that society defines for the two sexes contributes considerably to the stability of adolescent adjustment.

The body is particularly valued and becomes the core of later self value because it is the source of pleasure and pain and because it is the tool or vehicle for achieving satisfaction. Not only does satisfaction take place within the body but also the body, after skills of grasping, locomotion and control of the eyes have been acquired, becomes a tool for attaining satisfaction.

In later development extensions of the body become important and anything that extends the effectiveness or control which is originally a bodily function then can be called mine. In this way our tools, toys and possessions serve as extensions of the body and help to widen the sense of self. Clothes become closely identified with the body and in fact determine the shape and character of the body which we present to the outside world. Later on our position and our wealth become further extensions of the body. A boy's pockets will contain valued possessions which enhance his prestige and give him a sense of greater power and control. Even our ideals and social values can be thought of as extensions of what was originally bodily functions. Inasmuch as we value our bodies and do what is necessary to preserve and protect them, the body image becomes the basis of sympathy and we learn to value the bodies and possessions of others as we have learned to value our own.

Development of thinking. It is difficult to trace the beginnings of thought processes because their origins are shrouded in obscurity. The thinking processes of adults are studied largely through the help of language but before language is developed one has to depend upon observation and considerable speculation. There is no doubt that the language which is used in describing infantile modes of thinking is largely picturesque and inaccurate if the terms are to be used as they refer to similar adult phenomena. Infantile thinking is referred to in terms of omnipotence. Because the child is so helpless and because he achieves his satisfactions through the assistance of other persons he depicts himself as a kind of Aladdin who only has to rub his lamp and the powerful genie comes to do his bidding. The infant finds that his cry will bring him succor, and helpless as he is, he feels all-powerful. As long as there is no concept of a separate object or person there is contentment in this feeling of unlimited power. Later in development speech may substitute for the cry or for other gestures and signs by which the infant learns to control other people. This feeling of the magic power in the spoken word continues in many persons into later life and we have the use of incantation and prayer as a mode of meeting overwhelming need. It is only an easy transition to the belief in the omnipotence of ideas and there is a form of psychosis in which a person believes that he has extraordinary power through the influence of his ideas.

The development of the ego destroys the infantile illusion of omnipotence. As the distinction between the self and other persons develops it becomes necessary for the infant to recognize his own weakness in comparison with the greater strength and skill of other persons. Growth of the self seems to require a clearer realization of the weakness and littleness of the ego. Even as the ego increases real strength and power as the child learns skills which enable him to master his surroundings, so there is at the same time a gain in familiarity with weaknesses and limitations.

Mature Thinking. It is not the place in this section to make a thorough analysis of the thinking process when it is fully developed, but merely to point out some of the origins of thinking. Thinking may be considered as an experimental living through or trying out of a course of action mentally, before committing oneself to it in actuality. It is anticipation in fantasy of what is probable. Thinking originally serves the purpose of social adaptation and only later can it be divorced from its original function and become a pleasurable or defensive activity in itself. The intellect, then, is the ego's tool for solving problems, particularly social problems.

Psychologists have thought of the intellect as being primarily a function of innate neural structure and organization. However, recent clinical data would indicate that the intellect is also a function of developmental experience. Intellect, for instance, depends upon stable selffeeling and adequate functioning. The person who has to struggle with attitudes about himself is hindered from giving his attention to external problems. To maximize a child's functioning intellect, his selffeeling and self-valuation must be maximized.

Logical thinking presupposes a strong ego, and is a matter of character as well as of intellect. Effective thinking involves the capacity to postpone action. In order to think effectively one must be able to tolerate tensions. It is usually found that the strong thinker is also the individual who is rich in counter-cathexes, that is, in interests which run counter to his natural impulses and which keep them in check. It takes courage and mental freedom to notice something not generally accepted. To be able to think effectively one must also be able to distinguish between a painful past and a hopeful future. One must be able to endure recalling the disappointments of the past as well as to look ahead to the future without the dread which memories of the past lead one to expect.

The strong thinker is ready to judge reality on the basis of experience with a minimum of interference from his needs and desires. Logical thinking implies the faculty of considering phenomena objectively rather than in relation to the self. The individual who finds that he is personally involved in an issue which is being discussed in a group will not be able to consider the issue freely and objectively. His own involvement prevents him from full freedom in considering all of the factors. The individual who is personally involved is unable to consider the needs of other persons on a par with his own. It is for this reason that it is difficult for members of a family to think objectively with regard to family problems and issues. Each family member has his own interests at stake in any issue that may come up and this makes it difficult for him to consider the interests of the family as a whole, apart from his own individual needs. Effective thinking can take place only when confidence and security have been developed and are present.

One criterion of maturity is independence. It is characteristic of the dependent child to look to his parents for assistance in working out problems. When he goes to school he expects assistance from his teachers and reluctantly takes responsibility for the accuracy of his own work. He must continually look to others for verification. It is a mark of maturity to be able to tackle a problem independently, to try out the various possibilities without assistance and to have one's own inner criteria of success. But the good thinker never wholly cuts himself off from communication with others; rather he draws suggestions and ideas from every possible source.

Although thinking helps an individual to adjust to reality, it may also take on other functions. Thinking may serve as a defense against the individual's attempts to avoid his painful and dangerous impulses. The ego can use thinking as a sublimation in adjusting to reality. Blos [21] describes an adolescent boy, Paul, who is struggling with the conflict to remain a child, to retain his position with his mother, and to grow up and become more mature in his relations with his peers. He puts aside, however, facing this dilemma directly, and attempts to work it out through his interests in mathematics and language and his endless debates on philosophical and religious issues. Overstressing the intellectual helps

[21] Peter Blos, *The Adolescent Personality* (New York: Appleton-Century-Crofts, Inc., 1941).

the individual adopt an ascetic attitude and at the same time carries with it a high amount of social prestige.

Rôle of language in the development of the ego and the self. Notwithstanding the importance of language in aiding in the integration of the ego it is apparent that the ego begins to take form long before language appears. To be sure, thinking before language is extremely rudimentary. Thinking that takes place before language must be based on kinesthetic, visual and auditory cues and the symbolic nature of the reactions must be of an extremely rudimentary form. However, it is believed that every single thought, even in the adult, before it is formulated in words, has come through a prior wordless state. Before the thought receives its verbal formulation it is present in inner tensions which indicate the need expressed and the direction of the activity which is indicated. However, acquisition and the rational use of speech become decisive steps in the formation of the ego. After the first year when speech normally becomes effective the growth of the ego accelerates. Speech helps to anticipate events more precisely, effectively and realistically. There are many who believe that the ego achieves its integration and consolidation only after there is thinking on a conceptual basis, that is, when it becomes symbolic and verbal.

Awareness of self. Philosophers have been intrigued by the distinction between consciousness and self-consciousness. Consciousness refers to the general vividness and sensitiveness of our experiences when we are awake and give our attention to what goes on about us. Self-consciousness is a partial aspect of the whole realm of consciousness when attention is given to the self. Self-consciousness involves a backward look. When an act is performed it may be conscious but not self-conscious. Self-consciousness comes after the act as one turns back to look at it, to recall and to think about it. It is even possible to take a third step and to look back at our own self-awareness so that one can be conscious of his own self-consciousness. In general, the looking back and recalling of an experience seems to have a higher degree and intensity of conscious awareness than adheres to the original experience. Self-consciousness comes around the age of two although it has its vaguer beginnings before this time. At the beginning the self is recognized only as a self-assertive feeling. The first sensations of the self come through the kinesthetic proprioceptive sensations, and it is only later that awareness of and reference to the body and the mental processes makes self-consciousness a more vivid experience.

We perhaps should make a distinction between the self as *perceived* and the self as *conceived*. Certainly the self as perceived comes earlier. A baby begins to explore parts of his body with his eyes and his hands and learns to identify them by name and by touch. To be able to integrate these separate sense impressions into a concept of the self as a separate entity comes later. The "I" concept develops only as maturity and the advent of language make conceptualization possible. The concept of the self comes after the recognition and conceptualization of others. As Mead [22] has emphasized we tend to respond to ourselves as others have responded to us. As a matter of fact our concept of ourselves is built up very largely from the reactions and attitudes toward us expressed by others. A child develops self-feeling in part by taking on the rôle of other persons. As a child identifies himself with his parents and his brothers and sisters and attempts to copy them in his methods of eating, dressing, playing with toys and the like, he develops more definite feelings of himself.

Although the development of the concept of the self marks a step forward in development, at the same time it may temporarily interfere with adjustment. As the baby shifts his attention from the mastery of the world about him to attention to himself he may become for a brief time more self-centered and hence more difficult in his social relations. It is during this second year that negativism and resistance develop and undoubtedly this is in some way due to the growing awareness of the self as a separate entity with independence from others. Too much attention to the self will interfere with adjustment to the world at all stages. Frequently the child who is prevented from feeling secure to explore about him is thrown back to undue attention to himself and his body to the detriment of his adjustment to the world about.

Another distinction may be made between the self as conceived and the self to be realized. In childhood concepts of the possibilities of the self begin to develop as parents and teachers point out the direction of possible growth and emphasize goals to be striven for, and an ego ideal (which according to our terminology should be called a "self ideal") begins to take form. The self as conceived and the self to be realized are not identical. One attitude may play upon and influence the other and the two attitudes may conflict with one another.

STAGES OF EGO DEVELOPMENT

During the first year, the infant makes a beginning at establishing independence from its mother. He begins to perceive the mother as a separate person and likewise makes a beginning of sensing himself as a person. In his helplessness the infant has to rely upon such devices as crying to command the attention and services of others. At ages two and three there is a beginning of ego competence as the toddler begins to run about and manipulate objects and people for his purposes. Recognizing his helplessness he projects his fantasies of greatness onto

[22] G. H. Mead, op. cit.

his parents. At this stage the child comprehends only the external shape and appearance of phenomena without ability to give a rational explanation of them. His thinking operates by making comparisons and by seeing the analogies and likenesses and differences between phenomena.

Not until the age of four or five does the child's thinking mature so as to take on the form resembling that which it will have as an adult. The child becomes interested in personal relationships. He becomes aware of the relationships between his parents, is curious about them, and reacts to them as his own interests dictate. He wants to understand these relationships and his own relationship to others. It is at this stage that the first conceptions of causality and logic begin to appear. Now the child is able to consider phenomena somewhat objectively without referring them at all times to his own needs and desires. Negativism is replaced by growing social adaptability.

However, few individuals become wholly independent of parental support of authority in their thinking by integrating the scientific point of view into all of life's compartments. It is significant that even the most distinguished scientists who have long ago cast aside dependence on others in their bold explorations into unknown territory may still cling to presumptions which they docilely accept in the more homely aspects of living in which they are not "expert."

If the emotional problems at the age of four and five have been successfully worked through the normal child then passes into a stage—known as the latency period—in which a certain stability is achieved. Because he has resolved his emotional problems the normal child during the years from six to twelve can devote his attention to learning about the world around him and to perfecting motor and social skills and establishing self-control. The child who has not successfully worked through the earlier emotional problems will continue to struggle with these throughout this period of middle childhood.

Development of the ego in adolescence. Adolescence, however, tends to disrupt this equilibrium, at least in our culture. As new drives come into prominence the ego is confronted with new tasks of adjustment and integration. First of all, the ego has to adjust itself to physical changes in this last stage of growth. The ego must become familiar with these new physical phenomena and learn to accommodate itself to them. Since the body is representative of the self the adolescent boy or girl feels doubts and confusions about the self and is either plunged into overconfidence or into feelings of inadequacy.

In adolescence there is a repetition of the infantile struggle with the basic drives of love and hate. At times these drives appear to get out of hand and there is a continuous attempt to master them and to bend them toward the demands of adult living. The ego is afraid of and hostile to these drives because they represent a recrudescence of the earlier oedipal struggles. Erotic demands become increasingly powerful and if the adolescent was confronted with guilts and doubts over these same erotic impulses in infancy, they may trouble him in adolescence. With some adolescents these drives may get out of hand but in other cases they may be strongly repressed. Likewise the adolescent ego fears aggressive and hostile impulses, particularly if there are remnants of the conflict and guilt over them coming down from the oedipal conflict. Like the erotic impulses, these aggressive drives may also break over and get out of hand during adolescence or they may be severely repressed. The adolescent may doubt his right to and ability to love or his worthiness to be loved. Likewise he may have doubts about his manliness and vigor or about his ability to stand up to those who challenge his stamina.

The ego may be strong or weak during adolescence according to the strength it inherits from its infantile experiences. Intellectual interests help the adolescent boy or girl to master the excitement from the new driving forces at this period.

Flightiness is a well known characteristic of adolescence which again represents the ebb and flow of the struggle of the ego to gain the upper hand over surging forces within. Stability in adolescence may be helped or hindered by the aid given by adults. If the adolescent is associated with tolerant and accepting adults who at the same time give their firm coöperation in helping him control his impulses, ego development may proceed normally. If, on the other hand, adults are unnecessarily repressive, demanding, critical or punitive, the adolescent boy or girl may be forced to side with his impulses in combating these adults who are his enemies. This striving for adult stability is not accomplished easily and the struggle may persist over several years.

During this period, the individual is striving to work out a new concept of the self which leaves behind the dependence of childhood and attains the independence and self-direction of maturity. New self-ideals which may persist throughout life are taken on during adolescence for this is the period when ideals are adopted. Status values are increasingly derived from age contemporaries in contrast to the ideals which stemmed from parents in earlier life. Self-values also are subject to modification during the adolescent period. At the beginning of adolescence, as threats to the older established self-values begin to appear in consequence of doubts concerning his ability to meet expectations of himself and of others, there is an increased selfishness and the boy or girl becomes more self-centered. The ability of a boy or a girl to take on more altruistic interests and to participate in group activities is a sign that adolescent development is proceeding normally.

In old age the ego must make still another adjustment. As one's powers begin to wane and one's importance to others diminishes there arises a distinct threat to the self. It requires a special strength of character to give up responsibilities of middle life and to gracefully accept the facts of aging with the inevitable debasement of the self. Individuals with resources for continued activity and production are best able to maintain their self-respect as their powers diminish.

EDUCATIONAL IMPLICATIONS

The development of the ego may be considered the main task of education. Education should be concerned with helping individuals to make better adjustments to their social surroundings. Education should be concerned with more effective perceiving, more effective thinking, and more effective acting. Too often schools forget that their task is helping boys and girls grow up to be more efficient men and women. They become so immersed in the details of the process of growth that they forget the larger aims. Schools may become concerned with the development of such isolated skills as reading, writing and arithmetic, without providing that these skills be directed toward developing increased competence in the affairs of life. But modern education recognizes that these skills have a functional value and makes provision for the development of them in the situations in which they are to be used. The process of growth is one of changing from dependence on others to dependence on one's own efforts, decisions and control.

The ego of the child should be respected at every stage of growth, even from the first year. It is easy to forget that even the very young child is striving to attain competence and that his efforts to attain mastery should be respected from the beginning. The ego grows by exercise and a child should be provided with the opportunity of exercising all of his ego functions. He should be encouraged to attend to objects about him, to become curious about the relations of things, to think about the issues that confront him in daily living, to consider alternate plans, to anticipate the outcomes of various actions, and to learn to make rational decisions concerning them. The child should be given an opportunity of acting out freely rather than being discouraged from experimenting and exploring.

Parents should recognize that the ego grows gradually and slowly. Ego functions follow a natural sequence in development and it is unwise to attempt to force them. There is never reason to regret waiting until a later time to encourage a child to undertake new forms of learning. What the child might attempt to do today he can also do equally well, if not better, next week or next year.

Parents and teachers should give a child as much freedom for choice, decision, and learning by experience as he can stand. Here there must be moderation between two extremes. On the one hand, a mother who dreads a child's growing up and wants to keep him dependent as long as possible may attempt to delay the passage of each stage of a child's development. Such a mother will wean a child late, will dread the time when he leaves home for school and later in adolescence will resist every effort of the child to become independent and make decisions of his own. The other extreme is found in those parents who shove the child ahead. These parents seem to be threatened by a fear that the child will not grow up and are constantly urging the child to take more initiative and responsibility that he is ready for. Children who are over-protected will sometimes attempt to do things on their own in crude and unreasonable ways. On the other hand, children who are thrust ahead before they are ready will seem to lean back and require more than ordinary care and urging. It is believed today that the best results are achieved when more rather than less care and nuturing are given at each stage. The emphasis today is placed on the importance of the feeling of confidence and security, for it is believed that children who feel most secure are the ones who will dare to experiment and explore the most.

Children should be encouraged to be active and to become participants in enterprises rather than to be passive and recipients. It is too easy in many cases for parents to assume responsibility and do things for the child (because they can be done more efficiently) than to give the child the opportunity of trying things out for himself. Families and schools should include children in a discussion of difficult problems which have to be faced and in the making of plans. Children will learn best when they are given an opportunity to participate in the common activities of the group.

The harm that comes from ridicule and criticism to ego growth probably needs no emphasis and yet in countless instances parents and teachers vent their hostility on children by these methods and thereby frighten or shame children from exploring or thinking or acting.

The place of authority and dominance in ego growth is often misunderstood. To be sure a certain amount of dominance from one's elders is necessary for a child's acculturization. However, it is easy to carry the practice of domination too far. Autocracy in any human relation discourages self-direction and self-control and these are the aims of ego building. Much more is to be expected for ego development from a democratic organization of the social group in which respect is felt by all the members for each other, in which freedom of thinking and action is given to all and in which there is mutual assistance and participation in family activities. Children will learn more in the process of fitting into social expectations through the process of sharing than through dominance from above. However, in those instances in which a child has lived in an authoritarian atmosphere, liberation from control may place too heavy a burden on the immature ego. The shift from authoritarian controls to more democratic forms of control must proceed gradually and cautiously to make sure that the immature egos are not given more responsibility than they can manage.

Fries [23] has pointed out a number of factors to be considered in selecting experiences for ego building. She is particularly sensitive to congenital and constitutional differences in personality from her studies of new-born infants and warns on the one hand against forcing and inconsistency in the handling of the slow and lethargic child, and, on the other hand, points out the necessity of restraint and correction of the over-active child. In planning ego building experiences, physical status must be considered as well as mental capacity. Gifted children present peculiar problems in ego development because of the disparity between their ability and their emotional immaturity. Gifted children frequently can solve problems on an intellectual basis before they are emotionally ready to meet new situations. Other factors to be taken into account are the age of the child and special experiences such as travel, being under the guidance of a nurse, or a severe illness. Fries also suggests that one must look ahead to the results intended as a result of ego building experiences and they must be planned to fit the child into the culture in which he will probably live as an adult. Of special significance is the adult's attitude toward the child. Every child deserves being under the care of an emotionally mature adult who will not respond by envy on the one hand, or disappointment on the other, at the progress the child makes in his development.

Aids to the development of thinking. Many of the points already made apply with particular force in encouraging the development of thinking. If children are to grow in their ability to approach situations thoughtfully they must be given freedom to think for themselves. It is so easy to think for a child because his attempts to think are so clumsy and ineffective, but learning takes place only through exercise and if a child is to mature in his ability to think he must be given the opportunity of practicing thinking.

Children will learn a lot by being permitted to participate in the thinking activities of others. Since thinking is something that does not take place openly where it can be seen or heard, it is especially important for parents to carry on their thinking in ways in which a child can participate. A child will be helped greatly in his growth in thinking if he

[23] M. E. Fries, "The Child's Ego Development and the Training of Adults in His Environment," in *The Psychoanalytic Study of the Child*, Vol. II, pp. 85–112 (New York: International Universities Press, 1947).

can witness or participate in free discussion and the parents are wise if they will engage in lively discussion and encourage the children to join in with them.

Children should be praised for their attempts to think rather than belittled or criticized because their efforts are childish and ineffective. Children around the age of four, perhaps, do not need to be encouraged to ask questions but at least they should not be discouraged from asking them. Children's questions should be considered seriously and reasonable answers should be given. Naturally a parent cannot answer children's questions all day long but when attention can be given to the child's questions, the child should receive the satisfaction of a thoughtful and attentive answer.

Parents should admit their own limitations in thinking and if necessary should admit their errors and inconsistencies. Too often parents are afraid that they will lose the respect of their children if they admit any errors or limitations in their thinking. On the contrary, if parents will be natural with children with regard to their own thinking, children will then realize that their own verbal efforts are not unlike those of their parents and they will be encouraged to try to approach problems thoughtfully as their parents do. Rather than losing the respect of their children by admitting errors, parents actually help children to appraise them more realistically.

Children should not be forced to find reasons for all of their actions. To demand explanations encourages rationalization and chicanery. Children should be free to think without undue pressure, and parents should avoid distorting the thinking of their children by making unreasonable demands upon them.

Ego development can be aided by relieving children from the threat of punishment. Punishment, or the threat of it, is one of the prime conditions for the arousal of anxiety. Anxiety, if it becomes at all intense, puts pressures on the growing ego to mitigate it and to build defenses up against it. The ego should be free to meet problems in the real world about rather than to have to divert some of its energy to protecting itself from threats made against it. Parents, therefore, in the interest of ego development, should use positive methods of freedom and encouragement so far as possible and should avoid the threats arising from punishment.

Children should be encouraged to adopt a realistic conception and attitude toward themselves. Learning to accept one's own limitations as well as to appreciate one's assets is an important step in ego development and will make ego functioning more realistic. Accepting one's limitations in the sense of humbling oneself unnecessarily and belittling oneself becomes a defense mechanism only when the individual finds it necessary to defend himself in this way against attacks. Naturally parents should not belittle the child or put unusual demands on him which will necessitate self-belittlement as a defensive measure. Accepting one's limitations can be constructive when it is done realistically.

THERAPEUTIC IMPLICATIONS OF THE EGO

In cases where ego development has been retarded or distorted and there are cracks or weaknesses in the ego structure it may be necessary later in life to give the adolescent or the adult help in strengthening his ego functioning. This process of bolstering the ego in contrast to the natural process of ego development is known as *psychotherapy*. Freud, who has set the pattern for our present psychotherapeutic practices, did not recognize the importance of the ego until late in his career. His first efforts at curing emotionally sick people was directed toward the reduction of symptoms. Later, however, as his perspective broadened he saw that in order to help a person who is mentally sick it is necessary to treat him as a whole personality rather than in terms of separate bits of behavior.

The task of psychotherapy is to provide the best possible conditions for ego functioning. Usually the hindrances are not to be found in the external environment but in certain blocks and conflicts within the individual. Just as ego development is a process of becoming less dependent on others and becoming more self-directing and dependent on one's self, so psychotherapy, too, has these as its goals and it attempts to help an individual pick up where his development stopped in early life and continue with the maturing process. The ego resists change because any change becomes a threat to its stability and its integration. So a considerable part of the task of psychotherapy is to provide sufficient security so that an individual will dare to let go of some of the elements of his ego organization in favor of more effective and mature ego controls.

It is an interesting point that psychotherapy itself must work through the aid of whatever ego strength the person has already acquired. Without some ego structure there would be very little with which to work and one would have to start a process of psychotherapy on a very low level of functioning. To the extent that a person has certain elements of ego strength—the capacity for self-control, some adeptness at reality testing, and a certain degree of ego integration—there is a foundation on which to build. In psychotherapy ego strength is artificially given at the beginning of the process through identification with the therapist who in his own life exemplifies good ego functioning and with whom his client may identify.

Function of relationship in psychotherapy. The patient is helped to attain ego strength in large measure by the relationship which is built up between him and the therapist. Since the ego of the neurotic has remained immature, frequently because of insecurities in the early years of life, it is necessary to provide such security in the relationship between therapist and client which will enable ego growth to continue from points where it stopped developing. This means that the therapist must avoid any trace of threat in the form of criticism, belittlement or disagreement with not only the client's behavior but also his attitudes and thoughts. It is a well known principle of psychotherapy that the therapist must be convincingly accepting of the client in every respect. A critical, belittling or hostile attitude on the part of the therapist will defeat his purposes from the outset. Not only must the therapist be accepting but he must also be permissive which means that he must not attempt to steer or guide the client into ways that he (the therapist) believes would be desirable. Rather he should wait until the client has accumulated sufficient ego strength so that he himself can control and guide his own behavior. In practically every case, particularly of neuroses, the fault lies not in the client's ignorance of what is expected of him but in the failure of his ego to guide and control behavior along desirable lines.

Goals of psychotherapy. One important goal of psychotherapy is to loosen the hold of the superego on the individual. This does not necessarily mean that the superego standards and demands should be diminished but that they should operate in a less tyrannical fashion. The individual needs to acquire a flexibility with regard to his superego standards, and the feeling that he deserves punishment when he does not come up to his standards should be reduced. The healthy individual maintains standards and control of behavior but feels less guilt and self-abnegation when he does not totally live up to his own self-expectations. With a less tyrannical superego, an individual is better able to reconcile his superego demands with the demands of reality.

The principal tasks in all forms of psychotherapy is to incorporate into the ego structure unconscious contents that have been withheld and which are consequently unacceptable and cannot be integrated into the total ego structure. Psychotherapy may be thought of as a process of education by which the ego is helped to tolerate impulses and drives which the superego rejects as bad or infamous, particularly those that had their origin in infancy and which persist only as unconscious fantasy. To be more specific, it is not uncommon for neurotic individuals to express in their dreams distinct death wishes toward individuals with whom they are closely associated as, for instance, members of the family. Some psychotherapists regard these death wishes as remnants of attitudes held in early life and long since disregarded and repressed in favor of more socially accepted attitudes which constitute the superego. The task of psychotherapy is to help the individual acknowledge these deeper feelings and impulses, to recognize their fantastic nature, to see on what a thin foundation they were based, and how utterly unrealistic they are at the present time. As these unconscious impulses are thus brought to light, and their infantile bases exposed, their tenuousness helps them to dissolve into thin air and their grip on the personality is lessened.

However, these unconscious elements were originally made unconscious because such thoughts and impulses were not tolerated by parents and teachers in earlier years and increasingly to recognize them would be anxiety-provoking. In order to defend the ego against anxiety, resistances are built up against the recognition of these unconscious impulses. The task of therapy is principally that of breaking through these resistances which serve as a barrier to the conscious recognition of the impulses which are thus kept out of conscious awareness. However, even after the resistances are broken through and the ego is helped to become aware of inner trends of which it was not aware, there is still the necessity of a process of re-education in which the ego is encouraged to give up the repressions which it has so long harbored. Psychotherapy involves a splitting of the ego whereby a reasonable side which is responsive to reality works in coöperation with the therapist against the defensive side which is attempting to keep unconscious elements from exposure to the light of awareness.

There are two types of mental disorder for which psychotherapy is extremely difficult or impossible. Highly self-centered and selfish individuals have difficulty in establishing a trusting relationship with any other person. If there is no part of the ego which can work with the therapist the therapist has no handle with which to begin his work. The other group of individuals are those with psychoses who have so isolated themselves and withdrawn from reality that they have no part of the ego which is accessible and which can coöperate in regaining mental health. The psychiatrist who wishes to work with psychotic patients on a therapeutic basis must be content to work with whatever small fraction of the rational ego is left with which he can get into contact.

Process of psychotherapy. In psychotherapy the client is called to coöperate with the therapist against other elements in the self which are working at cross purposes with the rational. There must always be a change in the ego if it is to remain and deal with painful impulses. Rogers [24] in his method of non-directive therapy, advises patience while the client, through his own efforts but aided by the tolerance and acceptance of the therapist, works out a new perception of himself and gradually finds tolerance for forces within which enables him to reorganize his attitude toward himself and become more self-directing. Psychoanalysts believe that except in the mildest cases of ego disturbance

24 C. R. Rogers, *Counseling and Psychotherapy* (Boston: Houghton Mifflin Company, 1942).

this non-directive method would be ineffective. The psychoanalyst works through interpretation, principally the interpretation of the patient's resistances, by pointing out to the patient, how through his rationalization, his projections and other forms of evasion, or through his acting out, he is avoiding facing unpalatable truths about himself. As the patient is able to accept these interpretations and understand the defensive nature of his behavior it becomes increasingly possible for him to face and accept those actions, feelings and defenses which he was formerly unable to accept.

To the extent that an individual is aided in recognizing and accepting his feelings his ego becomes stronger and is better able to deal on a more rational and constructive basis with the daily situations which he has to meet. As an individual is helped to recognize and accept forbidden feelings and impulses they become less threatening and dangerous. Superego standards with regard to them may not change but the ego becomes less afraid of these superego demands. To put the matter more simply, a child may still believe that it is wrong to strike or harm another person but he is better able to accept his feelings of anger against others, and the very acceptance of these feelings reduces their strength. However, the exposure of unconscious feelings always arouses anxiety and anxiety is never easy to bear.

If the pain of the anxiety which exposure of unacceptable parts of the self might arouse is too intolerable the ego may refuse to use the worker and break off treatment. This outcome is seen in many instances when parents bring their children to the clinic for help with regard to their handling of them and the worker, in talking to the mother, helps her see that the children's problems are related to her own problems. As this insight breaks through, guilt may be aroused which becomes so intolerable that the mother is unable to permit the child to come for treatment and breaks off the process. Or in other cases where the mother is willing to let the child come for treatment, she is unwilling to explore her own relationship to the child's problem because of the guilt which it arouses.

No process of psychotherapy should be undertaken without a preliminary diagnosis of the nature of the difficulty. In some cases the individual's problems are the result of some immediate traumatic experience which has temporarily impaired the ego's functional efficiency. In such cases a type of supportive therapy is called for which will give the person being treated support until he is able to face his situation and make adequate adjustment to it. However, some clients may attempt to interpret their own problems as though they represented a temporary impairment because of their resistance to recognizing its neurotic background. It is true that during the war many men with otherwise stable personalities were temporarily unnerved and disorganized by severe traumatic experiences. Ordinarily, however, when an individual is broken by some overwhelming experience one should suspect a weakness in the character structure which has a longer history and which must be taken into account in repairing the damage.

QUESTIONS FOR DISCUSSION

1. Elaborate the statement made in the text that the ego is a social product.
2. How does the psychotherapist go about strengthening the ego of a person?
3. It has been stated that the ego is subject to educational influences, but that the superego is relatively impervious to outside influences. Discuss this abstraction. Does this mean that the superego once formed cannot be changed?
4. What is meant by "ego strength"? What are some of the criteria of ego strength?
5. Can the ego ever deteriorate or breakdown? What are some of the signs of ego breakdown?
6. It has been stated that the self is a focus of value around which other values are organized. Discuss this point of view in terms of self-esteem and feelings of inferiority.
7. Do you find signs of infantile modes of thinking in adults?
8. Repression has been spoken of as an ego function. How can you reconcile the fact that the ego takes responsibility both for making effective adjustments with its environment and also for setting up inhibitions and repressions?

RECOMMENDED READING

1. ALLPORT, G. W., "The Ego in Contemporary Psychology," *Psychological Review*, 50 (1943), 451–478.
2. BALINT, MICHAEL, "Ego Strength and Education of the Ego," *Psychoanalytic Quarterly*, 11 (1942), 87–95.
3. FENICHEL, OTTO, *Psychoanalytic Theory of the Neuroses* (New York: W. W. Norton and Company, 1945).
4. FREUD, ANNA, *The Ego and the Mechanisms of Defense*, The International Psychoanalytical Library, No. 30 (London: Hogarth Press, 1937).
5. FREUD, SIGMUND, *The Ego and the Id*, The International Psychoanalytical Library, No. 12 (London: Hogarth Press, 1927).
6. FRIES, M. E., "The Child's Ego Development and the Training of Adults in His Environment," in *The Psychoanalytic Study of the Child*, Vol. II, pp. 85–112 (New York: International Universities Press, 1947).
7. MURPHY, GARDNER, *Personality* (New York: Harper and Brothers, 1947).
8. NUNBERG, HERMAN, "Ego Strength and Ego Weakness," *American Imago*, 3, No. 3 (1942), 25–40.
9. SHERIF, MUZAFER, and CANTRIL, HADLEY, *The Psychology of Ego Involvements* (New York: John Wiley and Sons, 1947).
10. SYMONDS, P. M., "How Do Good Habits of Thinking Begin?" *Childhood Education*, 23 (1947), 309–314.

XXI

Normality

MEANINGS OF NORMALITY

Difference between normal and abnormal principally one of degree.
After this long analysis of the process of adjustment, it may be fitting to
close by an attempt to describe the well-adjusted person and to define
the criteria of normality. In the first place, it is generally agreed that the
difference between the normal individual and the pathological individual is mainly quantitative and not qualitative. The pathological individual does not differ from the normal in some quality or essence which he
possesses but the normal person does not. Neither does the normal possess certain qualities that the poorly adjusted person does not. The difference is merely one of degree. Every normal individual has potentialities of poor adjustment and carries about within him shreds and remnants which, if enlarged and magnified, would carry him over to pathological abnormality and maladjustment. These, of course, are the remnants of childhood reactions which in the normal person have been
outgrown and covered with more mature forms of adjustment.

In like manner, the abnormal person has the capacity for development
which will make him a normal and well-adjusted individual. Exception
to this statement must be made in the case of those individuals who
are suffering from organic tissue damage, destruction, or deterioration.
An infection of the nervous tissue, the growth of a tumor, damage by
the cutting or crushing of the nervous tissue, interruption of the blood
supply, or introduction of chemical substances into nervous tissue offer
insurmountable obstacles to normal adjustment; but if there is no tissue
or organic barrier, the only difference between the normal person and
the abnormal is a quantitative one. The common superstition that insanity is inherited and that one is destined to mental maladjustment if
there is some predecessor in the family who is mentally deranged, is without basis, as shown by the very inconclusive clinical and experimental
studies of the inheritance of insanity.[1] An understanding of the dynamics

---

[1] Norman Cameron, "The Functional Psychoses," in J. McV. Hunt, editor, *Personality and The Behavior Disorders* (New York: The Ronald Press, 1944), Vol. 2, Ch.
XXIX, 862–863.

of human adjustment permits us to see how insanity may be caused by the experiences of life and hence makes it unnecessary to search for an explanation in heredity. It is true that the chances for an individual's making normal adjustments are less favorable when his parents were poorly adjusted persons, but even in these instances the necessity of maladjustment is not inevitable, and except in cases where there are tissue disturbances, every individual has within himself the capacity for achieving a normal life. Freud once said, "Nothing is pathological— only when you cannot explain it." When mental disease was not understood, it was feared. Now that science is gradually accumulating knowledge concerning mental adjustments and their nature is better understood, there is less tendency to think of behavior deviates as pathological.

Normality described in terms of balance. In the normal person the forces in personality find a more satisfactory balance than in the abnormal. In the abnormal certain characteristics may be exceptionally strong or exceptionally weak. Certain traits and characteristics may dominate the rest of the personality, making for eccentricity. In the normal person, however, no one characteristic overbears the rest to produce an unbalanced, distorted, or twisted personality. In the normal there is a balance between the drives, the ego restraints, the superego restraints or urges, and the defenses against anxiety. In the abnormal some one or more of these forces may be exceptionally strong and overpowering. In the normal individual there is a balance between the demands of society and the wishes of the individual. These two forces work coöperatively and are in harmony. The normal person finds a cultural outlet for his basic drives. Perhaps in his vocation he finds a way of expressing some basic urge which is socially acceptable and gives him the feeling of making a worthwhile contribution to society.

The normal person represents a fortunate combination of traits, whereas the traits in the abnormal person, while each may be acceptable in itself, are out of balance and conflict with one another.

Normality as maturity. Normality can be thought of as the goal to be achieved in adjustment in maturity. The common man thinks of pathological conditions in terms of demoniacal possession or moral deviations. It is probably more helpful to think of pathological conditions in an individual as fixation, regression, and immature functioning. The abnormal person is simply one who has not grown up. He is still acting in infantile or childish ways. Practically every abnormal characteristic in an adult will be found also to be a normal reaction in a child or infant. One expects little children to be negativistic, to show intolerance when frustrated, to be untidy, to hit, bite, or scratch another person without compunction. When an older person does these things, we think him strange or odd. So normality consists in working infantile wishes and anxieties through to a satisfactory conclusion. These infantile trends become resolved; they become socialized and integrated within the individual.

Normality as maturity has no upper limit and hence cannot be a fixed concept. There is no limit to the extent to which a person can socialize his tendencies, learn to tolerate frustration, gain wider understanding of reality, learn to love more objectively. This, too, should be a heartening concept of normality for everyone. No matter at what stage he is in his adjustment, he can take steps toward achieving a more mature development, resolving infantile tendencies, and developing a more socialized and integrated adjustment.

Normality in terms of adequate functioning. Normality can also be thought of as the degree of hardship and strain a person can undergo and adjust to successfully without disorganization. Some persons become disturbed and upset at the slightest frustration. They must live sheltered, even, comfortable lives in order to make a "go" of things. On the other hand, there are individuals who can undergo terrific hardships and taking them in their stride, stand steadfast as a rock. Even these individuals may "break" when the tension becomes too great, but ordinarily they can take a great deal of buffeting and affliction. In the London air raids it was found that some children, particularly those coming from stable families, could come through severe bombings without nervous symptoms, while other children from less stable and loving homes developed serious neurotic signs. The normal person is one who overcomes severe threats and frustrating conditions; the abnormal person is one who makes ineffectual adjustment to even slight frustration. Among some of the strains which serve as tests of normality are death in the family, childbirth, loss of money or property, physical illness, and loss of work or position. An unstable individual may be bowled over by any of these. He may be forced into a deep depression or melancholy, or he may suffer a nervous breakdown which incapacitates him from carrying the normal burdens of family and work. The normal individual, too, may be expected to have brief depressions and to show discouragement and tension; but he snaps out of these conditions more quickly, and they do not disorganize his normal contacts and effectiveness.

Normality as a compromise between inner and outer demands. As this book has pointed out in many places, the crux of the adjustment problem lies in integrating the inner impulses, urges, and wishes with the demands of social living. These forces not infrequently run into headlong conflict, and the normal person is the one who finds compromise solutions for these conflicts. A number of such solutions have been described in these pages. A person may manage his conflicts by the *substitution* of one goal or solution for another. He may *compensate* for lack or failure in one direction by an overdevelopment in another. He may *sublimate* his desires by finding modes of expressing them which are, at the same time, in harmony with social goals and the expectations of the culture. He may work out some kind of *compromise* by which in a single act he may receive a token fulfilment of his desires which at the same time does not violate social sanctions. Every compromise means some sort of mutual concession, and the normal individual is one who is able to give up some of his wishes and at the same time yield something of the strictness of his moral standards. The normal person can practice *renunciation* of his desires without feeling deprived or becoming emotionally disturbed in the process. It is the abnormal person who feels that his desires are imperative. The normal person is able to *desensitize* his wishes so that they cause him less hurt if their fulfilment is denied.

Horney [2] finds that it is impossible to define normality in terms of behavior itself, inasmuch as the same behavior may be normal or pathological according to its meaning for the individual. Behavior is normal when it represents a straightforward and satisfying adjustment to the outer world. Behavior is abnormal, on the other hand, when it represents an attempt to escape from anxiety, inferiority, and inadequacy. Behavior which serves these purposes becomes a shield, a buffer, and a façade to protect both the individual and society from recognizing the emptiness and inadequacy beneath. Normal adjustment is realistic and straightforward; neurotic adjustment is false and insincere.

Finally it should be noted that normality and good adjustment cannot be absolutely defined. There is no one standard of normality that applies equally to all times and places and cultures. The criteria of normality must also vary from individual to individual. Each person makes the only adjustments possible for him in the light of his constitutional inheritance, the effect on his character of the experiences which he has undergone, and the circumstances under which he must currently operate. The reformer must aim at some goal of perfection. But there is no such universal goal of adjustment; rather, each individual must work out the most adequate and satisfying adjustment possible for him.

CRITERIA OF GOOD ADJUSTMENT

It is our purpose in the following section to indicate a number of criteria of good adjustment. It would be helpful if good adjustment could be boiled down to a single concept which an individual could carry about him as a phrase or catchword and apply as a measure of his success in living. The process of adjustment, however, cannot be defined within a single concept. Accordingly, it must be defined under a number of different headings, each one of which represents a different

[2] Karen Horney, *The Neurotic Personality of Our Time* (New York: W. W. Norton & Company, Inc., 1937).

aspect of the total adjustment process. These several concepts of adjustment will be put down roughly in the order of importance, although in strict terms this is not possible, for each phase of adjustment is important in itself.

Integration. The first criterion of good adjustment is freedom from inner conflict. A well-adjusted person presents a solid, unbroken front to the world and is free from competing trends within. He has resolved his early ambivalence. His tendencies to love or hate are not annulled because the expression of one of them is blocked by the interference of the competing trend. A well-adjusted person can love freely and can hate with equal candor when the occasion demands. The opposing trends have been successfully repressed or in some way displaced or sublimated. In particular, the Oedipus conflict has been satisfactorily resolved. Tender feelings have taken the place of early sensual feelings, and identification has taken the place of hostile rivalry. There has also been a spread or displacement of these feelings from the parents to many other persons, with a consequent dilution of intensity.

Integration also means the resolution of conflicting personality trends. There is no severe dissociation. The integrated person could not possibly be both Dr. Jekyll and Mr. Hyde. He adopts compatible goals, that is, goals which permit him to live with harmonious purposes in an open and forthright manner; he is forced to expend little energy in fighting undesirable trends within himself. In the integrated person the superego is in harmony with the basic drives. His superego is not so strict and incompatible with his ego that it overloads his ego with guilt. The things that he wants to do are also the things that his conscience tells him are right to do. He carries through his tasks, therefore, more from pleasure than from a sense of duty; or, to put it in another way, his duty is a thing that he wants to do. The individual for whom duty is onerous is the one who is struggling with conflicting trends within himself. The integrated person, then, has achieved a reconciliation of freedom and discipline. What he does arises more from the ego, that is, from his candid acceptance of his behavior as appropriate for the conditions, than from a blind sense of obligation.

The integrated person has resolved the conflict between his selfish and his social goals. His social goals are also his personal, and therefore his selfish, ones. He takes pleasure in social behavior because in the expansion of his personality the well-being of others is included in his own well-being.

It is probably true that the integrated person is one for whom these ideals are more or less conscious. They are not primitive ideals but represent the end of a long maturing process, one which can come only after mastering the conflicts which inevitably rise in the process of maturing. In short, integration is an achievement to be won.

Integration shows itself in ability to concentrate one's energies on a single goal or at least on a small group of harmonious and compatible goals. One thinks of the integrated person as the one who is on fire for a cause and who has deep loyalties and vivid enthusiasms. The integrated person is one who takes things seriously rather than playing at them. What the integrated person does is very much a part of his whole life rather than some superficial attachment which he puts on and off like a garment, to be entered into as the occasion demands, but to be laid aside when the group is dispersed. This latter is a picture of the shallow and superficial rather than the integrated person.

The energy of the drives of an integrated person is expended on the outside world for effective adaptation. The neurotic, on the other hand, through the necessity for repression and the consequent energy which must be used in maintaining the repression, is debarred from normal outlets in living. He who fights himself least has the most energy to expend on the outside world.

Ego development—effective intelligence. The well-adjusted person is one who has learned to apply his intelligence to the effective solution of the problems of living. The highest evidence of successful adjustment is getting along in the world around one, particularly with one's fellowmen. The well-adjusted person draws lessons from his defeats and failures in order not to repeat the same errors on another occasion. He learns to make intelligent compromises, renunciations, and substitutions as his drives and wishes meet resistance.

Effective adjustment means the sublimation and socialization of basic unconscious impulses and drives. The well-adjusted person has the capacity to plan. There is an interesting relation between goals and planning. First of all, a man decides that he wishes to build a house— that is his goal. Then he employs an architect to draw up plans for his house. He tells the architect what his needs are, the number of persons in his family, and the kind of lives they live, and then the plans are drawn up to meet these needs, the price the man is willing to pay, and the conditions of the market. In like manner, the well-adjusted person is able to make plans for the successful accomplishment of his goals in terms of his needs, on the one hand, and the conditions of his life, on the other. The behavior of the well-adjusted person is rational; that is, it makes sense. It can be explained. It represents a step on the way toward the successful achievement of one's goals.

This second criterion of good adjustment, effective intelligence, shows itself in the capacity to work and in one's efficiency and adequacy in work. The well-adjusted person finds a reasonable enthusiasm, satisfaction, and pleasure in his work. He enjoys attacking and overcoming obstacles. He revels in the solution of problems. He knows how to work when working and how to play when playing and does not confuse the two. He does not attack his work as a dilettante or make it a compulsive and disagreeable necessity.

Along this same line the well-adjusted person has worked out for himself a sane and constructive philosophy of life which includes a broad and realistic outlook on the world about him. The narrow-minded person who shuts his eyes to conditions and sees things through false and distorted perspective is unable to formulate worthy goals or to make effective plans for reaching them.

Acceptance of reality. A third criterion of good adjustment is ability to accept *reality*, particularly the reality within. The person who is well adjusted recognizes the reality and inevitability of the conditions to which he must adjust. Freud has discussed adjustment in terms of the *pleasure principle* and the *reality principle*. The pleasure principle dominates infancy, when there is failure to recognize the conditions imposed by outer circumstances. Only as a person modifies his longings, on the one hand, and his mode of satisfying them, on the other, to the conditions imposed by outer reality, is he making a good adjustment. The well-adjusted person learns frustration tolerance, that is, the ability to postpone satisfactions until conditions are ripe to grant them.

The most important kind of reality which must be faced and accepted, however, is the drives, fears, and inadequacies within the self. A person must learn to face the reality of his inner nature however much he has been taught that certain trends within himself are bad, evil, immoral.

An army colonel with wide experience in dealing with men once stated in the writer's hearing that he could trust a man who had insight into his own weaknesses. The successfully adjusted person learns the necessity of giving up impossible wishes. He learns continence and is not beset by an excessive need for indulgence. He develops the capacity for effective inhibition when this is called for, or he puts his wishes to work on realizable goals and substitute satisfactions, accepting the reality within himself, dropping his defenses, and letting fall the shams and disguises by which he tends to cover up and conceal the inadequacies within.

The person who has made good adjustment learns to accept unavoidable pain, humiliation, or loss. When trials come he meets them squarely and frankly. Since he does not have elevated notions of himself, he has little to be disappointed in when disillusions arrive. He does not get a swelled head and lose perspective in understanding who he is or what he stands for. John Wesley Dafoe, for many years a Canadian editorial writer, was once offered a knighthood. He retorted, "Me a knight? Why, I tend my own furnace and shovel snow off my porch."

Since a well-adjusted person adopts goals which are achievable in the light of his talents and capacities, it is necessary for him to assess his abilities and talents correctly and without over- or underestimation. The well-adjusted person is not afraid to get on the scales to see how much he weighs, to view himself in the mirror, to listen to a record of his own voice, to take various psychological tests by which he can learn his mental abilities, or to have an analysis of his personality trends. Indeed, he wishes to know the facts about himself so that he can establish goals which are reasonable in view of his capacities. The average man would perhaps be wise if he did not aim to become a champion athlete or supreme court judge. On the other hand, a man of superior talents would profit by knowing of these abilities and by making the most effective use of them. The well-adjusted man does not magnify his successes, and, at the same time, admits his limitations; in particular, he avoids tendencies toward perfectionism which would be foolish whatever his talents or abilities.

Acceptance of reality also means the absence of excessive fantasy. The man who lives in the world about him and derives his satisfactions from life's experiences does not have to depend on fantasy fulfilment of his wishes. Normality also implies that exaggerated and distorted infantile fantasies have been tested and corrected in the crucible of reality. In particular, the superego, instead of being highly fantastic, becomes more nearly in accord with the expectations of the parents and the community in general.

Responsibility for self. Otto Rank [3] in his discussion of therapy has made much of the point that the well-adjusted person is one who can accept responsibility for himself. This is another phase of maturity. The little child is one who has things done for him. His parents decide what he shall eat and wear, when he shall go to bed, and what he shall learn. It is a token of maturity that a person is able to manage himself and make decisions with a minimum of worry, conflict, and advice-seeking. Of particular importance for good adjustment is the ability to take responsibility for one's own feelings. The maladjusted child is one who is unable to accept the reality of his own feelings. He must project them onto others either by attributing hostile impulses to others or by retaliating to the hostility which he feels others hold toward him. It is a real achievement to be able to accept responsibility for one's own fears, dislikes, and hatreds, as well as one's loves and admirations.

The well-adjusted person is at home with himself and manages all aspects of his personality as one drives a four-horse chariot. He has self-control and capacity for inhibition and restraint.

A person successful in adjustment is characterized by independence. He is able to say, "No" to situations that may provide only temporary satisfaction. He is able to restrain himself from putting up a wager which gives him a momentary thrill but may result in a loss he can ill afford.

[3] Otto Rank, *Will Therapy;* and, *Truth and Reality* (New York: Alfred A. Knopf, 1936, 1945).

He is able to say, "No" to excesses which provide only temporary **excitement** but do not afford lasting satisfaction. On the other hand, he is able to say, "Yes" to the unpleasant that promises ultimately to prove beneficial. He can take temporary sacrifices, postpone temporary pleasures, and endure temporary hardships for the sake of more enduring satisfactions. He is independent of group opinion in favor of his independent judgment, but he does not take an arbitrary opposition to whatever the group proposes. The well-adjusted person has no need for flattery. He does not have to be supported at every turn by group approbation but when the occasion demands can assert his independent opinion.

Emotional expression. *Happiness and Pleasure in Life—Subjective Sense of Well-Being.* So far these criteria of good adjustment have emphasized the controlling, restrictive, and inhibitive aspects of personality, but this is only one concept of good adjustment. The well-adjusted man is one who, in addition to these capacities for self-control, has a certain freedom of emotional expression.

The enjoyment of pleasures is a mark of good adjustment. It is commonly thought that there is something ignoble about pleasures and the epicurean is looked upon askance by his puritan brother. Be that as it may, the well-adjusted person should find pleasure in the simple biological operations of eating and sleeping. He should be able to exercise his elimination functions without shame or conflict. However, the well-adjusted person is not preoccupied with the body. He is not overly interested in the minute details of bodily function and does not become unduly disturbed when there is an upset or sickness. In particular, he does not dwell unnecessarily on his ailments and complaints, as the hypochondriac does.

Perhaps the criterion of happiness as a criterion of good adjustment should have been given earlier, but whether given early or late, the subjective sense of well-being is an important criterion. A satisfactorily adjusted person is content and maintains an adequate and satisfying emotional undertone. He has a sense of security which springs out of a feeling in childhood of belonging and of being wanted and which stays with him throughout life. He has feelings of adequacy and of being appreciated. Being able to handle feelings of difference is especially important so far as happiness is concerned. Many persons are bothered by status. They are continually comparing themselves to others. But this leads only to unhappiness. The well-adjusted person has adjusted his aspirations to reality, that is, the reality of what he can expect of himself in the light of his talents, social position, and opportunities. And he measures himself, not in terms of whether he won the race, but in terms of whether he did what he could reasonably expect of himself and whether he enjoyed himself in the process. The well-adjusted person has adequate self-esteem, self-confidence, and strength. He is free from excessive anxiety, depression, worry, guilt, and disturbing fears. He maintains a relatively even emotional tone characterized by neither excessive exuberance nor excessive despondence. He can be characterized as fearless, which means not only courage in the face of immediate danger, but that peace and stability which also presage freedom from anxiety over unresolved conflicts in the past. All these emotional feelings accompany the other criteria of good adjustment which have been described.

Relaxation. There is emotional warmth in the well-adjusted person's relationships. He is able to laugh and smile freely. One can tell the degree of relaxation by noticing the facial muscles. The tense individual is one whose face is drawn and stern.

One of the most important criteria of good adjustment is the ability to play, perhaps the most significant sign of all in the little child. One can gage a person's adjustment by the breadth of his interests in sports, games, and hobbies, and by his ability for self-expression in creative living. The well-adjusted person shows a normal curiosity, another important sign of good adjustment in children. It is a typical complaint of teachers that Johnny is not interested in anything but remains apathetic toward all of the activities the school provides. This is a tell-tale sign of adjustment problems. The well-adjusted person should be spontaneous, natural, and easy in his social relationships.

Ability to Love. Ability to love is an important criterion of good adjustment and usually is placed alongside ability to work. One who is well adjusted is able to enjoy erotic pleasure without feeling it is somehow bad or sinful. He is able to show affection freely and through bodily contact, with unrestrained feelings of pleasure. He can feel sympathetic with the other person and share his joys and sorrows unrestrainedly.

The ability to have free and full sexual experience is commonly spoken of as characteristic of the well-adjusted person. This criterion, however, must be judged carefully in terms of an individual's need for sensuality. For certain individuals with a background of considerable sensuous experience and with strong hormonal stimulation, sexual experience may be highly important. On the other hand, there are persons whose early experiences have been relatively unemotional and whose hormone output is subnormal for whom sexual experiences are not so meaningful or important. It must be recognized that erotic gratification is an important pleasure and hence good in itself. It should also be recognized that an adequate freeing and expression of eroticism also implies an adequate solution of aggressive problems. There are individuals for whom sex has been overdetermined and who feel the need for sex as a method of proving their adequacy. It is probably more true that the well-adjusted person is one for whom continence is possible than that he is one for whom sexual expression is a necessity. Indeed, mental health and the capacity for continence go together, rather than the opposite. Although adequate sexual expression is recognized as a sign of good adjustment, variations in terms of individual needs must also be recognized and can be contained in the concept of good adjustment. For many individuals probably it is more important to think in terms of a general balance of living than in terms of the ability to obtain complete sexual gratification. This should be a comfort to many persons who are forced to live lonely and continent lives and who, while denied this one pleasure which does stand out above others, find a net balance of still greater satisfaction in an ordered scale of living.

Ability to Show Anger. The well-adjusted person is also able to show anger when injured, or hostility and aggression when necessary or desirable. This phase of good adjustment is difficult for most persons to understand or accept. The evil of aggression is taught so early and so consistently that many persons are unable to think of any expression of aggression as related to what is good or acceptable. But this is not the case. Aggressive tendencies are so much a part of every person's equipment that it must, of necessity, be right to show aggression at the proper time and in socialized channels. But aggression should be neither unduly exaggerated nor inhibited. It is a supreme achievement of the ego to know when it is the part of wisdom to face and fight the world as well as when to inhibit one's aggressive tendencies. Naturally, the well-adjusted person has learned to socialize his aggression and to put his energies to constructive and socially desirable ends.

Emotional expression, then, should be neither too completely inhibited nor too violently exhibited. The well-adjusted person is one whose emotions are under control and who does not permit them exaggerated expression.

Social relationships. A well-adjusted individual is one who lives with others and enjoys social contacts and interests. It is a sign of maturity for object love to take the place of selfish love, that is, for one to love others for themselves and not merely for the advantage it may bring him. In the normal individual social deeds take the place of pain and suffering in the neurotic. The neurotic individual is at odds with his family and friends, but the normal individual lives bountifully in his social group. For him there is a spread of emotional contacts as his experiences in social living widen and deepen.

Good Rapport with Others. The well-adjusted person has good rapport with others. He is able to establish permanent friendships, relations with others that persist year after year through good weather and foul, through success and failure, finding more value in the person than in the person's status. He is able to show friendly feeling and social understanding. He is able to get along with other people, to understand them,

and to avoid distrust, jealousy, conflicts, and quarrels. He is characterized by tolerance and the ability to accept others whose beliefs, standards, and tastes differ from his. He is coöperative and can work with
others harmoniously and helpfully on joint undertakings. As Jones
points out,[4] friendliness is to be measured by the internal freedom of
such feelings and attitudes rather than by their quantity.

Not Too Unlike the Group in Which He Lives. The well-adjusted
person is not too unlike the group in ways the group feels to be important. In short, he is a citizen who makes the goals, purposes, and
ideals of the culture his own. The interests of the individual and of the
community merge and become inseparable. An infallible sign of good
adjustment is a person's acceptance by others. The child who is liked
by other members of the family, who is accepted by his teacher at school,
who is elected to offices by his peers, tends to be the well-adjusted individual. He finds socially acceptable outlets for his energy and yet fits
himself in with the group's wishes with a certain degree of docility and
obedience.

Recognition of Others. The well-adjusted person is able to recognize
the ability and independence of others. He is able to admit superiority
and merit in others, even when they surpass him in respects that are
important to him. Genuinely to admire others without unconsciously
feeling envious of them is a very difficult accomplishment and a difficult
criterion of good judgment. Another requirement is the capacity for admitting the independence of other individuals. Parents sometimes have
difficulty in admitting that their children are growing up or that they
are independent and responsible individuals so far as their maturity
permits. The institution of slavery is based on the lack of recognition of
the independence of other men. The well-adjusted person is one who is
able to recognize and grant the independence of others.

Capacity to Enjoy Society of Other Sex. In a previous section the importance of sexual expression was discussed. There it was stated that
while freedom in sex was desirable, sexual expression was not a necessity
but should fit into the total pattern of living. Of greater importance than
sexual expression for good adjustment is the individual's ability to enjoy
the society of members of the other sex, not to feel strange or ill at ease
in speaking, working, or playing with them, not to be overly aroused,
on the one hand, or repelled, on the other, but to accept them as rational
human beings.

Extroversion Better than Introversion. There has been some discussion of the normality of the extrovert as contrasted with the introvert. In
general, the outgoing, friendly, social person is better adjusted than the
individual who has turned upon himself and has withdrawn from con-

---

[4] Ernest Jones, "The Concept of a Normal Mind," *International Journal of
Psychology*, 23 (1942), 1–8.

tacts with others. However, this should not be interpreted as meaning that the reserved and remote individual is necessarily ill adjusted. Of more importance, perhaps, than the amount or kind of social contact, is the inner harmony and self-assurance of the individual, which may be characteristics equally of the introvert and the extrovert.

Consistency of personality. A person who has succeeded in adjustment maintains a course without deviation. It is no sign of maturity to lead a will-o'-the-wisp, flighty existence, to dabble, to touch experiences lightly, to be here today and gone tomorrow. One cannot accomplish effective adjustment in terms of well-rounded life without a certain amount of settling-down persistency and consistency. The well-adjusted person is characterized by the persistence and depth of his loyalties.

Adaptability. To counterbalance the last criterion one should add that a well-adjusted individual is also, to a degree, flexible, plastic, and suggestible. He does not hold a course too rigidly and inflexibly in the face of insurmountable obstacles. The well-adjusted person can make the essential compromises that occasions demand. His morals and his conscience are not too inflexible. It is admissible to have moral standards; but again they should be adapted to circumstances, and if the interests of the largest number would be served by some breach of long-established standards, then such a breach is called for. This kind of adaptability is well illustrated in the life of the much-loved jurist and esteemed member of the United States Supreme Court, Oliver Wendell Holmes, who was always ready to overturn precedent in the interests of human welfare. The well-adjusted person avoids limiting fixations. In particular he avoids emotional ties that limit his growth and development. It is well known that fixations of emotions on one's parents or other members of the family interfere with the establishment of relationships which enable one to take his place as a member of adult society. It is appropriate to establish fixed emotional relations to one's husband or wife and to one's children, for this is in the interests of taking an accepted place in society, with all the possibility for expanded growth that family life carries with it.

Emotional perception of world. The well-adjusted individual perceives his world as a warm, friendly place inhabited by pleasant, friendly, benevolent people. He is optimistic (even while he is realistic) in outlook and expects the best from all. That person has a distorted and unhealthy outlook on life who sees it filled with dangers, who sees the people around him as sinister, plotting, evil, untrustworthy, and selfish. To be sure, a child may grow up so sheltered as to be unaware that there are bad people in the world who may wish to hurt him. But there is a difference between this unrealistic perception and the distorted perception that fails to see and expect the best in people and looks only for the worst.

Capacity to refrain from self-injury. In the chapter, "Guilt and Self-

Punishment" it was pointed out that a common method of defending oneself from guilt is to inflict self-injury. This interference with one's pleasures and successes does not have a rational basis, and paying for one's faults, while a profound psychological process, does not have value in real adjustment. In the first place, a person should become aware of his tendencies toward self-injury and the motives back of them. He should then find ways of recognizing and admitting his guilt, of lowering his superego tendencies, of finding socially acceptable outlets for his impulses, and thereby of eliminating the necessity for self-injury and self-depreciation.

Ability to accept love. Along with the capacity to love others should go the ability to accept love from others. This is a basic need, the need for dependency and being loved by superiors. However, some persons find that it is a threat to their self-sufficiency to continue to be dependent on others. The very individuals who most want to be loved by others are those who rebuff the efforts of others to be generous to them. The well-adjusted person is one who is able to accept the generosity and devotion that others want to express to him.

Adequate drive. A criterion of good adjustment that should not be overlooked is possession of health and vigor. One cannot enjoy life or experience it to the full unless he possesses adequate and abundant health. In some respects this requirement underlies all others, for without health one is thwarted in all other satisfactions.

Removal of symptoms not important. In therapeutic work the goal is often the removal of symptoms for which the child is originally referred for treatment or for which the individual refers himself. Since these symptoms cause the original distress, it is only natural to think of adjustment in terms of their elimination. However, the symptoms are merely signs of poor adjustment and do not indicate the nature of the adjustment process itself. One would do well to judge the quality of adjustment in terms of ability to work, play, and love, to feel happy and contented, to accept reality, to express one's emotions freely, to exhibit normal inhibitions, rather than to pattern one's behavior according to any set formula or standards. Parents would do well if they thought of their child's development not in terms of specific habits and skills to be formed, but rather in terms of these larger goals of adjustment and maturity. The symptoms become serious only when they drain off large amounts of energy which ought to be applied to a more effective adaptation to the real world about. Symptoms in which dependence is prominent, as in drug addiction or alcoholism, are unfortunate handicaps, and in good adjustment they would be absent. But by and large, the goal of every individual should be the achievement of a good working relationship with the world in which he lives.

THE ACHIEVEMENT OF GOOD ADJUSTMENT

Just as some trees reach magnificent development because they have been nurtured on rich soil, have access to light, and are free from destructive pests, so some men grow up under conditions that foster good adjustment. The foundation of good adjustment lies in a stable and happy family. Education can contribute notably toward good adjustment, and the steps that education can take have been described in many of the chapters in this book.

The individual who is unhappy and who is handicapped in his adjustment by an unfortunate constitution and deleterious early-life experiences can be helped to become normal, happy, and well adjusted. The stunted or gnarled tree can be made more beautiful by enriching the soil around its roots, by cutting away the surrounding growth to provide more sunlight, and by pruning, trimming, and spraying. So the individual can be helped in his adjustments by changing in some way his conditions of living and by modifying his attitudes and tensions. An individual cannot expect to find happiness or to banish anxiety by wishing it or by ordering it or by the application of self-determination. It is the rare individual who can help himself by self-analysis. A maladjusted person can achieve health and normality only through the help of other persons who can introduce him to new conditions of living and institute a process of psychotherapy. Most persons find release to grow to maturity with the aid of family or friends, or if these are not sufficient, through the help of a trained counselor. No one need despair, for there is the possibility of better adjustment, happiness and normality for every person.

QUESTIONS FOR DISCUSSION

1. What does it mean to say that mentally disturbed persons differ from normal well-adjusted persons quantitatively but not qualitatively?

2. Why is it not possible to set down sharply defined standards of desirable adjustment?

3. One goal of psychotherapy which is stressed today is the attainment of self-direction. How does achievement of this goal carry along with it other important outcomes believed important to good adjustment? What might attainment of the capacity for self-direction miss if achieved only by itself?

4. If attainment of happiness and pleasure in life is a criterion of good adjustment, why is there suspicion that the adjustment of the out-and-out Epicurean and pleasure seeker is not enough?

5. Discuss the implications of the statement that the best criterion of the adequacy of sex adjustments is that the person should feel comfortable about them.

6. Is the reformer, radical, or revolutionary well-adjusted?

7. On page 397 there is the heading "removal of symptoms not important."

This is contrary to popular and expert opinion. Discuss this point of view. Under what conditions would one say that a person was "normal" who retained a "symptom"?

8. Discuss good adjustment in terms of self-acceptance.

9. It has been suggested on page 395 that the extravert is better adjusted than the introvert. What are the grounds for this statement? Does this mean that an introvert is a poorly adjusted individual?

RECOMMENDED READING

1. GLOVER, EDWARD, "Medico-Psychological Aspects of Normality," *British Journal of Psychology*, 23 (1932-1933), 152–166.

2. HACKER, F. J., "The Concept of Normality and its Practical Significance," *American Journal of Orthopsychiatry*, 15 (1945), 47–64.

3. HOWARD, F. E., and PATRY, F. L., *Mental Health* (New York: Harper and Brothers, 1935).

4. HORNEY, KAREN, *The Neurotic Personality of Our Time* (New York: W. W. Norton and Company, Inc., 1937).

5. JONES, ERNEST, "The Concept of a Normal Mind," *International Journal of Psychoanalysis*, 23 (1942), 1–8.

6. LAWTON, GEORGE, "What is a Well-Adjusted Person?" *Journal of Adult Education*, 10 (1938), 395, 396.

7. MASLOW, A. H., and MITTELMANN, BELA, *Principles of Abnormal Psychology* (New York: Harper and Brothers, 1941).

8. MORGAN, J. J. B., *The Psychology of the Unadjusted School Child* (New York: The Macmillan Company, 1926; revised edition, 1936).

9. RANK, OTTO, *Will Therapy* reprinted under title of *Will Therapy; and Truth and Reality* (New York: Alfred A. Knopf, 1936, 1945).

Index